WYNDHAM LEWIS

A Portrait of the Artist as the Enemy

Dichter. O sprich mir nicht von jener bunten Menge,
Bei deren Anblick uns der Geist entflieht!
Goethe, "Vorspiel auf dem Theater," *Faust I.*

Wyndham Lewis

A PORTRAIT

OF THE ARTIST

AS THE ENEMY

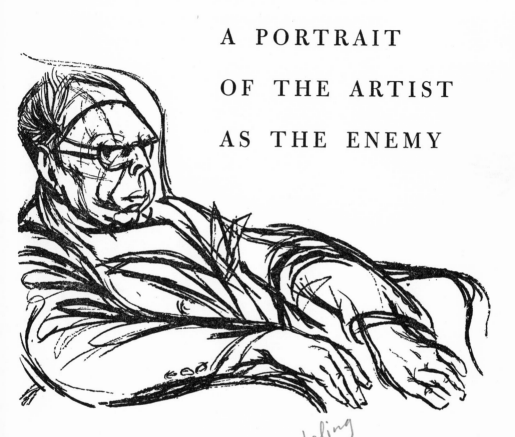

BY GEOFFREY *Atheling* WAGNER

New Haven: YALE UNIVERSITY PRESS, 1957

To the memory of my uncle

EDWARD WADSWORTH

who first introduced me to the work of Wyndham Lewis

Contents

Foreword

"THE MOST FASCINATING personality of our time" was T. S. Eliot's description of Wyndham Lewis in *The Egoist* for September 1918, an opinion recently reinforced in the Winter 1955 issue of *The Hudson Review* where he called Lewis "the most distinguished living English novelist." Speaking on the B.B.C. just after the last war, Geoffrey Grigson said: "If we could have a collected edition of Wyndham Lewis—a collecting of novels, stories, criticism, treatises, essays which have never been collected—we should understand, as perhaps we don't, his immense unity." V. S. Pritchett, on the other hand, denies this unity to Lewis' work; if one looks at the first and last sentences of any of his paragraphs, Pritchett asserts, "the two will rarely be found to have any logical connection."

The present study attempts to discover that logical connection. It is divided into four parts, roughly on the basis of the interest Lewis has shown in each field. All his writings are covered to date, although perhaps one point should be mentioned: I have not asked my printer to follow the atomic typography of *Blast*. The checklist which concludes this work, while it is perhaps the most thorough of its kind to be attempted, does not pretend to be definitive; I know from letters of Lewis I have examined that there is at least one item outstanding. The chronology of this list is only threatened, I believe, when I have been unable to trace month of publication in the usual way and the work in question has been relegated to the end of its year. The secondary sources simply gather a fairly arbitrary selection of works with divergent views on Lewis that seem worth preserving. In this listing the ordinary contemporary review is not included, although reference to such may be found in the text.

It is Wyndham Lewis' own contention that he has been a neglected writer, subject to a "conspiracy of silence." His views on this subject may be well known. As he has lately put it: "Let us say (not to indulge in truths that would lead straight to suits for libel) that the 'conspiracy' dates from 1913—it has been, as Mr. Ayrton says, long." This is a view he can scarcely take today, with his novels (both reissues and originals) pouring out annually on both sides of the Atlantic, being recommended by book societies and eulogized in special issues of little magazines, with the Tate Gallery staging a retrospective exhibition—an "apotheosis," as William Roberts has called it—of his work (and the Museum of Modern Art in New York featuring him regularly in shows of contemporary British masters), with *The New Yorker* devoting a seven-page article to *Self Condemned* (and *Time Magazine* one and a half pages), with *The Times Literary Supplement* in the course of a full-page panegyric on his work referring to *The Human Age* as "manifestly one of the great prose works of our time," with, finally, the last laurels of safe respectability descending on him in the form of a Civil List pension and an honorary degree from Leeds University. Indeed, during the course of my research, I have seldom encountered a more vociferous "conspiracy of silence" surrounding a contemporary writer. On the contrary, in his 1956 reissue of *Forces in Modern British Literature*, W. Y. Tindall believes that Lewis "has emerged from the precincts of fascism as the authentic voice of the postwar middle class."

However this may be, it is certainly true that there has been little scholarly work done on Wyndham Lewis, certainly nothing approaching the mass of serious studies that now hedge in, say, D. H. Lawrence. Nor has any bibliographical interest been taken in his work, as it has in the cases of Eliot, Joyce, and Pound. Moreover, there are letters which show Lewis somewhat dissatisfied by the kind of belletrist study that his work has so far drawn forth. It is also true that neither British nor American libraries have collected his work with much care. I could not help thinking it ironic that many of my slips requesting works by Lewis at the British Museum were returned to me marked, "Destroyed—By Enemy

Action." Lastly, this side of his work has not been made easier by his having a namesake; even supposedly immaculate sources, such as *Whitaker's Cumulative Book List* or the PMLA *American Bibliography* for 1955 (and the latter despite the article listed drawing attention to the similarity in names), both quite recently confuse our Percy Wyndham Lewis with Dominic Bevan Wyndham Lewis, chiefly known as a polite biographer.

Possibly, in any case, the "conspiracy of silence," if it existed, was justified; I shall not pass judgment on that, although I hope that the evidence adduced in these pages will be considered before others do so. Because of the heat of controversy that has always surrounded Wyndham Lewis, for better or worse, we needed, I felt, more light on him. We needed a "primer" to his work. For not only is he a writer who does not take the uninitiated with him into some of the more audacious of his critical forays, he constantly, every few years, rewrites his career or revises the opinions of earlier books. These are, in a word, "Destroyed—By Enemy Action." As I go to press, in fact, he has just rewritten *The Childermass* (i.e. Book I of what is now *The Human Age*), so that it is all the more important to record what he did write at the time. There is, in a word, no need to plead for Wyndham Lewis. He himself has been doing that for almost half a century. But exactly what he said, and when, these are questions that need honest and impartial answering, and for that reason much of what follows here is expository as well as critical.

Many people, friends of the Enemy and others, have helped me with this book, and my indebtedness on the bibliographical side is especially heavy. I read chiefly at the following libraries: the Bodleian and the British Museum, in England; in America, the libraries of Columbia, Harvard, Princeton, and Yale universities, and the New York Public Library. The staffs of all these proved characteristically courteous and generous. The principal collection of manuscripts by Lewis I examined was the so-called Carlow Collection, a large body of manuscripts, galleys, page proofs, and books bound for the late Lord Carlow by Stanley Bray of Sangorski and Sutcliffe; for permission to consult these I am indebted to A. Zwemmer. I was also allowed to read an unpublished satire by Lewis at the Houghton Library of Harvard University. I was further able to inspect a large number of letters from Wyndham Lewis to various individuals at the following libraries: the Lockwood Memorial Library at the University of Buffalo, the Sterling Memorial Library at Yale University, the Pierpont Morgan Library, and in the Berg and Quinn collections of the New York Public Library. For especial assistance, and for particular patience with my bothering them over small points, I am grateful to W. H. Bond, curator of manuscripts at the Houghton Library at Harvard, to Herbert Cahoon, curator of autograph manuscripts at the Pierpont Morgan Library, to Angus Wilson at the British Museum, to Sidney Ditzion of the Periodical Division of the Library of the City College of New York, and to Gene Magner, curator of manuscripts at the Lockwood Memorial Library at Buffalo.

On the more personal side, I need first to thank Mr. and Mrs. Wyndham Lewis most warmly for their hospitality to me on more than one occasion, and for their patience and courtesy in answering my many questions. My thanks are also due to the following, who acquainted me with helpful information, either in conversation or by correspondence: Lienhard Bergel, Frank Budgen, Herschel Chipp, Stanley Coffman Jr., Bonamy Dobrée, Douglas Goldring, Mrs. Patricia Graecen, Geoffrey Grigson, Nathan Halper, Mrs. Mollie Herbert-Dell, James Laughlin, R. A. Scott-James, Sir Osbert Sitwell, James Johnson Sweeney, and Miss Harriet Weaver. Peter Russell was kindness and encouragement itself throughout the period of my researches, and both he and Bertram Rota assisted me immensely in obtaining first editions of Lewis' scarcer works. My colleagues Clifford Josephson and Marvin Magalaner have been unfailingly sympathetic.

As regards academic direction, I owe a primary debt to my Oxford tutor Nevill Coghill who, although he is innocent of any influence over this study, first lured me into the groves of academe and under whose wing no scholar can come without being made both better and happier. Gilbert Highet, J. B. Brebner, and Mrs. Suzanne Nobbe, all of Columbia University, all cast their knowledgeable eyes over this manuscript in its early stages and improved it in small ways. Professor André von Gronicka supplied patient direction in my German researches, and Professor Jean-Albert Bédé in my French, while no one can take Justin O'Brien's course in contemporary French literature at Columbia without emerging considerably wiser. I should like to thank the Chairman of my Department, Edgar Johnson, for his patience with me during a very busy period in my career. To Professor William York Tindall I owe an enormous debt, not only for vigorously directing my researches into contemporary British literature, but for allowing me to draw continually from his vast store of informational detail; on the interpretive side he proved unwearyingly willing to lend my judgments some balance and perspective, without ever trying to impose on them his own. *Mentor mansues,* my thanks.

Finally, I owe the officers and trustees of Columbia University my gratitude for the award of the Lydig Fellowship in the Faculty of Philosophy, and the officers of the Edward MacDowell Association the same for a grant of assistance from its Fellowship Fund, both of which awards considerably eased the completion of this study.

GEOFFREY WAGNER

The City College
New York

Acknowledgments

I WISH TO THANK the editors of the following British and American periodicals for permission to reprint portions of this book that originally appeared in their pages: *The Catholic World, The Chicago Jewish Forum, The Journal of Aesthetics and Art Criticism, The Hudson Review, Modern Fiction Studies, The New Mexico Quarterly, The New Republic, Nine, The Romanic Review, The South Atlantic Quarterly*. The section dealing with the controversy between Lewis and Joyce was originally delivered as a paper at the 1955 meeting of the Modern Language Association of America in Chicago, under the aegis of Richard Ellmann.

Acknowledgment is gratefully made to the following publishers in England for their kindness in allowing me to quote from works by Wyndham Lewis to which they hold copyright: John Lane, Chatto and Windus, Cassell, Faber and Faber, George Allen and Unwin, Jonathan Cape, Eyre and Spottiswoode, Robert Hale, Hutchinson, Dent, Nicholson and Watson, George Weidenfeld and Nicolson (for Contact Books), and the present publishers of Lewis' work in England, Methuen. Acknowledgment is also gratefully made to the following American publishers for their similar courtesy: Alfred A. Knopf, Harper and Brothers, Harcourt, Brace, Robert M. McBride, Howell, Soskin, Doubleday, New Directions, and the present publisher of Lewis' work in America, Henry Regnery. I am also indebted to the Ryerson Press of Toronto for permission to quote from one work by Lewis to which they hold copyright. I am also similarly indebted to the editors and/or proprietors of those periodicals, extant or defunct, mentioned in the text, from which I have quoted unreprinted material by Wyndham Lewis. I am equally indebted to J. F. Littler of the British Broadcasting

Corporation for lending me typescript talks, originally transmitted via that organization. Lastly, I have to thank Wyndham Lewis himself for permission to quote from those writings of his in which sole copyright has reverted to him. And I am indebted to the principals and directors of those museums and foundations owning graphic works by Lewis, to which allusion is made in the text.

The drawing of Wyndham Lewis by Michael Ayrton which embellishes this volume is used by kind permission of Michael Ayrton and Methuen and Company, Ltd.

INTRODUCTORY

Introductory: The Men of 1914, the Detached Spectator, and the Joy of Protest

"From the start I have behaved *as if I were free.*" [*Rude Assignment,* p. 105.]

THE WRITINGS OF WYNDHAM LEWIS [1] can be divided in two, critical and creative, and it is the purpose of this study to relate the former to the latter. Of their relationship Lewis himself tells us that his "philosophic criticism," [2] as he calls it, grew out of his creative genius. But this reversal of the normal practice for a con-

1. In 1928 Lewis wrote: "at the outset of my career, I simplified myself to W.L. and cut off my christian attribute." He will therefore be referred to as Wyndham Lewis here.

2. This term may, I think, have been taken from Ramon Fernandez, whose essay "De la critique philosophique" (most of which appeared in *The Dial* for March 1927) forms the first chapter of his *Messages* of 1926, later translated by Montgomery Belgion. Lewis may have been introduced to Fernandez by Aldington's translation of his essay on Newman, which appeared in *The Criterion* for October 1924, the year when Lewis himself began writing for this periodical and when he started using the phrase.

Fernandez explains that philosophic criticism requires a critic of strong rational training and one who can find ideas sharply defined in the world of common sense; the public for this criticism should be "une élite capable de comprendre," such as Fernandez finds in Meredith's public. For Fernandez, the philosophic critic is unconcerned with formal aesthetics, but is interested rather in "une attitude devant la vie." Ramon Fernandez, *Messages* (Paris, Gallimard, 1926), pp. 31–3. His work should be a liaison between intelligence and reality and above all must join at some point with human experience: Pater is seen as the opposite of the true philosophic critic (ibid., pp. 210–16). This is precisely what Lewis' criticism aims to do, for it is nearly all concerned with problems of daily life, even the work on Shakespeare, his most "formal" piece of literary criticism, being filled with interpretations of, and judgments on, the contemporary scene.

temporary neoclassicist, according to Constant Bourquin in his book on Benda, makes it hard, though not impossible, to fit books like *Count Your Dead* or *Left Wings over Europe* into such an explanation. Perhaps what Lewis means is, as he puts it elsewhere, "I am an artist first, and a critic afterwards." [3]

In yet another place Lewis describes his work as formal (creative) and informal (critical), and he has further told us that his pamphlets—a term which for him apparently covers a work of over three hundred pages—were published in defense of his creative art. Again, it is difficult to reconcile his political books with this view, especially when he vacillates over the years in deciding what constitutes a "political" book.[4] But he is consistent in feeling that his criticism has been a wasteful expenditure of his creative gifts, necessary because of the nature of our times, and strident in order that such a minority view as his own might be heard in twentieth-century England.

However one may eventually feel about Lewis' own explanations of his writings, it would be rash to contest, surely, that he has been a "portmanteau-man" in the multiplicity of his interests and variety of his skills. Even those who dislike the use to which he has put these skills must honestly confess that this technical proficiency in two spheres, in literary and graphic art, has not been an ordinary gift in our time. Of the several estimates Lewis has made of himself, some decidedly flattering ("I have never been overburdened with the obvious forms of diffidence"), he has accurately described himself as "a writer who is a novelist, a critic, a politi-

---

3. Wyndham Lewis, *Men without Art* (London, Cassell, 1934), p. 130.

4. In one place he writes that he began his criticism in 1926, and one at once thinks of *The Art of Being Ruled* of this year as being principally concerned with politics. Wyndham Lewis, *Blasting and Bombardiering* (London, Eyre and Spottiswoode, 1937), p. 5. He himself sees it as such in ch. 30 of *Rude Assignment,* but he also calls *The Lion and the Fox* "my first political book." Wyndham Lewis, *Rude Assignment* (London, Hutchinson, 1950), p. 160. Confusingly, T. S. Eliot calls *The Lion and the Fox* an " 'anti-political' book." T. S. Eliot, "The Lion and the Fox," *Twentieth Century Verse,* 6/7 (Nov./Dec. 1937), unpaged.

cal pamphleteer, as I am: who has been engaged, as in my case, in the analysis of what is obsessional in contemporary social life; in composing satiric verse; exposing abuses in art-politics; celebrating in fiction picturesque parasites; in weighing to the best of his ability, contemporary theories of the State." [5]

If all this activity, critical and creative, arose from a single experience, it would be as well to glance briefly at this; and here there were, I think, three main influences on Lewis before, and contemporary with, his first writings. These were his periods spent in Germany, France, and then England in the first fifteen years of this century.

Born on November 18, 1882,[6] on a ship in the Bay of Fundy, the

5. *Rude Assignment,* p. 10.

6. There has been some difficulty about the date of Lewis' birth, two of the Sitwells alleging that Lewis himself is modest to the point of inaccuracy on this score. And they are undoubtedly correct. In the Quinn Collection in the New York Public Library a letter may be seen dated June 14, 1920, in which it is already evident that Lewis imagines himself much younger than he is.

On the basis of a letter in their possession, and acting in all good faith, the Library of Congress has adopted the date of Lewis' birth as 1886. This date is to be found in the Library of Congress Catalogue, despite the Thieme-Becker listing of 1884. Many American libraries and bibliographers (such as Kunitz-Haycraft and Manly-Rickert) have followed the Library of Congress. But Marriott early gave 1884, as did *Living Art* (New York, The Dial Publishing Co., 1923), a volume significantly printed in Germany. The date 1886 occurs as late as 1950 in Sherard Vines's *100 Years of English Literature* (London, Duckworth, 1950), p. 290. More recently, Scott-James, Handley-Read, and others have preferred 1884, in common with the current *Who's Who.* Bénézit also gives this date. And in the Catalogue to the Tate exhibition of "Wyndham Lewis and Vorticism" in 1956, the birth-date is still given as 1884, on the basis of "essential information" provided by the artist himself. Yet a change of date in *Who's Who* should surely arouse the suspicion of a scrupulous scholar, since the information for this compilation is submitted by the subject himself; I was further surprised, on verifying Lewis' years of study at the Slade School, at the extremely early age he seems to have enrolled in that institution.

Accordingly I checked the School Register of Rugby School, where the above and other facts may be authenticated, and are indeed likely to be accurate since they were either given by Lewis' parents, or by himself before any need for obfuscation arose. It but remains to add—did Joyce know that Lewis was born in the same year as himself when, in *Finnegans Wake,* he made him one of his twins?

son of Capt. Charles Lewis of Ealing (sometime of West Point), Wyndham went to Rugby in January 1897 and left in December of the following year to study at the Slade Fine Art School between 1898 and 1901.[7] For the next six years he was on the Continent, getting rid of "the bad effects of English education." Lewis first studied for a short while at the Heimann Academy at Munich, where Edward Wadsworth also studied, and his Munich pension is on record in the Carlow Collection of his manuscripts. After the period in Munich Lewis took a studio in the rue Delambre in Paris, traveling in the Low Countries and in Spain, and returning to England in 1909.

The only published Slade School memoir of Lewis we have is from Sir William Rothenstein, who says that Lewis came to read his poems to him and was at this time a man who "liked to shroud himself in mystery," an opinion confirmed by subsequent writers of memories, including Sir Osbert Sitwell.

To his period in Munich Lewis makes little allusion in his work, but it must have given him a firsthand knowledge of the German student type he was to satirize in the figure of Otto Kreisler of *Tarr.* For although he again met this kind of student in both Paris and London, Kreisler is essentially a German expatriate, who

---

In *Finnegans Wake* we read explicitly of the Shaun/Shem personae, "we were in one class of age like to two clots of egg." Meanwhile, Lewis' recent claim to have "won a scholarship at the age of sixteen" to the Slade should be modified. The information as to the place of Lewis' birth is taken from the file of an attorney who was at one time asked to assist Lewis in the completion of American citizenship papers.

7. My dates come from University College, London, where I am indebted to the Alumnus Secretary. Handley-Read, in the Chronological Outline to his *The Art of Wyndham Lewis* (London, Faber and Faber, 1951), gives a later year. But Handley-Read is not to be trusted. Although he assures us, in his provenance to this outline, that the details given have "been checked by reference to actual copies of the books, folios, or journals" in each case, seven works are misdated or mistitled of the few selected. Both issues of *The Tyro* are dated as 1924, when even *Rude Assignment* gives the correct dates for these. Hugh Kenner, in his *Wyndham Lewis* (Norfolk, Conn., New Directions, 1954), refers to this tissue of errors as "an invaluable Chronological Outline of Lewis's career."

hangs himself in a village on the Franco-German border, and the satire, as we shall see, is one on German manners.

The influence of Munich on Lewis was mainly graphic. This was the Munich that that latter-day Savonarola, Thomas Mann's Hieronymo, sees as the art city par excellence in "Gladius Dei," a delightful story to be found in the early *Tristan* collection. Mann's story opens with a fine description of Munich as art Mecca at the turn of the century, in the passage beginning "München leuchtete . . ." and continuing to describe the atmosphere among the young artists, models, and their friends at the time. Georg Fuchs, whose *Der Kaiser, die Kultur und die Kunst* was published in Munich in 1904 (and followed by his *Deutsche Form* in 1907), has also given us a lively general picture of the city at this period.

Fuchs reminds us, especially in his consideration of Wilhelm Busch, that Munich was at this time the seat of the German comic genius, of the celebrated *Witzblätter*. Both Christian Morgenstern (whose father was a typical Munich painter) and Willy Busch were publishing in Munich in these days, and it is of more than merely speculative interest to compare Busch's black-and-white illustrations to the *Fliegende Blätter* of the period with Lewis' first graphic work. Other artists contributing to this comic journal include Oberländer, Caspari, and Grätz, and Lewis certainly saw their work in the Munich satiric press, as he must that of Thomas Theodor Heine and the *Simplizissimus* group. A competent art critic could surely find the roots of his draughtsmanship not only in the German aestheticians like Wilhelm Worringer and Theodor Lipps but in the grotesque comedy of the Munich *Witzblätter*. The grotesque element of this satire, which pervades Lewis' first stories, was collected in Wilhelm Michel's *Das Teuflische und Groteske in der Kunst,* published in Munich in 1911.

It was Paris, however, whither Lewis repaired after Munich, that formed his critical mind more obviously. He has told us that "my literary career began in France," and that at the same time his interest in philosophy was awakened. It was out of his experiences in Brittany that his first published stories grew, while no closer clue to his critical development is needed than his admission that he attended Bergson's lectures at the Collège de France. For unlike Irving Babbitt or T. E. Hulme, Lewis does not further admit the French sources of his ideas.

In *The Masters of Modern French Criticism* Babbitt mentions with respect a work he had earlier told us caught his eye in a Paris bookshop, Pierre Lasserre's *Le Romantisme français,* a doctoral dissertation begun in 1903, completed in 1906, and published in 1907, quickly running into a second edition the next year. This dissertation, which did not receive the necessary *mention très honorable* from the Sorbonne jury, probably on account of its violent tone (Rousseau being characterized as a charlatan, debauchee, and maniac), was for P. Mansell Jones, surveying the period nearly a quarter of a century later, "the first 'text-book' of anti-romantic criticism."

Both Lasserre and "Agathon," pseudonym for Henri Massis and Alfred de Tarde, author of the equally contentious *L'Esprit de la Nouvelle Sorbonne* of 1911, are singled out for praise by Babbitt, and Lasserre, in particular, is an antiromanticist to whom he constantly returns. Both, or rather all three, men were *ligueurs* of the Action Française by this time, Lasserre having written his *Charles Maurras et la renaissance classique* in 1902. The organ of the political party called the *Action française,* a periodical of that name, started on July 10, 1899. But Charles Maurras, its leader, had been one of the signatories to the classical revival calling itself the *école romane,* whose manifesto appeared in the *Figaro* for September 14, 1891, and several of whom are considered by Pound in his *Instigations.* This was the Maurras who went to Greece to report the first modern Olympics in 1896 as a lover to his mistress; he went for *La Gazette de France,* to whose editor, Gustave Janicot, he dedicated his charming *Anthinéa* of 1901. Lewis confesses to having attended the famous gatherings at the Lilas, over which Maurras originally presided, and I have often wondered whether this was the model for the Café Berne of *Tarr*.

But the French classical revival, with which Lewis has so much in common, is not the école romane of Moréas so much as that group of young and rebellious spirits who gathered to resist romanticism and, as it developed, Bergsonism, in France in the first decade of this century, and whom MM. Girard and Moncel distinguish as consisting chiefly of Charles Maurras, Paul Bourget, Henri Massis, Ernest Seillière, Julien Benda, Pierre Lasserre, and Jacques Maritain.[8]

This group was a closely integrated one. Massis, to be author of a two-volume work on Maurras, was an official, and extreme, critic for the Action Française. M. le baron Ernest Seillière published his *Le Mal romantique* in 1908 and caused his name to echo through Babbitt's *Democracy and Leadership* and *On Being Creative*. In the vanguard of this revolt, Maurras himself was by 1905 author of three works all more or less directly damaging to the nineteenth-century romantic ideal. Benda, who more than any of these critics was Lewis' master, began to attack Bergson, and through Bergson Romance, in 1912,[9] while his friend Charles Péguy had begun his *Cahiers de la quinzaine* in 1900, several of which were anti-Sorbonnist and one of which (2ième cahier de la 15ième série) carried Benda's *Sur le succès du Bergsonisme*. Jacques Maritain published his *L'Évolutionisme de M. Bergson* in 1911 and his *Philosophie de M. Bergson* in 1913. In 1913 there also appeared Henri Clouard's

8. Henri Girard et Henri Moncel, *Pour et contre le romantisme. Bibliographie des travaux publiés de 1914 à 1926,* "Études françaises," onzième cahier, 1er février 1927 (Paris, Société d' Édition "Les Belles Lettres"), pp. 19–21.

9. Benda's *Le Bergsonisme ou une philosophie de la mobilité* first appeared in 1912. In 1913 Benda published his *Une philosophie pathétique* in the *Cahiers de la quinzaine,* and later his *Réponse aux défenseurs du Bergsonisme.* These last two works were collected in 1914 and can be found in the edition I have used of *Sur le succès du Bergsonisme.* I have used the sixth edition of *Belphégor;* the first was in 1918 but according to the "Avertissement" provided the work was mainly composed before 1914. In chapter 6 of *On Being Creative* Babbitt praises Benda, though he finds him inclined to misanthropy.

Les Disciplines: Nécessité littéraire et sociale d'une renaissance classique, calling for a renewal of intelligence in letters and citing Bergson as an anti-intellectualist. With this record in mind it is natural to find Lewis according Bergson a "blast" in *Blast No. 1* of the year following.

There are, of course, considerable differences between these critics. From Maurras and Maritain, in particular, Lewis has dissociated himself with justification. Yet as a revolt of the young against what they felt to be the tyrannous "romantic" academy of their elders, this neoclassicism obviously drew Lewis to it in Paris, just as it attracted Hulme when he was there. And its spirit is typically captured in "Agathon's" *L'Esprit,* largely a collection of previously published articles. Here we read that romanticism has atrophied in the hands of pedagogues. The Sorbonne's Faculté des Lettres is bitterly opposed to classical culture, while an overscientific methodology ("étude fantaisiste des textes") is being taught in the name of literary criticism. For "Agathon," as for his neoclassical colleagues, the classical genius *is* "l'esprit français." This is a criticism, of course, which Lewis does not push. It was only natural that after the Franco-Prussian War there should be an unusually large legacy of anti-German opinion in France. Maurras made use of this, and "Agathon" typically finds the Sorbonne tainted by a romanticism that is essentially Germanic. It is only the early Lewis who was persuaded of this view, and it gave him in Kreisler one of his greatest characters. The view lingers in *Time and Western Man* but is not carried through in quite the full-blooded manner of the French.

This second influence on the young Wyndham Lewis also captured writers in other countries, of course, even in Germany. Karl Joël, for instance, to whose "classical" artist Lewis bears great resemblance, called for a new assimilation of the classical spirit in German literature in his *Die Bedeutung unseres klassischen Zeitalters für die Gegenwart* of 1916, originally written in Basel. Fritz Strich is another German critic of this period who is tactfully forgotten by the French neoclassicists. And I shall try to show that Ernst and Lublinski were others. Meanwhile in Italy even Benedetto Croce recognized the new French classical revival in his *Brevario di estetica* of 1911 and found it, on the whole, justified.

There is no doubt, however, that in England this revival found eminent practitioners. At about the same time that it was publishing Lewis' first work, *The English Review* was giving space to both Jean Moréas and Paul Bourget. In its pages for June 1910 Bourget characteristically laments "cette funeste année," 1870, marked as it was by "l'installation en France du régime démocratique." Bourget goes on to deplore French writers from Voltaire to Victor Hugo, from Rousseau to Lamartine and Michelet, finally regretting that France could not produce in 1871 an Edmund Burke, a man Babbitt is to single out as a defender of traditional order against Rousseau in *Democracy and Leadership*. Hulme, Lewis' friend by now, and an avowed classicist of a sort, tells us how he attended a lecture on Racine in Paris heckled by irascible young students; Montgomery Belgion adds the information that these hecklers were indeed the famous, or infamous, *camelots du roi*. By 1914 Lewis was not only writing letters to *The New Age* in defense of Hulme but he was also, this year, lecturing beside him, a defense that bellicose philosopher should not have needed, for he was capable of suggesting "a little personal violence" in support of his views and of transfixing Lewis himself, a big man, on the railings of Soho Square to press home a point, as well as being provided, according to Michael Roberts, with an original Gaudier-Brzeska knuckleduster. Of his relationship to Hulme, Lewis has written: "We happened, that is all, to be made for each other, as critic and 'creator.'" Yet Hulme was in a dilemma in the matter of French antiromanticism. On one hand, he is the sympathetic translator and interpreter of Bergson (even, in *The New Age* for November 9, 1911, stoutly defending Bergson against the scurrilous charge of standing for democracy); on the other, writing as the militant "North Staffs" of the war years, Hulme is clearly indebted to the ideas of Maurras in his discrediting of pacifism.

Although French neoclassicism continued throughout the nineteen twenties, it was formed as a movement in France in the first decade of this century, the years so ardently dramatized in the enviably impartial *Jean Barois,* when Lewis met it firsthand. By the twenties Maurras is using it more and more as a camouflage for his political beliefs, as his letters to Raymond de la Tailhède show. Consequently it loses impetus, for as a political ideology contemporary neoclassicism has had little sympathy in France. This is surely shown by Maurras' own career. He came to prominence on the wave of understandable anti-German sentiment, but his party soon lost any popular context and never had any real representation in the Chambre des Deputés, while after the first World War the Action Française, though claiming to be Catholic to the core, was disowned by the Pope. Even "in the 'nationalistic' elections of 1898," writes Albert Guerard, "not a single anti-Semite was returned by metropolitan France. Drumont, the apostle of that hateful creed, had to seek a seat in Algeria."

The classical-romantic controvery is examined by Émile Henriot in the weekly *La Renaissance politique et littéraire* early in 1921, and two cahiers on the same subject were published by the Association des Études Françaises in 1928 and 1929, but it is hard to see it as a living issue in the way it had been earlier. The bibliography on neoclassicism, drawn up for the Association in 1927 by MM. Girard and Moncel, has a final appearance. New names, such as those of René Benjamin and Ramon Fernandez, join the roll call and creative writers continue, of course, to mirror the *débat,* but its boundaries are defined early in the century in France.

This is not to deny that there were other revolts against nineteenth-century European romanticism, but the neoclassicism Lewis is aligned with, together to some extent with those he likes to call "the men of 1914"—Eliot, Pound, Joyce, and himself—is that of the French critics mentioned, few of whom, except possibly Lasserre, add anything substantially new to their attack after the first World War. Clearly one can speculate on the causes of this anti-romanticism. Critical agreement seems to have been reached that it was an obvious reaction after a century of romanticism, a reaction speeded by the sociological ideas of the Action Française. Parenthetically, it is interesting that Bergson only becomes progressively anathematized. "Agathon," for instance, is at first temperate, but by 1913 calls Bergson negative and mechanical (Lewis' words for him later). Probably this was due to the fact that Bergson, lecturing at the Collège, was in a way a rebel against the Sorbonne, his candidature there having been refused in 1894 and 1898. We shall see how much Lewis borrowed from these French thinkers and we shall find his attitude admirably expressed in that now famous statement on the controversy by T. S. Eliot: "there may be a good deal to be said for Romanticism in life, there is no place for it in letters." [10]

Indeed the English antiromanticists tend to translate, rather than fabricate, antiromantic criticism. F. S. Flint, having helped Hulme to translate Bergson (if we are to believe Aldington), translated Massis' *Défense de l'Occident* in 1927, the very year in which Lewis showed himself so concerned as to the health of Western man. Aldington followed with his translation of Benda's *La Trahison des clercs*. Eliot, friend of both Massis and Maritain, guided, defended, and in some cases even lauded Benda, Maritain, and Maurras (his Coriolan) through the pages of *The Criterion* of the twenties. (In *The Literature of Politics*, an address to the London Conservative Political Centre published in 1955, Eliot confesses that he now sees some of Maurras' views as "deplorable.") The first chapter of Babbitt's *Rousseau and Romanticism* of 1919 is entitled "The Terms Classic and Romantic." Sir Herbert Grierson's Leslie Stephen Lecture for 1923 was on "Classical and Romantic," terms compared the year before in Germany by Strich. In 1934 both Lewis and Eliot published books, *Men without Art* and *After Strange Gods* respectively, in which there is reference to the debate. But I cannot see, beyond individual nuances here and there, much to challenge the contention that these English works prolong a battle fought out in

10. T. S. Eliot, *The Sacred Wood* (London, Methuen, 1932), p. 32; these essays were first published in 1920.

France earlier and in America, if we are to credit Robert Gorham
Davis,[11] later.

This brings us to the third influence on the young Lewis, namely
his first literary associations in London. His first publication was
in Ford Madox Ford's *The English Review*. Claiming that its title
was chosen by Conrad, Ford has given us many reminiscences about
this periodical. Harold Monro and Violet Hunt both assert that it
was founded in the first place to print a rejected poem of Hardy's.
Ford denies this story, stating that if any such idea existed it was
in the head of his colleague Marwood, but certainly Hardy's poem
"A Sunday Morning Tragedy" starts the first issue.

Apart from Ford's own inimitable memoirs, Douglas Goldring
and Violet Hunt have both recorded the beginnings of this influential review. It consisted of two schools of contributors; the
older, established generation included Conrad, W. H. Hudson,
Henry James, Hardy, Galsworthy, Wells (whose *Tono-Bungay* was
first printed in these pages), Meredith, and Arnold Bennett, while
"les jeunes," or the "haughty and proud generation" as Ford called
them, included among others D. H. Lawrence, Pound, and Lewis.
It was this younger generation, including also Flint, Norman Douglas, Eliot, "H.D.," Aldington, R. A. Scott-James, and R. B. Cunning-
hame Graham (some thirty years older than Lewis, of course),
whom Lewis met at 84 Holland Park Avenue, Ford's house and
editorial office.

The English Review was born in December 1908. Lewis met
Ezra Pound in 1910, according to Stanley Coffman.[12] This was,
then, after Pound had exerted some influence on his own, if we are
again to trust Flint's assertion, in *The Egoist* for May 1, 1915, that
the Imagist movement began in 1908 with Hulme's Poets' Club,
a club Flint earlier attacked for its pomposity and which did not
number Lewis among its members.[13] Coffman charts the beginnings

11. Robert Gorham Davis, "The New Criticism and Democratic Tradition,"
The American Scholar, 19, No. 1 (Winter 1949–50), 9–19.

12. Stanley K. Coffman Jr., *Imagism* (Norman, Okla., University of Oklahoma
Press, 1951), p. 18.

13. F. S. Flint, "The History of Imagism," *The Egoist, 2,* No. 5 (May 1, 1915),

of Imagism proper "in the spring of 1912," as we find them recorded in Aldington's *Life for Life's Sake,* despite the fact that
Pound calls the Imagists a school in 1909.[14] However this may be,
it seems that Lewis' return from the Continent at this time influenced Pound. Flint complains, for instance, that Pound "made
Imagism to mean pictures as Wyndham Lewis understands them,"
and Hugh Kenner believes that it was the increasing femininity of
Imagism, especially after the arrival in London of Amy Lowell
("Amygism"), that drove Pound to Lewis and his more masculine
Vortex. The anthology, officially uniting the Imagists, *Des Imagistes,*
did not appear until 1914.

In turn, Lewis' friendship with Pound would naturally lead him
from *The English Review* to *Blast* and the Great English Vortex.
Pound now saw to it, too, that Lewis could place his work in *The
Little Review,* for when he became London editor of this review
in 1917 Pound wrote to Margaret Anderson stating—what we also
find in his editorial for the May 1917 issue—that he wished to use the
review as a platform for Joyce, Eliot, Lewis, and himself, for, in
fact, the "men of 1914."

Similarly Lewis' meeting with Eliot, to whom, so he says, Pound
introduced him between the two issues of *Blast,* led to another
important association for him, that with the Egoist Ltd., with which
press he was to publish both *Tarr* and *The Caliph's Design.* Yet it
is worth recording that "Tarr" was accepted by *The Egoist* before
Eliot took over majority editorial control. The history of this important periodical is as follows; in *The New Age* for November

---

70–1. Flint's previous article, "Imagisme," *Poetry, 1,* No. 6 (March 1913), 198–
200, stated the principles of the movement, followed by "A Few Don't's by an
Imagiste" by Pound. But see also Ezra Pound, *Pavannes and Divisions* (New York,
Knopf, 1918), pp. 95–6.

14. Coffman, *Imagism,* pp. 4–5 (but cf. p. 154). Pound in one place calls the
Imagists "descendants of the forgotten school of 1909." Ezra Pound, Prefatory
Note to the "Complete Poetical Works of T. E. Hulme," *Ripostes of Ezra Pound*
(London, Stephen Swift, 1912), p. 59. Hugh Kenner takes Pound, as he takes
Ford, at his own word on the literary events of these days. Hugh Kenner, *The
Poetry of Ezra Pound* (Norfolk, Conn., New Directions, 1951), p. 56.

23, 1911, Harriet Weaver's *The Freewoman* is announced as to
be under the joint editorship of Dora Marsden and Mary Gawthorpe;
this became *The New Freewoman* and on January 1, 1914, *The
Egoist*. In the summer of 1916 we find Aldington and "H.D."
assistant editors, but with the former's removal to the front Eliot
took over in June 1917. "Tarr" began in *The Egoist* for April 1,
1916.

Among these many associations in the third formative period in
Lewis' early literary career, Ezra Pound was pre-eminent. Lewis
himself has consistently maintained that Pound was the animator of
the "men of 1914." Ford and Iris Barry both confirm this impression. Hugh Gordon Porteus claims this position for Lewis, but few
memoirs of the period substantiate him. John Cournos mentions
what an important literary meeting place Pound's flat was at this
time, while Stella Bowen recalls Pound's dinner parties at Bel-
lotti's in Soho, which Lewis attended. Not only has Lewis paid
tribute to Pound for his own indebtedness in this respect, but he
says that Eliot also met many, like Aldington, who were to be
influential on him, through Pound. And it was through Eliot that
Lewis met Joyce for the first time in the summer of 1920.[15]

Indeed, Lewis must have been too busy with his painting at this
time to have been so conscientious an "animator" as Pound. For
another short-lived literary association of the pre-first World War
era takes us into the field of Lewis' graphic art. During its brief
lifetime Goldring's periodical *The Tramp* published as well as
Lewis such writers as Flecker, W. H. Davies, Edward Thomas,
Arnold Bennett, and—Marinetti. To be reminded of Marinetti, and
of his spectacular visit to London when he gave a celebrated lecture
at the Doré Gallery in Bond Street, is to be reminded that, as Ford
puts it, "for a moment in the just-before-the-war days, the Fine,
the Plastic and the Literary Arts touched hands with an unusual

---

15. *Blasting and Bombardiering*, pp. 270 ff. Pound writes to Joyce that Eliot is
leaving for Paris around August 15, 1920. *The Letters of Ezra Pound, 1907–1941*,
ed. D. D. Paige (New York, Harcourt, Brace, 1950), p. 156.

intimacy and what is called one-ness of purpose." As we know, Lewis shared in this portmanteau period.

Handley-Read has it that Lewis' first exhibition was at the Ryder Gallery in 1909, but surprisingly he makes no mention of the famous "Post-Impressionist" show organized by Roger Fry at the Grafton Galleries in 1911. It was this exhibit, whose aims were summarized by Fry in *The Fortnightly Review* for May 1, 1911, that attracted Hulme to comment so vividly on the visual arts. To it Lewis sent his drawings for *Timon of Athens,* which he later published as a portfolio from the Cube Press, for if he did not, like Max Weber, write *Cubist Poems,* Lewis at least ran a Cube Press and painted Cubist rooms. Sir William Rothenstein has left us a chapter on this exhibition in his *Men and Memories, 1900–1922,* while Jacob Epstein has testified to the feeling of "intimacy" among the arts at this period, describing how he used to meet Hulme and Lewis and discuss art with them in 1912.

The war sealed this third period for Lewis. Although Lewis' name can be seen on the editorial committee of *Coterie* for December 1919, along with Eliot, Huxley, and Aldington, the war inevitably narrowed some of these friendships, as it ended Hulme's life a quarter of a mile from where Lewis' own battery was dug in, for Lewis allegedly enlisted in the Royal Artillery in 1915.[16] At the end of January 1917 Lewis is still in England, however, writing to John Quinn from Kent, although in *Blasting and Bombardiering* he writes about being at the front "throughout 1917." Ford recounts how he lost touch with Lewis after the war and he does not invite him to contribute to *The Transatlantic Review,* edited from Paris in 1924, nor is there any mention of Lewis in Stella Bowen's description of the first days of this review in *Drawn from Life.* If Lewis fell out with his first editor—and if one gives credence to Ford's memoirs—one can scarcely be surprised. For in the days of the con-

16. Handley-Read, *Art of Wyndham Lewis,* p. 37; here Handley-Read is corroborated by Lewis himself (*Blasting and Bombardiering,* pp. 91 ff.), while Pound writes to Lewis in uniform on June 24, 1916 (*Letters of Ezra Pound,* p. 83).

ception of *Blast,* Ford says, Lewis (whom he calls "D.Z.") and
Pound took him for a walk, during which Lewis is supposed to
have told Ford he was finished: " 'What people want is me, not
you,' " he thundered at Ford. " 'They want to see me. A Vortex . . .
I . . . I . . . I . . . The Vortex.' " [17]

There is little change in Lewis' critical opinions after 1920 and
he lives today in Notting Hill, Rotting Hill as Pound called it, the
place of his first meeting with Eliot through Pound. If it is true,
then, that his critical grew out of his creative work, it must make
any consideration of his criticism especially interesting as illumi-
nating his entire artistic genius. For it follows that if we resume
Lewis' criticism, we resume the purpose of his satire. And as we
inspect this criticism what we find is as representative a statement
of contemporary neoclassicism as can be found in any English
writer. In nothing is it more neoclassical than in its pretensions to
impartiality.

By the word "clerc" Benda designates the intellectual or thinker
who has, in the past, remained apart from practical necessity and
current controversy in an effort to safeguard lasting values; it is
this element of society which is, for Benda, especially guilty of
dereliction of duty today. Again and again Lewis claims to be this
kind of true clerc and, lest we might think him as deficient in ob-
jectivity as does Professor Häusermann (who finds him detached
only in name), Lewis reminds us over and over that he takes the
"outside" position, keeping his mind free of dogma and refusing to
mix thinking and acting (except inasmuch as thinking is one form
of acting). In *Blast No. 2* he called himself "an IMPARTIAL man
in time of war"; in 1926 he protests that he is "an independent
observer," and three years later an " 'impartial observer.' " It is
in politics, in particular, that he disarms us with the repeated as-

17. Ford Madox Ford, *Return to Yesterday* (New York, Liveright, 1932), p.
400: Ford repeats this story with minor alterations in his *Mightier than the
Sword* (London, Allen and Unwin, 1938), p. 282.

surance of classical detachment. "I fly the flag of no party"; [18] "I advance the strange claim (as my private *Bill of Rights*) to act and think non-politically in everything, in complete detachment"; [19] "I belong to no party"; [20] "Politically I stand nowhere"; [21] "I believe I am alone among writers today in advocating no partisanship in the political field"; [22] "I am called a rebel, I am called a reactionary, according to which boss of the moment I am facing, or whose dogs are barking at my heels" [23]—these are only a few such assurances culled from over the years, a heroic impartiality in politics that reminds us that the author of the Note to *Flowering Rifle*, Roy Campbell, has lately been seen as "a politically unattached poet" [24] by a writer for the British Council, Alan Ross. One could, in fact, continue indefinitely quoting Lewis' idea of himself as the detached spectator, if to do so might not give the uncharitable impression that he was protesting too much. One might, indeed, be led to be so lacking in impartiality as Professor Häusermann when one finds, for example, Lewis writing in the year he addressed the British Fascist party in *The British Union Quarterly*, "*Je constate*, that is all." [25]

Only occasionally does this mask of detachment slip off and we

18. Wyndham Lewis, *Left Wings over Europe: or, How to Make a War about Nothing* (London, Cape, 1936), p. 17.

19. Wyndham Lewis, *The Diabolical Principle and the Dithyrambic Spectator* (London, Chatto and Windus, 1931), p. 37.

20. Wyndham Lewis, *Rotting Hill* (Chicago, Henry Regnery, 1952), p. 54.

21. *Rude Assignment*, p. 77.

22. *Men without Art*, p. 263.

23. Wyndham Lewis, *Satire and Fiction* (London, The Arthur Press, 1930), p. 51. Answering an inquiry in *New Verse* in 1934 as to his political sympathies of the time, Lewis replied, "Politically I take my stand exactly between the Bolshevist and the Fascist—the gentleman on my left I shake with my left hand, the gentleman on my right with my right." And cf. "I have always hated any government" (*Rotting Hill*, p. 226).

24. Alan Ross, *Poetry 1945–1950* (London, Longmans, Green, 1951, i.e. 1952, see *DNB*), p. 22.

25. *Blasting and Bombardiering*, p. 244.

find him writing, "it is impossible to be non-partisan," [26] or, a more exact definition of his attitude, "I have an obvious interest in what I am writing about." [27] Strangely, while Lewis insists on his political detachment, he admits to being least impartial in his graphic art criticism, where he is actually more impartial, especially in his recent reviews in *The Listener*. The ideal of detachment, however, is an important classical principle for Lewis, who believes that when art, philosophy, and literature descend to the level of ordinary men, they are contaminated. If he is one-sided, it is as what he calls "a doctrinaire of art-independent of life."

This idea, of the creative individual keeping himself apart, was also behind Yeats' use of the mask. Richard Ellmann has shown what the mask meant to Yeats and, although Yeats used it in a special sense in *A Vision,* as one of the Four Faculties and the opposite of what he called Will, it was essentially employed as an ideal of impersonality or detachment, in keeping with the antiromantic movement. Yeats' use of the mask is part of what Ellmann calls "his policy of concealment of his more intimate self," and Ellmann notes, interestingly, that the word "mask" began to occur in Yeats' writings in the first decade of this century. In Yeats' case it was in consonance with his poetic movement away from his early romanticism.

For Yeats the mask was man's antiself, or *"antithetical* being," as he called it in *A Vision*. In *Dramatis Personae* he wrote, "I think that all happiness depends on the energy to assume the mask of some other self." Yeats further described the use of the mask in his *Autobiographies* as an explanation of true character, which is the sense of Pound's *Personae* (or even of Browning's). Thus we find that the manuscript of Lewis' *The Lion and the Fox* bears the subtitle "Or Shakespeare Unmasked." The artist as opposite of his creation is best expressed by Yeats in his poem "Ego Dominus

26. *The Enemy: A Review of Art and Literature, No. 2* (London, The Arthur Press, Sept. 1927), p. xxxi.
27. *Men without Art,* p. 118.

Tuus," a dialogue between Hic and Ille (Willie, as Pound called it), Ille concluding:

> "I call to the mysterious one who yet
> Shall walk the wet sand by the water's edge,
> And look most like me, being indeed my double,
> And prove of all imaginable things
> The most unlike, being my anti-self,
> And, standing by these characters, disclose
> All that I seek; . . ." [28]

But although Lewis has been typically neoclassical in hiding behind some fictional mask, this has not been what it was for Yeats —"the opposite of all that I am in my daily life." Writing of the Lewisian artist, Hugh Kenner says, "he doesn't quite believe in his lonely role (hence his interest in simulacra who manage to corrupt its austerity with a gratifying ration of vulgar power)." [29] It is through these simulacra, or disguises, that one is often compelled to present Lewis' critical opinions. For Lewis early advised the creative artist a variety of disguises. "The Code of a Herdsman," originally published in *The Little Review* for July 1917, is mainly a set of instructions to the Herdsman, or inspired artist, not to come down from his mountain to the herd without some mask or disguise. "Stagnant gases from these Yahooesque and rotten herds are more dangerous often than the wandering cylinders that emit them. See that you are not caught in them without your mask." [30]

Here the pun is made on a gas mask, of course, one Lewis liked

28. W. B. Yeats, *Essays* (New York, Macmillan, 1924), p. 484.

29. Hugh Kenner, "The War with Time," *Shenandoah, 4,* Nos. 2–3 (Summer/Autumn 1953), p. 22.

30. Wyndham Lewis, *The Ideal Giant, The Code of a Herdsman, Cantelman's Spring-Mate,* privately printed for the London office of *The Little Review* (1917), p. 36. In the text I adopt the spelling Cantleman. When this character first appeared in *The Little Review* (causing the issue to be confiscated by U.S. postal authorities), he was variously spelt. In *Blasting and Bombardiering,* however, where he is substituted for Thomas Blenner of *Blast No. 2,* he makes his last, full-dress appearance as Cantleman.

to prolong, for after an attack on him as the Enemy in *transition* for 1927 (a prolific year in Lewis' "canon"), he staged an imaginary conversation between himself ("L.") and the editors of *transition* ("P.A.J."), Eugene Jolas, Elliot Paul, and Robert Sage, in *The Diabolical Principle and the Dithyrambic Spectator.* In the course of this conversation "P.A.J." disgustedly accuses "L." of belonging to no party and, pressed to give himself some label, "L." terms himself " 'A Lewisite begging your pardon.' " Lewisite was the poisonous gas used by *both* sides during the first World War.

Nearly all the figures in Lewis' early drawings, especially those on the title pages of chapters or books, are masked; easily available examples can be seen in the prospectuses for *The Enemy* or the drawing for the section of *One-Way Song,* called "If So the Man You Are" and including the Enemy episode, showing an armored man accompanied by his *Doppel* or *sosie.* Again, we read that the characters in his play *The Enemy of the Stars* are masked, while the autobiographical Enemy himself enters the long poem *One-Way Song* with a mask on. The Herdsman is advised to adopt six different personalities to keep himself pure of the herd.

It is necessary to stress this because, by adopting at least six such personalities himself, Lewis makes it hard to take much of his criticism directly. Often some alias or alter ego intervenes and for that reason some of these should be sketched in briefly here, before rehearsing the criticism itself.

Chronologically, the first is Cantleman. Lewis calls Cantleman "my fictional diarist," while warning us not to confuse Cantleman with himself. But there are points of resemblance. Blenner-Cantleman is aged thirty-three, about Lewis' own age at the time of his first creation of the character. He is a retired first lieutenant with a beard and, typical of these antiselves, he has strong eyes, sharp sight among the blind crowds. He is, thus, a Crowd-Master, a man who does not want to "enter into league" with life. Cantleman is a military alias, and Lewis has confessed, "my politics bear signs everywhere of their origin in war." It is not pressing the comparison too far, I think, to recall Lewis' descriptions of his own visits to gunner O.P.'s during the war in *Blasting and Bombardiering*. Here, as gunner officer surveying in hostile detachment enemy terrain on which to direct his guns, Lewis must have felt an ironic symbol of his own literary outpost.

The "joy of protest" ingrained in Blenner is found also in William Bland Burn, another early alias and author of some "Imaginary Letters" from Petrograd to his wife Lydia in the first World War. The correspondence, in which Pound joined as Walter Villerant, characterizes Burn as a hater of the herd, or swine, and a man longing to change humanity back into men again. But it is the Enemy that is Lewis' most recurrent mask. This product of the Arthur Press—a name chosen for his own publishing house by Lewis since the word is the same in all languages [31]—advocates constant opposition, the wearing of many coats, the outside position as the only method of attaining truth in comtemporary society. In a world of sham, the Enemy seems to be saying, only revolt can constitute authenticity.

Lewis' periodical *The Enemy*, appearing toward the end of the twenties, was openly intended to sow discord. The editorial to Volume 1 defines the Enemy himself as "a solitary outlaw," the natural foe of modern times, opposed as these are said to be to genius. Although the Enemy has no politics, he is going to attack the indolence and apathy of the masses, in an effort to free the truly creative individual. The editorial to *No. 2* reaffirms this purpose, defining the Enemy's duty as opposition to all vested interests and pseudo-revolutionary trends in general, and in particular to the Time school and millionaire Bohemia. Later, in a newspaper article,[32] Lewis tells us that the Enemy is himself the true individual of our times and, as such, a man's best friend. A year later Lewis bids this

31. *Rude Assignment*, p. 205: Wyndham Lewis, *The Jews, Are They Human?* (London, Allen and Unwin, 1939), p. 48. The Abbé Brémond, a writer to whom Lewis refers with reluctant respect, introduced a new edition of Ulric Guttinguer's somewhat autobiographical *Arthur* in 1925, at the time when the Arthur Press started.

32. Wyndham Lewis, "What It Feels Like to Be an Enemy," *The Daily Herald*, No. 5082 (May 30, 1932), p. 8.

alias good-by in his one satiric poem *One-Way Song,* whose "Enemy
Interlude" furnishes us with the best description of the characterization:

> His balance is astonishing when you consider
> He has never sold himself to the highest bidder,
> Never has lived a week for twenty summers
> Free of the drumfire of the camouflaged gunners,
> Never has eaten a meal that was undramatic—
> Without the next being highly problematic.
> Never succumbed to panic, *kaltes blut* [*sic*]
> His watchword, facing ahead in untroubled mood.
> He has been his own bagman, critic, cop, designer,
> Publisher, agent, char-man and shoe-shiner.

He goes on:

> You must salute this outcast Enemy—
> Outcasted for refusal to conform
> To the phases of this artificial storm.

Stanza 15 of the part "If So the Man You Are," which Gilbert
Armitage thought as good as Byron,[33] has a section on the sham
of our everyday life very reminiscent of Hugh MacDiarmid's
"hokum" passage in *To Circumjack Cencrastus,*[34] and it is interesting to note that MacDiarmid, who would not normally be drawn
to Lewis' politics, gave *One-Way Song* a laudatory review at the
time.[35]

There are many other minor aliases. Ned, a political alias of
1937, calls himself a "Bolsho-Tory," meaning that he sits on both
sides of the fence at once, being both anti-Russian and anti-John

33. Gilbert Armitage, review of *One-Way Song, New Verse,* No. 7 (Feb. 1934),
16–17.

34. Hugh M'Diarmid, *To Circumjack Cencrastus or The Curly Snake* (Edin-
burgh, Blackwood, 1930), pp. 132–5.

35. Hugh MacDiarmid, review of *One-Way Song, Scots Observer, 8,* No. 381
(Jan., 1934), 10.

Bull. He has other sympathies, however, for he is pro-German (though denying being so, of course), springs to the defense of Hitler, and believes fascism to be "the nearest thing to Democracy." [36] Ned loathes usury and would welcome fascism to eliminate it and he wonders, sadly, why the English take to him so little. The supposedly uncommitted nature of the Lewisian alter ego, exemplified in the narrator of *Rotting Hill* (the only man impervious to the Rot and the only one who says "No" to his society), is also found in the "Deputy" in *Men without Art*. Kemp, of *The Ideal Giant,* a writer whose time is consumed with journalism and who is to be found in an arty restaurant, makes comments in sympathy with Lewis' own opinions during his pre-first World War Café Royal period. Kemp sponsors what Lewis often calls Cato's truth, or the expedient lie. Thus he tells his friend Fingal that he never lies and then at once poses as a war hero, saying "The Ego's worst enemy is Truth." This posing as a war hero is delightfully repeated in the person of the bogus Commander Perse (or Perce) at the end of *The Apes of God.* Ned, too, uses Cato's truth, and we find that he kills his patriotically English friend, Launcelot Nidwit, with it. As Kemp says, the status quo of contemporary Western society is a falsehood: "Self. Self. One must rescue that sanity. Truth, duty —are insanity."

This is orthodox Wyndham Lewis, for Kemp is simply saying that what we call truth is no truth, since our civilization is a fake. This, we shall see, is Percy Hardcaster's tragic lesson in *The Revenge for Love;* as he says to Gillian, " 'If you don't use *the lie* it is as if you made war upon a nation armed with bombs and gas with flintlocks or just with fists.' " [37] It is from this point on that Gillian

36. Wyndham Lewis, *Count Your Dead: They Are Alive! or A New War in the Making* (London, Lovat Dickson, 1937), p. 276.

37. Wyndham Lewis, *The Revenge for Love* (London, Methuen, 1952), p. 202. In general, I have used first editions of Lewis' works. The recent Methuen reprints, however, reproduce with fidelity, and only one or two minor corrections, the last edition of the work in question before the second World War. In the case of *Tarr* Lewis' extensive revisions are taken into account below.

begins to dislike him, for she is part of the sham herself. And so
Kemp tells Miss Godd, a murderess, "What I meant was that honesty
was a rhythm; it must be broken up." [38]

Some final masks should be mentioned. The first is Maj. Archibald
("Corkers") Corcoran whom we meet in *America, I Presume* gazing
with "Olympian detachment" on the New York crowds, "staccato
crowds" as he calls them later. There are many autobiographical
elements in this creation of 1940, the son of an army officer, married to a wife (a good cook) born in Maine, who leaves for Canada
and America shortly before the start of the second World War. An
interesting aspect of this characterization is the monocle "Corkers"
sports, imparting a symbolically militant appearance to his eye.
Indeed, his eye "explodes" behind his monocle, his eyeglass (or
"eyeglassed optical sentinel") has a "menace" in it. "Corkers" feels
very lonely and unique and at the end his wife, a celebrated mystery
writer (authoress of *Murder Is Fun* and *A Poppy in the Chocolate*),
leaves him. This duplicates the sundering of intellect (eye) and
emotion (woman), which there is at the end of *Tarr*. But Corcoran
is, of course, a stage John Bull, completely "sporting," though
playing the game in the English sense is more of a vice than a virtue
for Lewis. In one place, in fact, he suggests that his so-called impartiality is a highly unsportsmanlike gesture in a world like ours
where everyone is a phony: "It is rather disgusting of me, but I
am trying not to take sides . . . I shall go ahead, in my unsport-
ing way."

Secondly there is René Harding, the hero of *Self Condemned*,
who also leaves England for Canada at the same time as "Corkers,"
and then leaves Canada for the U.S.A. at the end of the book
(Lewis himself left Toronto for St. Louis and a number of little-
known portraits). "You see," René remarks at one point, "I think
in a manner in which one is not allowed to think. So I become an
outsider, almost a pariah." Father Card of *The Red Priest* should
also be mentioned. He is an ex-boxing Blue, with "the extremism of

38. *Ideal Giant*, p. 20.

the Asiatic." He is described as a "Man-Eating Man" (he kills a character called Makepeace), a "locomotive," and a "giant." One character in the book says of him: "He loathes everything, you see." It is not surprising that he desires "absolute loneliness," and finds it among the Eskimos, who kill him.

Lastly there is Snooty Baronet, Sir Michael Kell-Imrie, a Scot aged thirty-nine and nine months (about twelve years younger than his creator), and author of *People Behaving*. But the kind of behavior Snooty advocates by his actions, especially in his *acte gratuit* of shooting his best friend in the back, is anti-behavior. He indeed calls himself an "anti-man" and enemy of the human race. Physically, he is, like "Corkers" and like Lewis himself, six feet tall. Unlike Lewis he was wounded in the war and has a false leg and a plate in his skull. Thus he is semimechanical. His face frequently wears a "mask," he prefers "the One to the Many (whatever be the condition of the One)" and he refers affectionately to the genius of the Lewis-gun. What is more he laughs like Samuel Butler, a man he much admires as a fellow misanthropist. As usual he claims detachment: "To register the roar of storms you must yourself be just beyond their deafening circles."

Snooty's warning to his readers is surely one Lewis would want to give to any critic approaching his own opus: "Within the twilight of my race's days, the hostile silhouette (once that of tradition, of the hated next-door neighbour) grows vaster beneath our eyes . . . Expect nothing out of my mouth, therefore, that has a pleasant sound. Look for nothing but descriptions out of a vision of a person who has given up hoping for Man, who is scrupulous and just, if only out of contempt for those who are so much the contrary." [39]

39. Wyndham Lewis, *Snooty Baronet* (London, Cassell, 1932), p. 233.

PART I: POLITICS

"I am not a politician but an artist." [*The Jews, Are They Human?* p. 78.]

Chapter 1: A Study of the State

"With candour, and with an almost criminal indifference to my personal interests, I have given myself up to the study of the State."
[*Rude Assignment*, pp. 63–4.]

DURING the dinner party at Lord Osmund's in *The Apes of God* there is a discussion of contemporary literature, and one character inquires about " 'our solitary high-brow pur-sang Lewis?' " To which the reply is given that his activities are mere " *'teiloperationen.'* " Lewis is here unusually frank in describing his critical assaults, particularly in the field of politics. Yet, although these are indeed teiloperationen, they arise out of a common view of human society which he takes with him to all his writings.

What is politics for Lewis? Politics is the necessary government by force of the human animal in society. Believing with Machiavelli that men are not good,[1] Lewis sees politics as the instrument of power, used by individual or State to curb the masses. So politicians are to be classed with soldiers, or policemen, in that they are principally concerned with power—so much so, he once says, that intellectual equipment is a handicap for the contemporary politician.[2]

Being so concerned with power, the State, national or sovereign, functions on a lower level than the individual, an important attitude to emphasize from the start since it is typical of the neoclassicist in its

1. There are several key places in Machiavelli's work where we meet this, in particular the lion and fox episode in ch. 18 of *Il Principe,* and ch. 3 of the first book of the *Discorsi.* This distinction seems to escape James Burnham in his otherwise admirable study of Machiavelli.

2. Wyndham Lewis, *The Old Gang and the New Gang* (London, Desmond Harmsworth, 1933), p. 34.

opposition to the Platonic doctrine that the State can condition the individual. In all spheres the State acts as a restrictive influence on the individual, although of course he hints at the kind of State that might not do so, as we shall see. But politics, being concerned with power, is set on a lower plane of activity than that on which the true individual should operate. In short, "Politics are 'below' morals, below the reason," and "There are no *good* politics." [3]

There can be no objective truth in politics, Lewis asserts, since here participation alone gives knowledge, and participation means contact with that emotional animal, man. Today especially, since the undisciplined masses have been allowed into the political arena in the Western democracies, politics has put us in the keeping of the instinctual and violent, rather than of the rational, elements in our societies.

In *La Trahison des clercs,* a book Lewis calls "a modern classic," Benda gives three stages in the relationship between politics and morality; the first, when the moral was invited to determine the political; the second, when morals were to be dissociated from politics (as in Machiavelli); the third, when politics is to dictate morals (as today, especially in the politics of men like Maurras). [4]

Lewis begins his criticism of the contemporary scene from this last point of view, with the complaint that politics today implies a subordination of the intellect to practical ends and is thus inimical to the functioning of the true individual. Both Benda and Lewis explicitly agree with Romain Rolland's dictum: "Tous les États puent." Ned concludes, then, that politics is totally untruthful, a

3. *Rude Assignment*, pp. 62, 221. One should enter the occasional contradiction here. In one place Lewis will say that "Politics is a melodrama for teen-aged minds" (Wyndham Lewis, *America and Cosmic Man,* New York, Doubleday, 1949, p. 12); then we find him arguing that contemporary fiction must be steeped in politics to be an adequate reflection of reality (*Rotting Hill,* p. vii).

4. Julien Benda, *La Trahison des clercs* (Paris, Grasset, 1948), p. 183; this work originally appeared in 1927, but in *Rude Assignment* Lewis refers at length to this new edition, which includes a new preface recapitulating opinions previously expressed in *La Grande Épreuve des démocraties.*

lie opposed at every point to objective truth. This poses a fundamental, perhaps tragic, anomaly in Lewis' work; namely politics is base but today "Man, unless a very unusually fine specimen, is a 'political animal.' "

The reason why our age has become so cravenly political, in this sense, is that the true individual, whom Lewis defines as the abstract or quintessence of the group, with a life accordingly more intense than that of the group, has become lazy; as a result, the group or syndicalist ideal thrives. For the true individual must become increasingly energetic in an age like our own, when the body triumphs over intellect, "sensation" over mind (and woman over man). The general masses of mankind are less and less able to make this individual effort and consequently welcome political organizations that treat them like children.[5]

This is anticipating somewhat, but it is as well to make comparison with Benda from the start, for the whole argument of *La Trahison* is just this surrender of the disinterested intellect, either by treachery or sloth on the part of the clerc himself or by treachery on the part of the State toward the clerc. Benda here sees the intellectual conceding everywhere to immediate political interests, the chief of these being racial, national, and class passions. The organization of political hatreds (what Lewis calls "group-rhythms"), the tendency toward unreflecting action, the thirst for practical utility, championing of instinct over intellect, these are the main points of attack on contemporary society made both by *La Trahison* and Lewis' *The Art of Being Ruled*.

It was in this "key-book," as he himself calls it, that Lewis first outlined his view of human society. It is a society divided into two components, which must be kept apart. These two components, reminiscent of Nietzsche's master and herd, are defined in the same way by several of the French antiromanticists, especially by Lasserre in his work on Maurras and the classical renaissance. In *Time*

5. Wyndham Lewis, *The Art of Being Ruled* (New York, Harper, 1926), pp. 366–414.

and Western Man Lewis makes this a distinction between "persons" and "things" in the classical sense: *"Persona* for the Roman meant a free person only; a slave was not a *person,* but a *res* or *thing."* In *Paleface* this is elaborated as follows: "In Rome what constituted 'abnormality' was the being either a slave, a stranger or a minor (of whatever age) within the potestas of some head of a family. A slave and, originally, a stranger, a 'peregrinus,' was legally a 'thing' . . . All animals were naturally 'things'—a lion in the forest or a wild bee was a 'res nullius,' but a watch-dog or a slave was not 'wild,' so could not be affected to another person than his owner by capture." [6]

Although he contradicts himself as to who enjoyed the status of Roman persona,[7] Lewis generally refers in the "person" to the ideally normal, free, and (for him) formal element in the State, as opposed to the "thing" who is abnormal or "wild." This division possesses his thinking and is the structure on which his satire is based. In *The Art of Being Ruled* he advances the same division as between Goethe's Natures ("persons") and puppets ("things"), corresponding to the ruler and ruled in the authoritarian regime he urges in this work. In *Count Your Dead* we are referred to the Greek city-state, divided between " 'free men' " and "slaves"—the former constituting for Lewis "an authentic 'ruling class.' "

Of these two elements of human society, the "changeless Many" and the "changeable Few," Lewis finds the former in power today. Throughout his work he is unbending in his belief that the main body of humanity is composed of "things," idiotic units who have no desire to feel deeply or think clearly, "hallucinated automata," as he calls them, or larvae, performing mice, stereotypes produced by similar environments and like education. Man for Lewis is "by nature selfish and acquisitive"—it was not for nothing that Augustus

6. Wyndham Lewis, *Paleface: The Philosophy of the "Melting-Pot"* (London, Chatto and Windus, 1929), p. 70.

7. For example, he writes that only "the eldest male of a roman family" was a "person," but a page or two later he claims that "all roman citizens" were "persons" (ibid., pp. 70–2). Lewis used lower case type for nationalities, on the grounds that being English was no more worthy of a capital letter than being sick.

John called him "our new Machiavelli" [8]—and groups of men have neither the ability nor inclination to improve themselves. So we pick up, from book after book, references like the following: "In the mass people wish to be automata." "The mass of men ask nothing better than to be *Puppets*." "Men find their greatest happiness in type-life." [9]

Most neoclassicists share this view, that the masses want freedom less and less as the years go by, but Lewis has always felt especially strongly on the point. His idea of man as "a perfectly fixed and 'static'—corrupt, evil, untidy, incomplete—animal" [10] naturally drew him to Hulme's insistence on the doctrine of original sin. In the mass these animals are even more corrupt and incomplete: "A disciplined, well-policed, herd-life is what they most desire." What they least desire, says Lewis, is culture, and here he echoes Benda.[11]

Beyond this comparison one should not go, for few of the French antiromanticists, even Maurras, have been as extreme on this particular point as Lewis. It is perfectly true that one finds the view easily enough in Pound, Eliot, and others, but it would not be fair to say that one finds it pressed over and over again, as in Lewis. Pound's money pamphlets take the same view of the masses, while the Student in his *An Anachronism at Chinon* remarks, " 'Humanity is a herd, eaten by perpetual follies.' " [12] Nor is Eliot more sanguine on the subject: "the majority is capable neither of strong emotion nor of strong resistance," Eliot writes, and again, "at the moments when the public's interest is aroused, the public is never well enough informed to have the right to an opinion." [13]

8. Augustus John, *Chiaroscuro. Fragments of an Autobiography.* First series (London, Cape, 1952), p. 73.

9. *Art of Being Ruled*, p. 173; Wyndham Lewis, *The Doom of Youth* (New York, McBride, 1932), p. 93; *Rude Assignment*, p. 178.

10. *Men without Art*, p. 211.

11. Julien Benda, *Belphégor. Essai sur l'esthétique de la présente société française.* (Paris, Émile-Paul Frères, 1919), p. viii.

12. Pound, *Pavannes*, p. 18.

13. T. S. Eliot, *After Strange Gods* (New York, Harcourt, Brace, 1934), p. 60; T. S. Eliot, *The Idea of a Christian Society* (New York, Harcourt, Brace, 1940), p. 8.

To some extent such passages can be paralleled, of course, in Arnold's *Discourses in America,* and Eliot's lecture on Arnold at Harvard on March 3, 1933, began by a quotation from Norton to the effect that "the rise of the democracy to power" is "the rise of the uncivilized."

But Lewis is far more committed and does not trouble to hide behind that kind of evasive prose of which Eliot has shown himself such a master; such statements Kathleen Nott calls Eliot's "common evasive prudence which is so often nearly prudish," and Bernard Bergonzi describes them as "of such numbing ambiguity that they both demand and defy analysis." Not only are the "changeless Many" a crowd of useless "things" for Lewis, they actively detest freedom and long dearly for someone to take it from them: "Do most people really ever desire 'freedom'? . . . The answer . . . is an emphatic No! *Freedom* and *irresponsibility* are commutative terms, where the average man is concerned. The majority of men have to be persuaded or coerced into freedom . . . Ninety percent of men long at all times for *a leader.*" [14]

These words were written in 1936, and a second world war has not shaken the conviction they express. "The average man," he writes in 1950, "would rather rely upon somebody else . . . His will is feeble. He is always in search of a Leader (a Führer, a 'Strong Man')." The "changeless Many" still simply want to "hear 'their master's voice,' which it is their joy to obey."

There are two ideas subsidiary to this opinion; the first is that for Lewis, as not for Maurras or Eliot, the "changeless Many," or group of society comprised of "things," is composed of all social classes. "Curse abysmal inexcusable middle-class (also Aristocracy and Proletariat)," we read in *Blast No. 1.* Cantleman sees the English upper classes as " 'Arrogant and crafty sheep!' " William Bland Burn equally dislikes the "gentleman-animal," while in a story in *The New Statesman* for March 1, 1924, a character called Arouet Utchat, a clerk in an imaginary French dependency, writes

14. *Left Wings,* p. 294.

a document to his country's Senate attacking both upper and lower classes (he is at once arrested and flung into jail). Shakespeare's *Coriolanus* is taken to some extent by Lewis as a criticism of the English upper-class system in *The Lion and the Fox*. But nowhere is the "top-dog herd" (as Lewis called the upper classes in *Men without Art*) so abusively attacked as in *The Mysterious Mr. Bull*. This "unbiassed portrait of John Bull" which appeared in 1938 and was quickly translated into German as *Ein Tugendspiegel des Engländers* is a criticism of the repressive social machinery of the so-called English gentleman. John Bull, of this type, is depicted as a thoroughgoing imbecile who adulates idiocy and regards stupidity as an article of faith. So the herd of "things" is for Lewis drawn from all sections of society, being distinguished only by lack of intelligence; it is the "moronic majority" which dominates *The Human Age*. Yet, although it is important to make this distinction, as Geoffrey Grigson does in his sympathetic study of Lewis, it should not be exaggerated. There is no doubt but that the intelligence which alone distinguishes a "person" from a "thing" is more likely to be located for Lewis in the upper classes if only because they are more educated.

There is one place, and one place only to date, in Lewis' satire where he enters into an extended picture of the English working classes. This is at the funeral of Vincent Penhale's father in *The Vulgar Streak*. It is, to say the least, an unattractive portrait gallery —a drunken mother who refuses her husband solace in his last moments, a jealous sister (Minnie), a hypocritical elder brother —and the intention of the satire is indubitably to deride the indolence of the "changeless Many." The working classes ("the worst snobs of the lot") are here shown as totally unwilling to change their status of underdog in England, and there is, in harmony with this suggestion, the author's reflection on "the so-called working-woman, who in England does so little work." In the same way the story called "The Rot," the central piece of *Rotting Hill*, is designed to point up the English working man's laziness. We find this attitude even more extremely in Roy Campbell, whose extroverted and often beautiful autobiographies owe so much to Lewis' social criticism. So Campbell writes in *Broken Record* of the working classes: "I found them to be mostly treacherous; this probably accounts for the growing popularity of dogs in Europe, to make up for the lack of fidelity in servants." I am not interested in taking issue with this view, but it is necessary to advance it to balance the idea, put forward by Grigson, that Lewis attacks all social classes without discrimination. According to Lewis himself, he does, but the weight of his persuasion is against the lower classes, and sincerely so, for their "thing"-ness. What he is really criticizing in the "thing" is what Blenner-Cantleman calls the "Crowd-Spirit," the congealing of mankind into stupid groups, into what Maurras calls "le myriapode démocratique." The "thing" is only half-alive, if that. So Lewis will often write of "these masses of half-dead people, for whom personal extinction is such a tiny step, out of half-living into no-living, so what does it matter?" [15]

This brings us to the second point concerning his definition of the "thing." For Lewis takes with him to his satire the principles of seventeenth-century automatism, the Cartesian thesis (later modified by its originator) that the more animal an organism is, the more mechanical it is. And Lewis borrows also from Bergson's *Le Rire* in using as the food for laughter the human animal atrophied into a machine. The "thing" for Lewis is a cross between animal and machine, a Prole in fact, living in a blueprint of the present (*"The present man in all of us is the machine"*).[16] This "wild body," or "savage Robot" [17] as he calls the same element elsewhere, is therefore mechanical in a special sense. So Lewis uses "mechanical" to mean, as we would expect, mechanized, connected with actual machinery, and also to mean "thing"-like, that is, coerced by the environment or culture group, driven into the state of utter primi-

---

15. *Blasting and Bombardiering*, p. 115.
16. *The Tyro No. 2* (London, The Egoist Press, 1923), p. 35.
17. *Art of Being Ruled*, p. 170.

tivity and animality by lack of awareness and intelligence. In the *Phaedo* Socrates recounts his disappointment in the alleged intellect of Anaxagoras, which he finds "altogether forsaking mind" (Jowett trans.) by emphasis on mechanical matter. It is shortly after this that Socrates discusses the idea of man as vortex. If we did not concede Lewis too this terminology, we would only be confused by finding him calling the American Negro "mechanical," and criticizing D. H. Lawrence for championing the "mechanical" Mexicans. He also calls the African Riff, in his travel book *Filibusters in Barbary,* a machine in this special sense, as he does the ordinary English workman. Obviously Lewis sees that Negroes, Riffs, and Mexicans are less mechanized than white men; what he is saying is that they are "thing"-like, standing on the lowest rung of existence and, through no fault of their own, lacking in intellectual qualities. Unless one accepts this terminology, one cannot understand Lewis when he writes, of an emotional character like Bertha of *Tarr,* that "The machine, the sentimental, the indiscriminate side of her awoke."

So much for the "thing." What of the "person," that noble element of society, the quintessential core of the human individual rapidly disappearing because of our laziness and love of stereotyped life? First, the "person" is born, not made. A "thing" can never become a "person," and—"we are not all born Shakespeares." The "person" is the true individual, opposed to the social stereotype, free of group or class "rhythm," and the only element in the State who matters. "Personality is the only thing that matters in the world," he writes in his first book on Hitler, asking us to associate with "person"-ality shades of meaning embodied in the concept of Roman persona. Other neoclassicists use "personality" in the same privileged sense, but they usually take more care to carry their readers with them. The new humanism Maritain calls for should be, thus, *"personnaliste,"* in this sense, but Maritain gives a clear description of what his medieval and Christian "person" is: "Une personne, c'est un inverse de nature spirituelle doué de la liberté de choix et constituant pour autant un tout indépendant en face du monde, ni la nature ni l'État ne peuvent mordre sur cet univers sans sa permission." [18]

For Lewis this "person" is alone fully free. He is the form, or abstract, of the human being and a core, or cadre, of "persons" in the State will give us a governing elite from which the values of society should spring. Lewis denies proposing an elite, making distinctions to which I will come back below, but it is safe to say that for him a body of "persons" will provide that "gifted few" which Babbitt hoped also to see at the head of the contemporary State.[19] This "person" alone resists the "discontinuity" of class or race, and is frequently called the "Not-Self."

Clearly the Not-Self is associated with the classical "anti-self" of Yeats and others. Certainly it is for Lewis the *"antithetical being,"* in the sense that it is everything the ordinary man is not. In his attack on Spengler in *Time and Western Man* Lewis makes a passionate plea for "spatial" thought over "temporal" feeling, and writes, "what we *think* is not us, or is the Not-self." In 1925 he published an article explaining this principle and later printed this essay as a "commentary" to go with his play *The Enemy of the Stars.* Here we are told that the Not-Self represents real truth, and that such is death for the average man. The Not-Self is therefore hated by the majority: "It is an enemy principle." Housed in the intellect the Not-Self shows "the human mind in its traditional rôle of the enemy of life, as an oddity outside the machine." [20]

This is Babbitt's "distinguished person." Equated with truth, the property only of intellectual genius, the Not-Self is the only

18. Jacques Maritain, *Humanisme intégral* (Paris, Fernand Aubier, 1936), p. 17.

19. Irving Babbitt, *Democracy and Leadership* (Boston, Houghton Mifflin, 1924), p. 193.

20. Wyndham Lewis, *The Enemy of the Stars* (London, Desmond Harmsworth, 1932), p. 51. Lewis thought this an important description evidently, for he italicized it when first printing it. Wyndham Lewis, "The Physics of the Not-Self," *The Chapbook* (*A Yearly Miscellany*), ed. Harold Monro, No. 40 (London, Cape, 1925), p. 68.

element of society which really desires change, rather than "progress." The will of the masses, for Lewis, is conservative; they do
not desire change. In consequence, what we call revolution is merely
a difference in kind, rather than in value, a "horizontal" affair.
The indolent Many, therefore, desiring "progress" of this sort, are
what he calls "creatures of habit" rather than "creatures of
change." [21] True revolution, genuine social change, can only come
from the head of the State, where intelligence is lodged—"To *think*
being to *change*" is axiomatic for Lewis. If we follow this line of
reasoning we will see why preservation of the Not-Self is of importance to the whole of society; and we will better understand
One-Way Song which satirizes lovers of "progress," standardized
and unconscious creatures who are supposedly looking forward
but who, in reality, have "THAT BACKWARD FEELING" (this
is a pun on the popular Kruschen Salts advertisement of the time,
advocating "That Kruschen Feeling").

The Hegelian Not-Self is the epitome of the "person." Neither
Hugh Kenner nor Cecil F. Melville, who has made an intelligent
appraisal of Lewis' politics, agrees with this analysis, but it is undoubtedly "the Physics of the Not-Self." Our duty is to preserve
this heroic being. The man who gives in to the group, or "group-
rhythm," lacks identity, surrenders "continuity," and becomes a
prey to the fluxes of his time. He becomes "split," in the sense of
divided against himself, against those minute particles of the Not-
Self left within him. This type Lewis predicates as the Split-Man,
exemplifying him as Jamesjulius (James Joyce) Ratner of *The
Apes of God*. It should be made clear that this "split" is a longi-
tudinal cleft, as Horace Zagreus explains and as is shown by the
drawing at the beginning of Part v of *The Apes*, called "The
Split-Man" and characterizing Ratner. This creature, that is to
say, is divided against himself, possessed of Pound's "schismatic
tendency"; he is not split in the sense that he has two separate per-

21. Wyndham Lewis, "Creatures of Habit and Creatures of Change," *The Calendar, 3*, No. 1 (April 1926), 17–44.

sonalities, like Jekyll and Hyde. Some of the more absurd appellants at the Bailiff's Court in *The Childermass* are "split-men or half-men."

The idea of continuity, which this element of society is revoking, can almost be called a precept of the neoclassicist. For Eliot continuity of culture is virtually wisdom,[22] while Seillière discovers his regenerating principle ("raison") in the continuity of human experience.[23] Lewis agrees with these thinkers: "The more highly developed an individual is, or the more civilized a race, this *discontinuity* tends to disappear. The 'personality' is born. Continuity, in the individual as in the race, is the diagnostic of a civilized condition." [24] So Corcoran, at loose in America, notes with distaste the "discontinuity of the American psyche."

In the ideal State it is the function of the artist, Lewis says, to maintain our continuity. As he wrote in *Blast No. 2,* "the purest art is not tyrannic but is continuous," and art should ideally preserve our "differentiation of existence." Is not this the duty of Benda's clerc? Yes, with one distinction. Benda's clerc is the disinterested intellectual who presumably exists (though Benda does not say this) in all spheres of intellectual activity. I think Benda would admit an entirely impartial scientist as a clerc, but Lewis will not allow science the ability to maintain our continuity. In fact, for him it does the reverse. Science, especially when in the hands of Einstein, is on the side of the "thing" today, merging us all into "a mutually devouring mass," a criticism it would be rash to dismiss in the mid-nineteen fifties. Science uses the intellect "on the popular plane," keeping all down to a helpless norm, making it impossible for the Not-Self to emerge.

From the start of his career Lewis saw through the contemporary "individualist." No, the true individual today must be "an in-

22. Eliot, *Christian Society,* p. 41.

23. Ernest Seillière, *Pour le centenaire du romantisme. Un examen de conscience* (Paris, Champion, 1927), pp. 267–71.

24. *Art of Being Ruled,* p. 235. I have purposely selected another quotation to give the reader an idea of Lewis' special use of "person"-ality.

delicate interloper, a walking lie, a disturbing absurdity." And he, the gifted "person," must work for those beneath him since he represents that principle of authority delegated from the divine.[25] "I demand no absolute, except only God," he wrote in *One-Way Song* and, although he has opposed organized religion, he yields to the idea that there is a spiritual power related to us all, in the same way that the "person" is related to the "thing" in the social body. Thus, all the more reason that our terrestrial system should be authoritarian and hierarchic, in order to reflect the heavenly one more truly. For since it follows that if the "thing" gains too much power an imbalance will result, is it not in the interests of all that the white man's hierarchic system, with its strong sense of discipline, should be preserved? [26]

These are Lewis' general political principles. If they are not adhered to, as they are not today, ideological anarchy results, such as he criticizes through various writers, and we are faced with a series of contemporary excesses, or "group-rhythms."

25. This divine source of manhood is only occasionally hinted at in Lewis' work. It can be found throughout *The Art of Being Ruled,* in the recent *The Writer and the Absolute* (see p. 127), and in various pronouncements on graphic art I will instance below.

26. *Art of Being Ruled,* pp. 226 ff. Lewis' detachment is such that he can later describe his politics at the time of writing these words as that of a "straight 'leftwinger' " (*Blasting and Bombardiering,* p. 234), and the authoritarian regime he urges in *The Art of Being Ruled* as, later, a "classless society" (*Hitler Cult,* p. 21).

Chapter 2: The "Group-Rhythm"

"A class is a corral." [*Rude Assignment*, p. 178.]

UNIFORMITY of opinion in the State, of the type attacked by Benda in *La Trahison* especially when manipulated as a political passion, works against the principle of the Not-Self, and so the group is always loathsome to Lewis. "Yourself must be your Caste," is the advice to the Herdsman, reiterated nearly a quarter of a century later in *Anglosaxony*—"*ourselves* is our political principle."

In a lecture given at Brown University in 1926 Babbitt stressed the necessity for proportion and for the rejection of overemphasis in the true humanist (in his sense). The group-rhythm that Lewis describes, a coagulation of individuals into mass units, is an excess, and one which, moreover, leads to war—"wherever you have a *Class,* there you have a *War.*" Seillière, though a far more temperate writer than Lewis, equally finds the contemporary Western democracy susceptible to the group-rhythm, or "mysticisme de groupe." Using mysticisme in a special sense, as the invoking of abstract ideas in order to assist man in overcoming the exterior world, Seillière finds "mysticisme de classe" an attribute of democracy.[1]

Here, of course, we reach the real reason why Lewis spent so much time on attacking the contemporary group-rhythm, for it is an anti-authoritarian phenomenon. In *Rude Assignment* he defines his most disliked group-rhythms as five: class war (poor versus rich), sex war (woman versus man), age war (young versus old), lowbrow against highbrow, and urban man against agricultural

1. Ernest Seillière, *Le Romantisme* (Paris, Stock, 1925), p. 121.

man. Apart from the urban-agricultural war, on which he does not often take a stand, Lewis is here defining what he sees as warfare between emotional anarchy (poor, woman, young, lowbrow) and intellectual authority (rich, man, old, highbrow). One should perhaps further qualify this by pointing out that he never actually champions the rich as such, on one hand, while, on the other, the poor or working classes are so low in mentality for Lewis as scarcely to reach the level of lowbrows—in fact, he calls them " 'no-brows.' "

During the section of Lord Osmund's party in *The Apes* called "At the American Bar," the unpleasant Split-Man Ratner associates the poor, women, and young in his mind with "wild nature to be encouraged to flourish at the expense of contriving intelligent Man." Ratner feels a (ridiculed) pang of sympathy for "all oppressed classes—women, miners, children, Jews, horses, servants, negroes, frogs, footballs, carpets during Spring-cleaning, Zoo-reptiles, canaries and so forth." Roy Campbell, a writer Lewis explicitly admires and whom he has probably introduced into three of his satires,[2] has almost exactly the same catalogue in his Author's Note to *Flowering Rifle*. "Humanitarianism," Campbell writes here, "sides automatically with the Dog against the Man, the Jew against the Christian, the black against the white, the servant against the master, the criminal against the judge."

For in *Rude Assignment* Lewis omits one group-rhythm which

2. At the end of *Rotting Hill* some obvious friends of the Enemy are assembled, and include Roy Campbell (*Rotting Hill*, p. 260). This reference seems to have angered Campbell. Roy Campbell, "A Note on W. L.," *Shenandoah*, 4, Nos. 2–3 (Summer/Autumn 1953), p. 75. Augustus John suggests that Campbell was the model for McPhail in *Snooty Baronet* (John, *Chiaroscuro*, p. 114), an attribution Campbell accepts, for it is a fairly direct portrait. Roy Campbell, *Broken Record. Reminiscences* (London, Boriswood, 1934), p. 8.

Thirdly, Campbell claims that he sat for the character of Zulu Blades of *The Apes of God* (Roy Campbell, *Light on a Dark Horse*, Chicago, Henry Regnery, 1952, p. 220), although in *The Apes* itself Zulu is described as a "disgusting beast." Finally, Campbell is frequently praised by Lewis (cf. *Men without Art*, p. 160) and clearly has much in common with the neoclassical movement I am studying here. His interest in Mistral, for instance, is found in Maurras and again in Lasserre's *Mise au point* of 1931 and elsewhere.

he has often attacked, namely the race or color war of black against white, which is the thesis of *Paleface*. Indeed, "Race is the queen of the 'classes,'" he writes, and again, *"class* in primitive society always involves *race."* [3] Race, utilized politically, can be also a group-rhythm; this is what he means when, in *The Jews, Are They Human?* he associates sex with race. Both can be blind organizations of the human individual. Here I shall only examine the three group-rhythms that have principally attracted his attention, the color war, the age war, and the sex war.

In the case of the first, it must always be remembered that Lewis frequently pleads for better treatment for the American Negro who suffers, he says, "a monstrous social injustice." [4] In *Paleface*, however, a call is made to the white man to resist worship of the "underdog" in the name of the Negro. Lewis, after all, was writing on top of books by D. H. Lawrence and Sherwood Anderson in which the resources of the colored races on the American continent were highly admired. Lewis sees the American Negro as "racially a sort of Proletariat," and the criticism is made that the white races are suffering an inferiority complex vis-à-vis the colored. This growing sense of disbelief in himself on the part of the white man faced with black superiority (or "negro-worship")—a fantastic idea but to be found in Pound's *Indiscretions*—should be countered, Lewis advocates, by an *"esprit de peau"* among the white races. [5]

3. *Art of Being Ruled,* p. 234; Wyndham Lewis, *The Lion and the Fox* (New York, Harper, 1927), p. 306. The reader will also find in this latter book the statement that *"Class* in these adjustments is, of course, the great rival of *race"* (*Lion and Fox,* p. 295). But Lewis is consistent, for he goes on to explain that genius must be raceless and that all true personality must overcome "the mechanical ascendancy" (p. 296) of both class and race. He adds that social class, though involved with race, is more easily fixed and coheres more readily into the group-rhythm than race. Thus, in a sense, it is a "rival" of race.

4. *Rude Assignment,* p. 203; *America and Cosmic Man,* pp. 107, 196–7, 208. Further sympathy for the American Negro is shown in Wyndham Lewis, "American Melting Pot," *Contact Books, 2* (London, Contact Books, Weidenfeld and Nicolson, Oct. 1946), 58.

5. *Paleface,* pp. 7–21; Lewis' first reference to the idea of the racial "melting-pot" of America can be found ten years before *Paleface* in *The Caliph's Design* (London, The Egoist Ltd., 1919), p. 46.

Looking back on *Paleface* later Lewis denies that he was attacking the Negro race but asserts that he was laughing at the white man for permitting himself to be bamboozled into the idea that the colored man was his superior. This is a fair, if mild, description of the work.

At the bottom of it is Lewis' belief, so far from that of Anderson or Lawrence, that it is senseless to encourage Negro aspiration since the Negro has no cultural reserves in the true sense, and is simply infecting the world with lowered standards. Jazz is taken as symbolic of these and Lewis' dislike of Negro jazz, so popular of course in European café society of the twenties, is epitomized in the nigger-heaven episode of *The Childermass.*[6] In this work there are parodies of both D. H. Lawrence and Anderson, and one of the first things we meet in the Third City of *Monstre Gai* is a derided Negro band. For Lewis always associates jazz with the lower, emotional elements of society and so here the jazz band is staffed "with a mixed jewish and negro personnel." On the other hand, Starr-Smith, the well-disciplined blackshirt of *The Apes,* feels no affection for the Negro behind the American Bar at Lord Osmund's (unlike the other characters), and we are explicitly informed that he was no friend of "Tropical Man."

The "imperialism of Black serfdom" is what Lewis tells us in 1950 he was criticizing in *Paleface*. The work itself, by setting out to counter cultural productions on behalf of the Negro, is a neo-classical attempt to redress a balance. For Lewis' sense of justice suffers at the sight of "the literary Borzoi big-guns of Mr. Knopf" stampeding us into hero-worship of the Negro, an adulation sponsored primarily by the socialist: "it is *conscience* that makes cowards, or saints, or just sentimental pinky-pinky *Palefaces* of us."[7] The idea that the color war is the fault of the socialist is used elsewhere, but neatly reversed to suit another argument, so that in *America and Cosmic Man* Lewis alleges that the socialist is responsible for for racial discrimination in America.[8] Yet, although the socialist is

6. Wyndham Lewis, *The Childermass:* Section i (London, Chatto and Windus, 1928), pp. 168 ff.
7. *Paleface*, p. 6.
8. *America and Cosmic Man,* p. 197.

sponsoring Negro culture, as well as racial discrimination, we also read here that "the Capitalist . . . is the natural protector of all colored people, because they work for less money." This would conflict with Pound's idea, expressed in a recent money pamphlet, that the freeing of Negro slaves in America was due to "usurocracy" (Campbell also writes, "No colour feeling ever existed until slavery was abolished"), but it provides a convenient introduction to that habit of mind with which Lewis puts all his enemies in one camp. Often one's immediate impulse is to reject these extreme ideas, tossed out to *épater le bourgeois,* as ridiculously rococo social history, but one should be on one's guard against this. For what Lewis is criticizing in the group-rhythm is opposition to the intellect and, if one cannot go with him all the way in his criticism of the Negro (as when in 1936 he complains that England is sponsoring Negro aggression), certain of his arguments in this connection are suggestive. He strongly objects to the harnessing of these groups, such as the Negro or the young, in the interests of big business, because he sees that the commercial capitalist will be interested in keeping the group down in a state of unthinking acquiescence, usually by means of popular culture. Here Lewis is often thought to have made valuable criticisms of our society in advance.[9]

The age war is the organized strife between emotional youth and intelligent old age. Youth, like the Negro or woman, is opposed to tradition and discipline; all are concerned with attacking the father-principle of authority.[10] Benda similarly criticized the

9. I am thinking of a work like Herbert Marshall McLuhan's *The Mechanical Bride* (New York, Vanguard, 1951), a recent lively criticism of popular culture in America, which expresses indebtedness to Lewis' early criticisms at many points (pp. 68, 92, 102, 108, 143–4.) I am also indebted to Professor J. B. Brebner for calling my attention to the interest in Lewis' theories about popular culture taken by the late Dean Harold A. Innis, of the University of Toronto (as was McLuhan). *The Bias of Communication* and *Changing Concepts of Time,* both by Innis, contain unindexed reference to Lewis.

10. Wyndham Lewis, *The Doom of Youth* (New York, McBride, 1932), pp. 60, 104, 201, 253. Lewis, *The Old Gang and the New Gang,* p. 19. This latter work was published as a "sister-book" the year after *The Doom of Youth,* which was in

organization of youth for political purposes,[11] but to follow the youth war in France would mean engaging with ambiguous writers like de Montherlant, Saint-Exupéry, and that "romantique dompté" (as André Maurois calls him), de Lacretelle. And in any case Benda does not go as far as Lewis in claiming that capital encourages the youth war (as it encourages feminism) as a reduction in the rational faculties it has to face. As an appeal to the irrational the youth war is encouraged both by big business and the social revolutionary.

In 1932 Lewis published *The Doom of Youth*, in title a parody on Alec Waugh's *The Loom of Youth*. The work attacked the encouragement of intense consciousness of youth, in an endeavor to reverse the values of experience. For youth, trained, militarized, rigidly organized (and organized to appear spontaneous and unrigid), was being pitted against individual genius.[12] It was becoming "mechanical." This exploitation of youth Lewis laid at the door of the Futurists and the Italian Fascists in the first instance, but the period following the first World War was everywhere fertile in "youth-politics," since the male principle, representing authority, had shown itself capable of being overthrown. The result was that youth and woman could more easily take hold of values. And he has again found this situation (utilized by Jean-Paul Sartre) after the second World War.[13] Briefly then, "youth-politics" aims to shorten human life by insistence on being young (the "doom" of

England quickly withdrawn from publication. The second short book, however, adds little. Roughly speaking, it defines the "old gang" as the old school of capitalist politician (such as Baldwin), the "new gang" as the new kind of politician emerging (the dictators), a distinction to be found also in ch. 8 of *The Doom of Youth*. Pt. I of *Old Gang and New Gang* is written in a deliberately "nursery" style, both to marry with the subject matter and, as Lewis mischievously suggests, to assist critics. Pt. II largely consists in an elaborate discrediting of Erich Maria Remarque.

11. Benda, *Trahison,* p. 91.

12. *Doom of Youth,* pp. 138–42; ch. 15, Pt. II, is entitled "The 'Group' *Versus* the 'Individual.' "

13. Wyndham Lewis, *The Writer and the Absolute* (London, Methuen, 1952), p. 56.

youth), to level genius, break up family life, encourage precocity
and radicalism, extinguish the true individual, effeminize values,
and turn youth into a unique value at the same time as (in fact)
abolishing it, a *divide et impera* policy on the part of big business
aimed both at cheap labor and an uncritical consumer public.[14]

This "study of Youth seen as a *class*" is made use of in Lewis'
satire, particularly in the character of the fatuous young "genius,"
Dan Boleyn of *The Apes,* and in the horrible Third City of *The
Human Age.* But in its critical applications Lewis is not always
consistent. For if we pick up *Rude Assignment* of 1950 we find,
as we might expect, Hitler described as an arch youth-politician,
dragooning youth for militant purposes even more savagely than
had Baden-Powell in the Boy Scout movement. If we refer to *Hitler,*
however, we find Lewis actually *praising* Hitler's youth-politics.
Hitler's youth, at the start of the thirties, is "Youth with its eyes
wide open!" [15] Hitler is depicted as making youth more sensible
and informed (the book carries an illustration of German youth
watching "democracy" at work in the Reichstag) and, above all,
anti-Communist. In the same way, in 1927, Lewis had expressed
the hope that the organization of youth might be made fruitful
by the Action Française which was presenting youth with a purpose.
Later, in *Men without Art,* he was to bemoan the lack of serious
purpose in British youth.[16]

This kind of inconsistency, or philosophical acrobatic, naturally
casts doubt on Lewis' sincerity in political criticism, but before
we spring to attack him we should bear in mind that his first
book on *Hitler* appeared mainly as a series of articles in *Time and
Tide* in 1931, after a visit to Germany the year before. A glance
through the periodical press in England at this time soon shows
that few understood the direction Hitler was to take. In 1932,

14. *Doom of Youth,* pp. 259–65.

15. Wyndham Lewis, *Hitler* (London, Chatto and Windus, 1931), p. 99.

16. *The Enemy No. 2* (London, The Arthur Press, Sept. 1927), p. xxvii; *Men
without Art,* pp. 249–50.

the year after *Hitler,* Lewis is openly critical of the German youth cult,[17] and he repeats this criticism in the year following.[18]

It is in *Hitler* that we are told that, like the age war, the sex war is rooted in revolutionary humanitarianism, backed by the *Geldmensch.* Lewis had previously made the same criticism in *The Art of Being Ruled,* while in *Time and Western Man* he indicted Sex beside Romance, asserting that the classical world was untroubled by any "sex-cult." On this subject, by arraigning woman under the general head of what the French neoclassicists like to call "le mal romantique," Lewis stands closely beside the French critics mentioned.

But it was a German, Karl Joël, who anticipated this side of French antiromanticism in 1896, in a work devoted to criticizing the influence of women in philosophy. Joël warned: "Zwei Gafahren scheint das zur Rüste gehende Jahrhundert den kommenden zu vererben: den Feminismus, die Verweiblichung der Kultur, und den Barbarismus . . . beides sind Todeswege für die Kultur." [19]

Tarr was to think precisely the same: "Surrender to a woman was a sort of suicide for an artist." And when Tarr reflects "God was man: the woman was a lower form of life," we realize how deeply under the spell of French neoclassicism this book was written. Tarr early associates Sex with Romance in his conversation with Butcher, and Sex itself appears for him, after all, in the form of Bertha and Anastasya, creatures both German and female. The shadow of Madame de Staël stands behind both characterizations.

Although Seillière saw woman at the head of romanticism, it

17. *Doom of Youth,* p. 5.

18. *Old Gang and New Gang,* pp. 17–19; however in *The Doom of Youth* we again find him suggesting that German youth politics could be a satisfactory development, if youth can be made serious thereby (p. 247), and he reasons that in any case Hitler's youth politics are not nearly as belligerent as Communist youth politics (pp. 66–70).

19. Karl Joël, *Die Frauen in der Philosophie* (Hamburg, Verlagsanstalt und Druckerei A-G, 1896), p. 53.

was Maurras and Lasserre who devoted more space than any of their colleagues to this question. Maurras' *Le Romantisme féminin* is often an attack on woman as agent of "le mal romantique." Lasserre devotes a chapter of his *Le Romantisme français* to "Le Sacerdoce de la femme." For Lasserre here the female of the species has been overemancipated. Masculine intelligence is everywhere abdicating before feminine instability and emotion. The sane man is usually concerned with the real, the weak, romantic woman with the ideal (especially with the ideal of happiness).[20] Lasserre alludes to Nietzsche's remark that if you are going to make love to a woman, take your whip with you. As Lewis often mentions this also, it probably explains Tarr's treatment of Bertha. Like Lasserre, Benda also associates women with sensation, modern woman adoring sensation in a way entirely foreign to her seventeenth-century French forebear. *"Toute l'esthétique moderne est faite pour les femmes,"* [21] writes Benda. And it is perhaps from Benda that Lewis borrows most here. Characteristic male chauvinism can be seen in Benda's early *L'Ordination* or *Les Amorandes* (while in Germany the neoclassical von Scholz's even earlier *Der Besiegte* features a hero who brings death to the sexual embrace). In Benda's *L'Ordination,* which first appeared in Péguy's *Cahiers de la quinzaine* in 1911 and 1912, Félix, the hero, has the same Tarr-like entanglement with sensation, in the person of Madeleine: "L'esthétique de l'amour reste toujours l'esthétique de la chaîne et des larmes," Félix concludes; "l'esthétique de l'amour a été faite pour les femmes." [22] He quotes Nietzsche and yearns for "la vraie vie intellectuelle." It is essentially, of course, the well-known Swiftian antithesis: "when I began to consider that by copulating with one of the Yahoo species I had become a parent of more, it struck me with the utmost shame, confusion, and horror." Sir Thomas Browne

20. Pierre Lasserre, *Le Romantisme français* (Paris, Mercure de France, 1907), pp. 155–72.

21. Benda, *Belphégor*, pp. 112–13, 211–14.

22. Julien Benda, *L'Ordination* (Paris, Èmile-Paul, 1913), pp. 58–9.

had wished "that there were any way to perpetuate the World without this trivial and vulgar way of union." Nor is T. S. Eliot entirely free of this anti-feminism; the death of some woman recurs in his work from *Sweeney Agonistes* to *The Cocktail Party*. Needless to say, none of these writers would find anything to quarrel with in Lewis' belief that feminine values today are "the most featureless, boneless, softest, the most emotional." [23]

Nor would they but approve Tarr's attitude toward women. Tarr's talk with Hobson at the start of *Tarr* is most interesting in this respect, and its revision for the second edition only shows Lewis intensifying Tarr's antagonism to romantic womanhood. " 'Sex is a monstrosity' " is, for example, a remark Tarr makes *twice* in the second edition.[24] Sex (sensation) is the opposite of art (intellect); Tarr says: " 'How foul and wrong this haunting of women is!—they are everywhere—confusing, blurring, libelling, with their half-baked gushing tawdry presences! It is like a slop and spawn of children and the bawling machinery of the inside of life, always and all over our palaces.' "

Women for Tarr, being emotional and "jellyish," are close to the animal, and therefore "mechanical." This bias is particularly noticeable in the early Lewis. The Herdsman is advised, "As to women: wherever you can, substitute the society of men." In the same year (1917) Ker-Orr, the central character of *The Wild Body* stories, says, " 'Sex' makes me yawn my head off." It is true that the idea recurs, but it is mitigated, and in *Rotting Hill* we scarcely meet it. But what so clearly shows the French neoclassical influence on *Tarr*, as nowhere else in Lewis' work, is its thesis of emotional Sex being an especially German appetite. As opposed to Tarr, the intellectual Englishman who abhors this kind of Sex, the German Kreisler believes in "the efficacity of women." Kreisler likes women (nay, rapes them), and this is one reason why he

23. *Doom of Youth*, p. 210.
24. Cf. Wyndham Lewis, *Tarr* (London, The Egoist Ltd., 1918), p. 8; *Tarr* (London, Chatto and Windus, 1928), p. 7.

is drawn to the emotional Liepmann circle (originally spelt Lip-
mann or Lippmann). Nor can the nationality of either Bertha or
Anastasya be considered accidental. To the English reader of the
time Bertha would recall one of their principal enemies, the famous
Big Bertha artillery piece, symbol of Teutonic barbarism that fired
on the city of the intellect, Paris, from a distance of seventy miles,
while Anastasya is described in the Prologue to the first edition as
"the Munich German Madonna."

The dislike of woman as an agent of Romance occurs somewhat
in other satires, but not to the same extent. No women appear in
The Childermass, and in *The Human Age* they are kept in what
is called "a pen *incommunicado.*" [25] In the recent *The Red Priest*
we read of Mary Chillingham: "For such a woman to be able to
think was as rare as to find a famous man, undominated by his
fame." And Mary is later caused to vomit, by one of her husband's
actions.[26] Contact with the female kind is such a capitulation to
the animal that there is literally no instance in Lewis' work of
happy, fruitful sexual love between man and woman, as there so
supremely is in Joyce's work. "Cantleman's Spring-Mate" is the
only story by Lewis in which sex is nuclear, and even Cantleman
reflects that women are "spies or enemies." *Snooty Baronet* has
some reference to sexual love, but Snooty, we find significantly
enough, is made physically sick by the act of copulation, due to
his trepanned skull, a head wound suffered in the war. This directly
recalls Tarr, of whom we read, "Women's psychic discharges affected
him invariably like the sight of a person being sea-sick." Thus,
Val's bed to which Snooty is drawn is likened to a dentist's chair,
her bedroom is a "bedridden cabinet." Jack Cruze, of *The Revenge
for Love,* unusually interested in women for a leading Lewis character, is called a "love-machine." [27] Sometimes this antagonism to

25. Wyndham Lewis, *The Human Age* (London, Methuen, 1955), p. 192.

26. Wyndham Lewis, *The Red Priest* (London, Methuen, 1956), pp. 90, 241.

27. *Revenge for Love,* p. 197. Jack, who absconds with Jill in this book, is
obviously an unsympathetic character. To say that Lewis identifies with him

Sex will lead to its being sublimated in another form; in the story
"Sigismund," for example, Deborah's sexual appeal lies in her palms
(recalling Rose Godd of *The Ideal Giant* or Turgenev's hand
fetichism),[28] while in another story a character called Pringle gets
his sexual pleasure vicariously, out of hiring rooms.

In passing, one should perhaps note that nearly all Lewis' women
characters are fat, sleepy, indolent, and soft, in physical appearance, presumably in keeping with their mental make-up. Rose
Godd, Deborah, and Bertha are all large. Hotshepsot, of *The
Enemy of the Stars,* is "a big girl with a big roll in the hips." Lily
of *Snooty Baronet* is "sultry about the joints." [29] Anastasya, however, is enormous. " 'What a big brute,' " Tarr thinks, noticing that
she is "statuesquely genuine." One could continue the roll call indefinitely—Maddie of *The Vulgar Streak,* Gillian of *The Revenge
for Love,* the "obese groceress" Lewis met on his travels in *Filibusters
in Barbary*—they are all large, and usually so in their posteriors.[30]
Occasionally this quirk will harmonize almost perfectly with the
symbolization; the description of the peasant girl (Old Spain) at
the beginning of *The Revenge for Love* is thus one of the best
individual descriptions in Lewis' prose. Perhaps the explanation
is given by Lewis when he says, in *The Doom of Youth,* "I favour
the abundant asiatic hip—I prefer its volume for my pictures to
the lean gothic flank of the Flemish or English." This would coincide
with Vincent's predilection in *The Vulgar Streak* where April Mallow is "on the heavy side," but Vincent "liked them heavy."

Lewis in fact takes the French antiromantic suspicion of woman
about as far as it will go. Sex is associated with everything he dis-

---

strikes me as little short of ridiculous, but this criticism was recently made.
Steven Marcus, "The Highbrow Know-Nothings," *Commentary, 15,* No. 2
(Feb. 1953), 189.

28. Rose has *"large muscular hands"* at which Kemp stares (*Ideal Giant,* p.
26).

29. *Snooty,* p. 128. And Gillian is a "highbrow lily" (*Revenge for Love,* p.
113).

30. William Bland Burn is characterized by a protuberant rump.

likes, including what he calls "Time," which we shall see is largely romanticism. So we read, in this vein,

> Sex is of the same clay as Time!—of the same clay
> Since both are in their essence but *One-Way*
> Time is the one-way dimension: sex its tart
> And subtle biological counterpart.
> But even Sex is Time, too, in a sense—
> That chronological burgeoning of men's.
> Is it not the sex-magnet eyeless that gives
> That one-way motion to a thing that lives—

He continues to describe Sex as another "Front" for the One-Ways who are therefore "eyeless," since they can only blindly see the interior turmoil of emotional life. In the same way we find that the crowd Blenner-Cantleman is opposing is both female and blind, and by merging with it the male "embraces Death." [31]

In this dislike of woman Lewis has gone into social psychology, seeing sexual inversion (of both sexes) as another contemporary anti-authoritarian phenomenon. Again this criticism provides him with the pabulum of much satire, as it provided Roy Campbell with one of the themes of his *Georgiad,* published in 1931 and containing a defense of *The Apes of God.* More recently, Nigel Dennis seems to have been similarly inspired in the multiple-sex passages of his *Cards of Identity.*

The increase of war in our society, Lewis proposes, makes women feel that their reproductory function is being negated, on one hand, and makes men feel that the institution of manhood is being caricatured, on the other. The wake of a world war brings with it "sex-transformation" ("shamanization"), implying a general withdrawal from responsibility on the part of both sexes and an over-all effeminizing of cultural values. In short, after a world war, women

31. *Blast No. 1* (London, John Lane, the Bodley Head, June 20, 1914), p. 94. The sympathetic Don Alvaro sees women as "blind as bats" (*Revenge for Love,* p. 9).

become "anti-he-man perverts" and men, finding their role as slaughterers of the species "unprofitable," react by turning to Sodom. This inversion establishes a "shaman." [32] Resulting principally from a yielding of the disenchanted male to the female (concomitant with the male's guilty conscience at having kept woman subservient for so long), it acts as a receipt for irresponsibility. Lewis closes the argument with his customary indictment of commerical interest: big business is interested in the shamanization of culture since the machine age demands a neuter gender. The neuter (or Florabel, to pick up current American parlance), being principally emotional, is uncritical, and thus a natural consumer for the capitalist system. The "shaman" is a "sham-man" in all senses of the word.

Lewis took this criticism characteristically far, claiming that, like the Negro, the contemporary shaman has established an hegemony of taste. The male invert has developed norms more feminine than any woman (*"plus royaliste que le roi"*), the Sodomite is leader of a disciplined host, and like "revolutionary" politics sexual perversion has set up an orthodoxy in our midst. The balding "Lesbian-Ape," characterized in Part VIII of *The Apes,* with her hatred of men, fulfills criticism of this nature to be found in *The Art of Being Ruled.*[33]

"The 'homo' is the legitimate child of the 'suffragette,' " [34] Lewis has written more than once, meaning that both share in the disintegrating processes going on in our society and that both imply an "instinctive capitulation of the will on the part of the ruling

32. In *The Lion and the Fox,* which contends that Shakespeare may have been a "shaman," Lewis defines this word as follows: "A *shaman* is a person following the calling of a magician or priest: and the word *shamanization* that I have employed would refer to a shaman (the most typical of them) who had in addition transformed himself." He finds the same phenomenon after the second World War (*Rude Assignment,* p. 177).

33. E.g. "the stupider, more excitable kind of woman will revenge herself on those things towards which she has always been in a position of veiled hostility" (*Art of Being Ruled,* p. 252).

34. *Rude Assignment,* p. 177; similar statements can be found in *Doom of Youth,* pp. 207–11.

male sex." [35] This is echoed almost word for word at the end of
the first part of *The Childermass* when a member of the Action
Française enters, a Greek who clearly stands for masculinity since
he is called Alectryon (meaning cock), and who opposes the liberal
and Bergsonian Bailiff. " 'Homosexuality is a branch of the
Feminist Revolution. The pathic is the political twin of the suffragette,' " Alectryon declares. He goes on to explain that the
invert or "shaman," springing from the Puritan revolution, is today
mobilizing his forces in the destruction of all that is best in the world.

The group-rhythm, then, is for Lewis one of the most important aspects of contemporary social decay. Negroes, youths,
and women stand for emotion and intuition, for the overthrow of
rational authority and the introduction of irresponsible anarchy.
A body of French neoclassical criticism cites woman as romantic
in this sense, but nowhere in France was the Negro so culturally
suspect as in *Paleface*. And Lewis' impeachment of woman is
more personal—which he frankly confesses ("I'm not the man that's
sensitive to sex").[36]

It is not hard to see a principal weakness in the neoclassical
attack here. French scholars like Faguet, for instance, faced with
the over-all indictment of the nineteenth century as romantic, had
little difficulty in drawing attention to literary elements in the last
century, such as the Parnassian movement, which were more classical than romantic. Nor can the inclusive charge of woman as
chaotically emotional allow for the Renaissance poetess, with her
clarity of definition and adoration of the classics, let alone for a
writer like Jane Austen. In the case of Karl Joël, who liked hard-
and-fast periods, concluding generally with the turn of succeeding
centuries, these weaknesses become glaring.

Yet they show us that Lewis is here making a political, rather than
cultural, attack in his criticism of the sex war and youth politics.

35. *Art of Being Ruled*, p. 277; Lewis produces the same anecdote to illustrate
this point in both *Snooty*, p. 26, and *Rude Assignment*, p. 174.

36. Wyndham Lewis, *One-Way Song* (London, Faber and Faber, 1933), p. 34.

It is, after all, the General, in the Walpurgisnacht scene of the first part of *Faust,* whom Goethe makes say:

> Denn bei dem Volk, wie bei den Frauen,
>   Steht immerfort die Jugend oben an.

Lewis is attacking a symptom of political instability and he admits, in one place, to believing that the extension of the franchise to women has dreadfully decreased the common political sagacity. Frequently called masculine himself in both painting and writing, Lewis has, however, shown considerable respect, and even affection, for the female form in his graphic art. One has only to consider the fine head of Madge Pulsford, of 1920, or the two full-length portraits of women reproduced at the end of *Rude Assignment,* to sense this. And with characteristic panache he has apologized to the ladies for his somewhat savage criticism of their sex: "I'm sorry if I've been too brutal girls!" [37]

37. Ibid., p. 33; this is a line Edith Sitwell takes up in her *Aspects of Modern Poetry.*

Chapter 3: The Democratic Conceit

"It is the 'democratic' conceit that is at fault, is it not?" [*Paleface,* p. 73.]

IN APPLYING those general beliefs already examined to European society of our day Lewis' main criticism has been that our so-called democracies are—in the words of T. S. Eliot—"wormeaten with Liberalism." [1] Nineteenth-century liberalism vulgarized compassion and propagated the "democratic humbug," or "democratic handicap." [2] From 1926 until a few years ago, when he slightly modifies his view on this point, Lewis finds this kind of liberalism everywhere ending in totalitarian oppression. "Things are done, likewise, in the name of liberty, that are, in truth, the promptings of oppression," he wrote in *The Art of Being Ruled*. In *Light on a Dark Horse* Roy Campbell echoes this today: "Far more people have been imprisoned for Liberty, degraded and humiliated for

---

1. T. S. Eliot, *After Strange Gods*, p. 12.

Lewis uses the word "liberalism" in two senses. Liberalism of the nineteenth-century sort is used in a pejorative sense, but he tells us that *"Western* connotes Liberal" and that "the twentieth century Left Wingers repudiated the Western norm." What does he mean by "Western"? He answers: "the 'Western' of our title is given no more definition than what naturally inheres in the something that still characterizes our Western environment, as opposed to others distinct in tradition and outlook" (*Time and Western Man*, p. 9). Good liberalism, then, is "Western" in the true sense, traveling a "graeco-roman highway" lit by the beacons of "Darwin, Voltaire, Newton, Raphael, Dante, Epictetus, Aristotle, Sophocles, Plato, Pythagoras" (*Rude Assignment*, p. 192).

2. *"Disgust has been vulgarized"* (*Art of Being Ruled*, p. 89; and see pp. 56, 87–8, 146).

the sake of Equality, and tortured and murdered in the name of Fraternity during the last thirty years than in the previous thousand under less hypocritical forms of despotism." [3]

This idea, that democracy and autocracy are close, may be hard for some of us to receive, but unless we allow it, we cannot understand much of Lewis' political criticism. For from the start Lewis could see no freedom in the kind of freedom of which the European democrat today boasts. This can be seen in a talk he gave in 1935.

The burden of this broadcast talk is in diametric opposition to the *Areopagitica* of Milton. Milton's belief, at that time, was that if truth and error were let loose in the same arena, truth would invariably prevail. By taking the reverse view, Lewis here sees freedom of the press as simply freedom for "*intellectual* Jack-the-Rippers." [4] "Universal suffrage and universal education" have lost us our liberties today. Why so? Because common education provides a mere stereotype (or "thing"), whose subsequent freedom to vote is "meaningless"—"So 'democratic' government is far more effective than subjugation by physical conquest." Until this caricature of freedom is banished, man cannot be free. "Free means just nothing," says Arghol in *The Enemy of the Stars*. "Democratic politics possess a magic property," we read through the reflections of a sympathetic character in *Self Condemned*, "they are able to turn a nobody into a somebody."

Now this idea of democratic freedom being a mere technicality, and a cloak for totalitarianism (of England of the thirties Lewis writes "No Party-state could be more autocratic"), has been a principal political criticism of the neoclassical intelligentsia. Paraphrasing Lord Acton in a summary fashion in *Democracy and Leadership*, Babbitt writes: "Rousseau himself, as we have seen, would force people to be free. The attempt to combine freedom with

3. Campbell, *Light on a Dark Horse*, p. 133.
4. Wyndham Lewis, "V," *Freedom* [by various hands] (London, Allen and Unwin, 1936), p. 53.

equality led, and, according to Lord Acton, always will lead to terrorism." [5]

Eliot is more circuitous: "By destroying traditional social habits of the people, by dissolving their natural collective consciousness into individual constituents, by licensing the opinions of the most foolish, by substituting instruction for education, by encouraging cleverness rather than wisdom, the upstart rather than the qualified . . . Liberalism can prepare the way for that which is its own negation: the artificial, mechanised or brutalised control which is a desperate remedy for its chaos." [6]

Benda, less vociferously though (for me) more cogently, argues the same in *La Grande Épreuve des démocraties*. By placing "liberty" above life and being, the modern democracy is for Benda both antihumanitarian and warlike.[7] Lewis goes further, calling the egalitarian political ideal criminal and misanthropic. Even in *The Red Priest* we find England called "a sort of Methodist's model of Russia." These critics allow little flexibility to the democratic belief. Eliot derides the "Equality of Opportunity dogma." Lewis calls this the revolutionary orthodoxy and to it I will return below.

In particular, this charge of "dictatorial" democracy has been leveled by Lewis at a number of contemporary politicians. In America Franklin D. Roosevelt has borne the brunt of this attack. Since "it is always a doctrinaire libertarianism that ushers in despotism," Roosevelt is often referred to as a "democratic autocrat." This "Club-man Caesar" (as Dos Passos also calls Roosevelt in *The Grand Design*) has developed an astute, anti-Jeffersonian autocracy in the U.S.A., reminding Lewis of the politics of Frederick the Great, whom he calls, elsewhere, a degenerate crook and an

---

5. Babbitt, *Democracy and Leadership*, p. 127.

6. Eliot, *Christian Society*, p. 13.

7. Both Lewis and Benda quote Matthew 10.34 in support of this view. It is, however, one that contradicts the idea of nonresistance for which both men equally criticize contemporary democracy. Benda's *La Grande Épreuve* is largely concerned with assigning the defeat of France in the second World War to the pacifist nature of its democracy at the time.

"arrogant homosexual tyrant." The dislike of Roosevelt is balanced by admiration for the authoritarian temper of Hamilton. For Lewis, "poor Hamilton" had to suffer for believing what is neither wicked nor stupid, namely that "a democracy necessarily is a corrupt and disorderly type of government." [8] Or, as we read in *The Enemy of the Stars,* "To have Humanity inside you—is that to keep a doss-house malgré soi?" Similar criticisms can be found at the beginning of Pound's *Jefferson and/or Mussolini,* where we read that Woodrow Wilson was filled with "power lust." All the same, one can say that Lewis has never gone so far, in his criticism of America, as the Bernanos of 1931 who could fear the rise of "some little Yankee bootblack, half Anglo-Saxon, half Jew, a marmot with a rat's head, with Heaven knows what taint from a Negro ancestor hiding in his infuriated marrow."

If it is specific politicians Lewis attacks in America, he has tended to criticize in English politics the parliamentary system. In 1929 he called the English Houses of Parliament a "Talking House," [9] picking up this label for chapter 7 of *Rotting Hill* (entitled "The Talking Shop"). Now, as then, Lewis attacks the English Parliament for being a "fake antique," for providing a spurious Tweedledum-Tweedledee charade in the name of difference of opinion. We find him most open in this criticism in an article published in Germany in 1937. This tells us that England is composed of a *"grosse sanfte Mitte"* (the "Big Soft Centre" he ridiculed in *The Mysterious Mr. Bull* of the next year). The English Parliament, runs this argument, stages a sham fight. Ninety per cent of the Lower House never open their mouths, and so the Englishman's vaunted freedom to vote is a farce—though not such a bad thing, Lewis adds, since he has never set great store by universal franchise.

8. *America and Cosmic Man,* p. 145. I should enter a caveat here. In one place it is Hamilton's "indifference to power" (p. 146) that makes him great for Lewis; in another, we read that "Lincoln was at least as much of a centralizer as was Hamilton; and they both had the same guiding principle—Union and Power" (p. 147). Nor does the last "power" refer to national strength.

9. *Diabolical Principle,* p. 88.

The English love of moderation in politics is far from heroic, it is actually cowardly, the fear of any extreme. Baldwin is assailed as the product of this system. Guilty of an overthrow of royalty comparable to that accomplished by the Russian revolutionaries, Baldwin is depicted as the arch political hypocrite, totally cynical (and when Lewis wants to discredit Hitler, in his second Hitler book, he says he has the sincerity of Baldwin).[10] As he fairly puts it in *Time and Western Man:* "My criticism of 'democracy,' again, was of 'democracy' as that is understood to-day; and it was based on the conviction that democracy is neither free, nor permits of freedom." [11]

Once again, Lewis sees himself as the Enemy, his idealism expressed in opposition. For nineteenth-century liberalism, existing by this parliamentary humbug, has become the established English status quo. Accordingly it carries a complacent air—"every one to-day is *somewhere* on the Left." This point, that "a repressive 'Leftwing' orthodoxy" persists in our democracies, is one he labors, and it constitutes his chief attack on American and European intellectuals, the class Hitler similarly stigmatized as the lost intelligentsia. Other neoclassicists, like Maurras,[12] have liked to make this same criticism of an orthodoxy of the left, as did "Agathon" if we substitute left wing for "Agathon" 's "républicaine." [13]

10. Wyndham Lewis, "Insel und Weltreich," *Europäische Revue,* XIII Jahrgang, Heft 9 (Sept. 1937), 699–707. Wyndham Lewis, *The Hitler Cult* (London, Dent, 1939), pp. 120–1. Baldwinian "Liberty" is also scathingly denounced in *Count Your Dead,* pp. 55–6. In 1952 Lewis juggles with the difference between "freedom" and "liberty" in taking issue with Sir Herbert Read, but in the body of his work he uses freedom in a normal way. When he crosses swords with Sir Herbert Read, he is allegedly championing true liberty against the "freedom" of Attlee England, a technical or legal freedom, or, as Lewis puts it, a freedom to be ill housed, ill clad, and regimented (*Writer and Absolute,* pp. 23–7).

11. *Time and Western Man,* p. 137.

12. Charles Maurras, *Romantisme et révolution* (Paris, Nouvelle Librairie Nationale, 1922), p. 83; this useful edition includes *L'Avenir de l'intelligence, Le Romantisme féminin,* and other characteristically Maurrassian works.

13. "Agathon," *Les Jeunes Gens d'aujourd'hui* (Paris, Librairie Plon, 1913), p. 110.

The "dead level of liberal-pink orthodoxy" (or "rebel 'fixation' ")
Lewis finds in European democracies includes the rich; in *The Art
of Being Ruled* he wrote, "It is only the wealthy, intelligent or
educated who are revolutionary or combative." Gillian puts this
point of view in *The Revenge for Love:* "It is we so called 'intellectuals' of the upper-classes, who are the only real Communists
. . . When a workman becomes a Communist he only does so
for what he can *get!* . . . he brings with him all his working-class
cynicism, all his underdog cowardice and disbelief in everything
and everybody." [14]

In *Broken Record* Roy Campbell says the same. In this work,
which even sees Springbok rugby being "bolshevized," we read of
liberal ideas that "For the last two hundred years reformers and
agitators have been pumping workmen with these ideas until there
are no more workmen left, only a crowd of self-righteous martyrs
with the hallucination that everybody is under some obligation to
them. Extremely difficult and over-precious poets write propaganda
for these martyrs whose only ambition and daydream is to become
'dirty little bourgeois' themselves." [15]

If, then, Lewis sincerely believed that socialism in our society
has become obligatory, he is once again behaving like a good neoclassicist in endeavoring to correct a balance by championing what
he calls the *"unradical"* position of "poor old 'Reaction.' " Several
characters in his work, like Laming of *Rotting Hill,* are seen as
occupying a near-revolutionary position by being on the political
right. The revolutionary orthodoxy of "unprogressive 'progres-
siveness' " is what he is satirizing in the form of the One-Ways of
One-Way Song. Stanza 19 of the "One-Way Song" Canto itself
characterizes the "Fronts" as unreflecting units, standardized revolutionaries, puppet-like busybodies playing at social change, dolts

14. *Revenge for Love*, p. 225. In 1938 Lewis sees the British Labour party as
callously indifferent to the poor. Wyndham Lewis, *The Mysterious Mr. Bull*
(London, Robert Hale, 1938), p. 105.
15. Campbell, *Broken Record,* p. 44.

who "strut and pant in insect packs." "How we One-Ways stink / Of progress!" we read and, when Lewis describes the song of the "Fronts" as "the lament of *Not-to-be*," he means that such people are totally unaware, do not exist. This repressive orthodoxy of opinion has been particularly the case in literature (he does not attack painters in this way): "From Shelley to Shaw in England it has been rather the rule than the exception for a writer to be a destructive political revolutionary idealist." [16]

Here Lewis, closely concerned, becomes intemperate. It is true that Benda denounces the contemporary clerc for utilitarianism. And we may find in Conrad the idea that the average political revolutionary is simply "a brazen cheat." [17] But for Lewis any writer on the political left has adopted the position solely out of self-interest, in order to gain materially from the revolutionary orthodoxy. This criticism is summarized when he looks back on his career in 1950: "ours has been in the West a generation of hypocrites . . . a generation that has shown less care for men in the mass than any for a great many centuries, combining this demonstrable indifference to the welfare of the generality with never-ceasing hosannas to the Common Man: a generation of power-addicts who put on a red tie with a smirk, climb upon the back of the Working Class and propose to ride it to a new type of double-faced dominion." [18] Campbell also, in *Light on a Dark Horse*, attributes all socialist instincts to "base sham, and hypocritical self-seeking," but Lewis seems to have felt bitterly about this as far as it concerns the literary profession: "the same petty calculation," he writes in 1950, "that led the average intellectual to hoist himself on to the marxist bandwagon now prompts him discreetly to drop off it."

This bias was demonstrated in one of the most acrimonious at-

16. *Diabolical Principle*, p. 140.

17. Joseph Conrad, Author's Note, *The Secret Agent* (New York, Doubleday, Page, 1923), p. ix.

18. *Rude Assignment*, p. 142; cf. "Most socialist doctrine in the case of the older men is rooted in christian teaching: with the young it is rooted in power impulses" (p. 138).

tacks Lewis has made on any writer, namely his chapter on George Orwell in *The Writer and the Absolute*. Orwell is represented here as cynical and self-seeking. Having "succumbed to the fashionable pink rash" at Eton, Orwell "obtained so much kudos" out of socialism that he continued to indulge in it as "Slumming." He went to the Spanish Civil War "for no very serious reason," merely taking up socialist attitudes "to keep step with everybody else." Orwell got financial advantage out of his political position, just as Lawrence did out of being the son of a coal miner. Two points should be taken into account here; first, Orwell was undoubtedly popular for what he had to say, rather than for the way he said it. (I am aware that some critics, like V. S. Pritchett, claim a "clear, direct" style for Orwell, but the same could be claimed for the work-a-day journalist.) Lewis knows that he has been unpopular for what he had to say, to the neglect of literary proficiency superior to Orwell's, to understate the case. Secondly, Lewis wrote his attack after Orwell had foolishly referred to him in *Partisan Review* as "a Communist or at least a strong sympathiser." [19] It was not for nothing that Lewis likened himself to Voltaire's malign animal who, when bitten, is so impolite as to bite back.

The revolutionary orthodoxy comes in for satire in *The Revenge for Love,* the premise of which is largely that revolutionary politics is a game. But it is chiefly in Lewis' criticism that we find the idea that this orthodoxy derives from another, namely what he calls "the evangelical heresy." For Lewis, as I shall elaborate below, it is the political consequences of the "well-thumbed Genevan Bible" that we are suffering today: "The moralist politics of Protestant Christianity was violently anti-authoritarian, in contrast with the Catholic philosophy." Yet the Jew also is "the Leader of the Liberal world." [20] For the French antiromanticists these origins had

19. George Orwell, "London Letter," *Partisan Review, 13,* No. 3 (Summer 1946), 323. Cf. Francis Fytton, "Laughter and Letters: Dominic Bevan Wyndham Lewis," *The Catholic World, 181,* No. 1,086 (Sept. 1955), 425: our Lewis seen as "perpetually . . . flirting" with communism.

20. *Count Your Dead,* p. 268.

the added advantage of making modern socialism un-French. Maurras, who like Toussenel traced Protestantism to the Jews, was especially strong on this point, and even the relatively cool Benda
finds contemporary egalitarian politics rooted in Anglo-Saxon Protestantism (though Benda grew critical of both Maurras and Catholicism). In passing, it is surely a tribute to Jacques Maritain
that he could, though a strong Catholic, see the evangelical basis
of modern democracy as good, on the simple grounds that it is
Christian. Europe's problem, Maritain wrote in 1943, was to
recover Christianity, and to this democracy was linked, so that
the general ideal of human dignity was fundamentally assisted by
"l'inspiration évangélique." [21]

But to most antiromanticists seventeenth-century Puritanism, and
the Sermon on the Mount, are mandates to irresponsibility. Christ,
by inviting the last to be first, Lewis says, resembled Nietzsche
asking everyone to become an aristocrat. Thus Jesus vulgarized
true freedom, which is the privilege of the few. Contemporary
socialism, continuing nineteenth-century liberalism, is a perpetua-
tion of Bible Christianity.[22] Being emotional and intuitive, rather
than intellectual and rational, this theological politics leads to
hatred, intolerance, and egotism. This criticism, made by Lewis
in 1926, is not changed in 1950. In fact, a year later, *Rotting Hill*
turns out to be a satire of State socialism derived from "bible-
religion." There are several places in this work where Lewis shows
that socialism of what he calls the "hard-boiled" type stems from
Jesus.[23] Father Card of *The Red Priest* further implements this
criticism.

For de Maistre, master of French antiromantic criticism, democracy was an awful visitation from God. In the face of "the
liberal opera-bouffe" of modern democracy, confronted with "the

21. Jacques Maritain, *Christianisme et démocratie* (New York, Éditions de la
Maison Française, 1943), pp. 33–67.

22. *Art of Being Ruled*, p. 326; cf. "In a democracy the business of the State is
conducted upon an oily pulpit note" (*Snooty*, p. 6).

23. *Rotting Hill*, pp. ix, 36, 48, 51, 52, 226.

european egalitarian masquerade" where "Liberty is manufactured with words," drenched in the "greasy incense to Mr. Everyman" and deafened by the "chorus of parrots" of the revolutionary orthodoxy, what alternative has Lewis held out for our society? The answer, in general terms, is an organized despotism with a caste system based on the intelligence.[24]

In 1926 Lewis wrote: "Instead of the vast organization to exploit the weaknesses of the Many, should we not possess one for the exploitation of the intelligence of the Few?" In 1948 he put the same view: "Were I to return to this earth five centuries hence, and discover a country the size of Great Britain ruled by a 'Premier' and half a dozen secretaries, I should know that the 'free society' so often said to be there was at last in actual being." [25] At the start of his critical career Lewis could see only two forces confronting the inhibiting hypocrisy of the democracies. These two systems of government, Fascist and Communist, were in charge of political initiative, Lewis saw, and were to be admired for their organizing abilities.[26] Possibly here was a chance that the "person" could be freed. "The disciplined *fascist* party in Italy can be taken as representing the new and healthy type of 'freedom,' " [27] he wrote in 1926. The Soviet also had taken "the wisest and sanest step . . . in curtailing the impossible freedom of art." [28] Both regimes, for admitting "that there must be a master," [29] were not only commendable but compassionate. Let us now follow in the paths to which Lewis was led by this early analysis.

24. *Art of Being Ruled*, pp. 387 ff.
25. *America and Cosmic Man*, p. 160.
26. *Art of Being Ruled*, p. 79.
27. Ibid., p. 152.
28. Ibid., p. 121.
29. Ibid., p. 95.

Chapter 4: A Compromise with the Herd

"Do not play with political notions, aristocratisms or the reverse, for that is a compromise with the herd." [*The Ideal Giant*, p. 33.]

IN APRIL 1929 T. S. Eliot grouped Wyndham Lewis with a number of writers who, in his opinion, "incline in the direction of some kind of fascism." [1] In this year Lewis described his own politics as "partly communist and partly fascist, with a distinct streak of monarchism in my marxism, but at bottom anarchist with a healthy passion for order." [2] When we are later told by him that "At no time, however, have I been in the least danger of falling in love with a political Star, or becoming excited about a Party," we realize that we are facing a certain ambiguity of statement, the same kind of confession of faith made by Eliot when he wrote that he was "royalist" in contemporary England. [3]

It would be safe, however, to dismiss Orwell's notion that Lewis has been in sympathy with Russian communism. It is true that in *The Art of Being Ruled* we find him writing, "in the abstract I believe the sovietic system to be the best," [4] but in the same book we read also, "I am not a communist; if anything, I favour some form of *fascism* rather than communism." [5] Moreover, *The Art of Being Ruled* pours scorn on Marx and pictures the Marxist politician as totally cynical and ruled by lust for power. Adverse

1. T. S. Eliot, "Commentary," *The Criterion, 8,* No. 32 (April 1929), p. 378.
2. *Diabolical Principle,* p. 126.
3. T. S. Eliot, *For Launcelot Andrewes* (Garden City, Doubleday, Doran, 1929), p. vii.
4. *Art of Being Ruled,* p. 381.
5. Ibid., p. 28.

references to communism, both in theory and practice, follow this book, and are maintained to date. In *Paleface* the Communist doctrine is "proletarian imperialism," considered inhumanity, with the Russian leaders "open professors of intrigue and herd-hypnotism"; in *The Doom of Youth* it is "the most fanatical anti-individualist creed that has ever seen the light." No, Lewis can fairly write in his recent *America and Cosmic Man* that "Communist methods outrage me, and always have." What is responsible for that sympathy for communism that does exist in *The Art of Being Ruled* is its affinity with fascism; both are political theories with points of strength for Lewis. Thus, "An extreme version of leninist politics . . . is fascismo," we read here, and again, "*Fascismo* is merely a spectacular marinettian flourish put onto the tail, or, if you like, the head of marxism." Benda also, in *La Trahison,* finds communism and fascism close and ascribes both to a common source (in his case, Sorel). We know that Sorel praised Lenin and was himself praised by Mussolini.

But nowhere is it more difficult in Lewis' work to sort out a consistent attitude than on this point. Even the most sympathetic recording of his ideas must admit recurrent contradictions; so we read, in the second part of *Hitler,* that fascism is true socialism. We know that socialism, for him, derives from seventeenth-century Bible-religion and from Jewry (Marx). But we remember being told in *The Art of Being Ruled* that Marx was really in support of capitalism, or of "a great bureaucratic hegemony, which would result in a world state on capitalist lines, but theoretically purged of capitalist oppression." This leads us to the idea Lewis often expresses, that Marx's function in society was similar to a sort of Marx Brothers hoax (recently, Stephen Spender has seen Auden, in *The Dance of Death,* making "Karl Marx look like one of the Marx Brothers").[6] It is for this reason Lewis likens Hardcaster, of *The Revenge for Love,* to Groucho Marx in *Rude Assignment.*

6. *Blasting and Bombardiering,* p. 17; *Jews,* p. 74. Stephen Spender, *The Creative Element* (London, Hamish Hamilton, 1953), p. 150.

Then we have further complications when, within a single book, he equates both communism and fascism, and communism and socialism.[7] Confusion is worse confounded when we read elsewhere that the method of seizure of power by "catastrophe" and bloody violence is that of the capitalist rather than of the Fascist,[8] and in another place that fascism is defined by George Washington, viz. political by means of military despotism.[9] Faced with these equivocations, we can only think of the instruction given the Herdsman at the start of Lewis' career: "Contradict yourself, in order to live. You must remain broken up."[10]

Yet even as one arrays these apparent contradictions it can be seen that, deviously, they can be traced to a coherent political attitude. In Lewis opposites reconcile themselves. He was the first English intellectual to see the similarity between Russian communism and fascism, though his view of the latter was elastic. Nor is the idea that Marx (a Jew) was out to perpetuate capital so violently unusual, for it was of course a tenet of Nazi thought also.[11]

Chapter 12 of Part XI of *The Art of Being Ruled* is entitled "Fascism as an Alternative" and is the secret of Lewis' interest in Fascist politics. For here Lewis believed that with the dictator in absolute command the clerc would be freed; political thinking would be lifted from his shoulders and his energies liberated for purely aesthetic duties. But even as one contends that this idea was responsible for the more rabid of Lewis' political books of the thirties,

7. Wyndham Lewis, *Anglosaxony: A League That Works* (Toronto, Ryerson Press, 1941), pp. 1–2, 23.

8. *Art of Being Ruled,* p. 50.

9. *America and Cosmic Man,* p. 134.

10. *Ideal Giant,* p. 36. The general reader, unacquainted with Lewis' basic beliefs, is likely to find contradiction after apparent contradiction in his work. Even when one knows his beliefs, some of these remain insoluble; cf. "Functional philosophies do not interest me a great deal" (*Rude Assignment,* p. 91) and "My writings possess this unity because they are functional" (p. 141).

11. *Hitler,* p. 175, and *Count Your Dead,* p. 230, are two typical examples of this belief. In the latter case we find Marx also behind "Americanism."

one is faced with another contradiction, for in 1935 he called State patronage of the artist, of the kind he had seemed to welcome in *The Art of Being Ruled,* "more deadly than puritanism." [12] Still, it was this idea, I think—together with the theory he advanced in 1929 that if you could persuade one class of people they were better than another there was a chance they would act in conformity with this belief—that seems to have led him to write in 1926, "for anglo-saxon countries as they are constituted to-day some modified form of fascism would probably be the best." [13]

Meeting this remark in 1926 one would naturally imagine that Lewis would view Italian fascism with sympathy. Such is not the case. Mussolini is consistently ridiculed, in 1927, 1929, and 1932; the charge that he has an "actor-mind" in *Time and Western Man* is typical of Lewis' feeling for "the italian potentate in the political Dime Novel of Modern Rome," as the Duce is called in *The Apes of God.* Actually, in his satire, Lewis often shows himself ready to poke fun at stupid traits by no means ridiculed in his criticism; it is true that the Fascist Starr-Smith of *The Apes* is almost the only man of good will in the work, but Starr-Smith is frequently found "broadcasting" in an obvious skit of Fascist oratory, while in *The Childermass* the Followers of Hyperides give what may be intended as a parody of similar rhetoric.[14] In the same way Eliot is thought to have included in *The Rock* a satire of Mosley, whom he praised in *The Criterion.* However it is certain that Lewis never saw the possibility of an intellectual elite—and the reader will have gathered by now that this is what Lewis is after in politics—in Mussolini's Italy, as did Pound.[15] There is only one place where

12. Wyndham Lewis, "Art and Patronage (I)," *The B.B.C. Annual* (London, British Broadcasting Corporation, 1935), p. 187. This is a severe criticism, when one knows what Puritanism means to Lewis. The whole of this article reverses ch. 12 of Pt. XI of *The Art of Being Ruled.*

13. *Art of Being Ruled,* p. 381.

14. *Childermass,* pp. 253–4.

15. I refer to ch. 3 of Pt. V of Pound's *ABC of Economics,* entitled "Dictatorship as a Sign of Intelligence."

Lewis shows any enthusiasm for Mussolini. In two articles in *The Calendar of Modern Letters* in 1926 he finds Great Britain "badly in need of a ruling class," suggests that "a Fascist nobility supply the long-felt British need," and urges an alliance between France, Italy, and the British Empire, an alliance which should find its rulers in Rome.

Why did Lewis have reasonably little use for Mussolini, when we know he wrote with enthusiasm of Hitler? Two answers are possible. In one place he differentiates Mussolini from Hitler by calling the Duce more Communist. Second, Lewis had seen Italian fascism express itself (expose itself, for him) on the level of art, in the Futurism of Marinetti. Lewis constantly criticizes Italian fascism as political Futurism (an early criticism repeated by Pound and Roy Campbell) and charges both Marinetti and Mussolini with being apostles of "action." He was eventually to see Hitler in the same light, of course, but the difference remains that Italian fascism was ushered in with an artistic movement, in which Lewis could recognize reprehensible traits, in a way that German fascism was not. Moreover, Mussolini's long article "Fascismo" for the *Enciclopedia italiana,* with its stress on youth ("Giovinezza, impeto, fede"), openly advocated principles with which Lewis would disagree. The explanation, however, is not entirely satisfactory, for it was in 1925, after Hitler's detention following the November 1923 *Putsch,* that the German parallel of this document, *Mein Kampf,* appeared, again filled with principles with which Lewis might be thought to disagree. Finally, as far as the British Fascist leader was concerned, Lewis showed little explicit sympathy. He drew a head of Mosley in the thirties but he did not invariably draw heads of those he admired (Ronald Firbank). It is true that in an article published in Germany in September 1937 he saw Mosley possessing "grosse politische Einsicht und Führereigenschaften," [16] but it cannot be said that he ever praised Mosley in the way T. S. Eliot did in his "Commentary" to *The Criterion* for April 1931.

16. "Insel und Weltreich," p. 701.

On November 29, 1930, Lewis writes to A. J. A. Symons from Berlin. As a result of this visit he published a series of articles dealing with Hitler and Hitlerism in *Time and Tide* early the next year. These he reprinted in *Hitler,* which Geoffrey Stone correctly calls one of the few "positive" political pamphlets by Lewis. Of course Lewis himself claims that he is writing this work as an "exponent," not as an "advocate," of Hitlerism. In *Blasting and Bombardiering* of 1937 he reminds us of this impartiality again; the book was simply a series of impressions of Germany given "as a spectator, not as a partisan." In the work itself, however, he confesses in one place to a "sympathy" [17] for the Nazi regime of the time, and such is what we most undoubtedly find.

Neither Junker nor Marxist, Hitler is presented here as one of the little men of mankind, a total expression of Germany, and a "man of peace" who, if left to himself, would be unlikely either to want to expand or to start a war. He has, however, not been left alone and therefore has been compelled to arm his party in self-defense. Here we meet a contradiction. Having furnished the Nazi stereotype of a corrupt Berlin—the infamous Eldorado nightclub figures prominently in this "scientific" picture of Berlin—Lewis alleges that the Nazis were "driven to arm" against Marxist gang terrorism. Yet he also says that "Any Nationalsocialist carrying firearms is expelled from the party," and claims that Hitler's total armament consisted of "mere knuckles not knuckledusters." [18]

In *Hitler* the Jewish question in Germany is called a "racial red-herring," and the English reader assured that Hitler would grow more tolerant of the Jews in time.[19] As this raises a passionate controversy, and since the charge of anti-Semitism has been laid lately at Lewis' door with considerable acerbity by a writer in *Commentary,* perhaps I should digress to consider it. In the first place

17. *Hitler,* p. 143.
18. Cf. ibid., pp. 18, 65 with pp. 47, 54, and with *Blasting and Bombardiering,* p. 235.
19. *Hitler,* pp. 35–43, 48.

it is presumably unsound to call a writer anti-Semitic on the basis
of his creative work. T. S. Eliot is author of the famous lines,

> The rats are underneath the piles.
> The jew is underneath the lot.

The Jew at the start of *Gerontion* (coupled with the sick archetype
of potency) may seem as unpleasant as Bleistein, but it would of
course be unwise to adduce a racial attitude from these characterizations. Similarly, those Jews that do occur in Lewis' satire usually
possess qualities he does not admire; one thinks of the unpleasant
art critic (who has anglicized his name from Reuben Wallach) or
of Isaac Wohl, one of the principal forgers, in *The Revenge for
Love*. In *The Apes* we find Archie Margolin described as a "militant
slum-Jew" or "Sham Yid" with a "mass-production grin." But I
do not intend to draw conclusions from these. In 1939 Lewis published *The Jews, Are They Human?* (following the successful *The
English, Are They Human?*) which is a direct plea for the Jewish
race. It attacks anti-Semitism, pays tribute to Jewish ability, and
criticizes current German racial theories. One can, more or less
kindly, speculate as to its sincerity, but it must be considered, and
considered as an apologetic writing on behalf of the Jews, before
calling Lewis anti-Semitic.

At the same time as acknowledging that Lewis often rebukes
anti-Semitism, one can allow that he dislikes qualities considered
as Jewish (to be found even in the late, guarded *Self Condemned*,
where we read of "a fat jewish-looking gentleman, with a lisp, a
large cigar . . . ," etc., etc.). In *The Red Priest* a character is
afraid lest Father Card lose his money and so "become the victim
of the Jews." Yet if so many of his ideological opponents are Jewish
(Bergson, Einstein, Marx, Gertrude Stein, and Joyce, who celebrated a Jew), his philosophic master, Benda, was a Czech of
Jewish ancestry. Nor can it be said that Lewis, like Lasserre, ever
attacked Bergson for his race (Bergson was more than once threatened with execution by the French neoclassicists in the press). No,

Lewis has often been careful not to offend on this delicate matter. The following passage in square brackets was deleted in the second edition of *Tarr:* "Rembrandt paints decrepit old Jews [, the most decayed specimens of the lowest race on earth that is]. Shakespeare deals in human tubs of grease." [20] In the margin of the manuscript for an article on art to go into *The Dial* in 1921, he marks a passage on the emotional nature of the Jew as not to be included.[21]

In fact, this criticism, that the Jewish psychology is feminine and close to that of the child, does escape Lewis in *The Doom of Youth* and is a leading neoclassical attack. Again, in an article in *The New Statesman* in 1924, he stages an imaginary conversation with a Jew, finding the Semite hostile to true individuality and characterized by "an almost morbid sociability, clinging gregariousness, and satisfaction in crowds." In other words, he here criticizes the Jew for indulging in a group-rhythm. It is the Jewish gregariousness Lewis dislikes in *Paleface* (a work praised by Eliot in *After Strange Gods*), repeating the criticism in 1937: "Jewish success is a triumph of organization, the subordination of the individual to the race." This aptitude for organization leads, like all group-rhythms, to war. Hence we find the neoclassicist attack on the Jews as "militant." Cantleman finds the first World War partly due to "the quarrels of jews." Similarly Gaudier-Brzeska, whose notebooks seem to have been definitely anti-Semitic, wrote in *Blast No. 1:* "The SEMITIC VORTEX was the lust of war." [22]

This attack, which refuses to allow for the fact that the Jewish race has had to struggle for its very existence in twentieth-century Europe, seems wild at first glance—especially as it was being made at a moment when (as Hannah Arendt's *The Origins of Totalitarianism* or Jules Isaac's more recent *Genesis of Antisemitism* shows)

20. *Tarr* (Egoist), p. 9; *Tarr* (Chatto), p. 9.
21. Lockwood Memorial Library, University of Buffalo. Is it deliberately that, when quoting a passage concerning world capitalism from the *Völkische Beobachter*, Lewis mistranslates the Nazi epithet for it, *"wucherischen,"* as "accursed"? (*Hitler*, p. 175.)
22. *Blast No. 1*, p. 156.

the call of Maurrasians for Jews to be circumcised "up to the neck" was being literally implemented. But one comes across it repeatedly. Even the comparatively temperate Benda in *La Trahison* indicts Jewish nationalism and facility for organization ("*nationalisme juif*"), as a prime political passion of the most dangerous sort. But in *Belphégor* he takes up the attack on the Jews as agents of Romance, made by so many French neoclassicists, and acquits them of this charge.[23] Lewis is closer to Benda and Maritain [24] on this vexed question than to the other antiromanticists mentioned. He has never gone as far, for example, as to find, with T. S. Eliot, "any large number of free-thinking Jews undesirable." [25] This remark, incidentally, eluded Eliot's usual vigilance in *After Strange Gods,* a work to which Pound has recently referred as follows:

> Eliot, in this book, has not come through uncontaminated by the Jewish poison.
> Until a man purges himself of this poison he will never achieve understanding.[26]

Nor can comparison be made between Lewis' attitude to the Jews and that of Charles Maurras. Maurras, in fact, here makes a neat association of many elements disliked by the neoclassicist. Both de Maistre and Comte, we know, had seen Protestantism and revo-

23. Benda, *Belphégor,* p. 155.

24. Jacques Maritain also wrote against anti-Semitism at about the same time as Lewis. Maritain's "L'Impossible Antisémitisme" appeared in *Les Juifs* in 1937, and this essay was expanded in a lecture given by Maritain in Paris on February 5, 1938, at the Théâtre des Ambassadeurs. This was collected into a book translated into English as *Antisemitism* (London, Geoffrey Bles, 1939); this appears to be substantially the same volume as *A Christian Looks at the Jewish Question* (London, Longmans, Green, 1939). Like Lewis, Maritain obviously detests the violence being meted out to the Jews at this time. More recently he has found Jewry part of the whole religious family which it is essential for Europe to try to preserve (Maritain, *Christianisme et démocratie,* p. 46).

25. Eliot, *After Strange Gods,* p. 20. Cf. Morris Freedman, "The Meaning of T. S. Eliot's Jew," *The South Atlantic Quarterly,* 55, No. 2 (April 1956), 198–206.

26. Ezra Pound, *A Visiting Card* (London, Peter Russell, 1952), p. 22.

lution as allied, a fairly common attitude in such minds. But Maurras goes one step further; not only are the Jews behind democracy, Jerusalem being the seat of revolution, but the Jews are behind Protestantism also: "Le protestant procède absolument du Juif."[27] In actual fact, there is nothing very original in this criticism, as those familiar with attacks on Milton's Zionism must be aware. Maurras probably pulled it out of Toussenel: "Qui dit Juif, dit protestant, sachez-le," exhorted Toussenel at the start of his huge indictment of the Jews.[28] Yet it is surprising to find Benda referring to this association and tending to agree with it.[29] Maurras has the same idea that we shall find in Lewis of the Semitic origins of contemporary Russian leaders, but his dislike of "ce messianisme de Juifs charnels, porté au paroxysme par sa démence égalitaire" is itself a paroxysm Lewis never allowed himself. In the French neoclassicist indeed we meet that habit of mind of blanketing everything disliked under an absolute. Just as the Communist calls any ideological dissimilarity "bourgeois," so the Oriental mind with these thinkers tends to be monotonously Semitic. The obviously suspect Plato, for instance, is charged by Jules Lemaître, in one

27. Maurras, *Romantisme et révolution*, p. 275. I have also used a convenient digest of his political views Maurras made in 1937—Charles Maurras, *Mes idées politiques* (Paris, Librairie Arthème Fayard, 1937)—where, on pp. 193–4, there is a characteristic syllogism. For Maurras suggests that the masses are all demagogues, and then that the Jews are all demagogues. Presumably, then, for this "thinker," the masses are all Jews. This is further complicated when we read Maurras claiming that the Dreyfus agitation was "subventionnée" by England. Charles Maurras, *Kiel et Tanger* (Paris, Nouvelle Librairie Nationale, 1915), p. 121; this work was first published in 1910.

28. Alphonse Toussenel, *Les Juifs, rois de l'époque: histoire de la féodalité financière* (Paris, Gabriel de Gonet, 1847), tome premier, p. iv. Louis Thomas' recent study—*Alphonse Toussenel, socialiste national antisémite* (Paris, Mercure de France, 1941)—contains at p. 95 the following proud assessment of Toussenel from occupied France: "Le malheur est que sa leçon fut inentendue des Français jusqu'au jour où les Juifs, poussant leur audace à l'extrême et jouant le tout pour le tout, risquèrent, en 1939, l'existence de la France en la lançant ignominieusement, à l'aveugle, dans la Croisade pour les Juifs. Dorénavant, Toussenel sera une de nos Bibles."

29. Benda, *Épreuve*, p. 72.

of his interminable volumes on *Les Contemporains,* with being
steeped in the Semitic Orient and inimical to truly "Aryan" Hellen-
ism; Seillière, though far more resigned on this point, also finds
Plato contaminated by the Jewish Orient in *Le Romantisme.* But
the ideal of racial purity of this sort has not been wholly European
in our century. The "métèques" (resident aliens) Maurras disliked
so are the same "degenerate breeds" whose multiplication in America Babbitt dreaded, and who prompted him to write: "Circumstances may arise when we may esteem ourselves fortunate if we
get the American equivalent of a Mussolini; he may be needed to
save us from the American equivalent of a Lenin." [30]

Yet if we conclude that Lewis has been more careful than these
intransigeants, we must equally remember that he has played with
the paradoxical and perverse idea that, like the Negro, the Jew
is in power, his supposed racial inferiority a myth, and that in
reality the Aryan is the victim of intolerance in our society. Even
as late as 1937 he makes reasonably light of the Fascist persecution of the Jews.[31] To be really generous, perhaps we can say that
this was due to a sincere belief (expressed in *Hitler*) that racial
bias breaks down class bias. Class feeling is a more restrictive
group-rhythm than race feeling; he retains this idea in *The Hitler
Cult: "The more racial feeling, the less class feeling."* This is the
only way we can account for his acceptance of the Nazi doctrine of
Blutsgefühl in 1931, for it is a doctrine one might think extremely
distasteful to him, and indeed it is so, when he comes to criticize
Hitler adversely in *The Hitler Cult.* Roy Campbell, of course, is
more open, writing in *Broken Record* of 1934, "I fail to see how
a man like Hitler makes any 'mistake' in expelling a race that is
intellectually subversive." In *Hitler,* too, the racial homogeneity
preached by the Nazis is a counter to American "negro-worship"
and an essentially healthy belief in "the necessity of a Central,
Western unified culture, and the necessity of an acuter and more

30. Babbitt, *Democracy and Leadership,* p. 312.
31. *Count Your Dead,* pp. 339–42.

jingo, if you like, race-consciousness on the part of all White Western Peoples." Hitler's Aryanism is not only desirable in its context, but should be extended. It is "the only sane and realistic policy in the midst of a disintegrating world." Hitler may well be announcing another Golden Age.[32]

Soon after the publication of this book derogatory references to Hitler may be traced in Lewis' writings; yet his interest in Hitler and Fascist politics continues strongly sympathetic through 1936 and 1937. The only interpretation I put on this is that Lewis was quickly aware of the damage *Hitler* did him in literary circles. In *One-Way Song,* of 1933, he refers to how the book has hurt his reputation, and makes the claim, to be repeated frequently, that *Hitler* (which was translated into German in 1932) was disliked in Germany. This may have been so, but in 1936 the British *Fascist Quarterly* could list *Hitler* as "still about the best study of the man and the movement." [33] And it was in this year that Lewis published *Left Wings over Europe,* where we read, unequivocally: "it is an undeniable fact that *democracy* is being practised in Germany at present, with surprising success. It was a pure parliamentary democracy that voted in—as nearly by democratic vote as it is humanly possible to get—and has periodically confirmed in power, the great patriot who is now 'Dictator' of the German Democracy." [34]

This "impartial" book consists of a defense of German and Italian politics of the time, an attack on the League of Nations, a record of Baldwinian "hypocrisy," an analysis of representative government as occult, usurious, and despotic, and of British democracy as an egregious sham. It concludes with a pretense of German

32. *Hitler,* pp. 184–9. In fairness, it should be added that even in this work Lewis shows some signs of dissatisfaction with Hitler's boast of the monopoly of greatness of Aryan culture. But by and large he does not seriously challenge it, and even uses the theory of diffusion of culture (which he had come across as a *Criterion* reviewer) to back the possibility of such a monopoly. In 1939, however, one of the many reasons for condemning Hitler is his denial of the genius of the Jews (*Hitler,* p. 97).

33. "Select Bibliography," *The Fascist Quarterly, 2,* No. 3 (July 1936), 583.

34. *Left Wings,* p. 298.

friendship for England. In short, it is a fully committed apology for Hitler.

In a long defense of Fascist foreign policy, Lewis dismisses the idea of the "German menace" and pleads that Germany be allowed to rearm, a view he directly contradicts when writing from Toronto in 1942.[35] In the same way the Abyssinian war was a "war of liberation," a course thrust upon Mussolini by Great Britain.[36] Germany is being encircled, Lewis claims; he defends Hitler's assumption of absolute power by judicious quotation of John Stuart Mill, instances the high degree of freedom within the Fascist states, and concludes with a diatribe against the Soviet leaders, "an indescribable mafia" ending nineteenth-century liberalism in a blood bath. Stalin is an "ex-bank robber" and Peter Fleming is quoted to the effect that all Russian leaders are Jews.[37] This prejudice, which Lewis shares with other neoclassicists, notably Maurras, occurs the next year in an article in *The British Union Quarterly,* formerly *The Fascist Quarterly* which had numbered Mussolini, Goebbels, and Mosley among its contributors. Addressing the British Fascists as "the Poor against the Rich," Lewis here writes: "You as a Fascist stand for the small trader against the chain-store; for the peasant against the usurer; for the nation, great or small, against the super-state." [38] The left-wing orthodoxy has "swallowed the

35. Ibid., pp. 105 ff. (and cf. p. 91, "the Germans . . . do not dream of attacking France"); Wyndham Lewis, "That 'Now-or-Never' Spirit," *Saturday Night: the Canadian Weekly, 57,* No. 40 (June 13, 1942), p. 6.

36. *Left Wings,* pp. 164–7 (e.g. "that the industrious and ingenious Italian, rather than the lazy, stupid, and predatory Ethiopian, should eventually control Abyssinia is surely not such a tragedy"). In 1939, when reversing these views, Lewis criticizes British policy over Abyssinia for exactly the opposite reason (*Hitler Cult,* pp. 140 ff.).

37. *Left Wings,* p. 138.

38. Wyndham Lewis, " 'Left Wings' and the C 3 Mind," *The British Union Quarterly, 1,* No. 1 (Jan./April 1937), 33. He repeats this idea in *Count Your Dead,* p. 322. No sooner had Lewis contributed this article to *The British Union Quarterly* than he again asseverated his complete political impartiality (*Blasting and Bombardiering,* p. 17).

The quotation in my text touches upon Lewis' attitude to the sovereign State. Since his views on nationhood are almost impossible to reduce to consistency, and

Spain of Moses Rosenberg without turning a hair." Moses, or Marcel, Rosenberg was the Soviet ambassador to Madrid at the time of the Spanish Civil War and is bitterly attacked by Lewis (for example, as a thief) in the same way that he bitterly attacked other philosophical enemies (Marinetti, we learn, got his wealth from a string of brothels in Egypt, and there is a suggestion that D. H. Lawrence died of a most unpleasant disease).

---

since little new enters his thought on this subject, I have thought it best to relegate them to this note. At first one would conclude that Lewis would be against nationalism, as another force in our world tending to align disparate points of view. The idea of the Arthur Press suggests this, and such is what we find in *Blast No. 2,* p. 72: "All Nationality is a congealing and conventionalizing, a necessary and delightful rest for the many." Later, he claims that his *Blast* period was antinationalist because he originally saw nationalism as antipathetic to art, a significant enough confession in itself. Wyndham Lewis, *Wyndham Lewis the Artist, from "Blast" to Burlington House* (London, Laidlaw and Laidlaw, 1939), pp. 15–17.

However, there are many other references during the twenties which show Lewis antagonistic to nationalism (cf. Wyndham Lewis, "A World Art and Tradition," *Drawing and Design, 5,* No. 32, Feb. 1929, 56); in this way, he parts company from Maurras and, indeed, in *Hitler,* contrasts Maurras unfavorably with the Führer, who is more democratic than the leader of the Action Française (*Hitler,* pp. 32–3, 45–6).

As Lewis becomes interested in fascism in the thirties, nevertheless, he sacrifices this early view and denounces internationalism, especially that represented by the League of Nations which is a "collectivism" of underdogs. Consequently, he can plead that the nation-State facing this "collectivism" resembles the individual trying to liberate his potentialities against the fabric of democratic society (*Left Wings,* pp. 144–8, 268–73). In 1937 the U.S.A., the U.S.S.R., Britain, and France have established a restrictive "monism," a moneylender's dream being heroically resisted by the decentralized "pluralism" of the Fascist nation-States (*Count Your Dead,* pp. 282–99). The sympathetic Don Alvaro, a fictional character of this time, detests internationalism.

In two recent volumes, *America and Cosmic Man* and *Rude Assignment,* Lewis achieves a spectacular volte-face of these views. He is now, he assures us, a " 'pure internationalist,' " much to the dismay of Roy Campbell incidentally (Campbell, *Light on a Dark Horse,* p. 203).

Briefly, then, Lewis moves from internationalism on behalf of art, to nationalism on behalf of Hitler, back to his present concern with "cosmic man" and a "world-society" (*America and Cosmic Man,* p. 189; *Rude Assignment,* p. 193; *Writer and the Absolute,* p. 145).

In 1937 we reach the peak of Lewis' interest in fascism, and it is necessary always to read *The Revenge for Love,* his principal political satire, against the background of these sympathies. In *Count Your Dead: They Are Alive!* Lewis commits himself on the Spanish question. Like other English writers, such as Edmund Blunden, Evelyn Waugh, Roy Campbell, and Lady Eleanor Smith,[39] Lewis here sees Franco as the legitimate aspirant for power. The book, which is composed of the notebooks of one Launcelot Nidwit given us by the autobiographical Ned, presupposes that British democracy is a sham—"The Death of John Bull" was erased from the title page of the first part of the manuscript. British democracy is taken as a Russophile tyranny: "all you have to say to Britannia is 'Hitler' and she sees Red! She clenches her fist, links arms with Blum and Litvinov, and is ready for anything." [40] The freedom of the press comes in for especial scorn once more. Not even Pound, in *Jefferson and/or Mussolini,* goes quite as far as Lewis here, when he suggests that the B.B.C. is on the side of the "Reds," and that in the U.S.A. the Hearst Press alone gives the truth. Baldwin has stifled public opinion and made England a tool in the hands of the Soviet, with the result that "we are about to go to war to make the world safe for Communism." [41]

The picture Lewis draws here of the situation in Spain is this: Franco, who has majority support, is fighting gallantly, with little money, against the overwhelming odds of his richly endowed adversaries, controlled by Moses Rosenberg. England and France have broken the Non-Intervention Agreement, though the Germans

39. Lady Eleanor Smith wrote at this time, "naturally I am a warm adherent of General Franco's, being, like all of us, a humanitarian." Quoted, Douglas Goldring, *The Nineteen Twenties* (London, Nicholson and Watson, 1945), p. 112. Lewis here uses such pro-Franco source material as Eleonora Tennant's *Spanish Journey* (London, Eyre and Spottiswoode, 1936), which contains a useful chapter on "The Red Terror."

40. *Count Your Dead,* p. 199.

41. Ibid., p. 219. Lewis evidently enjoyed this phrase, having used it twice before: Wyndham Lewis, "Notes on the Way," *Time and Tide, 16,* No. 13 (March 30, 1935), 457, and *Left Wings,* p. 66.

have come to the rescue of law and order and Hitler's manners are "diplomatically impeccable." Britain is sponsoring Red atrocities. The cure for the situation is to allow those countries explicitly opposed to communism, especially Germany, to rearm. This is the book, then, that Lewis calls in 1950 "a first-rate peace pamphlet."

In 1939 he reversed all these views in two works, *The Jews, Are They Human?* and *The Hitler Cult*. These works begin a trend of political thought he has maintained, with individual differences, until the present day. In late 1938 Eliot derided "the irresponsible 'anti-fascist' " who found "an emotional outlet in denouncing the iniquity of something called 'fascism.' " [42] But in March 1939 Lewis joined this irresponsible group.

The Hitler Cult calls Hitler warlike, vulgar, and romantic; he is a power politician, both a true bolshevik (on one page) and "a typical democratic statesman" (on another). As for Hitlerism, this latter-day *Sturm und Drang* movement is now an unsubstantial Gothic dream, living on stale slogans, mystical and nihilistic. This ideology of the mob, a copy of Marxism, is relentlessly anti-individual. Lewis takes up the Blutsgefühl idea and discredits it as a group-rhythm. In fact, it is clear that he is rewriting his earlier *Hitler*. Point after point, made on behalf of Hitler in the first book, is refuted, though there are some he wisely allows to die, such as his previous instancing of Czechoslovak persecution of minorities within their borders (in *Left Wings*). His subsequent satires reinforce this change of opinion; in *America, I Presume* an autobiographical character refers to Hitler as a "barbarous little mountebank" and "demagogue." [43] *The Vulgar Streak,* of 1941, is laid at the time of the Czech crisis and is clearly anti-Hitler; the villain of the book is a Fascist called Tandish. And at the end of *Rotting Hill* the narrator significantly makes his way to a fairground where, in a booth, he shoots down effigies of both Hitler

42. T. S. Eliot, "A Commentary," *The Criterion, 18,* No. 70 (Oct. 1938), 59.
43. *America, I Presume,* pp. 59, 293 (and see p. 33). Hitler is a "touchy mountebank" in *The Hitler Cult,* p. 111.

and Mussolini, and finally makes his peace with Britannia by dropping a threepenny bit in her mug. The Fascist-like Hyperides, from the first version of *The Childermass,* is killed off brutally at the end of the recent *Monstre Gai. Self Condemned* is even boringly anti-Hitler.

But we must remember that this *was* a change of opinion for Lewis. We cannot accept his own word, in *The Hitler Cult,* that he saw through Hitler from the start. In *Anglosaxony: A League That Works,* published in Canada in 1941, he again contradicts previous support for Hitler, but is here more honest perhaps in claiming that as soon as he understood fascism it had no attraction for him.[44] Cecil Melville, replying in 1931 to Lewis' *Time and Tide* articles on Hitler, suggested that if Lewis really knew what Hitler stood for he would never support him. It is only fair to remember this volte-face, however, if we are to assess Lewis in the general perspective of contemporary British literature. He has repeatedly stated, in recent volumes, that he was one of the few British intellectuals who saw through Russian communism from the start; but the disillusioned "pinkos" and "Bloomsburies" could, I suppose, add that they saw through fascism from the start.

Alas, "men are as the time is," as Edmund says in *Lear* and, in case there should be thought to be cant in these recantations by Lewis, it is only fair to him to bear in mind that complete changes of political opinion by writers have been a feature of our time. In 1952 Sir Herbert Read reprinted in *The Philosophy of Modern Art,* without notice of alteration, an essay on surrealism first published in 1936. "Surrealism, like Communism, does not call upon artists to surrender their individuality," we read in 1936. In 1952 this sentence reads, "Surrealism does not, like Communism, call upon artists to surrender their individuality."

Moreover, those of the left at the time Lewis was writing on

44. *Anglosaxony,* p. 35. In this work Hitlerism is criticized as too much the doctrine of "action," but in *Hitler* Lewis had hoped that Hitlerism would prove the doctrine of *intelligent* "action."

Hitler seem to have been so somewhat inadvertently: Arthur Koestler, for instance, whose conversions and reconversions have filled volumes, "was carried by the tide; my impulses and decisions were a reflection of those pressures, but not a conscious reflection." [45] Although Stephen Spender has lately written that "I failed to find myself convinced by Communism," he describes his acceptance of membership of the Communist party in *World within World* and it is rather haphazard: "I accepted this proposal, and Pollitt at once gave me a membership card." [46] Mary McCarthy describes herself as a "mere trifler" with such ideas in the thirties.[47] John Lehmann's *The Whispering Gallery* could also be cited here. Nor can Lewis' political attitude of these days be called any more arrogant than that of writers of totally different beliefs. Koestler has recently stated, in effect, and Mary McCarthy seems to agree,[48] that at this time the left wing was right and the right simply wrong: "We were wrong for the right reasons; and I still feel that, with a few exceptions—I have already mentioned Bertrand Russell and H. G. Wells—those who derided the Russian Revolution from the beginning, did so mostly for reasons that were less honorable than our error." [49]

Of the "men of 1914," Joyce, Lewis, Pound, and Eliot—the first dead, the second blind, the third mad, and the fourth an O.M.— only Joyce seems to have been able to keep apart from the political passions of our times and live the life of the true clerc. The question of a writer's political affiliation must remain outside the scope of this study, but what an acute dilemma it has been for the neoclassicist. Maurras died in (comfortable) imprisonment. Pound is

45. Arthur Koestler, *Arrow in the Blue* (New York, Macmillan, 1952), p. 270.
46. Stephen Spender, *World within World* (New York, Harcourt, Brace, 1948), pp. 122, 192.
47. Mary McCarthy, "My Confession—Part II," *The Reporter, 10,* No. 1 (Jan. 5, 1954), 31.
48. Ibid., p. 30.
49. Koestler, *Arrow in the Blue,* p. 274; and cf. in this connection pp. 234–6, 256–8.

in a lunatic asylum. A lesser writer, William Joyce, who published in the British Fascist press at the same time as Lewis, ended his life on the gallows. It has even been asserted of Yeats that "In the political field, his opinions were quite definitely of a Fascist order." [50] And to Yeats, Lewis' criticism sounded true. In 1927 Yeats wrote of Lewis, "I am in all essentials his most humble and admiring disciple." [51]

It is easy enough to ridicule these opinions a quarter of a century later. W. Y. Tindall has done this in the case of D. H. Lawrence "among the Fascists," showing how Lawrence's Mexican writings were recommended as Fascist apologia by Rolf Gardiner. Some distinctions should be made, however, before we pass judgment too easily. Lawrence, Yeats, and Campbell were all men who hungered for the human relationship in an increasingly urbanized society. Yeats loved aristocrat and peasant, while *Broken Record* is a *cri du coeur* for the feudal relationship of serf to lord, working inside which the poet could so directly manipulate mythology. So Yeats wrote Fascist marching songs (and rewrote them, too) for the Irish contingent which was to fight on the same side as Campbell's "Christs in uniform" in the Spanish Civil War. So Sacheverell Sitwell wrote his *Canons of Giant Art* of 1933 "in praise of Fascist Italy." This is one thing; it is quite another to make a critical analysis of the Fascist position, as did Lewis, and then support it with a number of books like *Hitler, Left Wings,* and *Count Your Dead.* In such works Lewis asks to be judged as a political thinker, as Lawrence never did, and we can justifiably repudiate the philosophy of these books if we want to, without making a literary criticism. We are simply repudiating the neoclassical political approach, one designed to act as outrider for certain literary values, just as Hitlerism was reciprocally an aesthetic slipped over into the political sphere (Goebbels wrote a Dostoevskyan novel at Heidelberg).

50. Grattan Freyer, "The Politics of W. B. Yeats," *Politics and Letters, 1,* No. 1 (Summer 1947), p. 13.

51. *The Letters of W. B. Yeats,* ed. Allan Wade (New York, Macmillan, 1955), p. 734; and cf. W. B. Yeats, *A Vision* (New York, Macmillan, 1938), p. 4.

"The increase of the electorate, in Britain, is the destruction of Democracy," [52] T. S. Eliot wrote in his article on "The Literature of Fascism" in *The Criterion,* adding a few years later that "humanitarian zeal" (which Campbell calls "moral perversion") is "always dangerous." [53] Sometimes one wonders at the size of the vacuum inside which neoclassicism has existed in our century; now, after the second World War, with the contestant European nations panting in their corners, is surely the time for the pep talk from the seconds. But Eliot, Benda, and their colleagues have remained silent, or meekly repetitive, on politics. Neoclassicism seems to have little regenerating faith to offer, and its lack of contact with real political issues is brought out best by the barren aridity of *Notes towards the Definition of Culture.*

In conclusion, it would be uncharitable, of course, to associate any of the neoclassicists mentioned above directly with fascism. "I am no Fascist," Campbell writes, referring to an article of his in *The Fascist Quarterly.* Perhaps, therefore, the final word on this problem in the case of Lewis should be left with Eliot, who in 1937 wrote: "As for Mr. Lewis's politics, I see no reason to suppose that he is any more of a 'fascist' or 'nazi' than I am." [54]

52. T. S. Eliot, "The Literature of Fascism," *The Criterion, 8,* No. 31 (Dec. 1928), 281.

53. T. S. Eliot, "A Commentary," *The Criterion, 11,* No. 44 (April 1932), 467.

54. T. S. Eliot, "The Lion and the Fox," *Twentieth Century Verse,* 6/7 (Nov./ Dec. 1937), unpaged. Stanley Edgar Hyman, *The Armed Vision* (New York, Knopf, 1948), p. 87, explores the (obviously absurd) idea of Eliot being in any way a Fascist. See, for an instance of this latter, Leslie Woolf Hedley's "Fascism and Modern American Poetry" in *Contemporary Issues* vol. 8 (1956), where we read: "The thing Eliot lacked that both Maurras and Pound had was the courage to come out and admit he was a fascist."

Chapter 5: "Mister Ivory Tower"

" 'You, of course,' said a woman acquaintance in St. Louis once, 'are Mister Ivory Tower.' Probably I shrugged off that silly remark."
[*Rude Assignment,* p. 100.]

AT THE END OF *Tarr,* Tarr says, " 'The Many they are the eccentric —what do they matter? . . . Curse curse the principle of Humanity.' " Describing himself as a successor to the Nietzschean Superman, Tarr leaves Bertha, with her "democratic" face, and imagines himself as "this capricious and dangerous master . . . similar to Wellington breakfasting at Salamanca while Marmont hurried exultingly into traps: they were of the same metal [enemies of demagogues and haters of the mob]." [1]

Like Lewis, Tarr wanted to see "great individuals" in the world. Anastasya was "too big." Tarr's treatment of both Bertha and Anastasya, both feminine, emotional, and democratic, brutal as it may seem, is necessarily so and is in the spirit of Pound's statement: "There is no misanthropy in a thorough contempt for the mob. There is no respect for mankind save in respect for detached individuals." [2] " 'All effectual men,' " Tarr says, " 'are always the enemies of every time.' "

If Lewis' faith in certain "positive" political trends of our time was deceived, his basic idea of a successful society does not alter. Only the "person" matters; the idea of the common good is a fallacy, for

1. *Tarr* (Chatto), p. 318; the material in square brackets was inserted into the second edition.
2. Ezra Pound, *The Little Review Anthology,* ed. Margaret Anderson (New York, Hermitage House, 1953), p. 102.

"There cannot be any 'good' common to an unorganized mob of 'things.' " A healthy society will only result from the formation of a cadre of "persons" at the head of the State. This elite, "personal" in the true sense, must rule by a hierarchy that is *"perpendicular":* Ned says, "I prefer a Democracy more like a pyramid, and less like a morass." England, Lewis tells us, reached world eminence through an "enterprising minority, of magnificent leaders," whereas "The vast face of the *Massenmensch* [*sic*]—the enormously magnified visage of the Little Man—is a degeneracy . . . such magnifications are inartistic." Or, as he put it in *One-Way Song,*

> Against the grain, we henceforth must discount
> This sleepy people petted and 'all-found.'
> Unless, unless, a class of leaders comes,
> To move it from its latter-day doldrums.

Eliot, calling himself as had Babbitt a "thoroughgoing individualist," [3] has also like Carlyle and Arnold (not to mention Ortega y Gasset) referred to the necessity of stirring the pampered masses of the modern democracies out of their apathy by means of a few individuals. Maurras, in turn, has said the same, but the elite Maurras called for was an "élite héréditaire," and Lewis has always put intellectual before hereditary values. Since the whole of his political criticism, as I see it, hangs on the theory of an elite, it is perhaps only natural that he disclaims ever having held this notion. In 1950 he writes: "The more intellectual minority proposed here as the occupational nucleus of a partitioned-off *area of creative development* as it were, at the apex of a massive human group, takes with it no effluvium of éliteness, at least not as conceived by me."

This intellectual elite, who should abstain from contact with the "human herd," is symbolized by the Herdsman, whose "chief function" is to remain apart, on his mountain. The herd beneath him, after all, is stampeding to death. As Maurras put it, "La

3. T. S. Eliot, *Selected Essays* (New York, Harcourt, Brace, 1950), p. 425; Babbitt, *Democracy and Leadership,* p. 143.

Démocratie accourt donc, les yeux bandés, au cimetière." ⁴ Thus both Maurras and Lewis have seen inequality as a necessity for mankind *in its own interests.*

What Lewis often calls "the politics of the intellect," then, is nothing more complicated than the formation of an intellectual elite. And his solution for contemporary human society does not alter, except in particulars, from *The Art of Being Ruled.* Uniformity must be resisted, humbug exposed, associational life with its system of syndics everywhere combated in the name of the Not-Self, politics must cease to dominate the field of speculative endeavor, and creative intelligence must guide the world. For "The life of the intelligence is the very incarnation of freedom." ⁵ The intellectual elite, then, is the "ideal giant" or brain of society, which Kemp proposes and which is also hinted at in the form of the "universal" artist of *Blast No. 2.* There is a long plea for this "creative minority" inserted into the recent *Self Condemned.*⁶

To this summary should be added the rider that in any such society the "thing" will be content to serve the "person." For only a "person" may enjoy a right, and "human," we are told, meant for the Greek or Roman the willingness "to abide by a set of rules." Thus a stranger, lion, and bee were abnormal, or "wild," since they had not overtly recognized the laws of the dominant society; they had not acknowledged social necessity, that it is the privilege of the "thing" to serve the "person." ⁷ These views, forming Lewis' ideal of human society, are gathered at the end of *The Childermass* when Alectryon, his very name suggesting the dawn of a new social era upon the West, puts the case for the elite against the Bailiff's liberal-

4. Maurras, *Idées politiques,* p. xxiii. Maurras frequently finds democracy a kind of death, as well as a mandate to barbarism.

5. *Art of Being Ruled,* p. 448.

6. Wyndham Lewis, *Self Condemned* (London, Methuen, 1954), pp. 79–96.

7. It would merely complicate Lewis' argument here to introduce the case of the Roman slave. The slave was in the special position of only having recognized the laws of the dominant society under duress; he was thus "normal," for Lewis, in that he lived by the rules of this society and served the "person," but he was "wild" or "abnormal" in that he did so at the point of the whip.

ism ("liberally loving and even worshipping black red and yellow men as his brothers and teachers").

The ideal of an elite is a premise of neoclassicism and rests largely on the idea that order, authority, discipline are the foundations of a good society. For Maurras, indeed, order was a sacred syllable, an echo of Comte heard in the silence of the night. Not "organisation" but "ordre" is Maurras' call; for the Greeks, he reminds us, knew that things in themselves were worthless and that it was only in their order that value lay. Authority, for Maurras, is as important as beauty and genius, tradition as vital as sun and blood. Lasserre and Babbitt do not disagree here, while for Pound it is the "will toward *order"* that marks out the great individual, like the Duce; Pound puts this view in *Jefferson and/or Mussolini,* the last word of which is "order." Eliot, who has consistently advocated more authority in the State, gave his *For Launcelot Andrewes* the subtitle of *Essays on Style and Order.* Lewis, who in one place admits that all his work has been on behalf of order, pleads for authority in the State as in art.[8]

The neoclassicists are, in fact, most closely allied in this matter of the elite and of "order," a word Sir Herbert Grierson especially associated with the classical in his now famous essay "Classical and Romantic." Eliot, though denying Lewis any "positive theory," [9] finds him close to Benda and Babbitt. Robert Gorham Davis detects Babbitt's roots in Maurras, while Folke Leander has made a close comparison between contemporary American humanism, as represented by Babbitt and Paul Elmer More (to whom Eliot paid tribute in *The Criterion* for July 1937), and Seillière. In fact, Leander finds them "identical." [10]

8. *Jews,* p. 74; Wyndham Lewis, "The Artist as Crowd," *The Twentieth Century,* 3, No. 14 (April 1932), 12. This periodical recalls a literary society of the thirties, called the Promethean Society, to which Lewis may or may not have belonged, but which numbered men like Hugh Gordon Porteus and whose aims appear to have been Lewisian, if not Lewisite.

9. Eliot, *Selected Essays,* p. 419.

10. Folke Leander, *Humanism and Naturalism* (Göteborgs Högskolas Göteborg, Elanders Boktrycheri Aktiebolog, 1937), p. 61.

Yet only in the broadest boundaries should Seillière be linked
with Lewis. Seillière is author of a large *oeuvre*, much of which is
concerned with a special view of "imperialism." This, Seillière says,
is man's desire to dominate nature, his *"libido dominandi,"* as he
calls it (from St. Augustine), likening it to Nietzsche's *Wille zur
Macht.*[11] This "imperialism," or "élan d'expansion vitale," is praise-
worthy if balanced by reason, or by that "synthèse de l'expérience
humaine" which Seillière equates with reason. Elsewhere, Seillière
calls reason the synthesis of knowledge and experience,[12] or what
most of us call tradition. Reason and logic, Seillière says, issue
from experience, producing what he calls "raison-expérience." Without this quality imperialism turns into mysticism. By mysticism—
and Benda employs the term with the same special referent in *La
Trahison*—Seillière means the search for the divine, or noumenal,
in man's libido dominandi. Primitive, intuitive, usually fanatical,
this "mysticism" may be a tonic for action, but to be fruitful it must
be accompanied by "la raison grandie avec le savoir" and "le conseil
de l'expérience sainement interpretée de notre passée." In his book
on Lawrence, Seillière finds Lawrence's "vitalism" to be this kind
of misguided "mysticism," or "impérialisme irrationel," which is
romanticism.[13] But where is this reason located? Seillière answers,
"dans certains individus d'élite ou de choix." But although Seillière
approaches Lewis in this way, although he sees romanticism as
evil (in his fourth volume on "imperialism"), although in his book
on Baudelaire he can scarcely tell which has done French literature
the most harm, Victor Hugo or Baudelaire, he is yet ready to

11. Seillière, *Le Romantisme,* pp. 9–10; Ernest Seillière, *Romantisme et démocratie romantique* (Paris, Éditions de la Nouvelle Revue Critique, 1930), p. 21.

12. Seillière, *Romantisme et démocratie romantique,* pp. 26, 33, 141.

13. Benda refers to Seillière's theory of imperialism and mysticism, calling the
latter *"dynamisme."* Although Lewis equally dislikes what Benda means by "dynamisme," he never uses the English "dynamism" in a special sense like this. It
is as well to note this before tackling Lewis' art criticism. With Seillière, Benda sees
this form of libido dominandi as a necessary part of life, but hopes that it may be
soundly restrained. (Benda, *Épreuve,* p. 217. There is a misprint on this page.
Benda himself refers the reader to p. 45 for his discussion of Seillière's views. This
should read p. 85, however.)

criticize excessive rationalism. In passing, one notes that the indictment of these stock villains, Hugo and Baudelaire, under "le
mal romantique" neglects the aims of the romantics of the eighteen
thirties. The idea of an intellectual elite may be found in the
preface to *Hernani* (as it can, what is more, in the work of that
socialist, H. G. Wells).

Lewis' dissociation of himself from the idea of an elite may,
indeed, be due to his dislike of the chauvinist and hereditary nature
of such an elite, as proposed by certain of the French antiromanticists. Maurras, Lasserre, and "Agathon" agree here. Lasserre, for
instance, who ameliorated his views concerning romanticism and
cooled toward Maurras, retained his national bias to the end. One
of his latter works *Des Romantiques à nous,* of 1927, opens with
a denunciation of the un-French nature of romanticism. Of course,
there may be some truth in this idea, although many critics feel
that in France the romantic movement reached its most fruitful and
brilliant heights; yet we should not associate Lewis with it. On the
whole, he does not consider any one nation more intelligent than
any other today. All have their faults, for him. "Agathon," also,
attacking Gustave Lanson for his egalitarian system of education,
wants to train the masses "par l'exemple des meilleurs, du petit
nombre" in *L'Esprit de la Nouvelle Sorbonne,* and proposes *"le
type nouveau de la jeune élite intellectuelle"* in *Les Jeunes Gens
d'aujourd'hui,* but he too is filled with nationalist prejudice. Lewis
was no more happy with a nationalist elite than was Babbitt, or
Benda.[14]

As regards its hereditary nature he parts company from Maurras
and Eliot. And perhaps this is why Eliot, though finding the French
"an insolent people," has yet been able to praise so highly the
Action Française. Maurras continually insisted on hereditary values,
as located in family, monarchy, State, and Church.[15] Eliot has also

14. Benda not only is critical of Maurras himself throughout *La Trahison* but
also criticizes the whole neoclassical love of order which he finds linked to war.

15. When Lewis criticizes Maurras, he usually does so on the grounds of
"action." It is fair to say that Maurras held a different view of "action" (see the

admitted to being a "royalist," but since he has more than once expressed dissatisfaction with critics who refer to this statement, it might be as well to look elsewhere for this principle. It may be found quite early: "A real democracy is always a restricted democracy, and can only flourish with some limitation by hereditary rights and responsibilities." [16] More recently Eliot has specified his elite, a community of Christians maintaining the official body of belief in the State (which sounds like the British Council). Indeed, Eliot will allow no alternative to this view other than totalitarianism: "If you will not have God (and He is a jealous God) you should pay your respects to Hitler or Stalin." [17] Chapter 2 of *Notes towards the Definition of Culture* ("The Class and the Elite") further clarifies that this Christian elite should be the repository of cultural values, and this view, of the close correlation between art and religion, is something Lewis would not like. Eliot's elite, which we should instantly elect and which should live in leisure (of the old kind), is to overlap with the dominant or governing elite, again hereditary: "The governing élite, of the nation as a whole, would consist of those whose responsibility was inherited with their affluence and position." [18] To which we may reply: *Quis custodiet ipsos custodes?*

Eliot's elite may be close to that of Maritain [19] but it is not the

name of his movement) from Lewis or Benda. But Lewis also praises Maurras in a number of places. Like Hulme, Maurras for Lewis helped to correct the idea that the average man was good (*Blasting and Bombardiering*, pp. 109–10). It may be true, as Mansell Jones writes (P. Mansell Jones, *Tradition and Barbarism*, London, Faber and Faber, 1930, p. 81), that Maurras has been one of the few today to have produced a new philosophy (though I personally would contest this); but if one is simply after novelty in thought, one need only repair to a lunatic asylum.

16. Eliot, "Literature of Fascism," p. 287.

17. Eliot, *Christian Society*, p. 64.

18. Eliot, *Definition of Culture*, p. 85.

19. Maritain, *Humanisme intégral*, p. 266. Although he called for a new elite in this work, as in *Christianisme et démocratie* in the last World War, Maritain is not entirely innocent of the evasive purple passage in lieu of a definition of this elite (cf. *Christianisme et démocratie*, p. 86). Maritain is opposed to an "égalitarisme

elite of Lewis or of that "libertarian," [20] to use Eliot's word for him, Ezra Pound. And it was for his secular heresies that Eliot criticized Irving Babbitt. For Eliot, Babbitt's Confucianism was "a deracination from the Christian tradition," [21] and the new American humanism "alarmingly like very liberal Protestant theology of the nineteenth century," [22] in *The Forum* for July 1928. The real danger in Babbitt's humanism was that it might become an alternative to religion, rather than a servant of it. In his obituary notice of Babbitt in *The Criterion* for October 1933 Eliot regrets that Babbitt's mind remained "obdurate" to the Christian religion to the end, and "Second Thoughts about Humanism" adds little beyond further fear of the Protestant nature of American humanism.

Like Lewis, Babbitt bewailed the "disappearance of leaders" today. Using the word "imagination" as the faculty which sought out unity in the diversity of life,[23] Babbitt wanted an "imaginative conservatism" to counter the unchecked use of phantasy (Rousseauian romanticism). The "critical humanism" [24] he called for was to employ the faculty of discrimination (for Lewis, roughly the intellect) to check contemporary excesses—Maurras often uses the word "critique" in this sense. This humanism was, of course, sternly opposed to humanitarianism. In *La Trahison* Benda distinguishes

niveleur" and is not so romantically optimistic as to attribute good sense to the common man. He hopes for a "humanisme héroique" and proposes that the new elite come equally from lower and upper classes (Maritain, *Christianisme et démocratie*, pp. 89–90, 108). Like Benda, Maritain detests entirely practical politics, which he calls *"politicisme,"* but he does not seem to lay as much stress on the intellect as does Lewis, and he condones force in a way that neither Benda nor Lewis would (Maritain, *Humanisme intégral*, pp. 281–4).

20. Eliot, *After Strange Gods*, p. 45. Would this reference be the reason for Pound's attack on Eliot for this book, already cited, in *A Visiting Card?*

21. T. S. Eliot, *The Use of Poetry and the Use of Criticism* (London, Faber and Faber, 1933), p. 132.

22. Eliot, *Selected Essays*, p. 422.

23. Babbitt, *Democracy and Leadership*, pp. 10–13; Babbitt develops his special use of "imagination" more fully in *On Being Creative*.

24. Irving Babbitt, *Rousseau and Romanticism* (Boston, Houghton Mifflin, 1919), p. 382.

between true and false humanitarianism; the quality is good when it is humanism, that is a disinterested, intellectual interest in the human animal in the abstract. But the love of human beings in the concrete is generally a sentimental compromise, modern humanitarian politics sailing under the flag of practical considerations. Both Babbitt and Lewis would agree to this, but Babbitt's social justice was bound up in his idea of the "ethical," and in this Lewis would not share. Babbitt's "ethical will" presumes that art, the aesthetic will, must acknowledge a superior force, just as Eliot's elite presumes that art should serve religion. I am not arguing for or against these philosophies, but for Lewis art must be supreme. He is far closer to the nineteenth-century aesthete than he likes to imagine. So he would not be happy with Babbitt's elite, as when Babbitt writes: "The ethical State is possible in which an important minority is ethically energetic and is thus becoming at once just and exemplary." [25]

For Lewis the "person," or Not-Self, is above ethics, beyond morals. These are for the animal kingdom, for the "thing": "Dogs, horses, cats and cows are the natural, and the true, clients of the moral philosopher, I believe." So, in a word, we can say that Eliot criticized Babbitt for not being religious enough and Lewis criticized him for being too religious. Finally, in passing, I should note that T. E. Hulme's "humanism," which I shall examine below, was entirely different from Babbitt's. In the political questions posed by neoclassicism Hulme was divided. He defends Bergson—and for the same reason that Lewis attacks him [26]—but in *The New Age* for November 9, 1911, agrees with Lasserre's antiromanticism and is drawn to the Action Française. Finding "the fixed and constant nature of man" his classical ideal, Hulme dislikes what he calls social progress upward and, as "North Staffs," is a militant anti-

25. Babbitt, *Democracy and Leadership,* p. 309.

26. Hulme defends Bergson as opposing the world of mechanical determinism. T. E. Hulme, *Speculations* (London, Routledge and Kegan Paul, 1924–), pp. 143–69; T. E. Hulme, "Notes on Bergson—III," *The New Age, 10,* No. 4 (Nov. 23, 1911), 79–82. In *Time and Western Man,* as well as elsewhere, Lewis arraigns Bergson as "mechanical."

liberal who takes extreme issue with Bertrand Russell in *The New Age*.

The whole question of neoclassical political thought requires a sociologist, as much as a literary critic, for its interpreter; and it can hardly be supposed that the present critic, who spent six years of his youth uniformed to combat a politician Lewis liked to think "classical" (Adolf Hitler),[27] would be able to achieve total impartiality. Indeed, these problems are so much with us as I write that the inclination is not to criticize neoclassicism at all, for fear of being at once placed in the opposite camp by the reader. But the existence of these extreme antiromanticists, attacking what Léon Daudet called "le stupide dix-neuvième siècle" (and Pound, in *Gold and Work,* "the infamous century of usury") for what its writers would never have supported today, is enough, in the words of W. Y. Tindall, "to establish the romantic character of our age."[28] Surely this is testified by the very impossibility of the claims made by the neoclassicists. It may have been a reaction against the romantic politics of Rousseau, but to be of consequence a reaction must bring with it something from which the suffering society may take suck. And Régis Michaud, inspecting the movement from a fund of knowledge and experience far greater than my own, concludes that the whole neoclassical and anti-Sorbonnist movement in France was traditional. Of course, there is nothing wrong with being traditional. Traditions usually contain some elements of value in order to become such, and the resolutely antitraditional temper can produce as repressive an orthodoxy of opinion as ever an "Agathon" saw coming from the Sorbonne. But Michaud finds neoclassicism a social philosophy that makes no effort to meet contemporary conditions.[29]

As regards any judgment on Lewis' own share in the movement, as far as its politics is concerned, perhaps an article in *Experiment,*

27. *Hitler,* p. 184.
28. William York Tindall, *Forces in Modern British Literature 1885–1946* (New York, Knopf, 1947), p. 106.
29. Régis Michaud, *Modern Thought and Literature in France* (New York, Funk and Wagnalls, 1934), p. 262.

a periodical edited from Cambridge (England) at the end of the twenties, puts the case fairly. The editors of *Experiment,* calling themselves "Five" and including William Empson and J. Bronowski in their ranks, are happy that Lewis sets out to think, but "deplore that he has chosen so often to communicate the process rather than the result." [30] "Five" go on to liken Lewis to Benda in that both men only seem able to comment and observe, rather than conclude. L. Rudrauf, a French scholar, has made precisely the same criticism of Seillière, that he is an observer rather than architect of philosophy. And if this is true of other neoclassicists, we must remember that it is just this point Bergson makes in *Introduction à la métaphysique,* namely that observation from the outside enables you to analyze, but not to attain, reality.

"Five" suggest that Lewis is in the dilemma of disliking any association of art and politics and of insisting on art being close to reality. Yet our reality, for better or worse, has been a political reality. So, forced against his will into association with politics, Lewis has formulated a politics impossible to realize today. Because of this his political criticism is possessed with contradiction, for "the politics of the intellect" (of art, for him) is an anachronism now, if it were not so for the past five hundred years in Europe. "There are no *good* politics," but today we must live by their laws. Calling himself *"a man of the tabula rasa"* with an *"ahistoric"* mind, Lewis admits that he would have liked to have lived in "a society in which I was beneath a law." But not beneath our laws. It is not unfair to say that he has seen no one else apart from himself capable of the revolution necessary for that "tabula rasa," or of that formulation of acceptable laws under which men might live freely. One is forced to admit the truth in that criticism of Lewis' politics made both by Frank Swinnerton [31] and T. E. Lawrence,[32] both friendly

30. "Five," "Wyndham Lewis's 'Enemy,' " *Experiment,* No. 3 (May 1929), p. 2.

31. Frank Arthur Swinnerton, *The Georgian Literary Scene* (London, Heinemann, 1935), p. 476.

32. Quoted from letters to Sir William Rothenstein, thanking him for sending copies of *The Enemy* to T. E. L. in Karachi. Sir William Rothenstein, *Since Fifty* (London, Faber and Faber, 1939), p. 70.

critics and the latter a man who leapt Lewis' garden wall to meet him, to the effect that Lewis has attacked all not of his party, and that since his party consists of himself alone he has been kept busy. As Arghol puts it in *The Enemy of the Stars,* "Anything but yourself is dirt."

Ultimately, the lesson of Lewis' political criticism is that a writer should not indulge in political criticism. It is amazing, in fact, that a man so sensitive to words could use them so wildly and irresponsibly. It is indeed a "bloody crossroads," as Lionel Trilling so suggestively puts it, where art and politics meet. Lewis has paid for trespassing here. Apart from anything else, the works we have been considering, some of them distinctly ephemeral, have meant an enormous waste of time and energy for the author of *The Apes of God* and the artist who could draw "Surrender of Barcelona," and who had made his place in the history of painting secure by 1920. In general terms, however, Hugh Kenner puts the case against Lewis best here when he writes that "The polemics exalt a rhetorical kind of knowing over a grasp, in depth, of what there is to know."

PART II: ART

"Reality is in the artist, the image only in life, and he should only approach so near as is necessary for a good view. The question of focus depends on the power of his eyes, or their quality." [*Blast No. 1*, p. 135.]

Chapter 6: A Sort of *Life*

"Art at its fullest is a very great force indeed, a magical force, a sort of *life,* a very great 'reality.' " [*The Diabolical Principle and the Dithyrambic Spectator,* p. 69.]

IF WE CAN SAY that for Wyndham Lewis the function of art is to depict reality, we need to fortify ourselves at once with a host of definitions. Let us first say that reality can best be represented by a plastic art relying on form, and in particular on the line. The apprehension of reality, which is human awareness, is always to be accomplished for Lewis from the outside, and he immediately accords the painter the highest position in the arts. This can be found in a number of places, in an article in *The English Review* for January 1922, in the encyclical delivered to Zagreus (the key to *The Apes of God*), and throughout *Time and Western Man.* In his attack on Spengler in this last work he puts the contrast, to be repeated by the sympathetic Greek Hyperides, in *The Childermass,* between "classical," external painting and "romantic," internal music. He would have agreed with Hulme who wrote that "an art like music proceeds from *the inside."* Spengler is "musical." He attacks the principle of the hard outline, as do Bergson and Einstein. So, riding roughshod over any particular distinctions on this point, neglecting a composer like Bach, for instance, Lewis writes in *Time and Western Man:* "the line (or 'drawing,' in whose repudiation by his faustian spirit you see, above, Spengler exulting) is the Classical; whereas the aerial perspective, chiaroscuro, is the *musical* invention of the germanic North." [1]

1. *Time and Western Man,* p. 290.

"Je haïs le mouvement qui déplace les lignes!" Lewis tells us he said to Marinetti, and his own practice certainly substantiates this. Contrasting Lewis' method in painting with that of the Cubists, Patrick Heron writes in *The New Statesman and Nation* for January 12, 1952, that in his own work Lewis "finds the outline first."

If art, then, is to depict reality, what is the formal relationship between art and life? Here, like his character Kemp, Lewis maintains from the first that art is stronger and more important than life. "The Artist's OBJECTIVE is Reality," we read in *Blast No. 1* (when Lewis had arrived at his purely abstract phase), to which is added, "The 'Real Thing' is always Nothing." If we watch Lewis' use of inverted commas, we will not find him contradictory on this score.

Life, in other words, "reality," is merely the material to be manipulated by the intelligent artist. "Deprived of art . . . Life instantly becomes so brutalized as to be mechanical." [2] We must remember that the man who wrote this was also to be author of the statement, "Merely by living we contaminate ourselves." [3] There are two important essays where Lewis develops these views, "Vortices and Notes" in *Blast No. 1,* [4] and "Essay on the Objective of Plastic Art in Our Time" in *The Tyro No. 2.* To summarize these essays is simply to paraphrase Wilde's *Decay of Lying* or some of Whistler's aesthetic. Only artistic life, the life of the intelligence, is true life. The only reality exists in the artist's intellect. Nature, uninterpreted, can only be a mirror of general abasement, a photograph of a degenerated condition. Nature by itself is insignificant, unimportant, and the inspired artist is told, in *Blast No. 2,* that he must rearrange nature, or "ENRICH" abstraction. "Dissociating vitality from beef," the artist must reach the essential, life.

One could prolong the association between these ideas and much

2. *Blasting and Bombardiering,* p. 262.

3. *Hitler Cult,* p. 173.

4. "Vortices" is respelt to "Vorteces" in one place (*Blast No. 1,* p. 127), but I have adopted Lewis' more usual spelling here.

nineteenth-century aesthetics (especially those of Whistler or Baudelaire), for we have the same idea of the artist as privileged individual, supreme interpreter, rewarded indeed by a place in heaven, as in Baudelaire's *Bénédiction* or Stefan George's *Ich forschte bleichen eifers nach dem horte.* But a distinction arises as to the manner in which the rearrangement of reality is to be brought about; for Lewis there is only one tool the artist can and should use, namely the intellect. And the intellect makes its presence chiefly felt in the eyes. "The act of creation," Lewis states, calling intellect here the will, "is always an act of the human will." [5] He goes on, in this interesting essay in *The Tyro,* to describe what for Wilhelm Worringer is "empathy"; but that feeling of significance, or enjoyment, we may have in observing nature, at watching a river or a star, is for Lewis only the art impulse ("the situation that produces art"). The act of art itself is a transcending of this situation by means of the intellect, and in a " 'civilized' " time, one unafflicted with democratic pretensions that is, the onlooker would see a new reality, artistic truth, in the apparent distortion, or "abstraction": "One is to display a *strange* world to the spectator, and yet one that has so many analogies to his that, as he looks, startled into attention by an impressive novelty, he sees his own reality through this veil, as it were, momentarily in truer colours." [6] In passing, one notes that this is where Lewis leaves Babbitt again. Babbitt's "critical humanism"—by which we may alone seize reality—was to be a "coöperation of imagination and intellect," as opposed to the unrestrained use of the former faculty Babbitt saw in the romantic movement (following the separation of fancy, imagination, and judgment, reason, in the eighteenth century). In *Democracy and Leadership* Babbitt writes of "the supremacy of will." But although he attaches an appendix on this subject, it is not easy to

5. *The Tyro No. 2* (London, The Egoist Press, 1922), p. 31. This power, Lewis has more than once confessed, is supernatural in origin—"That the artist uses and manipulates a supernatural power seems very likely" (*Time and Western Man,* p. 198).

6. *The Tyro No. 2,* p. 33.

define what Babbitt meant by "will." Still, it is certain that the humanism he proposed was bound up with an inner spiritual life and would "subordinate intellect to the ethical will." [7] The "ethical self" was Babbitt's principle of inner control, or check, and to "ethical will" the intellect was finally subordinate. It is hardly necessary to evidence how strongly Lewis would disagree with this last conception and perhaps Babbitt knew this, for he saw a Lewis drawing in Eliot's flat as "a piece of incoherence." [8]

The declaration of war on life by art [9] which Lewis soon proposed does not mean that the artist should cease to live. Far from it. We are told of the Enemy in *One-Way Song* that "He knows to live comes first." Elsewhere Lewis protests, "Do I enjoy watching a man drink a glass of beer as much as I do drinking it myself?" But it does mean that the realm of art is sacrosanct, the preserve alone of the intellect. For, after all, only "a very small number of inventive, creative men are responsible for the entire spectacular ferment of the modern world." [10] In art, as in politics and philosophy, only "the exceptional individual" matters. "Art is a fluid moving above or over the minds of men," [11] Pound wrote in *The Spirit of Romance,* and again, "The arts are kept up by a very few people." [12]

The heresy of what Lewis calls the "dithyrambic spectator," then, is the invasion of the inviolable artistic stage, or dance, by the

7. Babbitt, *Democracy and Leadership*, p. 195.

8. Montgomery Belgion, "Irving Babbitt and the Continent," *T. S. Eliot. A Symposium* (London, Editions Poetry London, 1948), p. 52. Perhaps this reaction explains why Babbitt wept at the first Cézanne he saw. That is to say, one is never sure whether Babbitt wept with dismay at the "incoherence" of the Cézanne, or with joy at seeing classical principles reintroduced into painting. The latter reaction would have been more nearly Lewis', we shall see, but I fear that it was the former which moved Babbitt to tears.

9. For one of Lewis' many statements on the proximity of art and war in his mind, see *Blasting and Bombardiering*, p. 67. On the flyleaf of the copy of this work which he inscribed for Lord Carlow, we find him writing, "I send this war-life."

10. *Time and Western Man*, p. 141.

11. Ezra Pound, *The Spirit of Romance* (London, Dent, 1910), p. vi.

12. Ezra Pound, *Imaginary Letters* (Paris, Black Sun Press, 1930), p. 3.

spectator—"audience-participation," as he also called it. The second part of *The Diabolical Principle and the Dithyrambic Spectator* [13] is a discussion of a work that pretends to show art and ritual close, the consequent involvement of the spectator in the act of art being for Lewis another aspect of the democratic conceit. The spectators must be kept off the stage, else art will be corrupted. Philosophy (Spengler, especially) and politics are afflicted with this heresy today, but it is chiefly in art that Lewis finds the onlooker mixing in forms of reality which should be above him. This leads everyone to want to be an artist, particularly the rich who can afford the leisure therefor; this creates the millionaire Bohemia he excoriates in *The Apes of God*. For, although he uses "ape" in another, special sense, the characters in this work are dithyrambic spectators, apes or impersonators of the godlike artist; this is perhaps epitomized in the character of Dick Whittingdon, a satire of the late Richard Wyndham. Reciprocally, the heresy makes for child art, since art is degraded by having to cater for what the onlookers, the masses, want, and the masses, Lewis knows, simply want to be children, "resolute and doctrinaire Peter Pans." Thus the heresy is partly a political phenomenon: "Communism is the influence that, entering the theatre, causes the spectators to swarm on to the stage and all become actors." [14]

In "the excellent *Belphégor*," as Lewis calls it, we also find the idea of the dithyrambic spectator. Observing that the mixture of art and life is bad, Benda finds too much of our art emotion itself and sees before him "une *abolition de distinction* entre l'artiste et les choses, d'une dissolution de sa personnalité dans leur âme, à

13. Although we find Snooty Baronet defining the mind as the diabolical principle, or inveterate enemy of the passionate flesh, Lewis refers in this title to romantic "diabolism." He is thinking particularly of *transition*, and of its review of a reissue of Lautréamont's *Chants de Maldoror*.

14. For examples of this heresy in Lewis' satire, see *Apes*, pp. 258, 265–6; *Revenge for Love*, p. 327. For Tarr, woman is the inveterate dithyrambic spectator, " 'the arch-enemy of any picture' " as he puts it to Anastasya. *Tarr* (Chatto), p. 302.

l'évanouissement de tout jugement." At about the same time
Ramon Fernandez was making the same complaint: "Une grande
partie de la littérature de notre XXe siècle est dominée par cette
confusion de l'art et de la vie." And one can find the same in other
neoclassicists. But in Bergson's defense one should remember that
he pleaded that the great comic artist should remain detached, in
Le Rire, while the different domains he accorded intellect and intuition in *L'Évolution créatrice* are also forgotten by the antiromanticists. In his doctoral dissertation, *Essai sur les données immédiates
de la conscience,* Bergson again showed the danger of mixing static
intelligence (Paul) and dynamic intuition (Pierre).

But in this dislike of art and life Lewis is closer to the German
aestheticians, and particularly to Wilhelm Worringer, than to
Whistler or Baudelaire. I will go into this below; here it is enough
to point out that for Worringer "der primitive Mensch" (first of
his four distinctions in human culture) lived at odds with life, from
which he abstracted life in the truest sense. The art of primitive man
existed inasmuch as it was removed from, and an ordering of, the
chaos of the world around him. Oriental art refined this condition
and, in turn, Egyptian art was "überorientalisch." [15] For Worringer,
then, the artistic significance of abstract art relied on its absence
of life; its line was accordingly a result of the will, rather than of
the senses. "Gothic" line, however, is for Worringer sensuous and
organic, a flow continuing that of the body. By contrast: "Die
Linie der primitiven Ornamentik ist geometrisch, ist tot und
ausdrucklos. Ihre künstlerische Bedeutung beruht einzig und allein
auf dieser Abwesenheit alles Lebens." [16]

For Worringer, as for Lewis, this kind of abstract art is geometric,
masculine, and unconcerned with sex: "Starrheit, unmenschliche,
aussermenschliche Starrheit ist das Zeichen dieser Kultur." [17] This

15. Wilhelm Worringer, *Ägyptische Kunst* (München, Piper, 1927), p. 7.
16. Wilhelm Worringer, *Formprobleme der Gotik* (München, Piper, 1912), p.
35.
17. Worringer, *Ägyptische Kunst,* p. 106.

idea, of the reduction of chaotic "life" to the deathlike stillness of artistic (or real) life, is most important to emphasize before approaching Vorticism. And it is an idea Lewis takes furthest when examining Professor Elliot Smith's researches in Egyptian mummification: "Indeed, in dynastic Egypt, *art* comes nearer to being *life* than at any other recorded period: and apparently for the reason that it was *death*."

This paradoxical statement can be clarified in this way; art only exists in its abstraction from the so-called alive, or spuriously alive, since what we call "life" (the life of "things," or machines) is a kind of death, a decease of the soul, that is. In the case of Egyptian mummification (which is, after all, an attempt to control time), art has taken over entirely, for here the fully conscious artist is unimpeded by the fluxes of "life," his sitter being dead, and yet he is working on the product of life itself. Eccentric as it may seem, this is what Lewis says: "Into the egyptian *living death,* again, a good deal of the *rigor mortis* has passed. And that suits art admirably. It asks nothing better than a corpse, and it thrives upon bones. Did not Cézanne bellow at his sitter, when he fell off the chair, 'You're *moving!* Les pommes, ça ne bouge pas!' " [18]

Lewis is not saying that this kind of art is the greatest of all time, but that theoretically its conditions are ideal. At once this view opposes the romantic one of bestowal of a soul on nature. So Bertha is a pantheist in *Tarr.* And Bertha here derives from Benda's criticism of Bergson's pantheism and from Lasserre's *Le Romantisme français,* where Lasserre finds pantheism a Germanic synthesis of progress and false nature.[19] It is in this context that the important,

18. *Diabolical Principle,* p. 181. In this analysis Lewis goes on to claim that for the mummifier artist "The EYE was the last thing to resist his ingenuity." Once he had mastered this, however, his mummy "lived," that is, it became wholly art. Cf. the quotation in my text with the Lesbian-Ape's instruction to Dan Boleyn (*Apes,* p. 231).

19. Lasserre, *Romantisme français,* p. 537. At the end of this work Lasserre develops an interesting attack on pantheism in various guises, much of which may be found in Lewis also: Lasserre here criticizes political pantheism (fanati-

and otherwise difficult, conversation between Tarr and Anastasya at the end of *Tarr* must be read. Anastasya asks Tarr:

> "What is art?—it sounds like Pompous Pilate!"
> "Life with all the humbug of living taken out of it: will that do?"
> "Very well: but what is life?"
> "Everything that is not yet purified so that it is art."
> "No."
> "Very well: *Death* is the one attribute that is peculiar to life."
> "And to art as well." [20]

In the revision of this passage from the first edition, we find an intensification in the thesis. Anastasya has been given a new speech, in which she says, " 'the artist has to hunt and kill his material so to speak.' " Tarr's remark that life has a soul has been excised. When a character called Affie dies in *Self Condemned*, René reflects of her: "How dignified and how *real*." [21] The idea of deadness, of Worringer's total abstraction (ridiculed in *The Childermass*, incidentally, when a painter rejoices over a severed head, as it is also ridiculed in Huxley's *Point Counter Point*), is what Tarr desiderates for graphic art:

> deadness is the first condition of art. The armored hide of the hippopotamus, the shell of the tortoise, feathers and machinery, you may put in one camp; naked pulsing and moving of the soft inside of life—along with elasticity of movement and consciousness—that goes in the opposite camp. Deadness is the first condition for art: the second is absence of soul, in the human and sentimental sense. With the statue its lines and masses are its soul, no restless inflammable ego is imagined for its interior: it has *no inside:* good art must have no inside: that is capital. [22]

cism), aesthetic pantheism (love of the norm, rather than of the beautiful), and "panthéisme du coeur" (dilettantism).

20. *Tarr* (Chatto), p. 302.

21. Wyndham Lewis, *Self Condemned*, p. 301.

22. *Tarr* (Chatto), p. 303. One should enter a caveat here. Although no *human* soul should show through a work of art, yet art presumably has its own soul,

In *Time and Western Man* Lewis repeats Tarr's views as his own: "The dead ossature—*that* is the region of the human will," and again, "I vie with Professor Moore in wanting things *solid* and wanting them *dead.*" This deadness, we are told, is the only way the artist can be realistic: *"deadness,* above all, for the fullest, most concrete 'realism,' is essential." [23] This is not so perverse as it sounds; reality is only in the artist's mind. The "reality" of our world, on which his inspired intellect should play, is the world of common sense. Here experience is to be credited over appearance, speculation to be decried, and the basis of truth sought in belief rather than in the intuition or imagination. Reality, the reordering of "reality," is the preserve of the higher individual, or "person"; "reality is to be sought in the self or the person." Henri Clouard makes a very similar claim for the benefit of the French neoclassicist, and its political parallels stand out clearly. For collective truth ("reality") is no truth, since the opinion of a lot of "things," tossed together, is valueless: "when we 'get together,' and clash and fuss, scrutinize and sift, we frequently arrive at a point at which *collectively* we become convinced that the rose is *not* red."

From this collective fuss the private mind of the "person," the inspired artist, abstracts a static permanence which is aesthetic verity. " 'Death is the thing that differentiates art and life,' " Tarr says, and in an article not long after Lewis refers to this "deadness," calling it the painter's "immortality," or "a sort of death and silence in the middle of life. This death-like rigidity of the painting or statue . . . is one of the assets of the painter or sculptor." [24]

This still center at the heart of our busy life is the idea of Vortex for Lewis. It is the principle of unity in the maelstrom of our life's diversity. Babbitt frequently writes of a similar "centre" in life, associating it with "oneness." The creation of this ultimate, still

---

since it is performed in interests other than those of this world, as Lewis often confesses.

23. *Time and Western Man,* p. 212.

24. Wyndham Lewis, "The Credentials of the Painter—I," *The English Review,* *34* (Jan. 1922), 36.

center is the consummate act of creation for Lewis. It is "The Art of the Great Race"; it is "DOING WHAT NATURE DOES," [25] that is, truly creating. Or, in the words of Babbitt: "To look to a true centre is, on the contrary, according to the classicist, to grasp the abiding human element through all the change in which it is implicated." [26]

25. *Blast No. 2,* p. 46.
26. Babbitt, *Rousseau and Romanticism,* p. 391.

Chapter 7: Lyrical Enthusiasm about Defeat

"In my criticism of 'L'école de Paris' I have never gone so far as to get out of sympathy. But from that time as a philosophy it has seemed to me uncreative. It makes the best of a bad job, perhaps: and we all do that, after all. It is only when people insist too much that it is a *good* job—that it is not a *pis-aller* with foundations that are unreal and highly unsatisfactory—that I grow restless. Wildly to acclaim disaster is the worst type of defeatism. There is nothing so bad as lyrical enthusiasm about defeat." [*Rude Assignment,* p. 159.]

IF WYNDHAM LEWIS' Vorticism was a correction of contemporary excess, what elements did it set out to correct? Lewis' criticism of modernity in the graphic arts is a criticism of those trends he dislikes in politics. The French Impressionist movement, especially, is the diagnostic of a romantic and uncivilized time ("Impressionism is too doctrinally the art of the individual"). Although in *Blast No. 1* he concedes Impressionism value in accustoming the public to a brighter palette, in insisting on light (though this reached a cul-de-sac, for him, in pointillism), essentially the French nineteenth-century movement in painting was guilty of that heresy we have examined: "The impressionist doctrine, with its interpenetrations, its tragic literalness, its wavy contours, its fashionable fuss, points always to one end: the state in which life itself supersedes art." [1]

We can excusably leave further analysis of this movement, for Lewis simply challenges Impressionism as nineteenth-century romanticism, and pass on to the present. In doing so, Cézanne should be excepted. For, in common with André Lhote and other critics,

1. *The Tyro No. 2,* p. 31.

Lewis rejoices to see classical principles being reintroduced in the work of Cézanne. Cézanne is "something like a pure Classic," and again, "an heroic visual pure." [2] This feeling he does not get when faced with the post-Cézanne Cubist movement. This, Lewis paradoxically asserts, is too photographic a style for his taste.[3] I shall return to this, but I cannot help feeling that it was as an ugly distortion of nature (such as Victor Stamp seems to be indulging in, when we meet him in *The Revenge for Love*) that Lewis really disliked this movement. Handley-Read and Patrick Heron both independently see Lewis' own drawing as opposite in method to that of the Cubists who, far from reaching the hard outline first, work from within, they suggest, proceeding outward from the sensation of a plane—"infilling," Handley-Read calls it.

Allowing for the occasional personal crotchet elsewhere, the burden of Lewis' criticism of graphic art is to be found in his destructive pamphlet, published with The Egoist Ltd. in 1919, called *The Caliph's Design. Architects! Where Is Your Vortex?* This passionate plea for the divorce of art and "style" is one of the least strident and most impressive of all Lewis' critical works, and it seems to have received the best press of any of his books (*America and Cosmic Man* received the worst). *The Piccadilly Review* (Ford Madox Ford), *The Athenaeum* (J. Middleton Murry), *The Cambridge Magazine, The New Europe, The Spectator,* and *Arts Gazette,* all praised the argument of this pamphlet, if quarreling with its literary style. The daily papers seem to have been equally polite, unusually so in their case over a Lewis work, *The Times* for Novem-

2. *Caliph's Design,* p. 71. In *Blast No. 1,* p. 137, Cézanne is called an "imbecile." This is certainly not typical of Lewis' comments on this painter, and I cannot account for it, beyond pointing out that the first *Blast* was concerned to advance English painting beyond that on the Continent and therefore Cézanne may have been included in the general indictment of French painting.

3. *Wyndham Lewis the Artist,* pp. 75–7. But in *Men without Art,* p. 203, Cubism seems to have evinced a brief awakening of classical tendencies. I discuss this below.

ber 13, 1919, even finding him "too favourable" to Picasso! Of course, some of this approval can be put down to the fact that superficially *The Caliph's Design* can be read as a conservative appeal to "stop the rot" coming from Paris.

One of the principal manifestations of this "rot," for Lewis, has been the love of novelty, a criticism shared with French neoclassicists. Maurras attacks our love of the novel, and our facility for accepting spontaneity as genius, in *L'Avenir de l'intelligence,* and Benda, making the same criticism in *Belphégor,* adds that our love of novelty is due to the increased luxury of living today. What Babbitt called "the cherishing of glamour," then, is for Lewis the "apriorist heresy"—apply a formula to nature, and a novelty will start forth, we will be confronted with a "system of surprises." This is a prime danger in aesthetics today, the danger that only the new may have prestige. It is a form of spiritual indolence, Lewis says, in the sense that the modern artist is too lazy to approach nature in the classical (external) manner and so seizes whatever in nature will confirm his own inner theories. This tendency André Lhote also calls *"apriorisme"* both in his *La Peinture: Le Coeur et l'esprit* and his admirably intelligent articles in *The Athenaeum* after the first World War, and for Lewis it finds a dupe in D. H. Lawrence.

T. S. Eliot, who thought Lawrence's work that of "a very sick man indeed," found *Paleface,* where this heresy is chiefly considered, a "brilliant exposure." [4] Since Lewis wrote that *Paleface* was "my reaction at the time to Lawrence (D. H.)," the work can presumably be taken, on one level, as an exposure of Lawrence's apriorist heresy. Such it is. Lawrence is guilty of having imported his own philosophic ideals into his interpretation of the American consciousness, of proselytizing about the Indian *Geist,* of inviting a victory of emotion over mind. Lawrence's writings are destructively committed "on the side of the oppressed and superseded, the underdog." Seillière goes nowhere near as far as this in his book on

4. Eliot, *After Strange Gods,* pp. 63, 66.

Lawrence, but he makes a close connection between Lawrence and Klages, another alleged enemy of the intellect and author of a study of Stefan George published in 1902. The year after *Paleface* came out Lawrence was highly impolite to Lewis in an introduction to Edward Dahlberg's *Bottom Dogs,* while for Lawrence's real attitude to the Negro his derogatory review of Carl van Vechten's *Nigger Heaven* should be read.

This mention of an apriorist writer is necessary here, because the equivalent in painting is the principal disease of art in our time. Hungering after sensation as we do, setting up novelty as authenticity, we approach the world around us in a blind, apriori manner, with the result that we are easily deceived by two trends—the cult of the child, and that of the primitive. Here Gauguin stands in for Lawrence.

Gauguin, "a vulgar tripper by the side of Cézanne," shares in that kind of romanticism which champions Asiatic exoticism over European rationalism. Lawrence, Gauguin, Baudelaire, Zola, Stevenson (an impeccable black list for the neoclassicist) have "ruined us with their *dreams."* This decadent and defeatist exoticism, of which Dada is also part,[5] is a tendency Lewis hoped Hitler would cure in 1931. Gauguin, ridiculed at the Café Berne in *Tarr,* is characterized in *The Caliph's Design* as

> this absurd bechevelured figure daubing pretty colours, like a malicious and stupid urchin, on every idea that had been pronounced moribund, and that was destined for the dustbin. But clearly this individual, this masquerader, this bag of schoolboy conceits, this old-clo merchant, loaded with rusty broadswords, Spanish knives, sombreros, oaths, the arch-priest of the romantic Bottle, was not an artist-type. Gauguin was not an artist-type. He was a savage type addicted to painting. He was in reality very like his sunny friends in the Marquesas

5. *Wyndham Lewis the Artist,* pp. 46–8. And Lewis here adds the criticism that a movement like Dada is bad since it gives the art world just the chance it is looking for not to take art seriously.

Islands. He was in as limited a way a savage as an American negro is typic, or a Jew over-raced and over-sexed.[6]

Among the French antiromanticists, Seillière was strongly opposed to this same primitivism (*"naturisme"*), but "cette école régressive" of modern art which Seillière sees as seriously risking its sanity includes Van Gogh and Cézanne. The whole appendix to Seillière's *Le Mal romantique,* entitled "Le Romantisme dans l'art contemporain," reads more like the art criticism of a retired colonel than of a sensitive aesthetician, so that I cannot think this aspect of the neoclassical attack Seillière's forte.[7] André Lhote, on the other hand, though milder in his criticism than Lewis and clearly more concerned to help his reader than state a point of view, is somewhat similarly opposed to Gauguin in his *Parlons peinture,* while obviously enjoying discipline and geometrical order in painting and, in *La Peinture,* welcoming the hard line and "réalisme solide" of Cézanne.

For Lewis this pictorial primitivity is one with the cult of the child (linked to "youth-politics"). He has always opposed child art and in *The Listener,* shortly before he went blind, derogatorily reviewed an exhibition of children's paintings, pointing out that their qualities were inspired by the adult. He has been especially critical of Sir Herbert Read in this respect—Sir Herbert replying with damnation of Vorticism [8]—the story "My Disciple" in *Rotting Hill* being a skit on the kind of art Read likes. Here an art teacher (*né* army sergeant) called Gartsides, deriving his authority from Read, sets his pupils loose in the emotional world Lewis loathes; for them, "Art was *doing what they liked.*" Babbitt, in the section of *The New Laokoön* called "The Theory of Spontaneity," makes similar criticisms of child art. And if this attack on the primitive and

6. *Caliph's Design,* p. 37.
7. Ernest Seillière, *Le Mal romantique.* Vol. *4* of "La Philosophie de l'impérialisme" (Paris, Librairie Plon, 1908), 379–82.
8. Sir Herbert Read, *The Philosophy of Modern Art* (London, Faber and Faber, 1952), p. 44.

child in contemporary painting seem to us today unexceptional and unexceptionable, it must be remembered that Lewis' own art grew up against these trends. Thus, in the Catalogue to Roger Fry's famous "Post-Impressionist Exhibition" of 1911, where advanced styles in painting were first shown to a wide English public (and where Lewis himself showed), we read the following: "Primitive art, like the art of children, consists not so much in an attempt to represent what the eye perceives as to put a line round a mental conception of the object. Like the work of the primitive artist, the pictures children draw are often extraordinarily expressive." [9]

They are indeed, Lewis would say, but expressive of what? So, going from this exhibition to work in Fry's Omega Workshops, he soon found them too dilettantist for his tastes. There then followed Vorticism, in which his criticism of contemporary trends is especially partial. When he returned from the war, he began a period of art criticism, including some perspicacious articles in *The Athenaeum, The Caliph's Design*, and an important Foreword to his first one-man exhibition, called *Guns*, at the Goupil Gallery in February 1919. At this time he formed his "X" Group, to which E. McKnight Kauffer among others belonged, but he tells us later that this resurrection of Vorticism was undertaken "against my better judgement."

The criticism of this period is summarized in *The Caliph's Design*, which is a plea for classical principles in art as much as for anything. It is a plea for standards of beauty, rather than standards of executant genius. We are the first civilization, Lewis reminds us, to accept the ugly as the visual mode of our time. The great cultures of ancient China and Japan, however, saw life whole, in a way we refuse to, and would have considered our art either perversely insensitive or mere "rough popular art." This is precisely what Lasserre designates by aesthetic pantheism, the love of the average (or ugly) rather than exceptional (or beautiful) going hand in hand with revolution and romance. And to justify such

9. Catalogue, *Post-Impressionist Exhibition* (London, Grafton Galleries, 1911), pp. 11–12.

art as the painting of the common man, Lewis reminds us, is making an ethical, not aesthetic, judgment.

The Caliph's Design, which he later calls another *Blast* or "fight-talk," studies a contradiction, then, between executant vitality in modern painting and "a very serious scepticism and discouragement in the use of that vitality." The first part deals with architecture, taking, in Aristotelian fashion, the largest subject in the field, the city, first. Here, Lewis suggests, the Cubist contribution could most constructively be put to use. Again in 1940, writing in *The New Republic,* he sees modern abstract art as really a branch of architecture. If the architectural journals were unhappy with the rhetorical question of Lewis' title (one of them answering that fortunately they had not got a vortex), at least Lewis influenced McKnight Kauffer. *Blast No. 2* pleaded for abstraction in popular art, even in underground railway posters, and this of course was the direction Kauffer was to explore so rewardingly after the war.

What *The Caliph's Design* really challenged, however, was the whole development of studio art. Here Lewis found the most vulnerable point at which to attack the *école de Paris.* Choosing as representatives of modern painting such artists as Dérain, Matisse,[10] Kandinsky, Braque, Gris, and, especially, Picasso, Lewis finds this painting full of life in its executive skills, but fatigued in vision, even pessimistic in their application: "Listlessness, dilettantism is the mark of studio art. *You must get Painting, Sculpture, and Design out of the studio and into life somehow or other* if you are not going to see this new vitality dessicated in a Pocket of inorganic experimentation." [11] This view is maintained. In 1940 he writes: "The artist must, if he is to survive, come to terms with the people

10. Another ambivalent attitude must be recorded here. In *Blast No. 1,* p. 142, Matisse is highly praised. However, later, perhaps when Matisse had developed his characteristically distorted odalisques, Lewis classes him in the category of imbecile artist, to which in literature Gertrude Stein belongs. So we read, "The goitrous torpid and squinting husks provided by Matisse in his sculpture are worthless except as tactful decorations for a mental home" (*Art of Being Ruled,* p. 419).

11. *Caliph's Design,* p. 7.

at large, and no longer accept the role of a purveyor of sensation, or of a highbrow clown, to a handful of socialites." [12]

Picasso exemplifies this spirit. Although Lewis writes that his estimate of Picasso in *The Caliph's Design* refers only to the artist up to 1912 or 1913, we also find from the pamphlet that Lewis had visited the Picasso exhibition put on in London shortly after the end of the first World War and which drew somewhat similar, though far less severe, criticism from André Lhote. But Lhote defended Picasso from "apriorisme," and it must be borne in mind that Lhote, for whom Cézanne constituted "the first recall to classical order," [13] liked the resuscitated interest in David at this time, an interest Lewis explicitly deplores in *The Caliph's Design*. In Lewis, possibly from the authority of his own performance, we have the only significant English critic of this time making a thorough, thought-out rejection of Picasso and of the école de Paris. Clive Bell, who wrote scathingly of Lewis' own painting, and especially of R. H. Wilenski's praise of it,[14] showed the customary reverence when approaching Picasso in his articles entitled "Order and Authority" which began in *The Athenaeum* for November 7, 1919.

Having said this, one must hastily add that Lewis has always conceded Picasso great ability as a painter. Even in *The Caliph's Design* Picasso is a "great artist," "one of the ablest living painters," the painter of the future. Five years later he is a "very wonderful artist," [15] and a decade later still "superbly gifted," and so on. But Picasso is symptomatic. Technically gifted as he is—and Lewis sees him as a "performer" like Joyce—he exhibits that love of novelty and of the ugly which afflicts our art today. The source of his constant alteration in style is boredom and lack of belief; pro-

12. Wyndham Lewis [Letter], *The New Republic, 102,* No. 21 (May 20, 1940), 675.

13. André Lhote, "Cubism and the Modern Artistic Sensibility," *The Athenaeum,* No. 4664 (Sept. 19, 1919), p. 920.

14. Clive Bell, "Wilcoxism," *The Athenaeum,* No. 4688 (March 5, 1920), pp. 311–12.

15. Wyndham Lewis, "Art-Chronicle," *The Criterion, 3,* No. 9 (Oct. 1924), 107.

phetically, Lewis predicts in 1919 that Picasso will quickly tire of each new style he explores. In brief, Picasso is a mirror of his times like Joyce, "an interpreter rather than a creator" [16] as he wrote in 1940. For Lewis' criticism of Picasso has not altered. Reviewing a Picasso exhibition in London in 1950, he still finds Picasso "blamelessly highbrow," a "conjuror" he admires, but the possessor of an "almost smug vitality." [17] So Lewis criticizes in Picasso our own age. As with much of his criticism, there is a grain of truth in it, but Picasso can hardly be blamed for reflecting his age, when Lewis admires other artists who did the same in classical times. If Picasso had remained in, say, his celebrated "blue" period, which Lewis might call classical (though one cannot tell, as some critics see this period as hopelessly romantic), he would have been far less a painter than he is today, having run the gamut of practically every aesthetic expression of our time.

But as footnote to this criticism through Picasso of the intellectual bankruptcy of our times, one can happily add that in the discussion of Picasso in *The Revenge for Love* Tristram Phipps (who seems to own Vorticist paintings [18] and is thus probably a sympathetic artist) defends Picasso. Tristy feels "another conscience" (that of art) in the face of the attack on Picasso made by the politically conscious artist, Victor Stamp, and the pretentious Semitic art critic, Peter Wallace or Reuben Wallach.

At first glance *The Caliph's Design,* brilliant pamphlet as it is, seems torn by a contradiction fundamental to Lewis' entire art criticism. How can we align the high place accorded the artist with the detestation of "life" in Lewis' aesthetic? With one hand Lewis removes the artist from humanity lest he become contaminated by the herd, with the other he tells him to leave his studio and "live."

16. Wyndham Lewis, "Picasso," *The Kenyon Review, 2,* No. 2 (Spring 1940), 200.

17. Wyndham Lewis, "Round the London Art Galleries," *The Listener, 44,* No. 1135 (Nov. 30, 1950), 650.

18. Jack Cruze describes one on Tristy's wall as like "a blooming airplane crash in the middle of a football scrum" (*Revenge for Love,* p. 116).

The contradiction is only apparent. The artist's intellect, housed in the eyes, must remain aloof, apart from particular passion, but it must irradiate the whole world of nature, not merely that unrepresentative section to be found in the artist's studio.

Secondly, there is another seeming contradiction, in Lewis' own practice. But again it is possible to square this up with his critical beliefs. On the whole, it can be said that Lewis' art shows three styles, entirely realistic, semi-abstract, and fully abstract.

In the first group we find his portraits, especially those executed at St. Louis during the last war, and the two likenesses of T. S. Eliot, for the rejection of the first of which by the Royal Academy of 1938 Augustus John tendered his resignation to that body (he resumed membership two years later and the portrait is now at Durban). Lewis reproduces many of these heads in his autobiographical volumes and their success as regards design can scarcely be in doubt. The head of Ezra Pound shown at the Goupil Gallery in 1919, for example, drew praise from all sections of the press, *The Observer* for November 9, 1919, finding here "the synthetic reconstruction of personality in legitimate and pure terms of art."

In the second style we find external nature, including man himself, suffering some distortion. But the metallic, armored, machine-like figures that stalk this section of Lewis' work (cf. "Inca and the Birds," the last plate in *Rude Assignment*) are not really distortions for Lewis when we acknowledge his view of the human species. What is more, this artistic transcending of the world of "things," which he is giving us here, is by no means ugly—at least I am sure Lewis did not intend it to be so. The distortion is based on his philosophic beliefs: "We preferred something more metallic and resistant than the pneumatic surface of the cuticle. We preferred a helmet to a head of hair."

The third style offers the most serious contradiction to Lewis' expressed beliefs; that is the period of Vorticism, around the second decade of this century, when he banished nature altogether from his drawing and relied on form for his effects—a period we shall watch Hulme criticizing below, and which Yeats thought "stylistic arrangements of experience." [19] But this period, Lewis has repeatedly asserted, was only a temporary affair, primarily designed to drive English art ahead of that on the Continent. In this fully Vorticist work even the "gay intellectual shell" disappears and we are faced with the acrobatic of formal arrangements and shapes. Lewis retrospectively explains his intention here:

> In the year or two prior to World War I. I attempted totally to eliminate from my work all reference to nature . . . At that early period I reproached, even, the Paris school; of "nature-mortists," as I called them, for their inability to free themselves from the habit of naturalism. It was their practice to begin by painting a straight still-life, or figure (as *morte* as was the "nature-morte"), and then subject it to abstraction and distortion . . . If you are going to be *abstract,* I argued, why worry about a lot of match-boxes, bottles of beer, plates of apples, and picturesque guitars? Why not turn your back upon familiar objects altogether—since by the time you had finished your picture they had, in any case, almost disappeared? [20]

Such is the explanation for what he calls the "de-humanizing" of his art at this period, but it was only an interim period: "no one but an idiot—or a Dutchman, like Mondrian—would pass his life in that vacuum." [21] Virtually the same criticism is made in his Foreword to his 1921 exhibition, "Tyros and Portraits": "Again, abstraction, or plastic music, is justified and at its best when its divorce from natural form or environment is complete, as in Kandinsky's expressionism, or in the experiments of the 1914 Vorticists,

19. Yeats, *Vision,* p. 25.

20. Wyndham Lewis, Introduction, Catalogue, *Exhibition of Paintings, Drawings, and Watercolours by Wyndham Lewis* (London, Redfern Gallery, May 5, 1949), unpaged.

21. Wyndham Lewis, "Round the London Galleries," *The Listener, 43,* No. 1104 (March 23, 1950), 522.

rather than when its basis is still the French Impressionist dogma of the intimate scene." [22]

Those who know the history of Lewis' artistic development will know that after about 1924 (when, of course, he begins his strenuous literary criticism) he becomes increasingly less abstract in his painting, culminating in his call for a new naturalism—"Supernature versus super-real"—in 1939. He announced "The End of Abstract Art" in 1940, predicting that its cadaver will flicker on in decay for a few more years in America, and after the second World War his page in *The Listener* was remarkable for its hospitality to realist, or semirealist, painters like Francis Bacon, Edward Burra, Michael Ayrton ("classical" [23]), Ceri Richards, Keith Vaughan, and the Scottish painters (who appear at the end of *Rotting Hill*) Colquhoun and McBryde. To some extent, the phenomenon of total abstraction in Lewis' work may be attributable to two sources, first, as complete a reaction as possible to English academicism, and second, infatuation with the teaching of T. E. Hulme. Although Hulme, as we shall see, was not happy over total abstraction, Lewis has himself suggested this latter source in *Blasting and Bombardiering*. Total abstraction, after all, makes a telling contrast to the "romantic" view which places man at the center of the universe.

22. Wyndham Lewis, "Foreword: Tyros and Portraits," Catalogue, *Exhibition of Paintings and Drawings by Wyndham Lewis* (London, Leicester Galleries, April 1921), pp. 6–7. But Kandinsky is castigated elsewhere. As I have pointed out, I must simply try to preserve the unity of Lewis' argument and discount the personal crotchet that crops up occasionally and does not seem the representative of a sustained point of view.

23. Wyndham Lewis, Note, Catalogue, *Exhibition of Paintings, Drawings, Book Illustrations, and Designs for the Theatre by Michael Ayrton,* arranged by the Wakefield City Art Gallery (Yorkshire, May 1949), unpaged. Interestingly, Lewis here defines "classical" art as follows: "I have used the word 'classical,' by which I mean nothing more pedantic than the image purified of the sensational: such degree of timelessness as is involved in cleaving to perfection: a chasteness in colour (reaching at times in Ayrton's case the chill of a conventional austerity): a clarity in form, the shunning of the romantic blur and blotch, fastidiously dispensing with nineteenth century *atmospherics.*"

We are now able, I believe, to see as he would wish us to what he means by calling Cubism photographic. For although there are moments when Lewis seems to suggest that Cubism made a refreshing (and anti-Bergsonian) re-emphasis on form, he usually associates it with Impressionism. He does so in *The Athenaeum* in several places: "The particular decomposition and distortion of Cubism is a compromise, in one sense, within the dogmatic tradition of French 19th.-century naturalism." [24]

One need not agree with the interpretation Lewis throws on Cubism, but it helps us to understand what is otherwise a difficult criticism. One of the tenets of Impressionism, he claims, was "catching the Moment on the hop," that is, the artist's "photographing" a specific moment at a specific time and in a specific place. This, of course, is opposed to the classical ideal of permanence. He explains in *The Athenaeum,* and Lhote agrees, that the Cubist is attempting also to give this momentary feeling of the interior of the studio, "the *immediate* truth of the copy of *La Presse,* the morning coffee-cup, the roof seen from the studio window." But the Japanese print was aiming to achieve the static perfection of eternity. In just the same way he comes to criticize the Futurists, for a more extreme example of this romantic "immediacy."

Lewis' criticism of Futurism, from his "A Review of Contemporary Art" in *Blast No. 2* on, is most interesting, for Futurism had much in common with Vorticism. Futurism was anti-Cubist, even anti-Picasso, as was Lewis, but it contained elements obviously anathema to him, so that when Marinetti told him on their way to the Café Royal that he was a Futurist, Lewis could sincerely reply, "No."

The first Futurist manifesto ("Manifesto del Futurismo") appeared in the *Figaro* for February 20, 1909. It advocated speed, machines, the future, war ("We wish to glorify War—the only health giver of the world"), youth, and the destruction of museums:

24. Wyndham Lewis, "I. Nature and the Monster of Design," *The Athenaeum,* No. 4673 (Nov. 21, 1919), p. 1231.

We shall sing of the great crowds in the excitement of
labour, pleasure or rebellion; of the multi-colored and poly-
phonic surf of revolutions in modern capital cities; of the
nocturnal vibrations of arsenals and workshops beneath their
violent electric moons; of the greedy stations swallowing
smoking snakes; of factories suspended from the clouds by
their strings of smoke; of bridges leaping like gymnasts over
the diabolical cutlery of sunbathed rivers; of adventurous liners
scenting the horizon; of broad-chested locomotives prancing
on the rails, like huge steel horses bridled with long tubes;
and of the gliding flight of aeroplanes, the sound of whose
screw is like the flapping of flags and the applause of an enthusiastic crowd.[25]

Marinetti, better known himself as a poet and the editor of
Poesia rather than as a painter, immediately began a strenuous
lecture campaign, which early took him into the Lyceum Club in
London, for Marinetti was a rich man and traveled far and fast.
The "epileptic rhetoric," as Lewis calls it, of these lectures was
a distinctive feature of the Futurist movement and certainly impressed those English who heard them. When Marinetti lectured
at Bechstein Hall in London on March 19, 1912, for instance, *The
Times* tells us that his audience "begged for mercy." Epstein says
that when all else failed Marinetti used to imitate the sound of
machine guns on the podium.[26] But possibly Epstein was simply
deceived by what Stella Bowen calls Marinetti's "zoom-bang poetry,"
for the Futurist leader made a point of reciting poems now from
his subsequent collection called *Zang Tumb Tuuum*. These poems
were avowed attempts at typographical painting, or the *Klang-
gedichten* of Hugo Ball later, a form best utilized in our times by
E. E. Cummings perhaps, and worst by Kurt Schwitters in *transition*,

25. I use the translation contained in the Catalogue to the *Futurist Exhibition*
(London, Sackville Gallery, March 1912), p. 4.

26. Jacob Epstein, *Let There Be Sculpture* (New York, Putnam, 1940), p. 52.

and of which the following is a characteristically Marinettian example:

SOLE A RIPETIZIONE 20,000 PROIETTILI AL MINUTO
urzzzzzzz aaaaaaaaaaa
goia goia goia goia ancora ancora vendetta
ta ta ta ta ta ta ta ta ta ta ta ta ta

Goldring also attended one of these spirited meetings in London and describes Marinetti of the time as "a flamboyant personage adorned with diamond rings, gold chains and hundreds of flashing white teeth." [27]

The second Futurist manifesto appeared in April 1909 and was entitled "Tuons le clair de lune!" [28] It was an even more hysterical document than the first and actually gave the signal to the Futurists to open fire ("Attention! . . . Feu!"), for a cardinal point of this movement was the conversion of the salons into fields of battle. On February 11, 1910, there appeared the *Manifesto dei pittori futuristi* and on March 8 a spectacular exhibition and lecture series were given by the Futurists at Turin. On April 11, 1910, *La pittura futurista: manifesto tecnico* came out, Balla and Severini now joining Marinetti, Boccioni, Carrà, and Russolo as signatories.[29] Further manifestoes, and manifestations, followed, including a musicians' manifesto, a motion picture manifesto (Marinetti's *La cinematografia futurista*), and special, urgent summonses to dilatory Venetian and Spanish Futurists—Venice being reviled for its gondolas and canals. On March 9, 1911, Marinetti lectured in Paris at the Association des Étudiants de Paris, and in this year published *Le Futurisme*, a convenient compilation of these views. The next year the Futurists staged their international exhibition, their "*Putsch*," as Lewis calls it. From Bernheim, Jeune et Cie. in Paris

27. Douglas Goldring, *South Lodge* (London, Constable, 1943), p. 64.
28. F. T. Marinetti, *Le Futurisme* (Paris, Sansot, 1911), pp. 155–78. I base my date on Luigi Fillià, *Il Futurismo* (Milano, Sonzogno, 1932), p. 19.
29. Reprinted in Umberto Boccioni, *Pittura, scultura futuriste* (Milano, Edizione Futuriste di "Poesia," 1914), p. 189.

the exhibit went to the Sackville Gallery, in Sackville Street, London, in March 1912. In April/May it was on display at 34a Tiergarten-strasse in Berlin, and in September we find it at the De Roos Gallery, on the Rokindam, in Amsterdam, whence it moved to the Galerie Georges Giroux in Brussels.

Marinetti continued to propagate his doctrine by means of lectures. On November 17, 1913, he lectured to Hulme's Poets' Club, attacking Baudelaire, Flaubert, Wagner, and claiming H. G. Wells as one of his flock. But it was the two lectures Marinetti gave at the Doré Gallery in Bond Street the next year, the first on April 30, 1914, and the second on May 5, that fired Lewis and probably put the match to the fuse of *Blast,* as much as did the British Futurist manifesto *Vital English Art* (reproduced in C. R. W. Nevinson's *Paint and Prejudice*). To the second of these lectures Lewis took "a determined band of miscellaneous anti-Futurists," including Gaudier-Brzeska, Edward Wadsworth, and T. E. Hulme (all big men). They heckled Marinetti. Gaudier "put down a tremendous barrage in French," while the rest "maintained a confused uproar." As a big drum was being thumped behind the scenes to accompany Marinetti's poetry, it must have been a noisy affair, but—can we doubt that "the Italian intruder was worsted?" Ford, who liked to call himself "Grandfather of the Vorticists," recalls this lecture in *Thus to Revisit:* "Signor Marinetti shouted incredibly in the Doré Gallery, and a sanguinary war was declared at the Café Royal between those youths who wore trousers of green billiard cloth and whiskers and those who did not." [30]

If Ford embroidered the facts slightly here, he does point up that it was this lecture, on May 5, 1914, that touched off Vorticism. *Blast No. 1* appeared some one and a half months later. On September 18 Marinetti was arrested by the police in Milan for organizing a Futurist demonstration to try to get Italy to join in the war on the side of the Entente.

30. Ford Madox Ford, *Thus to Revisit* (London, Chapman and Hall, 1921), p. 176.

Le Futurisme, which provides a summary of Futurist "thought," is militant, anti-*passéiste* (the lovers of the past, *passatisti,* had been torn to shreds in the first manifestoes as well as in sympathetic periodicals like *Noi* and Papini's *Lacerba*), antiromantic, anti-Nietzsche (who admired the past), and definitely committed to the introduction of life into art as brutally as possible. As regards woman, Marinetti wanted a modern womanhood. *Le Futurisme,* thus, was prosuffragette, unlike *Blast* which was extremely rude to suffragettes. This dynamic view of the artist was simply reiterated by Boccioni in his *Pittura, scultura futuriste* of 1914, a work larded with black-type adjurations such as "Tot! . . . Tot! . . . Tot!" or the pleasantly Italianated "Hip! Hip! Hurrà!" Indeed, some of the earlier Futurist documents may well have been responsible for the typographical dynamite of *Blast.* Boccioni, as a good Futurist, was anti-Picasso and anti-Cubist—though claimed as a Cubist by Apollinaire in 1913.[31] Of course, there are works by Boccioni, Severini, and by Lewis himself which look distinctly Cubist, just as Lewis also tried his hand at the multiple-image Futurist picture at this time. The Cuban Cubist, Picabia, tried all styles.

As that sensitive critic Gustave Coquiot, no more friendly to Cubism than Boccioni, was quickly aware, however, the Futurists criticized themselves.[32] Even a sympathetic study like Rosa Clough's *Looking Back at Futurism* can really find little to praise in the movement as a whole. Lewis himself challenged Futurism on two grounds; as he fairly puts it later, "I heartily detested, and had violently combated, Marinetti's *anti-passéisme,* and dynamism."

James Thrall Soby, analyzing Vorticism, sees it anxious to announce the art of the future, but reluctant to break entirely with the past.[33] This is an accurate analysis. As we read in *Blast No. 1,*

31. Guillaume Apollinaire, *Les Peintres cubistes* (Paris, Éditions "Athéna," 1913), p. 84.

32. Gustave Coquiot, *Cubistes, futuristes, passéistes* (Paris, Librairie Ollendorff, 1914), p. 93.

33. James Thrall Soby, *Contemporary Painters* (New York, Museum of Modern Art, 1948), pp. 115–21.

"Our vortex is not afraid of the Past: it has forgotten its existence." [34]
Although, in several places, Lewis calls for an art to look entirely
ahead ("The Children of the New Epoch"), he criticized Futurism
for being too "Presentist"—*"The present man in all of us is the
machine."* This is not hard to follow. For Lewis the aesthetic personality is part of all time, and his energies arrive from all times
(he is, in fact, a vortex). The Futurists, then, by overemphasis, were
disrespectful to the future. Moreover, with their insistence on immediacy (catching the moment on the hop), they were no more,
despite their invective to the contrary, than another development
of Impressionism. So in *Blast No. 1,* much of which, I cannot help
feeling, was written with Marinetti looking over Lewis' shoulder,
figuratively speaking, Futurism is "the latest form of Impressionism."
He repeats this in *The Caliph's Design:* "The Futurists, and their
French followers, have as the basis of their aesthetic the Impres-
sionists generally . . . Their dogma is a brutal rhetorical Zolaism,
on its creative side, saturated with the voyou respect and gush about
Science, the romance of machinery engraven on their florid banner."
Pound, probably influenced by Lewis here, repeats the criticism
from *Blast No. 1.*[35]

But the "presentist" critique of Futurism is best explained by
reference to the paintings themselves. Here Balla gives good examples, in a work like "Speed of a Car Plus Light and Sounds,"
of what Lewis disliked. Severini's "Blue Dancer," Boccioni's "Dynamism of a Football Player" are others. Balla's painting "Leash
in Motion" shows a woman walking with her poodle, their feet a
blur of motion in a multitude of images rather like Duchamp's
famous "Nude Descending a Staircase," or an instructional picture
of Bobby Jones playing golf, the golfer's arms shown in every

34. *Blast No. 1,* p. 147. In *One-Way Song,* p. 102, we read, "give me England
. . . / Give me her Back," in the sense, here, of her past, as opposed to the
"front" (future).

35. Ezra Pound, "Vorticism," *The Fortnightly Review,* N.S., *573* (Sept. 1,
1914), 461, 468. *Gaudier-Brzeska. A Memoir by Ezra Pound* (London, John Lane,
the Bodley Head, 1916), p. 104.

position gone through during the shot. Russolo's "Plastic Résumé of a Woman's Movements" is the same. A Futurist sculpture at the Turin exhibition actually rolled its eyes. Boccioni's "Muscles in Quick Motion" was another similar "plastic ensemble." Lewis obviously detested this Bergsonian flux (as he must have detested the Futurist ideal of tactile values in art), but it was an undeniable influence of the time. Epstein confesses that he nearly connected a live pneumatic drill to the man in his famous sculpture "The Rock Drill" (which Hulme praised so highly),[36] but discarded the idea as too childish. Equally Benda refers to a Futurist painting showing a horse in motion having twenty feet and attacks this kind of art for assailing the very principle of art, the still absolute, symbol of eternity.[37]

Benda writes this in his *Sur le succès du Bergsonisme,* and of course this dynamism is just what Bergson calls his "mécanisme cinématographique" in *L'Évolution créatrice*—Boccioni frequently quotes Bergson with admiration. Lewis is likely to have been familiar with this theory, since Bergson was lecturing on it in the first years of the century, when Lewis attended the Collège de France lectures. Matter, Bergson here proposes, presents itself to us in a constant becoming, and the intellect can best trap it by a series of immobile, instantaneous "snapshots": "La méthode cinématographique est donc la seule pratique, puisqu'elle consiste à régler l'allure générale de la connaissance sur celle de l'action, en attendant que le détail de chaque acte se règle à son tour sur celui de la connaissance." [38]

---

36. T. E. Hulme, "Mr. Epstein and the Critics," *The New Age,* N.S., *14,* No. 8 (Dec. 25, 1913), 251–3. This issue carries a reproduction of Epstein's drawing for "The Rock Drill," a title Yeats misquotes (W. B. Yeats, *Autobiographies,* New York, Macmillan, 1927, p. 348) and Lewis employs in 1951 to compliment Pound (Wyndham Lewis, "The Rock Drill," *The New Statesman and Nation, 41,* No. 1048, April 7, 1951, 398).

37. Julien Benda, *Sur le succès du Bergsonisme* (Paris, Mercure de France, 1929), pp. 175–6.

38. Bergson, *L'Évolution créatrice,* p. 332.

This deplorable view of things, for Lewis, caused *Blast No. 1* to assail Futurism for being mechanical (Bergson having called the intellect this). The Futurist aesthetic was amenable to this attack. Roger Fry saw the Futurists ("journalists") in this way in 1919.[39] But Lewis went further than Fry; Futurism was too excitedly Latin in its love of the machine. This was what he called Marinetti's "Automobilism." Lewis' point was that there was nothing so very new or startling about the machine age for the Englishman. The "God-Automobile" was only too obvious a fact; as *Blast No. 1* put it, "Elephants are VERY BIG. Motor cars go quickly." His friend, and supporter, Edward Wadsworth, however, loved fast motor cars and had special "souped-up" Rolls-Royces built to his order, in which I recall traveling with terror as a boy. But England, Lewis protested in *The New Weekly* for June 20, 1914 (the day of the first *Blast*), "practically invented this civilisation that Signor Marinetti has come to preach to us about." In his earlier article on Marinetti in this same periodical Lewis had written: "As modern life is the invention of the English, they should have something profounder to say on it than anybody else." *Blast* firmly reasserted this. The Italians had suddenly emerged into the machine age; hence their childish excitement over the machine. While the Futurists, then, had done much to combat the "deadness and preciosity of the artists working in Paris," he wrote in *The Caliph's Design*, they had not assimilated the machine fully into the aesthetic consciousness and could not, therefore, make proper use of it in art.

Although one finds little of interest today in the Futurist gospel, it is only fair to point out that Lewis did their aims injustice. Several Futurists thought they were classical. Carrà specifically welcomed Cézanne as a new classicist in *Lacerba* and in the fourth number of *La ronda*. Rosa Clough shows how anti-Cubist the Futurists were (like Lewis). The Futurist critic Soffici, for example, was apparently incensed by the Cubist claim to be descended from Michel-

39. Roger Fry, "Fine Arts," *The Athenaeum*, No. 4658 (Aug. 8, 1919), p. 724.

angelo.[40] And in architecture a close comparison might be made between Lewis' views and those of Sant' Elia, as he expressed them in *Lacerba*.

In actual fact, if space were available, a close comparison could be made with certain of the group around *La ronda* in Italy between 1919 and 1923 and Wyndham Lewis. This group included men like Antonio Baldini, Vincenzo Cardarelli, Riccardo Bacchelli, one of his few contemporaries admired by Croce and whose early work (like *La città degli amanti* or the historical *Il diavolo al Pontelungo*) reminds one of Lewis, and Emilio Cecchi, the present encomiast for Hemingway (an enthusiasm perhaps anticipated by Cecchi's article on Stevenson in *La ronda* for February 1920). The immediate purpose of *La ronda* was to react against the Voce group, particularly as represented at the time by Papini and Prezzolini, for its cultivation of latter-day French decadence and its close ties with Futurism.[41]

In the second number of *La ronda,* in fact, Cecchi equates Futurism with Bolshevism in a penetrating "Communicazione accademica," to most of which Lewis would surely subscribe, and in the third issue the same critic writes perspicaciously on Benda, especially on *L'Ordination*. I Rondisti, who included Carlo Linati (praised by Lewis) translating Yeats and praising Pound (July 1920), regarded the Voce group as overgrown children, just as did Lewis; Cecchi wrote a satire on Futurism. Bacchelli contributed a note from Paris on Dada ("un male ebraico-rumeno che si chiama *Dada*"), and in an interesting essay called "Classicismo pittoresco" in the July 1920 number, Giorgio de Chirico praises

40. But Boccioni, *Pittura, scultura futuriste,* pp. 118 ff., however, sees the Cubists as anti-Impressionist.

41. A brief survey of these aims may be found as follows: Oreste Munafò, "Correnti odierne della letteratura italiana: La reazione rondista," *Italica, 29,* No. 4 (Dec. 1952), 235–44. Meanwhile, amusingly satirical biographies of several contributors to *La ronda* may be turned up between pp. 92 and 98 of the November 1919 issue.

the linear in Greek and quattrocento art, while disliking the disheveled baroque of his home town, Venice. A review of Babbitt's *Rousseau and Romanticism* in this same issue, incidentally, calls that author "pieno di sagacità *yankee,* di intelligenza nervosa e positiva." And so on. In short, the spirit of this brief "riscoperta di una civiltà italiana autóctona" is filled with as much "neoclassicismo" as Lewis could desire of the Italians of his time. The distinguishing factor of this neoclassicism, however, was that since Italian romanticism is largely antiromantic, a conscious return to the prebaroque tradition, we find a contemporary antiromantic reaction "returning" to the Italian romantics, like Manzoni and Leopardi. Thus *La ronda* rediscovered *Zibaldone* and through Leopardi's reflections on literature regarded the "novecento" as something very different from the romantic cliché put forward by Lewis and his ilk.

So it is interesting that for Pound Marinetti is a "corpse" in 1914, though in 1933 (in an article likening the Duce to Confucius) Pound supports Futurism. Political considerations clearly account for this change of heart. But Lewis, even in the heat of his interest in Fascist politics, was never happy with Futurism, constantly attacking it for being the politics of "action" and unguided emotion. "Marinetti's post-nietzschean war-doctrine became War, *tout court;* and then Fascismo, which as Futurism in practice is the habit of mind and conditions of war applied to peace."

How true to form, one feels if one knows I Rondisti, but not how quick Lewis was to see this in 1927. And a host of similar references can be found in the twenties. Why then, if he saw through Futurism, did he go on to support fascism? I have no answer. More recently, Lewis has given us another aesthetic squib, similar in form to *The Caliph's Design* but not nearly so excitingly original in matter. In *The Demon of Progress in the Arts,* put out in 1954 and running quickly into new printings, we are told that the visual arts are today endangered by extremism (defined as "a pathological straining after something which boasts of a spectacular *aheadof-*

ness"); that the rapid turnover in industrial trends is being duplicated in our artistic life; that artistic change, instead of being organic, is being artificially stimulated by interested "pundits" (Sir Herbert Read represented as "a Mister Abreast-of-the-Times for Everyman"); [42] that the artist's healthy curiosity has turned pathologic and that the artist himself, victim of technology, now only enjoys a technical freedom—"he is probably least free when most eccentric." [43]

There is more that is equally stimulating. When Lewis reports an acquaintance complaining that "we have to struggle just as hard today to do something . . . well, like painting a recognizable portrait . . . as formerly we had for years to struggle to be allowed to do something 'extremist,' " [44] a pertinent comment is made on the decline of portrait painting in our time. Lewis cannot feel that the "aesthetic excursionist," as he calls the extremist artist today, has any real "roots in the sensuous reality," for "whoever is able to create upon a canvas or a piece of paper a human figure containing the reality of life . . . is not likely to go off and satisfy himself by drawing with a ruler a lot of strips upon a canvas or paper." There is a section on the salvationist solemnity with which Americans dignify extreme art, and a dig at the Museum of Modern Art here recalls *America, I Presume.* The work ends with a discussion of Malraux, who Lewis thinks neglects the effects of the industrial revolution on art for certain political considerations. But *The Demon of Progress in the Arts* is disappointing. There is a weary exasperation that soon makes this squib fizzle out. The comparative analysis provided with the art of the cinematograph, a corporate endeavor, is wholly unsatisfactory, and is it true, one asks oneself, that "most painters have always come from working-class

42. Wyndham Lewis, *The Demon of Progress in the Arts* (London, Methuen, 1954), p. 50.

43. For Selden Rodman, in his subsequent *The Eye of Man* (New York, Devin-Adair, 1955), the extremist painter is also in this danger: "The more an artist strives for originality the less original he becomes."

44. *Demon of Progress,* p. 40.

families"? On the other hand, Lewis might here for once have strengthened his main case: the impermanence of much modern extreme painting would have done so, as would a realization that the "pundits" of today are responsible for extremism (if they are) because yesterday they were guilty of the reverse. Here a frustrated Lewis—for this pamphlet was written when he was blind—sees art on the verge of an "insane zero," a "clownish suicide," or "a nihilistic nothingness." [45]

The weakness of Lewis' art criticism as a whole is chiefly its (deliberate?) unfairness to Cubism—from which, after all, so much of his own art derives. Unlike Vorticism, Cubism had no organized *mystique*—indeed, boasted of its freedom from such, despite Lewis' imputation of "dogma" to Cubists—and its exponents were painters rather than writers. What is more, not only did it anticipate Vorticism by some years (Apollinaire dating the nomenclature from a derisive reference by Matisse in 1908) but it went on for some years, as we well know, and cannot easily be categorized. Like all vital art movements, it resists classification. However there are a few works, from practitioners and sympathizers, which do give us a general contemporary view of the movement's aims. These include *Du "Cubisme"* by Albert Gleizes and Jean Metzinger, Robert Delaunay's notebooks, and Apollinaire's *Les Peintres cubistes: Méditations esthétiques,* as well as Apollinaire's statements in the two erratic reviews of the period, *Montjoie* and *Les Soirées de Paris.*

Needless to say, Apollinaire, friend of so many of the Cubist painters assembled in their special room in the 1911 Salon des Indépendants, is a poetic rather than academic critic. Moreover, Apollinaire's view of nature in analyzing this painting was not held by all the painters themselves, least of all by Fernand Léger during his Cubist period. Here Apollinaire is in reaction to nineteenth-century pantheism—"trop d'artistes-peintres adorent encore les

45. *Ibid.*, p. 33, and *passim.* Sir Herbert Read may be seen, by the way, temperately disliking Benda in the Introduction to his anthology *The English Vision* (London, Eyre and Spottiswoode, 1933).

plantes, les pierres, l'onde ou les hommes." [46] The last word is challenging, but Apollinaire was clearly fascinated in this work with Einsteinian space and the fourth dimension. Answering the charges already made by this time against the overgeometric nature of Cubism, Apollinaire asserts that while the Greeks took man as the measure of perfection, the new art was to take the universe as such. But both Apollinaire and Gleizes agree that Cubism, far from presenting a given moment (as Lewis said), actually aims to create a moment of stasis into which is poured a series of unknown moments, from past, present, and future. And both men see Cubism as anti-Impressionist, though Gleizes goes further here than Apollinaire. As a good Frenchman Gleizes is ready to pay his respects to Impressionism, but he begins his study with criticism of Impressionism for its lack of formal qualities and for what Lewis largely criticized in the movement: "L'art des Impressionistes comporte un non-sens: par la diversité de la couleur il tâche à créer de la vie, et il propage un dessin veule et nul. La robe chatoie, merveilleuse; les formes disparaissent, atrophiées." [47]

Further, Gleizes has the same high praise for Cézanne as has Lewis, he likes the art of ancient China as much as Lewis, he emphasizes "esprit" and "volonté," space and the surface plane, and he detests "la foule" in a way to which Lewis could not take exception. Apollinaire, while critical of le douanier Rousseau, admires this painter's "ordre," mentions the art of Egyptian mummification with obvious interest, and claims that the new painters he is considering as Cubists are "plus cérébrales que sensuelles." Apollinaire, too, has the Futurists looking over his shoulder: "Nous n'errerons point dans l'avenir inconnu, qui séparé de l'éternité n'est qu'un mot destiné à tenter l'homme." [48]

As he shows in his poem "La Jolie Rousse," Apollinaire was

---

46. Apollinaire, *Peintres cubistes,* p. 6.
47. Albert Gleizes et Jean Metzinger, *Du "Cubisme"* (Paris, Eugène Figuière, 1912), p. 8.
48. Apollinaire, *Peintres cubistes,* p. 8.

clearly looking ahead, and welcomed painters like Le Fauconnier, André Salmon, Georges Deniker, and Jacques Villon, but he still sees great art as a meeting place of periods and movements.

If Lewis' art criticism is at times unfair, it is always lively. The progress of this demon in the arts is inevitably entertaining to observe. The same may be said, of course, for his political criticism. Yet here one has the pleasant task of referring to the series of reviews Lewis wrote as art critic for *The Listener* between 1946 and 1951, before blindness overtook him. On the whole these reviews, although eclectic, are tolerant and kind; at times, however, as in his praise for the work of Michael Ayrton, he is still wholly interested, and the note of propaganda spoils some of his writing on the lesser English realists. Still these reviews caused even Clement Greenberg, who holds no brief for Lewis and thinks Sir Herbert Read "an incompetent art critic," to call Lewis "a superb one." [49] In any case, even if one is totally opposed to this art criticism, one cannot ignore it, as one can safely ignore the political "thinking"; the former is always a bracing tonic.

49. Clement Greenberg, "Polemic against Modern Art" [Review of *The Demon of Progress in the Arts*], *The New Leader, 38,* No. 49 (Dec. 12, 1955), 28.

Chapter 8: The Puce Monster

"Such things as *Blast* have to be undertaken for the artist to exist at all. When you have removed all that is *necessarily* strident, much sound art-doctrine is to be found in this puce monster." [To Lord Carlow, with a copy of *Blast No. 1.*]

ON FEBRUARY 21, 1912, Roger Fry invited Lewis to join his Omega Workshops; in December of this year we find Lewis still exhibiting with the relatively conservative Camden Town Group at the Carfax Gallery. In the autumn of 1913 he broke with Fry and founded his own Rebel Art Centre with Kate Lechmere at 38 Great Ormond Street, off Queen's Street, London W.C. This center united principally the following artists: Frederick Etchells, Cuthbert Hamilton, Edward Wadsworth (later to help Lewis financially), Charles Nevinson, and Lewis himself. According to Virginia Woolf the Omega opened in July 1913, and the reason why Lewis broke from it is given in a letter, signed by Etchells, Hamilton, Wadsworth, and Lewis, alleging that "the Direction of the Omega Workshops" had secured a commission "by a shabby trick, and at the expense of one of their members—Mr. Wyndham Lewis." Fry retorted by accusing Lewis of "vindictive jealousy." [1]

Lewis was at this time asserting his individuality in a series of mural paintings. He decorated Ford's study, and several private houses, as well as the walls of his own center. His famous "Cubist Room" done for the Countess of Drogheda's London house, at

1. Virginia Woolf, *Roger Fry, an Autobiography* (London, Hogarth Press, 1940), pp. 192, 194. The account Lewis himself gives visitors of this break with Fry is put, with an almost touching credulity, in John Rothenstein, *Modern English Painters* (New York, Macmillan, 1956), p. 26.

40 Wilton Crescent, with its jet ceiling, ebony chimney glass, and Vorticist mirrors, was opened to an astonished public. Violet Hunt has described Lewis' Rebel Art Centre alleging that Lewis even advised the faithful on how to dress. The most spectacular of all his murals, however, were for the nightclub called the Cave of the Golden Calf, owned by Madame Strindberg (Strindberg's third wife), later to be the Cabaret Club in Beak Street. Here, the ceiling supported by Epstein columns, the walls (as Sir Osbert Sitwell puts it) "hideously but relevantly frescoed" [2] by Lewis, were danced what Edgar Jepson calls "Vorticist dances." Jepson, to whom Ford dedicated *The Marsden Case* with its almost certain description of this "pink cell" of a nightclub, tells us that "not only could you dance there those obsolete Vorticist dances, the Turkey Trot and the Bunny Hug, but between the dances you could observe violent, Vorticist assaults on the drama." [3]

The program for one evening at the Cave I saw included Margaret Morris and her "Greek Children Dancers," a veil dance, and "A Breton Wake."

Violet Hunt was reminded of "raw meat" by Lewis' murals here, and she goes on to describe them in a passage that strongly recalls the description of the "Wheelwright's Yard" in *The Enemy of the Stars:* "Bismarckian images, severings, disembowellings, mixed pell-mell with the iron shards that did it, splashed with the pale blood of exhausted heroes." [4]

Both Aldington and Ford mention the Cave affectionately in their memoirs, as does Augustus John (who has described Madame Strindberg with gusto). Pound, who was living at this time at 5 Holland Place Chambers, in Church Street, Kensington, complains in November 1913 that a "bloody guardsman" had removed his hat from the cloakroom there. And of course Imagism ran beside Vorticism, Pound linking the two in *The Fortnightly Review* for

2. Sir Osbert Sitwell, *Great Morning* (London, Macmillan, 1948), p. 208.

3. Edgar Jepson, *Memories of an Edwardian and Neo-Georgian* (London, Richards, 1937), p. 155.

4. Violet Hunt, *I Have This to Say* (New York, Boni and Liveright, 1926), p. 267. *Enemy of the Stars*, p. 6. The Wheelwright is Arghol's uncle.

September 1, 1914. Possibly the Cave was not entirely innocent of the influence of the "idéisme" of the celebrated Valentine de Saint-Point, whose strange dances, accompanied by geometric shadows thrown on a screen, had been a feature of Paris nightclubs in 1908 and 1909. But it was here, *chez* the Golden Calf, so Violet Hunt alleges, that the Rebel Art Centre held its evenings, the invitation for one of them reading, "The Manifesto of Rebel Art will be read to the sound of carefully chosen trumpets."

In early 1914 Etchells, Hamilton, Wadsworth, Nevinson, Lewis, and Epstein exhibited together, constituting the Blast group. Lewis described the group in *The Egoist* as "a vertigineous but not exotic island, in the placid and respectable archipelago of English art. This formation is undeniably of volcanic matter . . . The work of this group of artists for the most part underlines such geometric bases and structure of life, and they would spend their energies rather in showing a different skeleton and abstraction than formerly could exist than a different degree of hairiness or dress." [5] Both Lewis and Aldington say that Pound invented the word "Vorticist" for this movement, and Pound tells John Henry Quinn this, in a letter dated March 10, 1916, where he writes enthusiastically of Lewis' art to this future collector: "The vitality, the fullness of the man . . . Nobody has *any* conception of the volume and energy and the variety . . . It is not merely knowledge of technique, or skill, it is intelligence and knowledge of life, of the whole of it, beauty, heaven, hell, sarcasm, every kind of whirlwind of force and emotion. Vortex. That is the right word, if I did find it myself." [6] Gaudier-Brzeska, who shared Pound's enthusiasm for Lewis' work, is also joined in print with this group. John Cournos, however, places Gaudier outside the movement in a letter to Horace Brodzky; [7] but Pound contests this. However this may be, it is

5. Wyndham Lewis, "The Cubist Room," *The Egoist, 1,* No. 1 (Jan. 1, 1914), 9.

6. *Letters of Ezra Pound,* p. 74. Cf. for similar enthusiasm, Pound, *Pavannes and Divisions,* pp. 109, 110, 148, 245, 246, 250, 251, 254.

7. Quoted, Horace Brodzky, *Henri Gaudier-Brzeska, 1891–1915* (London, Faber and Faber, 1933), p. 166.

obvious that Gaudier's sympathies (e.g. his love of the art of ancient China) place him alongside Lewis. Hugh Ross Williamson classes Gaudier as definitely "of the Greeks." [8]

Writing to Amy Lowell, Pound now says that the *Blast* dinner (which Gaudier attended) is to be held on July 15, 1914. In *Gaudier-Brzeska. A Memoir* he writes that it was originally intended for the 7th, but on Wednesday, July 15, the *Blast* dinner was held at the Dieudonné Restaurant in Ryder Street, St. James's—a restaurant name (taken from the famous chef, Dieudonet) to reverberate through Pound's *Pisan Cantos*.[9] One trusts that it did not resemble a Futurist dinner ("We throw the table over . . . toc toc toc toc toc toc toc . . . He vomits. They vomit. They laugh" [10]), but it seems to have been a lavish affair for in the Carlow Collection there is an invitation card on which a characteristically practical Lewis has worked out the large costs for himself.

In fact there were several *Blast* dinners, some of them, according to Goldring, being held at the Eiffel Tower Restaurant in Percy Street (for which Lewis had also executed murals),[11] the restaurant that had seen Hulme's Poets Club dine in dinner jackets in 1908.[12] The Carlow Collection also contains an invitation to a "Vorticist evening" for February 23, 1916. But the *Blast* dinner was that of July 15, 1914, when what Pound called "the great MAGENTA cover'd oposculus" had burst on the literary and artistic scene.

Blast No. 1,[12a] with a page area of $12'' \times 9\frac{1}{2}''$ and the title angled to resemble lightning across the cover, appeared not long be-

8. Hugh Ross Williamson, "Portrait of an Artist," *The Bookman, 80,* No. 477 (June 1931), 153–5.

9. Glenn Hughes miscalls this restaurant the Dieu Donnes, and seems to confuse the date of the Vorticist dinner. Glenn Hughes, *Imagism and the Imagists* (Stanford, Calif., Stanford University Press, 1931), p. 36.

10. Marinetti, as quoted in Rosa Trillo Clough, *Looking Back at Futurism* (New York, Cocce Press, 1942), pp. 167–8.

11. Goldring, *South Lodge,* p. 70. Peter Keenan claims a hand in these murals.

12. Ezra Pound, *Polite Essays* (London, Faber and Faber, 1937), p. 8. Flint assailed the pompous dress of this Poets' Club in *The New Age*.

12a. A name suggested by C. R. W. Nevinson (if we are to believe *Paint and Prejudice*).

fore the outbreak of war and announced the necessarily short-lived Great English Vortex. To some extent, as Lewis tells us in *Time and Western Man,* it was aimed at the Royal Academy and thus continued, if it accelerated, the spirit of the New English Art Club. In 1914 also Pound was proposing his College of Arts, with Lewis on its "faculty," for the spreading of this new gospel. In March 1915 (not June or May as per Sir John Rothenstein and the Tate Gallery respectively) a Vorticist exhibition was held at the Doré Gallery and included paintings or drawings by Wadsworth, Lewis, Charles Nevinson (who was to be dropped for being too "Futurist," according to Peter Keenan),[13] and William Roberts, as well as sculpture by Jacob Kramer, Gaudier-Brzeska, and Epstein (who showed "The Rock Drill"). In July of this year the second, and only subsequent, issue of *Blast* appeared, its color changed from the sanguinary puce of the first number because, as Lewis explained, too much liquid of that hue was being shed at the time—"*BLAST* finds itself surrounded by a multitude of other Blasts." In 1933 a short-lived periodical of this name started in New York, publishing William Carlos Williams among others, while in 1954 H. M. McLuhan produced *Counterblast* from Canada. In 1956, during the Vorticist exhibition at the Tate, William Roberts produced in an acerb pamphlet what may well be the final blast, namely "Blast Vorticism!" This pamphlet is an attack on Lewis for arrogating to himself so much of the space in the Tate exhibition and for making such large claims for himself so long after the event.

The principal feature of the first publications was the series of "blasts" and "blesses" they contained, probably suggested by the fifty-seventh of Blake's *Proverbs of Hell,* "Damn braces. Bless relaxes." Although Lewis has since told us that he looked on the inclusion of Imagists in his Vorticist organ as *"pompier,"* the manifestoes of *No. 1* were signed by R. Aldington, Arbuthnott, L. Atkinson, Gaudier-Brzeska, J. Dismorr, C. Hamilton, Pound,

13. Peter Keenan, "Memories of Vorticism," *The New Hope,* 2, No. 6 (Oct. 1934), 6.

W. Roberts, H. Sanders, E. Wadsworth, and Lewis himself. Ford had prose in the first number, poetry in the second. Rebecca West contributed a story to *No. 1,* while Eliot had some unindexed poetry in *No. 2.* Lewis himself has explained that the "blasts" were anti-Victorian and proclassical (if we allow "classical" to carry those referents I shall align for him below under this head): " 'Bless the Hairdresser' . . . exalts formality, and order, at the expense of the disorderly and the unkempt. It is merely a humorous way of stating the classic standpoint, as against the romantic." [14]

Critics have liked to approach the "blasts" in this way, suggesting that those elements which curb nature are chiefly praised. Tindall puts this view in his *Forces in Modern British Literature, 1885–1946.* Certainly this classical restraint is the context Pound imposes on the period later, in *Pisan Cantos:*

> in whom are the voices, keeping hand on the reins
> Gaudier's word not blacked out
> > nor old Hulme's, nor Wyndham's.[15]

Up to a point this interpretation seems satisfactory, but it should not of course be taken as a cut-and-dried explanation. *No. 1* for instance, blesses castor oil and the Pope, both of whom presumably curb nature, but Madame Strindberg and Kate Lechmere, who perhaps did less to keep their hands on the reins, are blessed. The sea is blessed, as well as things of the sea, throughout both issues. Moreover, *No. 2* blasts "birth-control," which certainly curbs nature. Perhaps the answer to these objections is to be found in Goldring's *South Lodge* where we read that the list of "blasts" and "blesses" was drawn up at a prepublication tea party held in Lewis' studio in Fitzroy Street. Goldring alleges that the blessed were often simply the friends of contributors, especially of Ford. This might account for the Catholic tinge, Ford being a "Roman."

14. *Blasting and Bombardiering,* p. 43.
15. Ezra Pound, *The Pisan Cantos* (Norfolk, Conn., New Directions, 1948), p. 57.

The blasted, Goldring goes on, were mainly leading figures or things outliving their publicity. Violet Hunt adds the information that some of these names were deliberately misspelt.[16] Thus *No. 1* blesses "Bearline" (Henry Baerlein). The blessing of the sea I attribute to two sources; first, Edward Wadsworth, who went into the navy in the first World War, and later decorated the "Queen Mary," had a great love of the sea, and a volume he illustrated for Etchells in 1926 [17] shows the accurate and detailed knowledge of sailing ships he possessed; second, there was the patriotic element of the movement. So Lewis writes in the prologue to The Egoist Ltd. *Tarr:* "we should long ago have been swamped had it not been for the sea. The habits and vitality of the seaman's life and this vigorous element have protected us intellectually as the blue water has politically."

In general, Aldington's contemporary review of *Blast No. 1* still seems one of the best. It was a periodical, Aldington wrote in *The Egoist,* "in which the distressing and cow-like qualities of the nation are successfully blasted, and the admirable, unique and dominating characteristics piously blessed." [18] For there is nothing complicated about the Vorticist desire to liberate English art from Victorian sentimentalism: "We do not want the GLOOMY VICTORIAN CIRCUS in Piccadilly Circus." *Blast No. 1* aimed, Harriet Monroe writes, "to blow away, in thick black capitals half an inch high, the Victorian Vampire." [19] In *If This Be Treason* Pound says that it marked "the end of XIXth. century unsurocracy and mercantilism." [20] But while the Vorticists stood for emancipation from the English past, they considered that similar sentimentality could result from being Futurist—"We stand for the Reality of the Present

16. Hunt, *I Have This to Say,* p. 215 (where she adds a further misspelling herself).

17. Edward Wadsworth, *Sailing-Ships and Barges of the Western Mediterranean and Adriatic Seas* (London, Frederick Etchells and Hugh MacDonald, 1926).

18. Richard Aldington, "Blast," *The Egoist, 1,* No. 14 (July 15, 1914), 272.

19. Harriet Monroe, *A Poet's Life* (New York, Macmillan, 1938), p. 355.

20. Ezra Pound, *If This Be Treason* (Siena, privately printed for Olga Rudge, 1948), p. 30.

—not for the sentimental Future." If this would seem to conflict with Lewis' "presentist" critique of Futurism, it does not really do so:

Life is the Past and the Future.
The Present is Art.

Vortex was a rushing together of ages and art forms, "this strange synthesis of cultures and times," as Lewis called it in 1929, "the first projection of a world art." [21] Violet Hunt tells us that Lewis said to her at this time: "You think at once of a whirlpool. At the heart of the whirlpool is a great silent place where all the energy is concentrated. And there, at the point of concentration, is the Vorticist." [22] At this still center, both of the fluxes of life and of the concatenation of artistic periods, is what Pound calls the "point of maximum energy." The artistic will presides at this heroic place. "IT IS THE **VORTEX** OF WILL," declaims Gaudier, as he promises to "present my emotions by the ARRANGEMENT OF MY SURFACES." Lewis repeats this emphasis on will, in *Blast No. 2*, and the last words of the first issue hurl the claim at us:

Will and Consciousness are our
VORTEX.

This emphasis on energy and vitality, which was reinforced by the rhetorical vigor of the typography, was in direct opposition both to Royal Academicism and Cubist studio art. For Pound, in *No. 1*, Vorticism is "the most highly energized statement," while Gaudier seems to scream at us "VORTEX IS ENERGY!" But although Wadsworth retained this emphasis in his Unit One period in the thirties (as in his conversation, also, with Eric Newton in *The Listener* for March 20, 1935), and although Gaudier repeats it in his notebooks, I suspect that it was principally for Lewis a premise that all this energy should be solely intellectual energy.

21. Wyndham Lewis, "A World Art and Tradition," *Drawing and Design, 5*, No. 32 (Feb. 1929), 56.
22. Hunt, *I Have This to Say*, p. 211.

"Action" is a word Lewis always associates with emotion, and the first cardinal point of the *Blast* manifestoes was, "Beyond Action and Reaction we would establish ourselves." He repeats this in *No. 2:* "Our point is that he [the Vorticist] CANNOT have to the full the excellent and efficient qualities we admire in the man of action unless he eschews action and sticks hard to thought."

For Lewis, the energy concentrated in the center of this whirl-pool is artistic (or, for him, intellectual) activity. And it is to be aimed at trapping "some essential," to get to "the essential truth." Pound, in his article in *The Fortnightly Review,* agrees: the emphasis, he repeats, is on *"primary form"* rather than on "second intensity": "Vorticism is art before it has spread itself into flaccidity, into elaborations and secondary applications." And he goes on: "The image is not an idea. It is a radiant node or cluster; it is what I can, and must perforce, call a VORTEX, from which, and through which, and into which, ideas are constantly rushing." In his "ideo-grammic" method Pound is in the same revolt against Impres-sionism in the arts. Neither Pound nor Lewis wants *Einfühlung.* Pound (whom Gilbert Highet calls "a silly poseur and a third-rate poet") is looking for what he tells us in *Guide to Kulchur* Con-fucius demanded, "a type of perception, a kind of transmission of knowledge obtainable only from such concrete manifestation." [23] And in his memoir of Gaudier-Brezeska, where Hugh Kenner rightly observes that "the whole of Pound is present in embryo," [24] it is "intellect" Pound admires in "the men of 1914."

"The Siberia of the Mind," as *Blast No. 1* called England, does not seem to have been unduly disturbed by Vorticism. After all, London had had some three years of Marinetti, on and off, by now; and indeed, reviewing *No. 1, The Times* seems glad that it is a healthier movement than Futurism.[25] How much, then, was this art movement worth?

23. Pound sometimes spells "ideogrammic" with one *m.*

24. Hugh Kenner, *The Poetry of Ezra Pound* (London, Faber and Faber, 1951), p. 58.

25. "Blast," *The Times,* No. 40,564 (July 1, 1914), p. 8.

Some Vorticist apologists, usually to be found outside England, make extravagant claims for the blasters. Hugh Kenner believes that Vorticism was "the only time since 1600—when a congeries of masters was doing things in English that had not been done better on the continent." [26] Another critic, Av Teddy Brunius, has been equally enthusiastic, writing from Sweden.[27] To my mind Thrall Soby presents the most balanced view, and one which Lewis himself would not contest, namely that Vorticism was a liberating influence of great consequence for England, throwing English painting into the main stream of advanced European art, but it was far from an exact discipline.

The first part of this judgment was exactly what Lewis himself stated in *The Tyro No. 1* ("Roger Fry's Rôle of Continental Mediator") and in *The Dial* for the same year, 1921. Later, in his auto-biographical volumes, Lewis restated his complaint of the English facility for accepting the école de Paris as superior to English art. One should not underestimate Lewis' contribution in this respect. Only by looking at what there was in England before he staged his Vortex can one see his achievement here. Looking back on the period, Paul Nash tells us that in the spring of 1913, despite Fry's efforts, "the doctrine and practice of the New English Art Club represented all that was most typical of modern art in England." [28] Despite the fact that a few advanced artists like Roberts, Wadsworth, and Lewis himself showed with this Club before 1914, Lewis realized that it had fossilized. The New English Art Club began in the Marlborough Gallery in 1886 as a protest against Royal Academicism, and Whistler was a member of its first selection committee. It showed Sargent, Wilson Steer, and Sir William Orpen,

26. Hugh Kenner, "Remember That I Have Remembered," *The Hudson Review,* 3, No. 4 (Winter 1951), 603.

27. Av Teddy Brunius, *Pionjärer och Fullföljare i Modern Engelsk Konst, Lyrik och Kritik* (Stockholm, Natur och Kultur, 1952), pp. 17, 18, 27, 28, 30, 40, 57, 71, 75, 89, 126.

28. Paul Nash, *Outline* (London, Faber and Faber, 1949), p. 166. There is also an interesting article on Post-Impressionism and Futurism by H. E. Bates in *The Calcutta Review* for January 1916.

among others, and was for George Moore, in his *Modern Painting* of 1900, a go-ahead institution. But by the time of *Blast* its membership was chiefly academic, and it was the outlet for painters like Muirhead Bone, Conder, the sadly overestimated Sickert, and Harold Gilman (whom, however, Lewis admired), rather than for really creative and experimental art. By the nineteen twenties the juries for its exhibitions read like catalogues announcing the Slade School faculty—Henry Tonks, Randolph Schwabe, William Rothenstein, D. S. MacColl—and the dead hand had fallen.

Secondly, Lewis never claimed that Vortex was an exact discipline. It was a necessary interim. It "hustled the cultural Britannia, stepping up that cautious pace with which she prefers to advance." And Britannia was certainly goosed up the gangplank to Modern Art. Clive Bell detested Vortex. Pound's "primary form" was here of chief consequence. For, as Lewis pointed out in 1939, Vorticism sought forms directly expressive of vigor. Instead of sentimentalizing the machine, like the Futurists, Vortex went straight to the static ("the hard, the cold") *spirit* of the machine. Instead of worshiping the machine in flux, Vortex dominated the machine, by seeking its conceptual form. In *The Diabolical Principle* Lewis writes that we live in an age when "machinery went straight to nature and eliminated the middleman, Man." Thus the machine represented to the Vorticists the "form" of certain qualities, usually the principle of energy. A motorcar was a quintessence of energy, or speed, for the sake of which natural or quasi-natural elements (steel, glass, rubber, and so on) had been abstracted to make a functional form, and a form in which emotional subjectivity, Einfühlung, was minimal. The purely functional machine, Lewis wrote in *The Art of Being Ruled,* comes close to artistic abstraction. Later, in the section of *One-Way Song* called "Engine Fight-Talk," he satirizes these ideas as having gone too far in the thirties. Possibly these views persist today in the younger realist painters, like Michael Ayrton or Colleen Browning, who enjoy affirming the line instead of dissipating it (like the American "action" painters) in their art. But they persist more obviously, surely, in functional architecture;

and, writing in *The Architectural Review* in 1934, Lewis admits
that Vorticism was *"a substitution of architecture for painting."* [29]

On the whole, however, as Lewis later wrote, Vorticism had only
time to be a program. There are letters—especially some to Mc-
Knight Kauffer in 1919 concerning the formation of the "X" Group
of artists then—that show Lewis did not regard it as more at the
time. Amusingly enough, it has found its place, in delineating a
period, in several novels. In *Antic Hay* (which is mentioned in
The Red Priest), for instance, Theodore Gumbril Junior dreams
of owning a Lewis drawing, and one suspects that Lypiatt, with
"a face that ought by rights to have belonged to a man of genius,"
is a cruel parody of Lewis himself. (At Lypiatt's exhibition Mr.
Mercaptan says the word *Argal,* possibly a variant through the
grave-digger in *Hamlet* of Arghol.) In Waugh's *Vile Bodies* Johnnie
Hoop designs his invitations like *Blast* manifestoes, while at the
end of *Lady Chatterley's Lover* Duncan Forbes shows his Vorticist
paintings to Mellors ("They show a lot of self-pity and an awful
lot of nervous self-opinion, seems to me," Mellors remarks).[30] More
recently, Angus Wilson's *Anglo-Saxon Attitudes* concerns itself
with a scholar who was supposedly a friend of Lewis; here "a
graduate of Minnesota University and North-Western University"
is preparing a thesis on "The Intellectual Climate of England at
the Outbreak of the First World War," most of which is to be
devoted to D. H. Lawrence and Wyndham Lewis. If Vorticism,
then, is regarded as a stimulant (and a much-needed one) rather
than as a logical aesthetic, it has its place in the history of English
art. And to round out this sketch of "Lewis (Pictor)," as he liked
to call himself to Lord Carlow, it is interesting to glance at the reception accorded his art by T. E. Hulme.

29. Wyndham Lewis, "Plain Home-builder: Where Is Your Vorticist?" *The
Architectural Review: A Magazine of Architecture and Decoration, 76,* No. 456
(Nov. 1934), 156.

30. David Garnett, from a larger authority than my own, believes that Duncan
Grant was here the model for Duncan Forbes. David Garnett, *The Flowers of
the Forest* (London, Chatto and Windus, 1955), p. 37.

Chapter 9: The Intelligent Few

"Art always has been, and within limits must remain, the monopoly of the intelligent few." ["The Credentials of the Painter—2," *The English Review, 34* (April, 1922), 394.]

LEWIS has admitted that he saw Hulme as his mentor in art. What did Hulme have to say about Lewis' painting? First, we must agree that Hulme saw two different types of art, broadly corresponding to two different types of civilization. In fact, I have often thought it wiser to direct newcomers to Hulme to his art criticism before his philosophy of history, for Hulme was to my mind a sensitive art critic—he understood at once the most advanced movements of his day—with a bigoted *Weltanschauung* in rationalization of his cultural beliefs. So, when in *Speculations* Hulme tells us he is giving us Worringer's cultural periods, the reader should not take him at his own word; actually Hulme simplifies Worringer's cultural periods, reducing them arbitrarily.

Worringer, who is in turn indebted to Lipps (on whom Hulme was composing a book before he was killed), suggested three kinds of aesthetic man—"Der primitive Mensch," "Der klassische Mensch," and "Der orientalische Mensch,"—all prior to the modern period which he broadly defines as Gothic (though his reader should jettison any of the usual referents for this word). For Worringer, the first of these categories, primitive man, lived in a state of dualism with the natural world, and his art was an abstraction or call to absolute values in a shifting and incomprehensible universe. For this primitive man, art, Worringer suggested, was avoidance of life and resentment of nature. He is the perfect antipantheist. As

Worringer puts it: "Vom Leben verwirrt und geängstigt, sucht er das Leblose, weil aus ihm die Unruhe des Werdens eliminiert und eine dauernde Festigkeit geschaffen ist. Künstlerisch schaffen heisst für ihn, dem Leben und seiner Willkür auszuweichen . . . Von der starren Linie in ihrer lebensfremden abstrakten Wesenheit geht er aus." [1]

The rigid line—"starr" and "Starrheit" are words that are used constantly in this connection by Worringer—is the primitive's reduction to order. For Worringer this attempt to stabilize the world outside reached its high point in Oriental man. With the arrival of classical man on the scene, man and his world tend to unite harmoniously. No longer tortured by perception, no longer at odds with nature, classical man—wretch that he so obviously was for Worringer!—actually begins to enjoy life and, in his art, to idealize nature. It is at this point that Einfühlung enters into art appreciation.

It is in *Abstraktion und Einfühlung* that Worringer clarifies Einfühlung, which both Hulme and Sir Herbert Read translate as "empathy" ("imaginative projection of one's own consciousness into another being," according to Webster). Einfühlung is the enjoyable projection of the consciousness into a work of art, the consequent recognition of one's own emotions in it, and the general feeling of elation at such recognition—"Selbstgenuss." [2] It is, in other words, the way most people approach a painting today. Abstraktion is the reverse process, a withdrawal to calm and order, "Selbstentäusserungstrieb." [3] For both Worringer and Lewis the art of Abstraktion reaches its high watermark in Oriental man. For Hulme it seems to be at its best in Byzantine art. This Oriental is closer to the primitive than is Hellenic man. To some extent he still has the primitive's dislike of "life," but with the difference that he is contented with (rather than fearful of) the state of dualism, since he

1. Worringer, *Formprobleme*, p. 16.
2. Wilhelm Worringer, *Abstraktion und Einfühlung* (München, Piper, 1948), pp. 17–26.
3. Ibid., pp. 27–37.

has a transcendental, instead of immanent, view of the universe. For this Oriental man there is an exalted destiny, and the supernatural sources of life are admirable rather than horrible. In Oriental man the primitive's terror of nature is raised to respect and he feels humility before the eternal forces.[4]

This condition, so close to Lewis' own views stated in Chapter 6, produces not only abstract art but great abstract art, an art sharply outlined and wedded to the hard line: "Wie die Kunst des Urmenschen ist auch die Kunst des Orients streng abstrakt und gebunden an die starre ausdrucklose Linie und ihr Korrelat, die Fläche."

This division, between Abstraktion and Einfühlung, is the application Hulme puts on contemporary art in *The New Age*. So on January 15, 1914, Hulme finds "a new constructive geometric art," and singles out Lewis, Etchells, and Nevinson as its practitioners, welcome correctives to Roger Fry's post-Impressionism. Hulme now reacts quickly to what he sees. In his next article he elaborates the two kinds of art he finds before him, one "geometrical and abstract," the other "vital and realistic." Hulme here uses the word "vital" in a special sense, a "vital" art being not one filled with vitality in our usual use of the term but an art that takes pleasure in the reproduction of natural things (Einfühlung).[5] Hulme then goes on to object to the thesis, which he later (like Lewis) partially concedes, that extreme abstraction becomes academic, a mere mannerism. Granted, he continues, that the "vital and realistic" artists always need contact with the natural world, "geometrical and abstract" art is a creative process of another kind, concerned mainly with the method of expression. In passing he rather con-

---

4. Worringer, *Formprobleme*, pp. 24–7.
5. Hulme, *Speculations*, p. 53. "Vital and organic" art is characterized for Hulme in its difference from Byzantine or Egyptian art, and is unable to achieve "an austerity, a monumental stability, and permanence, a perfection and rigidity." Byzantine art, a separation-from rather than a joining-in, for Hulme, was non-"vital," and expressed "a kind of contempt for the world." (*Speculations*, pp. 9, 57, 77, 92.) It is scarcely necessary to point out how Lewis would sympathize with this view.

tradictorily holds up Cézanne as a model of this latter style—yet, linear as Cézanne may have been, he generally represented some aspect of the outside world. Meeting this contradiction in Cézanne Hulme seems to be led to admit that the artist must have contact with nature at some point, although nature need not be the source of his imagination ("There must be just as much contact with nature in an abstract art as in a realistic one; without that stimulus the artist could produce nothing").[6]

It is fascinating to watch Hulme grappling with these controversies so much in advance, and it is interesting to notice that he takes a midway point, coinciding considerably with Lewis' views in *The Caliph's Design*, and in tacit approval of the second of Lewis' own painting styles I mentioned above, his semi-abstract method.

So, coming on Kandinsky and total abstraction, Hulme is less happy. This emphasis on pure form, which he also finds in Lewis, David Bomberg, and Wadsworth (who praises Kandinsky and links him to the art of the East in *Blast No. 1*), is abstraction for its own sake, Hulme says, an excess and therefore a romantic heresy. Although he likes Lewis' drawing "The Enemy of the Stars," Hulme now finds invalid the banishing of all emotion for the sake of an intellectual interest in shapes.[7]

In an article on Bomberg Hulme moves further over to this side, and criticizes the Rebel Art Centre. The human mind, Hulme writes here, can only *"edit,"* not *"create,"* forms; for the abstract design to be valid, some contact must be made with the external world, for form alone does not produce an aesthetic emotion specific to form. Rather, abstraction simply touches off "ordinary everyday human emotions" by a new means, and therefore both artist and onlooker must be in touch with nature.[8]

Epstein, of course, fulfilled the requirements of this criticism

6. T. E. Hulme, "Modern Art—II, A Preface Note and Neo-Realism," *The New Age*, N.S., *14*, No. 15 (Feb. 12, 1914), 467–9.

7. T. E. Hulme, "Modern Art—III, The London Group," *The New Age*, N.S., *14*, No. 21 (March 26, 1914), 661–2.

8. Hulme, "Modern Art—IV, Mr. David Bomberg's Show," *The New Age*, N.S., *15*, No. 10 (July 9, 1914), 231–2.

better than any of the *Blast* group, and Hulme rose quickly to the sculptor's defense in *The New Age,* while Epstein executed that noble head of Hulme by which most of us remember the philosopher today. Hulme does not seem to have allowed Lewis the period of Vorticism as a necessary interim phase. Perhaps at the time Lewis himself was uncertain how long an interim this style was to be. Pound, on the other hand, is far more satisfied with art being a mere arrangement of shapes than Hulme, though Pound puts some odd interpretations on Lewis' art, calling it "nearly always emotional" and then going on to liken it to Bach. In general, what Hulme saw in Lewis' art was a healthy change to that "austerity," "bareness," "structure," which he hoped were characteristics of an entire cultural change. As he put it, Lewis' pictures turned the organic (Einfühlung) into the nonorganic (Abstraktion). Yet however persuasive the Worringer-Hulme aesthetic may be in its obvious welcome to Vorticism, it has obvious flaws. Hulme, who did not share Lewis' emphasis on beauty,[9] never explains why the satisfaction of a human need in art, as in Einfühlung, must necessarily be bad, for Abstraktion, the reordering of a chaotic universe, was certainly the satisfaction of a need for primitive man.

In conclusion, Lewis' own aesthetic is haunted by his sociological ideals. Art, a timeless thing, its values universal and static, must remain apart.[10] It proceeds only from "the exceptional individual,"

9. Hulme, *Speculations,* p. 84, where we read, "We naturally do not call these geometrical arts beautiful because beauty for us is the satisfaction of a certain need, and that need is one which archaic art never set out to satisfy." Cf. "our goddess is Beauty" (*Blast No. 2,* p. 79).

10. For Lewis, as for Benda, artistic truth should be objective, rather than functional. One should note, however, that Lewis occasionally denies that an artist can be truly impersonal; we find this denial in the encyclical given to Zagreus, and Zagreus himself later says that the paraphernalia of detachment in an artist may simply be a cloak for prejudice (*Apes,* pp. 125, 259). Lewis takes up this point in his book on Shakespeare, and I have confined it to this note because it does not really touch his main convictions. What he is really saying in *The Lion and the Fox* (pp. 284–91) is that the artist should have something to say, he should not be entirely uninterested in and uncommitted on the problems of his age; but the artist must remain apart from the action involving these problems: "Artistic creation is always a shut-off—and that is to say a *personal*—creation" (*Lion and Fox,* p. 286).

or (in a much-quoted sentence) "It is a constant stronghold, rather, of the purest human consciousness." [11] In his two articles on "The Credentials of the Painter," where he places the painter above all other artists as being attached to truth by the sense of sight, Lewis actually makes the suggestion that art should impose all laws of value in human society. This, we shall see, is what sharply distinguishes his thought from that of contemporary Thomism, for Lewis could never allow art to be used in the service of religion. Art for him is religion itself. And the system, the set of laws, under which he repeatedly asserts that he would have liked to work is one of intellectual aesthetic values. But not all artists wish to work within such a set of laws, especially as interpreted by Wyndham Lewis. In 1939 Sir William Rothenstein, who gives a generous estimate of Lewis' graphic work, adds: "If ever the Fascist party should come into power in England, I imagine Wyndham Lewis as the chief state artist; as Poet Laureate, Ezra Pound." [12]

The association, though suggestive, is not a happy one, for Lewis has never directly attached his creative art to the service of any Fascist, or indeed of any organized, politics. But like Benda he has consistently maintained that art *cannot* flourish in a contemporary democracy and that the artist must remain the obligatory enemy of that democracy.[13] " 'Our classifications,' " Tarr says, " 'are inartistic.' " Again Tarr declares, " 'You can't have "freedom" both ways and I prefer the *artist* to be free, and the crowd not to be "artists." ' " For Benda too the triumph of sensation over reason, hand in hand with our apriorist contemporary conscience, has fatally crippled the artistic and intellectual in our lives.[14] Or, as Lewis, makes Tarr say, " 'It is the artist's fate almost always to be exiled among the slaves.' "

11. *Time and Western Man,* p. 39.
12. Rothenstein, *Since Fifty,* p. 254.
13. Benda, *Épreuve,* pp. 134–6.
14. Ibid., pp. 58, 137, 162; Benda, *Trahison,* pp. 25–6.

PART III: TIME

"Exclaim with me: 'Oh World, oh Life, *oh Time!'*
And make each thought with *busybody* rhyme!"
One-Way Song, p. 123.

Chapter 10: The Many against the One

"On every hand some sort of *unconscious* life is recommended and heavily advertised, in place of the *conscious* life of will and intellect . . . the crowds were pitted against the Individual, the Unconscious against the Conscious, the 'emotional' against the 'intellectual,' the Many against the One." [*Time and Western Man,* pp. 318–20.]

IN HIS attack on what he calls "time" Lewis is simply criticizing romanticism in its contemporary garb. The "time-philosophers" he singles out as having chiefly "presided at, and speeded, the dissolution of an ancient culture" are writers rather than painters. It is true that Picasso is criticized in *Time and Western Man,* but on the whole it is literature, unfolding in time, rather than painting, unfolding in space, with which Lewis here has to do.

Time and Western Man is the principal English document in the whole neoclassical movement to arrest the attrition of what was considered to be "Western Man." Eliot's fear of the "hooded hordes," which he connects by footnote with Hermann Hesse's prediction of philistinism overcoming Europe in *Blick ins Chaos,* was part of a general fear of European dissolution by many intellectuals after the first World War and the Russian revolution. Indeed, Henri Massis' *Défense de l'Occident* appeared in Flint's translation in England the same year as *Time and Western Man.* Of course, there is much in Massis' work with which Lewis would disagree. "Asiatisme" and "bolchevisme" are the main forces weakening Europe for the Catholic convert Massis. Lewis would be unlikely to concede Massis the former peril (especially not as German orientalism, by now), because his graphic beliefs have usually led him to write well of the Orient. And although Massis links "asiatisme" and its evil influences with Proust and Gide, he is not *principally* concerned, as Lewis obviously is, in criticizing ideas of dissolution through literary practitioners. Still, Massis defends what Lewis defends in the name of the West: "Personnalité, unité, stabilité, autorité, continuité, voilà les idées mères de l'Occident." [1] "Time," for Lewis, is the opposite of these qualities. But Lewis wrote to Lord Carlow, and confessed in *Time and Western Man* itself, that he was exposing reprehensible elements in Western thought through authors, showing the concepts he chiefly opposes in operation on the plane of literature. And in the same way Benda claims that since a literature has been erected on Bergsonism, one has to analyze this canker through the literature concerned. [2]

If this is the case, one can justifiably approach Lewis' attack on "time" on its literary side first, and then move behind the "time-philosophers" to "time-philosophy" itself. At bottom, there lies Lewis' conviction that time and motion are synonymous, and that imperfection is synonymous with both. Zagreus says this; Lewis says this. And Yeats too, who approved of *Time and Western Man,* also seems to have seen time and subjective, or suggestive, literature as the same.

The root of Lewis' criticism of "time-philosophy" is to be found in a passage from *Time and Western Man,* which A. C. Ward also selects as the summary of his attack: [3] "The Time-doctrine, first promulgated in the philosophy of Bergson, is in its essence, to put it as simply as possible, anti-physical and pro-mental." [4] But for Lewis' "mental," here, we should of course substitute "psychological." The "mind," in the sense of the intellect, is what he imagines he is defending in the book. "Chairs and tables, mountains and stars, are animated into a magnetic restlessness and sensitiveness, and exist on the same vital terms as man. They are as it were the

1. Henri Massis, *Défense de l'Occident* (Paris, Plon, 1927), p. 11.
2. Julien Benda, *Le Bergsonisme ou une philosophie de la mobilité* (Paris, Mercure de France, 1913), p. 6.
3. A. C. Ward, *The Nineteen-Twenties* (London, Methuen, 1930), p. 68.
4. *Time and Western Man,* p. 449.

lowest grade, the most sluggish of animals. All is alive: and, in that sense, all is mental." [5]

This is exactly Benda's complaint about Bergsonism: "C'est le mouvement aujourd'hui qui est divin, le changement, l'absence de toute fixité." [6] Art alone, in Lewis' view, is able to confer the static on the objects it apprehends. For science is today constantly altering the objects under its scrutiny, and in one place Lewis actually demands that art should be the master of science, that the scientist should remain simply the "self-effacing highly technical valet" of the artist. And science, too, has today become popular, another dithyrambic heresy ("The audience participates fully: every one, from the smallest errand-boy, assists at the performance"). Naturally, this criticism has its political connotations for Lewis: "Science stands for the theory of *collective* life, art for the doctrine of *individual* life." In both *The Art of Being Ruled* and *Time and Western Man* Lewis alleges at length that science is manipulating the passions of the mob under a shield of bogus anonymity, and reducing us all to goggling children, a criticism it is difficult to ignore in, say, contemporary America. [7]

Since by this constant alteration, this continual revolutionizing of trends, science is "anti-physical," it devolves on the artist to safe-guard the intellect ("consciousness"). So it follows, then, that a literature interested in depicting subconscious states must be shunned; it is especially treacherous—the stream-of-consciousness technique is "a *public* stream." For Lewis personality is stability, and a literature of the subconscious, which he sees as the area of sensational life, threatens the principle of being, for "a man is only an individual when he is *conscious*." Here he argues side by side with all the more intelligent neoclassicists; in *Messages*, Fernandez writes, "L'image esthétique est irréductible à l'image psychologique." And thus we reach Lewis' severe, nay virulent, criticism of the "time-children," Gertrude Stein and James Joyce. Now admittedly

5. Ibid.
6. Benda, *Sur le succès du Bergsonisme*, p. 176.
7. *Art of Being Ruled*, pp. 4, 13, 266–7; *Time and Western Man*, pp. 313–19.

Lewis reviews in the same way a number of other writers under this head, but not only have I no space to deal with all these attacks individually, they are generally subsequent to, and derive from, the criticisms in *Time and Western Man*. His attacks on such diverse figures as Sartre, Virginia Woolf, D. H. Lawrence, or Faulkner ("moralist with a corn cob") add little new. The criticism of Hemingway ("the dumb ox") in *Men without Art* is an attack on the cult of "action" through this writer, a cult satirized earlier in *Tarr* in the person of Kreisler. In the Hemingway hero Lewis rebukes a civilization "where personality is the least thing liked" and which he sees rapidly approaching a military state. Lacking in will, the Hemingway hero (up to 1934, that is) was an objectionable representative of our society, a herdlike dolt *"to whom things happen"* (Zola's ideal of subjecting men and women to things). It is customary to shrug off this attack today, and Carlos Baker makes light of it in his book on Hemingway. In *Enemies of Promise* Cyril Connolly observes that "at the period at which Hemingway wrote his best books it was necessary to be a dumb ox. It was the only way to escape from Chelsea's Apes of God and from Bloomsbury's Sacred Geese." [8] Even so, it should be remembered that Lewis here opened up the one avenue by which serious attack is now made on Hemingway, such attack, that is, as dares to raise its head today. Actually, far more than Joyce, Hemingway is the total opposite of Lewis as a writer. In any case, is not Lewis' objection to Hemingway here an objection to Bergson, especially to Bergson's theory of *"perception pure"* as expressed in *Matière et mémoire?* [9] It is not unfair to say that Bergson was an ally of action; he saw knowledge and action (perhaps activity would be a better word) as intimately related, and indeed wrote, "Nous sommes faits pour agir autant et plus que pour penser." [10]

8. Cyril Connolly, *Enemies of Promise* (rev. ed. New York, Macmillan, 1948), p. 66.

9. Henri Bergson, *Matière et mémoire* (Paris, Félix Alcan, 1900), pp. 56–7.

10. Bergson, *L'Évolution créatrice*, p. 321.

Gertrude Stein, far more than Hemingway, exemplifies what Lewis is attacking in his thesis, "Subject as King of the Psychological World." Abdication of the intellect, deprivation of the external, physical, common-sense world of validity, suppression of authority, anarchy of the instincts, "an eternal mongrel itch to *mix,* in un-directed concupiscence, with *everything* that walks or crawls," these are the elements Lewis sees in the work of Stein and, to some extent, in that of Joyce, the prime "time-philosophers." Psychic concerns conquer physical veracity: "The distinction between sensation and sense-datum vanishes. You are forced to a fusion of the world of objects with the fact of apprehension, so that when you see a tree you *are* the tree." Stein is a dithyrambic spectator: "she, too, *became* the people she wrote about." Stein's infantilism drives Lewis to distraction. "The spurious child-language of Miss Stein, cadenced and said twice over in the form of the hebrew recitative," leads him to torrents of protest, which it is unnecessary to repeat here: "she writes usually so like a child—like a confused, stammering, rather 'soft' (bloated, acromegalic, squinting and spectacled, one can figure it as) child." In *Satire and Fiction* he writes, "Stein is just the german musical soul leering at itself in a mirror, and stick-ing out at itself a stuttering welt of swollen tongue." This child style, which Lewis believes to be derived from Isaiah, is political in effect: it is "the dark stammering voice of a social dissolution." For by this method, the instincts are invited to establish a dogma, matter is made to overcome mind, and the psyche conquers that principle of authority, the intellect.

The last is accomplished by Stein in her attack on the word, which is the literary representative of the intellect ("Hatred of the *word* goes hand in hand with hatred of the intellect, for *the word* is, of course, its sign").[11] Again, the French antiromanticists agree. Both Lasserre and Maurras (in *Le Romantisme féminin*) had al-

11. *Art of Being Ruled,* p. 404. Cf. "*Hostility to the word* goes hand in hand with propaganda for the intuitional, mystical chaos" (*Time and Western Man,* p. 352).

ready seen verbal experiment in literature an ally of a wider anarchy, particularly when in the hands of women or "métèques." Benda complains that Bergsonism sets up "la superiorité du vagissement sur la parole," [12] while Gonzague Truc, in *Classicisme d'hier et classiques d'aujourd'hui*, writes, "le classique . . . entend s'expliquer par la parole, non se purger par l'éclat des cris ou le hoquet des sanglots." [13]

Because of this, for attacking the intellect via language, Stein and Joyce are the chief representatives of decay in the name of "time." We shall find both collected and flayed in Lewis' satirical hades, *The Childermass,* and in this work the one thing the (unpleasant) Bergsonian Bailiff hates is the word, or *logos*.[14] This is the purpose of Lewis' satire in the second canto of *One-Way Song,* called "The Song of the Militant Romance." Stanzas ii-viii of this section of the poem show the romanticist speaking for the clattering, splenetic, and frenziedly anti-intellectual, and stanza ix concludes:

I sabotage the sentence! With me is the naked word.
I spike the verb—all parts of speech are pushed over on their backs.
I am the master of all that is half-uttered and imperfectly heard.
Return with me where I am crying out with the gorilla and the bird!

"The stammering ogress, 'Trudy' Stein," with her "gargantuan mental stutter," is not only guilty of the child cult for Lewis, she shares in its twin, imbecility. He frequently likens her work to the mouthings of madness, makes her persona vomit in *Malign Fiesta,* and in one place regrets that "The massive silence of the full idiot is, unfortunately, out of her reach."

It must be admitted that it is precisely for her cult of the child that Stein is often defended by her champions, like Edwin Muir or Laura Riding who calls Stein "the darling priest of cultured

12. Benda, *Le Bergsonisme,* p. 59.
13. Gonzague Truc, *Classicisme d'hier et classiques d'aujourd'hui,* "Études françaises," dix-huitième cahier, 1er mars 1929 (Paris, Société d'Édition "Les Belles Lettres"), p. 3.
14. *Childermass,* p. 200.

infantilism to her age." [15] Nor should, to balance Lewis' criticism, the idea of Stein as a representative of *transition* (which he continually throws out) be tolerated. It is a fact that *transition* published Stein faithfully, their first issue in April 1927 containing the famous line "suppose a rose is a rose is a rose is a rose." But in February 1935, after the publication of Stein's pseudo-autobiography called *Autobiography of Alice B. Toklas,* Jolas published a special supplement critical of her work and refuting her claims, allowing a number of French contemporaries to express their disapproval of her in a manner scarcely less disobliging than Lewis' own. *transition,* however, played a principal role in the controversy between Lewis and Joyce, and as this controversy involved two major literary intellects of our time, it would be best to look at it in detail.

15. Laura Riding, *Contemporaries and Snobs* (London, Jonathan Cape, 1928), p. 189.

Chapter 11: Master Joys and Windy Nous

"Master Joys of Potluck, Joys of Jingles, whom men called Crossword-Joys for his apt circumsolutions but whom the Gods call just Joys or Shimmy, shut and short.—'Sure and oi will bighorror!' sez the dedalan Sham-up-to-date with a most genteelest soft-budding gem of a hip-cough. 'Oh solvite me'—bolshing in ers fist most mannerly." [*The Childermass*, p. 172.]

LEWIS first met Joyce in the summer of 1920, taking him as a gift from Ezra Pound an old pair of shoes, shoes to appear, incidentally, in *Finnegans Wake*. The introduction, effected by Eliot, took place in Paris and resulted in the head of Joyce drawn by Lewis and reproduced in *Blasting and Bombardiering*. Both writers had previously published with The Egoist Ltd., and Joyce owned copies of both *Tarr* and *The Caliph's Design*. There are warm letters from Lewis to Joyce shortly after this, congratulating him on *Ulysses* and hoping the best for it. And in the first issue of *transition*, dated April 1927, Lewis signed the appeal protesting against Roth's piracy of Joyce's work. In September of this year, however, *Time and Western Man* appeared, expanding the previous attack on Joyce in *The Art of Being Ruled*. In December the editors of *transition* assailed Lewis with "First Aid to the Enemy," to which Lewis retorted with "The Diabolical Principle," first printed in *The Enemy No. 3* of January 1929. For already, in *transition* for September 1927, "Work in Progress" (or "warping process," as it is called in the *Wake*) had featured the famous lecture by that "spatialist" Welshman, Professor Jones, and in February 1928 the author of *Spice and Westend Woman* is ridiculed. But in "spice and westend woman" (or *Time and Western Man*) Lewis had concurrently jibbed at "the gathering material of a new book, which, altogether almost, employs the manner of Nash" [1] by Joyce. In June 1928 Lewis published *The Childermass:* Section I (or Part I, as it is the American edition), from which point on it can fairly be said that he has anathematized Joyce's work, while according it the first importance.

In his admirable book on Joyce published in 1941 Harry Levin pointed out that "Joyce has stuck his tongue out at Lewis in *Finnegans Wake.*" [2] About a decade later William York Tindall went into the personification of Lewis in *Finnegans Wake* a little more fully, but it is only more recently still, perhaps because of the rather obvious and much gentler caricature of Joyce in *The Human Age* (touched on at the end of this book), that contemporary critics in general have become aware of the controversy between the two men. Hugh Kenner, the Catholic apologist for Lewis, had obviously been aware of it, however, since he knew Lewis' work well, and in his brilliant *Dublin's Joyce* he has, with characteristic perspicuity, written the most extended examination of the Lewis-Joyce *débat* to date.[3] While being extremely indebted to it, I cannot always agree with his Shaun identifications, nor is he, one observes, very interested in dating the quarrel (indeed, it appears rather as a jolly lark between the two men in his pages). This last is worth investigating, all the same.

Already I have shown the almost simultaneous mutual satirizing by the two writers, and a glance at the epigraph to this chapter will reinforce this feeling. Joyce (or Joys) is here "the dedalan Shamup-to-date"; in *transition* for October 1927, eight months before *The Childermass,* Shem answered "the first riddle of the universe . . . when is a man not a man?" with "Shem was a sham." [4] Yet

1. *Time and Western Man,* p. 122.
2. Harry Levin, *James Joyce* (Norfolk, Conn., New Directions, 1941), p. 198.
3. Hugh Kenner, *Dublin's Joyce* (Bloomington, Indiana University Press, 1956), pp. 362–9.
4. James Joyce, *Finnegans Wake* (New York, Viking Press, 1947), p. 170.

this mention, so often used by Lewis against Joyce in *The Childermass,* may in turn have been taken by Joyce from *Time and Western Man,* for he is likely to have seen an early copy of this work in which Lewis refers to both him and Gertrude Stein as "shams." In the same passage above, "Joys of Jingles" refers us to Lewis' main charge, in both *The Art of Being Ruled* and *Time and Western Man,* that Joyce had merely copied Dickens' method of presenting the thought-stream of Alfred Jingle in *Pickwick Papers.* (Paul Shorey thought that Joyce's technique came from the battle soliloquies of Hector in the Iliad.[5])

Now, in "Juan before St. Bride's," Shem (as Joyce) is called "Mr. Jinglejoys," suggesting Lewis' Jingle of *The Art of Being Ruled* and *Time and Western Man* and Joys of *The Childermass.* This reference appeared in the summer of 1928; moreover, there is a likely reference to *The Childermass* by Joyce as much as a year before this, in *transition* for August 1927. The word "innocent," in the passage relating to *The Waste Land* and beginning "Premver a promise of a pril," is now closely followed by the word "massacre," a massacre of the innocents giving us, of course, the Childermass. However, Nathan Halper has spotted that the version of this chapter that appeared in *The Criterion* in 1925 contained only the word "innocent," and lacked "massacre." Thus between this year and August 1927 Joyce saw fit to add the latter word and give the passage one of its obvious present interpretations, namely the massacre of the innocent Joyce by Lewis' attacks (probably the one on *A Portrait*). Moreover, there had been two references in *Ulysses* to a "slaughter" of the innocents, the first through Bloom in the Lestrygonian episode.

Coincidental collocation or Joycean prophecy? Most probably, I suggest, oral information passing between the two men, since the same thing happened in reverse, and here the problems of dating become fascinating. In *The Apes of God* (or "massacre of the insignificants," as Lewis called it) Lewis characterizes Joyce as

5. Paul Shorey, *What Plato Said,* Chicago, Ill., University of Chicago Press, 1933, p. 64.

a second-rate writer and self-publisher called Jamesjulius (i.e. James Joyce) Ratner, a Jew and the "Split-Man" of Part v of this work. Zagreus, for example, tells us that he "emerged from the East End, with Freud for his Talmud," and when the absurd naïf Dan Boleyn (who has a father called Stephen in Dublin, by the by) meets him, we read: "He had never seen a Jew before—and he hoped from the bottom of his great Irish heart that he might never see one again!" A further parallel between Dan Boleyn and Anne Boleyn (on whose account, after all, the father of English humanism, Sir Thomas More, suffered) and the fact that the Joyce personae in Lewis' works are usually called "rats" tempt one to digress further in this direction, but the interesting thing here is that Ratner is editor of a high-brow weekly called *Man X,* which I take to be Lewis' Joycean pun on *transition* via the "official" photographer (and photographer of Joyce, too) for that periodical, Man Ray (X ray —*Man X*). In this journal "it was possible for Juliusjimmie to puff and fan that wan perishable flame of the occasional works of his old friend Jimjulius." And so on.

Now although Lewis had read and reviled *A Portrait of the Artist,* he had not seen *Stephen Hero* and could not have seen *in print* any overt reference to the "epiphany" of the inspired artist's moment of supreme apprehension, except for Stephen's fairly arcane reference to his "epiphanies on green oval leaves" in the Proteus section of *Ulysses* (which would not, in any case, have given Lewis the clue to a method of composition). Yet we can at once see that Ratner's method of writing is thoroughly Joycean, for Lewis at any rate. It is described as "auto-parley," or "automatic writing," consisting of "continual impassioned asides" and "thrilling words in isolation, of high-brow melodrama, and the rest of the 'sickening' tricks of the least ambitious, sham-experimental, second-rate literary cabotinage." What seems to me almost certain evidence, then, of some oral connection, or unpreserved letters, between the two writers is the fact that Lewis makes Ratner compose in a supposedly epiphanic manner, thus: "A factory. Two freemasons. A cloud threatened the tail of the serpent. A little child picked a forget-me-not. She lifted a chalice. It was there. *Epiphany.* There were three distinct vibrations." [6] It but remains to add, in this context, that Ratner, once called a "bilious greasespot," is perhaps the most unpleasant character Lewis has ever depicted. A "split-man" in the sense of lacking in cultural continuity, Ratner goes to Lord Osmund's party in a fancy-dress costume filled with associations all detestable to Lewis (Madame Blavatsky, D. H. Lawrence, Quetzalcoatl): "My very fly-buttons are allusive," he says proudly to himself, looking in the mirror at this get-up which reminds one also of HCE's outfit at the start of Book I, chapter 2 of the *Wake* ("HCE —His Agnomen and Reputation"), the Earl's costume later assumed by Shaun and not unlike the clothes Lewis is said to have sported in his own youth. "Masochismus, thy name is Ratner!" Zagreus says to him. Finally, to revert to my specimen passage as epigraph, Lewis' "shut and short" may throw back to the huge "SHUT" Shem's house has on it, just before the appearance of *The Childermass,* while we equally wonder if the "solvite" refers to the *"Solvitur!"* Shaun, in Joyce's work, had earlier given to Shem.

Of course, Lewis makes no pretense to academic standards when judging Joyce in *Time and Western Man,* but rather immediately classes him with all he dislikes most. He is guilty of what Professor Jones in the *Wake* calls "Demonocracy." "The method of *Ulysses* imposes a softness, flabbiness and vagueness everywhere in its bergsonian fluidity." [7] Other "time-philosophers," however, must be found for the genesis of this hateful work, and so we read, "This torrent of matter is the einsteinian flux." Bergson and Einstein. Well, either Lewis knew of Joyce's interest in these masters, or the latter's gift of prophecy was something he need not have joked about. For in *transition* for September 1927 occurs the lecture we now have in *Finnegans Wake,* given by the "spatialist" Professor Jones (as common a name in Wales as Lewis); Jones, as many have already recognized, partially prolongs the characterization of Lewis as

6. *Apes,* p. 156; italics in the text.
7. *Time and Western Man,* p. 120.

Shaun, although in the lesson chapter Shaun shadows into Yeats and Hopkins. When asked whether he would help a colleague like Shem, "a poor acheseyeld from Ailing . . . dropping hips teeth . . . the blind blighter," he categorically refuses. He is apparently something of a painter ("Every admirer has seen my goulache of Marge") and he begins a lecture on the "dime-cash problem." He dismisses the "sophology of Bitchson" (Bergson) as well as "the whoo-whoo and where's hair theorics of Winestain" (the who's who and where's here of Einstein). He refers to a "postvortex" lecture he has heard and, in particular, to Lévy-Bruhl, author in real life of *La Mentalité primitive,* a "time" man obviously as he supports the idea that the all (or "Allswill") is *"when."* Jones, on the other hand, in company with Professor Llewellys ap Bryllars, F.D. (another pseudoscholarly Welshman), finds "the all is *where* in love as war." [8] It is Professor Jones who, in the study period of the *Wake,* interrupts Dolph and Kev in an interpolation that paraphrases Parnell's statement concerning English suppression of Irish nationalist aspiration, and which Joyce seems here to apply to the arresting of Irish literary genius by English critics as in "that most improving of roundshows, *Spice and Westend Woman* (utterly exhausted before publication, indiapepper edition shortly)." By implication, then, Lewis here becomes "the beast of boredom," thus jibing with that other Shaun persona Yawn (*transition* for February 1928), whence Brawn, Jaunty Jaun, Don Juan, and so forth.

The important thing, for us, is Jones's reply to the initial question put. As Tindall has told us, Joyce was impartial on the subject of time versus space.[9] In the caricature of himself he made as Shem it is now clear that considerable concessions were made to Lewis' charges, for *Finnegans Wake,* alone among Joyce's works, shows him taking cognizance of criticism (including that of Rebecca West). Time and space came to represent for Joyce here one aspect of that duality by which modern life is haunted; in the *Wake* every

8. Joyce, *Finnegans Wake,* pp. 148–51.
9. W. Y. Tindall, *James Joyce* (New York, Scribner's, 1950), p. 92.

Shem has its Shaun—be it Lewis, Gogarty, Stanislaus, De Valera, Cranly, or whomever—and Yeats is one of the very few (in the lesson period mentioned) to become almost a full HCE, a Shem plus Shaun. Stephen had said that an aesthetic image is to be presented in time *or* space, both of which the artist may presumably employ. But Joyce was extraordinarily acute in his Lewis-Shaun identifications, for although neither of the two brothers could be adequate by himself (and they are indeed rescued by ALP in a union of the Muse) the Lewisian modulation of Shaun uses only space and refuses to come to terms with Shem. In his lampoon of Lewis Joyce was as fair as Lewis was unfair to him.

For, of course, Lewis' "Analysis of the Mind of James Joyce" is packed with contradictions. At one moment he says that *Ulysses* has classical affinities, the next he writes that it buries "the classical unities of time and place." With one hand he throws off the idea that Joyce, being "not so much an inventive intelligence as an executant," cares little for matter: "He is become so much a writing-specialist that it matters very little to him *what* he writes." Two pages later Lewis affirms that Joyce possesses "an appetite that certainly will never be matched again for the actual *matter* revealed in his composition." Nor can the arrogant picture of Joyce Lewis draws be very well reconciled with the notion that he has a "herd-mind," other than by some such philosophic perversity as that "The authentic revolutionary . . . will rebel against everything—not least rebellion." (Will he? one wonders.) Not only is Lewis' charge that "There is not very much reflection going on at any time inside the head of Mr. James Joyce" echoed by Harvey Wickham in *The Impuritans* ("Joyce never did much conscious thinking"), but Kenner has shown how Joyce put it in the *Wake:* "There was not very much windy Nous blowing at the given moment through the hat of Mr. Melancholy Slow!" Windy might here be used in the English sense of scared, while nous of course comes from the Greek word for mind.

No, at first glance all this seems like an almost deliberately obtuse misunderstanding of *Ulysses*. Yet, like Picasso, Joyce is highly praised by Lewis also; he is to be placed "very high in contemporary letters." In 1935 he is "a great literary artist." [10] In 1950 his work is *"of its kind* a masterpiece." [11] Still, Joyce shares with Stein in verbal anarchy, in the destruction of the personality on behalf of the psychic flux, in the lack of linear or plastic qualities in his prose, and in that mark of fashion—"the sign of the herd-mind." Lewis fictionally implements this criticism in *The Childermass.*

In the discussion of this satire at the end of the present study, it will be shown how Joyce appears as James Pullman, governess or nanny to Satterthwaite (Gertrude Stein). Here, however, it is pertinent to note that the former of these characterizations merges into Master Joys, a sly, sham, left-wing, pedantic writer with definite physical and literary associations with Joyce. "A cute little Cyclops with his one sad watery glim," he has "Vico the mechanical for guide in the musty labrinths of the latter-days to train him to circle true and make orbit upon himself." Joys freely admits that he is a fake, or sham: "arrah we're born in a thdrop of bogjuice and we pops off in a splutter of shamfiz or sham pain." The Bergsonian Bailiff of this work quotes Joys as follows: "Then as for that crossword polyglottony in the which I indulges misself for recreation bighorror, why bighorror isn't it aysy the aysiest way right out of what you might call the postoddydeucian dam dirty cul of a sack into which shure and bighorror I've bin and gone and thropped misself and all, since s' help me Jayzers oiv sed all I haz to say and there's an end of the matter?" [12] To this a character called Chris replies, "Oh capital sir! I recognize him!" It is not, in fact, hard to recognize the original of Joys, a "giltedged giltie conshie of a playboy of westend letters," who is, "half Orange and quarter Bog-

10. Wyndham Lewis, "Martian Opinions," *The Listener, 14,* No. 340 (July 17, 1935), 125.

11. *Rude Assignment,* p. 55.

12. *Childermass,* p. 175.

apple it is probable and in any case naturally half-hearted about Isis and Kadescha Papa and all that, not to say generally laodicean and a bit elegantly lily-languid as I knew, but his god is Chance and that as it chances is mine so as another narfter thort (talking all the time beeang ontong to you in the patois picked up in Targums, Titbits, Blicking Homilies, Centuruolas, Encyclepeeds, Boyle's Dictionary, the Liber Albus, Tamil and Lap Vademecums, set to the tune of the best Nash-patter)." [13] It is not hard when we recall that in *Time and Western Man* Lewis compared Joyce's technique with that of Nashe—thus in the *Wake* Professor Jones scoffs at "his craft ebbing, invoked by the unirish title, Grindings of Nash." Similarly, we observe that "Windy Nous" knew of Joyce's use of the celebrated *Tit-Bits,* the defense of which in 1881 by Newnes along the line "What the Public Wants" is frequently assailed elsewhere by Lewis himself. Finally, Joyce returned Lewis' skit on his accent; the ultra-British author of *Spice and Westend Woman,* wearing an Eton collar, opposes Irish upstarts in such terms as, "you must, how, in undivided reawlity draw the line somewhawre."

From these works, then, Lewis clearly shows himself familiar with *Ulysses,* "Work in Progress," and, most important, with *A Portrait of the Artist as a Young Man.* From the evidence of his close knowledge of Joyce's technical aims advanced above, I do not think it unfair to conclude that calling Joyce a "time-philosopher" was a *deliberate* misunderstanding, one with the attack on Eliot as a "pseudoist" in *Men without Art.* Few if any critics, however unfriendly to Joyce in the intention (as Rebecca West in *The Strange Necessity*), have chosen the basis of "time" on which to arraign Joyce's *oeuvre.* Most critics realize the reverse to have been true. Stuart Gilbert writes, "The structure of *Ulysses* (though to a less extent than that of 'Work in Progress') indicates that Joyce aspires to outsoar the category of time." [14] Claude-Edmonde Magny adds,

13. Ibid., p. 174.
14. Stuart Gilbert, *James Joyce's "Ulysses"* (London, Faber and Faber, 1930), p. 355.

"Right from *The* [*sic*] *Portrait of the Artist* Joyce is seen as essentially preoccupied with eliminating, through his description of it, the temporal succession of events from the world." [15] The simultaneity of time in *Finnegans Wake,* the representation of flux, a river, by a woman in the same work, are clearly in harmony with Lewis' aesthetic requirements; surely all the "men of 1914" were in harmony here, for April, month of change, was disliked by Eliot, while Pound actually called Joyce "classic." [16]

In short, unless we allow for the idea of malice, Lewis' criticism of Joyce as a "time-philosopher" is almost inexplicable; perhaps, indeed, it is the "cawraidd's blow" [17] dealt by Taff in the *Wake,* and so similar to that given Stephen by the English Private Carr in *Ulysses.* We notice that it is always the Shaun personification who is belligerent: thus Kev (whose police element reminds one of Lewis' attitude in *One-Way Song*) strikes Dolph, Chuff wrestles Glugg, and so on. For critics have by now arrived at some agreement that the conversation between Stephen and Lynch in *A Portrait* partly exhibits Joyce's own early aesthetic. Apart from the more obvious autobiographical elements, comparison can be made between Stephen's statements to Lynch and Joyce's own Paris notebooks, as given in Herbert Gorman's *James Joyce.*[18] Stephen refers, in fact, to "a book at home" in which he has recorded questions and answers such as Gorman publishes. Here Stephen calls the aesthetic emotion "static": "The mind is arrested and raised above desire and loathing." [19] He later returns to this idea of rest, which characterizes good art for him, and which we find in the Paris notebooks: "All art, again, is static for the feelings of

15. C.-E. Magny, "A Double Note on T. S. Eliot and James Joyce," *T. S. Eliot: A Symposium,* p. 209.

16. Pound, *Pavannes and Divisions,* p. 159.

17. Joyce, *Finnegans Wake,* p. 344.

18. Herbert Gorman, *James Joyce* (New York, Rinehart, 1948), pp. 95–100.

19. James Joyce, *A Portrait of the Artist as a Young Man, The Portable James Joyce,* edited with an Introduction by Harry Levin (New York, Viking Press, 1949), p. 470.

terror and pity on the one hand and of joy on the other hand are feelings which arrest us." [20] What Stephen calls "an aesthetic stasis" is the ideal reaction caused by a work of art. He then goes on to explain a theory of rhythm to Lynch and to elaborate his idea of art as "the human disposition of sensible or intelligible matter for an asthetic end."

Here the Paris notebooks are particularly interesting for in them Joyce puts a series of questions to himself, reduced in *A Portrait,* as to what constitutes a work of art, and it becomes clear that the necessary "human disposition" (the word is surely used in the French sense), producing the ideal "stasis of the mind," must to a large extent be brought about by the intellect. This is presented to Lynch by Stephen in terms of admiration of female beauty. Stephen's requirements of beauty, which are Aquinas' (wholeness, harmony, radiance), are those of the mind, which have appealed to different kinds of men in different stages of development, rather than being mere desire for reproduction of the species (emotion).

Joyce's own notations from Aristotle, as well as the library scene in *Ulysses,* show how much store Joyce set on the intellect from the first. Surely Lewis must have sympathized, when reading this scene, with Aristotle representing the rock of dogma facing Plato the whirlpool. But although Stephen well knows which of the two, Aristotle or Plato, would have banished him from his commonwealth,[21] Bloom of course steers neatly between this Scylla and Charybdis. Again, although Stephen and Bloom merge at the end of the work (Blephen and Stoom), the idea of Stephen standing for the Hellenic, the intellectual, the artistic, as against Bloom, the Hebraist, the sensualist, the scientific, should by rights have made Lewis far friendlier toward Stephen than he was, unless indeed he was incensed by their very merging.

Yet for Stephen, as for Lewis, the inspired artist had to remain

20. Gorman, *Joyce,* p. 97.
21. James Joyce, *Ulysses* (New York, Random House, Modern Library ed., 1934), p. 184.

godlike and apart, and the moment of epiphany, the artist's flash of supreme apprehension in which he should have utter faith, had to be a revelation of *"quidditas,* the *whatness* of a thing"—exactly, in fact, Lewis' "essential." It is described by Stephen as follows: "The instant wherein that supreme quality of beauty, the clear radiance of the esthetic image, is apprehended luminously by the mind which has been arrested by its wholeness and fascinated by its harmony is the luminous silent stasis of esthetic pleasure." [22] And, as I have emphasized, this moment of quasi-divine revelation, so Stephen suggests, may come about by an image presented in space *or* in time, for "What is audible is presented in time, what is visible is presented in space." There is no evaluative differentiation and it may have been this very impartiality, operating in the first of "Work in Progress," that decided Lewis that Joyce deserved an over-all diatribe. And this, too, is what surely distinguishes such artistic apprehension from Proust's "moment privilégié," with which it has been compared by Marcel Brion, for Proust's epiphanic moment, of which the *madeleine* episode is the most popularly known proto-type, was itself a moment in flux, changing even as presented.

Joyce's epiphany, although early unspecified, seems to have been rather an attempt to fix perception and appreciation. And in this fixing, this "disposition," the intellect is to operate considerably —this can be substantiated in the fuller description of the theory in *Stephen Hero* (which, again, Lewis would not have seen before *The Childermass*). Here once more we find statements that Lewis should by rights openly applaud. For Stephen, who is to tell the President that "My entire esteem is for the classical temper in art," does not yet want to make any facile association between classical and Hellenic. So he says:

> Classicism is not the manner of any fixed age or of any fixed country: it is a constant state of the artistic mind. It is a temper of security and satisfaction and patience. The romantic temper,

22. Joyce, *Portrait,* p. 479.

so often and so grievously misinterpreted, and not more by others than by its own, is an insecure, unsatisfied, impatient temper which sees no fit abode here for its ideals and chooses therefore to behold them under insensible figures . . . The classical temper on the other hand, ever mindful of limitations, chooses rather to bend upon these present things and so to work upon them and fashion them that the quick intelligence may go beyond them to their meaning which is still unuttered.[23]

Although we must not, of course, confuse Joyce (especially the later Joyce) with Stephen, as did Lewis who called that character "a neat, carefully-drawn picture of Joyce," it is nonetheless interesting to note that in *Stephen Hero* Stephen toys "with a theory of dualism which would symbolise the twin eternities of spirit and nature in the twin eternities of male and female." Shem and Shaun, Earwicker's two sons in the *Wake,* also personified as the schoolchildren Dolph and Kev, and again as the comedians Butt and Taff (obviously Mutt and Jeff) who turn into Mutt and Jute and into Muta and Juva, these stand for time and space, ear and eye, and in some measure for Joyce and Lewis. The two are, of course, representative of a classical antinomy; Lewis himself was not necessary to suggest it. But he proved extremely useful to Joyce in implementing it in the context of philistine (like Mulligan) to artist, of extrovert to introvert, of the stone of permanence to the elm of mutability.

There are a host of such uses throughout the book, from the moment when we first meet the two brothers as witness and accused in the early trial sequence that is to mirror the trial haunting Earwicker himself. Father's boy and ladies' man (Lewis replied by making Ratner cheaply popular with women), it is Shaun who tells the fable of the Ondt (space and the philistine) and the Grace-

23. James Joyce, *Stephen Hero* (Norfolk, Conn., New Directions, 1944), p. 78.

hoper (time and the artist), which Lewis would have read in *transition* for March 1928.

Here we begin by learning that the Ondt (Lewis) thinks the Gracehoper (Joyce) is wasting his time by writing works like *Ho, Time, Timeagen Wake!*—"What a bagateller it is!" he says. The Gracehoper, like Joyce (and ironically like Lewis now), is "blind as batflea." He has "tossed himself in the vico" and signifies "chronic's despair." But after mildly accepting the Ondt's reproof, he says:

> *"Your genus its worldwide, your spacest sublime!*
> *But, Holy Saltmartin, why can't you beat time?"* [24]

So for our purposes the lesson of the fable is once more that Joyce, in the Gracehoper, can see Lewis' point of view, but Lewis, in the Ondt, refuses to see his. Joyce seems to have understood his "Windy Nous" rather well.

Lewis is also useful to Joyce in the recurrent theme of plagiarism, built around the hidden, lost, or stolen manuscript of the *Wake*. Joyce must early have known how interested Lewis was in this; one of the main themes, if not the main theme, of "The Roaring Queen" (1936) is literary larceny. In the "Premver a promise of a pril" passage mentioned, for example, and referring to Eliot, "keepy little Kevin" (Lewis) is accused of plagiarism, but the accusation is nearly always in reverse. In the "Shem the Penman" section there is a long passage on Shem's "pelagiarist pen" which has been responsible for so many "pseudostylic shamiana" and "piously forged palimpsests." Elsewhere I have alluded to Lewis' idea that his *The Enemy of the Stars* had been used by Joyce for the Circe episode of *Ulysses*, whereat in the *Wake* Jones accuses Alderman Whitebeaver of plagiarizing his publications "to the irony of the stars." Later, when asked why he hates Shem so much, Shaun gruffly replies that one reason is "stolentelling" or "robblemint."

24. Joyce, *Finnegans Wake*, p. 419.

Nathan Halper, meanwhile, believes he finds a suggestion in the *Wake* that the *Time and Western Man* attack is itself in reality indebted to the Nausicaä episode of *Ulysses*. La Calumnia, the snake of schlangder, grows in the garden! As any Joycean knows, one could be lured into almost indefinite attributions of this sort. There are probably scores of allusions to Lewis in the *Wake* that I have not mentioned; Kenner cleverly identifies references to *Cantleman's Spring-Mate* ("cattlemen's spring meat" and "gentlemen's spring modes"), and I should add that the situation is further complicated by the presence on the scene of Joyce scholarship now of a real-life Professor Jones, William Powell Jones, author of *James Joyce and the Common Reader* (Norman, University of Oklahoma Press, 1955), to whom absolutely no reference is intended here, of course.

I have instanced how Shaun-Lewis refuses to come to philosophic terms with Shem-Joyce. This is perhaps not quite so. Joyce seems to suggest, at the end of Professor Jones's refusal, that two men like Lewis and himself, so closely united in so many ways, should cease to quarrel, for were they not both admirers of Aristotle: "were we bread by the same fire and signed with the same salt, had we tapped from the same master"? Again, "we were in one class of age like to two clots of egg."

Nor is this suggestion of an appeal for truce an entirely isolated one. In accepting the Ondt's reproof, the Gracehoper says that they are really twins. And in Book IV the Professor, who had earlier asked for the time factor (*"ill tempor"*) to be killed, is told to forget the controversy and have a drink. We are reminded that "in this drury world of ours, Father Times and Mother Spacies boil their kettle with their crutch."

These reconciliations of Shaun and Shem haunt us from the Pegger Festy-Wet Pinter passages until we read Shaum, as the two turn into a unified twin hero, like Stephen and Bloom or, indeed, like Butt and Taff at the end of chapter 3 of Book II who become *"now one and the same person."* But these resolutions remain philosophic and cyclic. The two touch—"equals of opposites"—

only to whirl outward again. In "Shaun before the People" the audience asks Shaun: "have you not, without suggesting for an instant, millions of moods used up slanguage tun times as words as the penmarks used out in sinscript with such hesitancy by your celebrated brother?" Furiously Shaun denies kinship with such a creature ("always cutting my prhose to please his phrase, bogorror" and "wordsharping"). Shem's language is beyond all propriety. There then follows the famous parody on Joyce's own life, and then Shaun claims that he could do better in his brother's style "any time ever I liked" if only it were not "to infradig." Although this last reference is thought by some to come from a Gogarty-Stanislaus modulation, it would also serve as Lewis' answer to Shem-Dolph's earlier, similar question, "I cain but are you able." For at the end, when the fight is played out between St. Patrick (Shaun-space-day-outside-eye) and the Archdruid (Shem-time-night-inside-ear), the Joycean Archdruid puts forward the theory of epiphany ("obs of epiwo") and to this, in what Campbell and Robinson see as Joyce anticipating criticism, the Lewisian St. Patrick says, "Punc." [25] Even Shaun, at the end, seems to relent a little: "I loved that man" he says echoing not so much Baudelaire as the use of that poet by Eliot (through whom the two "equals of opposites" had come together in the first place), "my shemblable! My freer!" But Shaun really dislikes Shem "For his root language." [26]

Even as cursory, and elementary, a résumé of the controversy between Lewis and Joyce as this has been will serve to show that, in the words of HCE, "skirts were divided on the subject." There

25. Ibid., p. 612. Surely Campbell and Robinson wax a shade oversubtle on this occasion, explicating the reference as follows: "Patrick's paragraph opens with the word 'Punc,' i.e. *Punkt,* period, that's an end to it." Joseph Campbell and Henry Morton Robinson, *A Skeleton Key to Finnegans Wake* (New York, Harcourt, Brace, 1944), p. 351. Admittedly *Punkt* recurs throughout *Ulysses,* once in the form of the vast period or full-stop omitted from the Random House edition (p. 722), but the more homely levels of Joyce's prose should be borne in mind also. Patrick's "Punc" here, antiphonal to the usual *Tunc,* simply means that Patrick thinks the Archdruid's theory punk!

26. Joyce, *Finnegans Wake,* p. 424 (*transition No. 12*).

are other aspects of the controversy, too, and that involving Lewis'
attack on verbal experiment in literature will be considered below,
in the chapter dealing with his satirical technique. Yet, why was
Lewis so bitter? He knew Joyce, and I have tried to prove that
he knew Joyce's beliefs. In the Paris notebooks there are hints that
beauty is *primarily* of intellectual apprehension and, in sensitively
elucidating these, H. M. McLuhan writes that "Joyce tends like Lewis
to reject the way of connatural gnosis and emotion favored by
Bergson, Eliot and theosophy, in which the emotions are used as
the principal windows of the soul." And McLuhan adds, "Compared
with Joyce, however, there is in Lewis a manichean abjurgation of
delectation." [27] But I have shown how in the *Wake* Joyce asks precisely this question of Lewis, through the personae of Shem and
Shaun. "Root language" is scarcely a sufficient answer for such
spleen. Joyce himself emerges from the controversy serenely impartial and heroically generous.

Above all, for his own sake, Lewis should not be judged by his
supporters who, like Roy Campbell or Hugh Gordon Porteus (or
even Geoffrey Grigson), have liked to see his work as a superior
correction of Joyce's. The point is that Joyce had written a *"time-
book,"* a symptom of a social malady, and it is behind Joyce's work
that we must look for what Lewis is attacking in the "mind" of
James Joyce. It is Bergson who here stands at the root of all evil—
"Bergson's doctrine of Time is the creative source of the time-
philosophy." [28] Bergson opposes "every form of intelligent life."
He stands on the side of intuition, of the feminine, of flux, and is
the spokesman, we read, of the way of life of the typical American
businessman,[29] as well (elsewhere) as being connected directly
with " 'red' revolution." [30] Pound (who called Bergson "crap" in

27. Herbert Marshall McLuhan, "Wyndham Lewis: His Theory of Art and
Communication," *Shenandoah*, *4*, Nos. 2–3 (Summer/Autumn 1953), 84–5.

28. *Time and Western Man*, p. 166.

29. *Art of Being Ruled*, p. 398.

30. *One-Way Song*, p. 122. Although Lewis attacks Bergson alongside of Russell, Russell himself was extremely critical of Bergson.

The Townsman), Benda, and Babbitt are all less concerned, like Lewis, to analyze Bergsonism than to denigrate it for its political repercussions. All accuse Bergson of allowing time (in the theory of "durée") to play havoc with space. In his *Les Pangermanistes d'après guerre,* Seillière likens Bergson to Spengler in this; [31] here we have what we might call, in the case of the French, the German "smear." Massis' hatred of "asiatisme" was in less rabid writers a fear of the disintegrating philosophies of Keyserling and Spengler.

Lewis adds little to this side of the Bergsonist debate, either on political or aesthetic grounds. He agrees with Fernandez that "L'objet artistique résiste à toute tentative d'assimilation aux fantaisies du sujet." [32] What Benda calls "l'esthétique du sujet" or "ipsèisme" [33] is simply Lewis' charge of the abandonment of perception for sensation in Bergsonism. As he puts it in *Time and Western Man:* "Perception, in short, smacks of contemplation, it suggests leisure: only *sensation* guarantees *action,* and a full consciousness that 'time is money,' and that leisure is made for masters, not for men, or for the old bad world of Authority, not the good new world of alleged mass-rule." [34] Restless intuition, excitable sensation, making events and objects transitory and subjective, threaten the static world of common sense, the realm of the intellect; so runs the argument. And it runs, may I say, over and over again through nearly five hundred pages of *Time and Western Man* to the point of total monotony, not to mention a "mental stutter" for which Lewis so derides Stein. This is one thing; it is quite another to associate Joyce with this viewpoint. When we know Joyce's aesthetic, such a charge cannot be considered serious criticism. It is not even good gossip. Its very extremism shows how far from the truth it is, for the further Lewis recedes from reality in his criticism the more eccentric his opinions become. If no one is listening to you, you have to shout.

31. Ernest Seillière, *Les Pangermanistes d'après guerre* (Paris, Félix Alcan, 1924), pp. 95–101.
32. Fernandez, *Messages,* p. 27.
33. Benda, *Belphégor,* p. 104.
34. *Time and Western Man,* p. 412.

No, what Lewis does is to make academically intolerable, and morbidly repetitive, Benda's *Le Bergsonisme,* first published in 1912. *Time and Western Man* is the English reply to *Time and Free-Will,* as Bergson's *Essai sur les données* was translated, and where we find the thesis that the intellect distorts reality if it unfolds everything in space. Both Benda and Lewis charge that Bergson, by denying knowledge of "mobilité" to the intellect, is poeticizing intuition, and desiderating action ("connaissance *vive*" in Benda's milder phrase) before consciousness ("connaissance *de l'abstrait*"). So Benda writes: "s'il est incontestable que 'nous qui *regardons* la ligne décrite par le mobile, nous ne *sommes* pas cette ligne,' réciproquement vous qui êtes *devenus* cette ligne, *vous ne pouvez plus la voir;* s'il est incontestable que notre raison reste nécessairement 'à l'extérieur des choses,' non moins nécessairement votre 'installation à l'intérieur des choses' a rompu tout commerce avec la raison." [35]

Let it be said, once and for all, that this is the summary of *Time and Western Man.* It is a pleasantly open charge, under which Lewis manages to indict a number of writers, but is Bergson guilty of it? Of course Bergson's philosophy suffers injustice at the hands of the neoclassicists and, in Lewis' case, injury is added to insult when we find him considerably indebted, as we shall, to Bergson's *Le Rire.*

Certainly Bergson early put an unqualified emphasis on intuition, in its ability to attain metaphysical reality. We find this readily enough in his *Introduction à la métaphysique,* brought to England by Hulme: "Il suit de là qu'un absolu ne saurait être donné que dans une *intuition,* tandis que tout le reste relève de l'analyse." [36] Intuition for Bergson is an effort of imagination and identification, of a kind often found in literature, an act of sympathy with and

35. Benda, *Le Bergsonisme,* pp. 101–2. But in fairness to Bergson, see Bergson, *L'Évolution créatrice,* p. 260.

36. Henri Bergson, "Introduction à la métaphysique," *Revue de métaphysique et de morale,* onzième année (Paris, Colin, 1903), p. 3.

merging in the constant flow of "durée." In *L'Évolution créatrice* he defines "durée" as follows: "La durée est le progrès continu du passé qui ronge l'avenir et qui gonfle en avançant." In *Matière et mémoire* he calls "le présent pur"—"l'insaisissable progrès du passé rongeant l'avenir." Thus the present tends to be a condensation of history, and memory is stressed as a vehicle for perception. Intuition, to attain truth, must plunge into "la mobilité de la durée" and listen to the heartbeats of the soul.

One can see how Lewis would honestly dislike this theory, for it is certainly an attack on what he calls the world of common sense: "L'état, pris en lui-même, est un perpétuel devenir." There is no Lewisian fixity. The state of objects in space must yield to their identity in memory—"notre *caractère*, toujours présent à toutes nos décisions, est bien la synthèse actuelle de tous nos états passés." But here, in *Matière et mémoire*, Bergson tends to attack the fixity of space only in that it is sometimes considered as anterior to motion. Bergson will not allow this view because it carries with it, of course, connotations of quality, conferring ultimate truth on space rather than on time.

Still, if one reads Bergson's section on intelligence and intuition in *L'Évolution créatrice*, he cannot be considered anti-intellectual, certainly not so blindly and stupidly inimical to the intellect as *Time and Western Man* makes him out. In this work, in fact, Bergson concedes that the intellect may sometimes be superior to the instincts in apprehending reality, especially conscious reality, though he denies it ability to grasp the subconscious. Like Lewis, Bergson wants the intellect to operate "sur la matière brute, en particulier sur des solides." He believes: *"Notre intelligence ne se représente clairement que l'immobilité."* [37] But Bergson goes on to call this play of the intellect on static matter mechanical, and he will not, of course, allow the intellect a place at the head of the faculties. For Bergson, intellect should cooperate with instinct in apprehending reality. This Lewis would never echo.

37. Bergson, *L'Évolution créatrice*, pp. 167, 169.

So Lewis, in common with his French neoclassical colleagues, pushes Bergson over into a position of leader of all the worst elements associated with romanticism. Such is the satire of Bergsonism in *The Childermass*. Such is intended in the characterization of Bertha in *Tarr*, for Bertha is an arch-figure of Romance, accompanied as she is by its fatalistic and disastrous effects. Bertha, who relies "on the authority of intuition," personifies the flabby, soft, emotional life. To take only one example, her face "withdrew with a glutinous, sweet slowness: the heavy white jowl seemed dragging itself out of some fluid trap where it had been caught like a weighty body."

In contrast to this "time-world" Lewis claims to celebrate in *Time and Western Man* "the 'spatializing' instinct of man." He is trying to stimulate "a philosophy that will be as much a *spatial-philosophy* as Bergson's is a *time-philosophy*." This philosophy he everywhere associates with the Greek or Roman ("the world of greek philosophy, the pagan exteriority" and "the God of the Roman faith"). It is "Classical Man" he says he is setting up against "Faustian," or modern Western Man, though he fails, unlike Lasserre, to make any distinction between the various Fausts here. Lewis' Faustian romantic is presumably Goethe's early Faust, striving for self-gratification. Since Lewis constantly claims that his philosophic beliefs are of the classical persuasion, it is worth while seeing exactly what he means by "classical" before considering his satire. So the "time-philosophers" are defended by the anticlassical Bailiff of *The Childermass:* " 'We are not Greeks the Lord of Hosts be praised, we are Modern Man and proud of it—we of the jazz-age who have killed sexishness and enthroned sensible sex, who have liberated the working-mass and gutted every palace within sight making a prince of the mechanic with their spoils, we deride the childish statecraft, the insensitive morals, the fleshly-material art, the naïf philosophy of the Hellene.' " [38]

38. *Childermass*, p. 261.

Chapter 12: On the Side of Common Sense

"I am on the side of commonsense . . . and my position, inasmuch as it causes me to oppose on all issues 'the romantic,' comes under the heading 'classical' . . . 'Classical' is for me *anything* which is nobly defined and exact, as opposed to that which is fluid—of the Flux." [*Paleface*, pp. 253–5.]

IN AN ADMIRABLY dispassionate article published in *La Nouvelle Revue française* for January 1, 1929, the centenary of French romanticism, Ramon Fernandez analyzes neoclassicism in France and England. He finds the classical-romantic antithesis factitious today and admits the debt of the antiromanticists to the romantic movement. Fernandez, for instance, is fair enough to make a welcome reappraisal of Proust from this point of view, pointing out that the abundant intelligence and "jugement" in Proust's work must preserve it from any facile condemnation as romantic, or, in Lewis' phrase, as that "cheap pastry of stuffy and sadic romance, with its sweet and viscous sentimentalism, which was manufactured with such success by Proust." Fernandez, in company perhaps with Joyce of *Finnegans Wake,* wants to supersede the old antithesis. He ridicules the (Lewisian) idea of "inhumanité" as the primary characteristic of classical art and contends that if the neoclassicists have enjoyed contemporary success, it has been a personal one.

Whether Fernandez is fair or not in his estimate of French neoclassicism, he is certainly borne out in England. In fact, he wrote his article conscious of the earlier discussion of this subject by Middleton Murry in *The Criterion*. Writer after writer on the classical side in England seems to find it necessary to restate the fruitlessness of classical and romantic labels. For the Pound of *The*

Spirit of Romance the terms are "snares." Eliot equally declines to accept the terms, in a work in which he likens classicism to orthodoxy and romanticism to heresy.[1] Elsewhere Eliot finds the difference between classical and romantic one between "the complete and the fragmentary, the adult and the immature, the orderly and the chaotic."[2] Although a declared "classicist in literature," and calling classicism in his review of *Ulysses* "a goal toward which all good literature strives, so far as it is good,"[3] Eliot refuses to accept the labels in his editorials to *The Criterion* for June and September 1927. In *Men without Art* Lewis does the same. All this is confusing enough, but it is not nearly so much so as the civil war that goes on within the English neoclassical camp. Joyce, while fulfilling almost every requirement of the contemporary classical writer for Lewis, is yet bitterly assailed by him. In the same work Lewis flays Pound as "a genuine *naïf* . . . a sort of revolutionary simpleton." Again in 1933 Lewis characterizes Pound as romantic: "Those snobbish baubles dived for by the scholar, silver-lip shells and those of the Smoky Beard, are pretty enough, but in the end they are as tiresome a *bric-à-brac* as the iron filings and scrap-iron of the fake factory school—though no one has made a better use of the Ocean bed of Time (where everything has suffered a sea change into something sumptuous and odd, however commonplace when it came to kick the bucket) than the indefatigable Ezra: and I should be one of his best customers, it is possible, like my friend Mr. Eliot, were not my tastes a little austerely 'classical.' "[4] Ezra replied in *Guide to Kulchur*.[5] And in the same way Pound heaped scorn on one of his greatest admirers, T. S. Eliot, both for his essay on

1. Eliot, *After Strange Gods*, p. 26.

2. Eliot, *Selected Essays*, p. 15.

3. T. S. Eliot [review of James Joyce, *Ulysses*], *The Dial*, 75, No. 5 (Nov. 1923), 482.

4. Wyndham Lewis, " 'One Way Song,' " [sic] *New Britain*, 2, No. 30 (Dec. 13, 1933), 121. The "fake factory school" probably refers to the New Signatures group of this time.

5. Pound, *Guide to Kulchur*, p. 234.

Jonson [6] and for *The Criterion*.[7] And we have seen that Eliot could not reinstate himself in grace by putting a Chinese jar in "Burnt Norton" or even by attacking "free-thinking Jews" in *After Strange Gods,* for Pound calls this latter work contaminated by the "Jewish poison." Not to be behind, Lewis sailed into Eliot in *Men without Art* as "The Pseudo-Believer" (I suggest that this is largely a religious controversy, Eliot moving toward religion as Pound and Lewis move away from it). Here Lewis denies Eliot any sincerity; Eliot's classicism is a comedy, a sham, but then Eliot is *"pseudo* everything." [8] He is guilty of "dogmatic insincerity," of "confusions and inconsistencies," and is to be linked with the Naughty Nineties and the diabolism of Mario Praz.[9] For Lewis, Eliot's radical ideas "show through the snobbish veneer." Lewis goes on to deplore "the essential muddle-headedness of this strange classicist and 'revolutionary' poet." It should perhaps be mentioned here, in passing, that

6. Ezra Pound, *How to Read* (London, Desmond Harmsworth, 1931), p. 49.

7. Pound, *Jefferson and/or Mussolini,* p. 56.

8. *Men without Art,* p. 77.

9. Ibid., pp. 203–4. In his "Note to the Second Edition" of *The Romantic Agony* (Oxford University Press, 1951) Mario Praz defends himself against Lewis' reference to the book in *Men without Art.* But it will be found that Praz quoted Lewis' offending passage more accurately in *The Times Literary Supplement* for August 8, 1935. In the Note Praz complains that Lewis calls his compilation a " 'gigantic pile of satanic bric-à-brac, so industriously assembled, under my direction [?], by Professor Praz.' " In *Men without Art* (p. 175), however, we read rather, "this gigantic pile of satanic bric-à-brac, so industriously assembled, under my directions (cf. *The Diabolical Principle,* etc.), by Prof. Praz." In his article on the classical revival in *The Bookman* for October 1934 Lewis calls *The Romantic Agony* "the historical dossier for my 'Diabolical Principle.' " In fairness to Lewis I should add that I have examined the manuscripts of this book in the Carlow Collection and the words "under my directions" do not appear in the handwritten MS. The suggestion of relationship Lewis wished to show was apparently concertinaed in galley proof. In galleys, also, he inserted a recommendation to read Praz's book, which is indeed highly praised on p. 171 of *Men without Art.* Praz was obviously stung by the references to this matter in Montague Summers' *The Gothic Quest* and Stephen Spender's *The Destructive Element.* But it is hardly likely that Lewis would want to call a work like *The Romantic Agony* his own.

Hugh Kenner assumes that this attack on Eliot was really just a huge joke, a "fantasia . . . as funny as anything in that chef d'oeuvre of polemic comedy *The Diabolical Principle*." In all honesty I cannot help feeling that this can safely be put down to sophistical whitewashing (perhaps rather similar to the same critic's allegation that Joyce was simply pulling Stuart Gilbert's leg in letting Gilbert think he was writing an authorized explanation of *Ulysses*). The attacks in *Men without Art* appeared as anything but funny to the recipients: Hemingway is said to have been infuriated by his, while a glance at *A Writer's Diary* will show just how deeply wounded Virginia Woolf was by the "fantasia" about her. In *Enemies of Promise* Cyril Connolly quite independently—Virginia Woolf, after all, had referred to Connolly's "cocktail criticism"—called *Men without Art* "bullying and unfair." As regards Joyce, Harry Levin in his book on that author refers to "the malice of Wyndham Lewis" in attributing the origin of Bloom's meditations to the diction of Alfred Jingle; a recent study of Joyce by Marvin Magalaner and Richard Kain also refers in this context to "the malicious retorts of Wyndham Lewis," and considers Lewis' attack on Joyce's sources as "the most malicious." None of this really matters very much, however, for one can virtually say that in an article in *The Bookman* at this time Lewis finds bogus classicism in every neoclassicist except himself. Faced with this internecine warfare, then, between writers one would normally imagine in perfect harmony, one can sometimes simply ask oneself if one is standing on one's head or one's heels. Yet this internal strife, matched in France to some extent perhaps over the Action Française affair, does seem to bear Fernandez out. Hugh Kenner may claim that "Pound, Eliot, Joyce and Yeats mark . . . a return to the Aristotelian benison," but it is an individual return, a personal success.

Lewis would have agreed with Yeats that Aristotle was "Solider," [10] but it would be incorrect to think of his classicism—*tel*

10. W. B. Yeats, "Among School Children," *The Collected Poems of W. B. Yeats* (London, Macmillan, 1934), p. 244. There is a corrupt American edition giving "Soldier Aristotle."

quel—as exclusively Hellenic. It is as well to mention this since French neoclassicalism tends to seek its authority in three periods, precisely the periods given by Sir Herbert Grierson for classical in his famous lecture of 1923, namely Periclean Athens, Augustan Rome, and the France of Louis XIV. Maurras, for whom to be a Roman was to be human and who early apostrophized Minerva, sees his classicism as Roman, Hellenic, and Catholic: "Dans l'ère moderne, la philosophie catholique se modèle de préférence sur Aristote; la politique catholique s'approprie les méthodes de la politique romaine. Tel est le caractère de la tradition classique. L'esprit classique, c'est proprement l'essence des doctrines de la haute humanité. C'est un esprit d'autorité et d'aristocratie." [11]

In *Mise au point* Lasserre has a chapter called "Le Destin de l'Occident," in which he claims, "il n'y a cause plus juste et plus belle que celle de la culture intellectuelle et esthétique gréco-latine." And Lasserre goes on to rally Frenchmen to their Hellenic heritage: "Enfin n'abusons pas du bel exercice qui consiste à déployer des drapeaux où s'inscrivent ces mots superbes d'Occident, d'hellénisme, de latinité, d'esprit français . . . Soyons nous-mêmes: occidentaux, latins, grecs, français." [12] Even Péguy equates the classical Greek with the French genius, in opposing to both the romantic German. The point of noting this here is to show how Lewis' graphic interests severed him from this view. The French fear of "asiatisme" (the yellow peril) is never translated in Pound, Lewis, or Hulme,[13] simply because these men admired Oriental art. Massis, on the other hand, finds the enemies of classicism Germany and the Orient—"la culture gréco-latine n'est donc pas pour l'Allemand une valeur fondamentale de civilisation." [14] Spengler and Keyser-

11. Maurras, *Romantisme et révolution*, p. 270.

12. Lasserre, *Mise au point*, p. 100. But Lasserre goes on to counsel against an excess in this direction.

13. For a convenient definition of Hulme's terminology in this respect, see Murray Krieger, "The Ambiguous Anti-romanticism of T. E. Hulme," *ELH: A Journal of English Literary History, 20,* No. 4 (Dec. 1953), 300–14. The definitive study of Hulme to date is undoubtedly the exhaustive, but currently unpublished, Columbia doctoral dissertation on him by Clifford Josephson.

14. Massis, *Défense,* pp. 65–6.

ling combine these elements for Massis, and it is interesting that in
Time and Western Man Lewis pays relatively little attention to
Spengler's supposedly "asiatic" romanticism. In fact, what Lewis
does is to defend the ancient Orient against Spengler, claiming that
Spengler distorts this civilization, "making Buddha swallow his
words, and Confucius learn to play the ukelele." Seillière, however,
in his *Les Origines romanesques de la morale et de la politique romantique,* traces the origins of romanticism to early Japan!

For Lewis classicism is antiromanticism. Consequently it is elastic in its particular definitions. The romantic he ceaselessly defines
as the unreal, the philosophy of the day-dreaming Many. But in his
chapter on the terms in *Men without Art,* and in his article on the
classical revival in *The Bookman,* he uses a number of words in
connection with the two. A brief listing of these may summarize his
position:

Classical	*Romantic*
objective	subjective
intelligence	emotion
permanence	flux
body	psyche
solid, defined, exact	misty, muddled
common-sense	undirected
impersonal	dishevelled
Aristotle	Bergson
order	chaos
rational	moralistic
universal	idiomatic
health	feeble, gloomy, sick
indifferent to originality *	love of novel sensations
static	drifting

* In the sense that the classical spirit for Lewis interprets the *Zeitgeist,* rather
than forming this for itself.

I have excluded the term Hellenic from the classical category above
because though Lewis admires the Hellenes he also writes, "my
'Classical' is not the Hellenic Age, as it is Spengler's." In *Men with-*

out Art he actually admits that he looks to ancient Egypt or Japan, *rather than* to Hellas, for his classicism. This was the Worringer-Hulme influence, but I would also venture a guess, namely that Hellenic classicism is more the expression of a corporate society than Oriental "classicism," and for that reason less likely to appeal to men like Hulme and Lewis. Grierson, on the other hand, finds this very love of expressing one's society a criterion of true classicism.

At first it appears that Lewis approaches Hulme's view of the matter (nor must we be put off by Lewis' charge that Hulme was a romantic,[15] for this is explained by Hulme's Bergsonism). The two certainly have much in common here. And on some points Babbitt joins them. Hulme, however, proposed "two conceptions of the nature of man." The first comprised man from St. Augustine until the Renaissance, the second from the Renaissance to the present day. Of course, the very term Renaissance is elastic, Professor Haskins arguing cogently for a renaissance in Italy in the twelfth century, but as Hulme uses "humanist" constantly for the second period, one presumes he must be thinking of the start of the quattrocento, the period of classical studies in Italy, of Petrarch and Boccaccio, and of the development in painting from Giotto and Cimabue. The first of Hulme's periods believed in original sin, the second did not. The first, the Middle Ages, was characterized by absolute values, the doctrine of original sin, and belief as the center of civilization. For Hulme this period expresses itself ideally in Byzantine art (usually considered from about A.D. 395 until the capture of Constantinople by the Turks in 1453). Austerity, rigidity, and disgust with living shapes are the leading traits in this art, Hulme tells us. The second period is the reverse of this. It is "vital." Far from being subordinate to absolute values, man now takes pleasure in an art and culture which reproduce human and natural forms, in which "all the emotions expressed are perfectly human ones," in other words the art of Einfühlung. For Hulme this is *toto caelo* wrong. "The humanist

---

15. Wyndham Lewis, " 'Classical Revival' in England," *The Bookman, 87,* No. 517, (Oct. 1934), 10.

canons are, I think, demonstrably false," he writes, and again, "I hold the religious conception of ultimate values to be right, the humanist wrong." [16]

Like Worringer, Hulme finds Egyptian and Byzantine art anti-"vital," and in fact opposed to the rot that set in with classical man —in the case of Byzantine art, with classical values as resurrected by the high Renaissance. Yet it need not confuse us when Hulme calls for a "classical revival," as he does, since he here uses the term as a correction of romanticism, and one inclusive of the qualities of his first period. Classical man is, thus, a "fixed and limited animal whose nature is absolutely constant." It is this clarion call in *Speculations* which draws Hulme's classicism to that of the Action Française (which Hulme explicitly admires). In other words one has to approach Hulme's classicism as a theory of two kinds, artistic (that of Worringer) and political (that of Maurras).

Hulme, indeed, breaks his second period ("humanist") down into two parts; contemporary romanticism, which is horrible ("like pouring a pot of treacle over the dinner table"), is an ignoble degeneration of man's interest in man of the Renaissance days. This latter was at least free, Hulme feels, from utilitarianism. It is this distinction, within Hulme's broadly "humanist" era, that makes it faintly possible for him to accept Bergson's theory of art, especially in what he calls its *"life-communicating* quality," which would otherwise seem to be everything Hulme despises. There are, of course, other, possibly more serious contradictions in Hulme's classicism. For me Hulme's outstanding defect is that he fails to explain why his "humanist" period (leading to "the state of slush in which we have the misfortune to live") ever came about, if the previous values, of the medieval period, were so absolutely superior.

The most damaging evidence, however, for the irrelevance of neoclassicist philosophy comes forward when these thinkers choose practical examples of their theories. In his notes on Sorel's *Reflections on Violence* Hulme classes Sorel as "classical in ethics." Hulme is just able to justify this by associating Sorel with his first period

16. Hulme, *Speculations,* pp. 31, 70.

of civilization by means of "the conviction that man is by nature bad or limited," scarcely a qualification we all care to see in our political theoreticians. Lewis finds a similar interpretation of the "classical" in another contemporary Nero, writing that "The Hitlerist dream is full of an imminent classical serenity." [17] And Maurras, in *Vers l'Espagne de Franco,* found the same "politique classique" in the Spain of *el Caudillo.* After this sort of thing, how easy it is to be persuaded by Benda who, in *Belphégor,* finds French neoclassicism "le romantisme de la raison" and a "besoin de l'excessif."

But if Benda turns the tables on the neoclassicists, the Germans complete the ruin. For here are—*horresco referens*—men like Ernst, Lublinski, Karl Joël, and others obviously enjoying classicism. And the chief weakness in the French attack, more flagrant than the neglect of classical elements in their own literature of the nineteenth century, was to deny the classical to a country which produced the author of their virtual manifesto—"Classisch ist das Gesunde, Romantik das Kranke."

Nowhere is Lewis' ignorance more exposed than here, in his absurd attack on the pan-German nature of "romanticism." A mere glance through Albrecht Soergel's historiography of contemporary German literature will at once reveal a stronger neoclassical movement than has existed in England since Lewis took up his pen.

The circle around Stefan George exemplified, as is well known, a kind of neoclassicism (including, in some of George's early poems, Lewisian Caliphs, Crowd-masters, hero-artists, and Padishahs) that later proved far too romantic for most Anglo-Saxons. Moreover, George (*Jahrbuch der geistigen Bewegung*) has attacked music more roundly than Lewis. Yet in many respects George was what Jethro Bithell has called "a Mallarméan Parnassian," and it is rather in others like Paul Ernst, Wilhelm von Scholz, Rudolf Pannwitz, and Samuel Lublinski that we find the bulk of Lewis' so-called "classicism" either anticipated or paralleled in the Germany it derides.

What is more, the creative side of these writers bears remarkable

17. *Hitler,* p. 184.

affinity with some of Lewis' satire. The tragic hero of Ernst's dramas of the first decade of the century, such as *Demetrios* or *Brunhild*, is to reappear later in Lewis' work, while the theoretical aspects of Lewis' neoclassical attack may also be found in these Germans. Ernst's glowing admiration for *Klassizismus,* as well as for Oriental literature ("Die chinesische Novelle hat die höchste Kultur"), is representatively seen in his *Der Weg zur Form,* a work with which neither Lewis nor Pound could properly disagree.[18] For Ernst here the great work of art is an act of will; he inveighs against false feeling, adulates Greek drama with its order and form, and compares the German stock with the Greek and Roman (as Maurras does with the French, as a matter of fact). Indeed, if there be any national bias in Ernst's work, and it is a dull one to reread today, it is in its reversal of Lewis' accusations as to the racial origin of the romantic spirit. In one passage Ernst thinks with evident distress from "unsere klassische Dichtung" to "die französische Revolution" and reverses Maurras in a sentence such as: "Das französische *conscience* ist weniger als das lateinische *conscientia.*" One other work by Ernst, *Der Zusammenbruch des deutschen Idealismus*, might also be brought up in this context. Throughout this collection of studies of the drama, addressed to the youth of the time and liberally peppered with platitudes, Ernst adulates the Greeks of the past—for their "form," [19] their application to reality, their understanding of what is true tragedy ("jenseits der Leidenschaft"). Samuel Lublinski's *Die Entstehung des Judentums: Eine Skizze,* or his foreword to *Tsar Peter,* mirrors these ideals. But what is particularly interesting in Ernst's *Klassizismus* is its growing suspicion of contemporary religious concepts— indeed its paganism (to be found in one interesting chapter on *Don*

18. Paul Ernst, *Der Weg zur Form* (München, Georg Müller, 1928), pp. 305–6, gives a characteristic definition of classicism and romanticism for the Germans of this group.

19. Paul Ernst, *Der Zusammenbruch des deutschen Idealismus* (München, Georg Müller, 1918), p. 100, perhaps best defines what the author means by this word.

Carlos)—which, of course, makes Ernst more than ever a pre-cursor of Lewis and Pound (not to mention Hitler) rather than of the contemporary French neoclassicists.

Lublinski, who wrote a sympathetic study of Ernst in 1913, and an Ernstian drama *Gunther und Brunhild* in 1908, published a rousing attack on the "Neuromantik" at this time in his *Der Ausgang der Moderne: Ein Buch der Opposition*. Like Ernst, Lublinski finds "die grosse und heroische Persönlichkeit" going under be-fore the tide of hypersensitive romanticism. Further, Lewis' propaganda against the youth cult can be found here in Lublinski's fears that romanticism reduces us to children, even in the political sphere.[20]

One final admirer of Paul Ernst might very well be mentioned here, and that is Georg Lukács, a sometime member of the George-kreis and now a leading Marxist critic (indeed, Ernst roundly as-sailed "bürgerliche Gesellschaft" with all the other writers of this group from the start). Perhaps the most interesting essay in Lukács' early *Die Seele und die Formen* is that on Ernst himself, entitled "Metaphysik der Tragödie." The whole of this essay breathes the spirit of contemporary German neoclassicism. Lukács here finds the "Neuromantik" uncongenial to drama (it is "ein poetisches Dumpf-werden des Menschen"), and he concludes with a stirring tribute to Ernst's *Brunhild*: "sein erstes 'griechisches' Drama. Das erste entschiedene Verlassen des Weges, den das grosse deutsche Drama seit Schillers und Kleists Tagen ging: des Vereinens von Sophokles und Shakespeare." The play, for Lukács, is full of a simple, Greek monumentality: "Auch die Haltung und die Worte seiner Menschen sind in ihrem tiefsten Wesen griechisch, ja vielleicht . . . grie-chischer als die mancher antiken Tragödie"![21]

20. Samuel Lublinski, *Der Ausgang der Moderne: Ein Buch der Opposition* (Dresden, Carl Reissner, 1909), pp. 54 ff.; cf. also the chapter on "Politik," pp. 235–47.

21. Georg von Lukács, *Die Seele und die Formen* (Berlin, Egon Fleischel, 1911), pp. 350–73. At p. 354 Lukács momentarily confuses Kriemhilde with Brunhild, and there is virtually a direct quotation from Ernst unacknowledged

Finally, for Karl Joël the classic of Goethe and Schiller, marked
by health, is ethos ("Herrschaft des Ethos"), while the romantic of
the sick Hölderlin, who championed Kronos, is pathos. Forgiving
Joël his rather Teutonically watertight compartments, the classicism of his *Wandlungen der Weltanschauung* is Lewis' classicism.
For above all Joël stresses that the classicist is not caught up in the
flux of time. He must be above time: "Doch damit stellt sich der
Klassiker eben *über* die Zeit." [22] The romantic spirit, on the other
hand, Joël sees in continual flux ("Strom"), going from extreme to
extreme, regarding historical movement as the most important: "In
der Romantik siegt Dynamik über alle Statik." [23] If one adds Joël's
classicism to Hulme's, one has a fairly good working hypothesis of
what Lewis predicated by the term. For Hulme, admiring Bergson,
did not particularly pit classicism against flux; but for Joël, as for
Lewis, the nineteenth century was the century of change, of irresponsible pantheism (the "Naturgott"), of the inharmonious marriage between "Gott und Natur, Tragödie und Satyrjauchzen, Macht-
trieb und Massenhingabe." As against this pathetic romanticism:
"Wahrlich, der Idealismus der klassischen Epoche war keine
Ausschweifung des Geistes, kein Schwärmen der Seele, kein schwel-
gender Selbstgenuss wie im Zeitalter der Empfindsamkeit, sondern
ein *ethischer Kampf*, eine schwere Selbstzügelung, eine ergreifende
Selbsterziehung." [24] Of course, I must not give my reader the impression that the French neoclassicists criticize *only* the Germans as
romantic. Far from it. In *Le Romantisme français* Lasserre finds
Hugo and Benjamin Constant chiefly responsible for the "naufrage
romantique" of the nineteenth century. And Lasserre's catalogue

---

at the foot of p. 333. Lukács' subsequent development is possibly evident here in
his longing for an *absolute* form, his dislike of "unsere demokratische Zeit," and
of excessive individuality in general. Cf. "Nur für eine abstrakt absolute Idee des
Menschen ist alles Menschliche möglich" (pp. 347, 370–1).

22. Karl Joël, *Wandlungen der Weltanschauung* (Tübingen, Mohr, 1934), 2,
347.

23. Ibid., p. 349.

24. Ibid., p. 279.

of romantic characteristics is similar to Joël's. It is worth quoting, as a breviary of all those traits opposed to what Lewis means by the classical: "Ruine psychique de l'individu, eudémonisme lâche, chimérisme sentimental, maladie de la solitude, corruption des passions, idolâtrie des passions, empire de la femme, empire des éléments féminins de l'esprit sur ses éléments virils, asservissement au moi, déformation emphatique de la realité, conception révolutionnaire et dévergondée de la nature humaine, abus des moyens matériels de l'art pour masquer la paresse et la misère de l'invention . . ." [25]

This, in a nutshell, is "time-philosophy" for Lewis. "Organic," "Faustian," "musical," "apocalyptic," "feminine," "dynamic," it is a philosophy he opposes in a series of negatives. Indebted to Spengler,[26] indebted to Bergson, he borrows from his enemies, inverting their convictions. For his is not a positive philosophical approach. It is what can be summarized as Stopping the Rot. And so he writes: "We fly to the past—anywhere out of this suspended animation of the so smugly 'revolutionary' present. Out of the detestable crowd of quacks—*illuminés,* couéists, and psychologists—that the wealthy death-bed has attracted, and who throng these antechambers of defeat; from all the funeral furnishers, catafalque-makers, house-agents, lawyers, money lenders, with their eye on the Heir of all the Ages, we fly in despair." [27]

25. Lasserre, *Romantisme français,* pp. 311–12.
26. In *The Canadian Forum* for June 1936 H. N. Frye briefly but persuasively outlines Lewis' indebtedness to Spengler, especially in Lewis' rather obviously similar anti-Bohemianism and in his sweeping "cultural consciousness" approach.
27. *Art of Being Ruled,* p. 25.

Chapter 13: A Thief of the Real

"It is as thieves only—a thief of the real—that we can exist, or as parasites upon God." [*Time and Western Man*, pp. 397–8.]

LEWIS has often been called a Thomist in all but name, and it would not do to conclude a summary of his philosophic beliefs without a mention of this. However, Geoffrey Stone, analyzing Lewis' ideas at the end of 1933, singles out his antagonism to religion as the chief point differentiating him from his French and English colleagues in the neoclassical movement. Stone seems to me perfectly correct, and once more, when Lewis' ideas engage with religion, we see why he has been called "Mister Ivory Tower."

For Lewis supposes the presence, if not of a deity, at least of some supernatural power, whose representative on earth is the inspired artist, or "person": "The Sistine Chapel Ceiling is worthy of the hand of any God which we can infer, dream of, or postulate. We may certainly say that God's hand is visible in it." [1]

The "sense of personality" ("the most vivid and fundamental sense that we possess") is delegated from the divine, and especially manifested in that feeling of separation and nobility felt by the artist. Lewis' God is the "supreme symbol" of "person"-hood; he is, in fact, literally a *"personal God."* [2] Thus the only part of our experience with which we may construct God is the intellectual, and to this art has the prerogative. "God is for us something to *think,* not *feel.*" [3] At once we see how he differs from the Christian for whom emotional experience may give access to God.

1. *Time and Western Man,* p. 401.
2. Ibid., p. 463.
3. Ibid., p. 397.

It is not oversimplifying Lewis' beliefs to say that for him intellectual and artistic faculties may alone fix for us the divine. Art is the supreme expression of God in our lives. And naturally he must quarrel violently with the Protestant ethic where "God has become merged in everything, the Kingdom of Heaven is running about inside every individual thing in a fluid ubiquity." This ignoble idea that every man may be entitled to grace leads Lewis, of course, to furious, repetitive attacks on Protestantism. It is hardly necessary to rehearse these diatribes, which reiterate the notion of a vindictive Christ, of a vitiating love of the "common good," and of Bible-socialism resulting in despotic totalitarianism. It is amusing, in passing, to note the paroxysms to which John Milton drives these humanitarians. In *Comus,* Lewis writes, Milton has made chastity worse than obscene and so is either being stupid or malicious. (In fact, the Lady in *Comus* expresses the principle of intellectual liberty motionless in the whirlpool of Comus' sensual rout that is precisely Lewis' Vortex: nor was Milton's position at the end of his life far from favoring an elite of Christian humanists.) Roy Campbell writes that Milton "in *Comus* attacks female virtue." [4] What Eliot calls Milton's "moral aberrations" [5]—so different, one supposes, from the "decorum" of Launcelot Andrewes' private life [6]— drive Pound to loathe Milton, to a "disgust with what he has to say, his asinine bigotry, his beastly hebraism, the coarseness of his mentality." [7] Milton, Pound elsewhere puts it, "shows a complete ignorance of the things of the spirit." [8] This bias can frequently be found in Lewis' fiction and it is principally on this score, for being "a Calvinist moralist," that he criticizes Faulkner.[9] In the Protes-

4. Campbell, *Broken Record,* p. 157.
5. Eliot, *After Strange Gods,* p. 35.
6. Eliot, *Selected Essays,* p. 299.
7. Pound, *Pavannes and Divisions,* p. 202.
8. Pound, *Polite Essays,* p. 200.
9. There is a reference to Vorticism in Faulkner's early sketch *Mirrors of Charles Street,* dated February 8, 1925, and William Van O'Connor even suggests that Faulkner may have been influenced by the "literary applicability" of Vorticism.

tant code, in short, Lewis can find no "compensating beauty such as you get in the great catholic mystics."

This is as far as Lewis approaches the Catholic position. "We should support the catholic church perhaps more than any other visible institution," he writes in *Time and Western Man,* and in *Paleface* he adds, "I find myself naturally aligned today, to some extent, with the philosophers of the catholic revival." Even in the recent *Rotting Hill* he considers that a purely Catholic Europe might still today provide a "practical and orderly society" rather than "the rabid indiscipline of parties." (Yet how often does he quote Montaigne's remark that a free government is "toujours agité"?)

In the chapter at the end of *Time and Western Man* called "God as Reality," his lengthiest consideration of this matter, he categorically denies the Catholic position. There are two main reasons why he is "unable to subscribe" to Catholicism. The first is that it looks too much to the past, and is therefore "as irretrievably 'historical' as the doctrine of Spengler." Under this charge Lewis specifically indicts Thomism—"to rely upon St. Thomas Aquinas at such a juncture . . . would prove in you a meagre sense of the reality." Maritain is here "a frantic, hallucinated, 'soul'-drugged individual." But let us allow that Maritain by no means advocates a return to the past, at least not in the sense Lewis imputes to him. He has openly stated that it would be ridiculous to try to relive the Middle Ages again today.[10]

The second reason why Lewis denies the Catholic creed is clearly aesthetic, and it is shared, rather more intelligently, by Fernandez. For Lewis sees the Catholic removing man's eyes from the base

---

I observed one parallel passage: at the end of *Rotting Hill* Roy Campbell is seen walking "as if the camp were paved with eggs"; at the end of the earlier *Light in August* Byron Bunch "goes on toward the truck, walking like he had eggs under his feet." In passing, too, one might note a mention of Gaudier-Brzeska in Faulkner's recent *A Fable* (1954).

10. Maritain, *Humanisme intégral,* pp. 149–51. Cf. *Time and Western Man,* p. 387, and *The Writer and the Absolute,* p. 37.

world of matter and fixing them on the world beyond. This he calls
"irreligious." He is able to do so, if we allow his view that our "godlike experience" results only from a feeling of separation of the
"person" from the "thing." In other words, matter provides part of
the religious experience for Lewis, or at least of that experience by
which we duplicate God's relation to us. "We are surface creatures
. . . It is among the flowers and leaves that our lot is cast." Only
by the play of the intellect on the surface of things, Lewis is saying
here, can we know the divine, only, in short, by being artists. Naturally, as I hardly need to point out, this cuts across the Catholic
view of redemption, and across the whole Christian conception that
God reveals Himself, if He wishes, to us all. Lewis says that He does
not: "I, of course, admit that the principle I advocate is not for
everybody . . ." Exactly.

Fernandez puts this dislike of Thomism on a far more reasonable
level. He objects that the religious outlook fails to provide a stable
objective world (Eliot's "objective correlative") for the apprehension of the aesthetic sensibilities: "L'objet, comme l'ombre d'un
corps aux différentes heures du jour, tantôt s'étend devant le sujet,
tantôt s'évanouit en lui." [11] It is this that makes religion a "time-
philosophy" for Lewis. Maritain's humanism, though based on human dignity and the rights of individual man, is concerned to place
God at the center of our lives, to make God our sole court of appeal,
a God to be apprehended for Maritain through the emotions as
through the intellect. He is concerned, as he puts it, to make life
"théocentrique" rather than "anthropocentrique." For Maritain
Lewis' religion is guilty of the sin of pride, of the "anthropocentrique" heresy, for here (with God as a sort of superintellectual and
artist) the Deity has become simply the guarantor of man's power
working out his own destiny on earth. Maritain's "humanisme intégral" is an attempt to put man in touch with God again, but to do
so by means of accepting the absolute and heroic values incarnated
in the Middle Ages.

11. Fernandez, *Messages,* pp. 26–7.

In the recent *Self Condemned* the hero René calls himself "a friend of Farm Street" (i.e. of the famous Catholic Church there), but this may be his French background. For undeniably Lewis sees religion as a sort of art, as he sees politics in aesthetic terms. "Laughter is . . . our 'god-like' attribute," he writes, in connection with satire, and one does not have to push him far to find him claiming that God is really a sort of supersatirist! Reference to the world of common sense, to known objects and facts, is essential to the working of art in Lewis' mind, as it is to Pound's "ideogrammic method," and so he refuses to allow a religion like the Catholic which removes our gaze from this world. We are most fully conscious, our faculties as human beings supremely extended, inasmuch as we are exercising our intellects. And the field where this faculty itself can operate at its best is the solid world of objective common sense. It is this play, a current sent out from the brain and flashing on the world of static reality, that is the highest form of life for Lewis and our nearest approach to the Godhead. We can now watch it at work in his fiction.

PART IV: SATIRE

"Satire is the great Heaven of Ideas, where you meet the titans of red laughter; . . ." [*The Wild Body*, p. 235.]

Chapter 14: The Immense Novices

"These immense novices brandish their appetites in their faces, lay bare their teeth in a valedictory, inviting, or merely substantial laugh . . . This sunny commotion in the face, at the gate of the organism, brings to the surface all the burrowing and interior broods which the individual may harbour." ["Note on Tyros," *The Tyro No. 1*, p. 2; also "Foreword: Tyros and Portraits," Catalogue, *Exhibition of Paintings and Drawings* by Wyndham Lewis (London, Leicester Galleries, April 1921).]

WYNDHAM LEWIS' first publication, called "The Pole" in *The English Review* for May 1909, has been variously described. In *South Lodge* Goldring tells us that Lewis presented himself at 84 Holland Park Avenue to find Ford in the bath, where he proceeded to read him "The Pole," not omitting to introduce himself as a man of genius. The story was instantly accepted. In fact, the last is the only part confirmed by Ford who says he took Lewis' story after reading the first three lines.[1] Elsewhere calling Lewis "D.Z." (and describing him as the swarthy, saturnine figure with tall hat and long hair that others provide for the Lewis of this period), Ford claims that "Poles" (as he calls it) was produced in manuscript form from all over Lewis' person, even from next his skin. He goes on to tell us that, offended at a suggestion that he should turn entirely to writing, Lewis presented himself at the office of *The Times Literary Supplement* and threatened to horsewhip the editor, should that gentleman be so unwise as to give Ford any of Lewis' books to review.[2] It is the first part of this story that Hugh Kenner gives us

1. Ford Madox Ford, *It Was the Nightingale* (Philadelphia, Lippincott, 1933), p. 323.
2. Ford, *Return to Yesterday*, pp. 388–91.

at the start of his study of Lewis; however, it is as well to remember that his contemporaries mistrusted Ford. Both David Garnett and Richard Aldington mention Ford's terminological inexactitudes, the latter writing that "strict veracity was not his strong point." [3] In his biography of Conrad, Gérard Jean-Aubry calls Ford "a pathological liar." And I should here perhaps mention in passing that in the Berg Collection of manuscripts at the New York Public Library there are letters from Lewis to the famous literary agent Pinker, showing that Lewis had already completed a novel by January 1910. He refers to this novel as *Khan and Company* and suggests using the pseudonym James Sed for it; later Lewis was to set his lawyer on Pinker. Certainly, however, *The English Review* saw the publication (after rejection by *Blackwood's*) of Lewis' first satire and there is an affectionate reference to the review in *Tarr*.

Although Goldring says the above incident (which he embellishes in *Odd Man Out*) took place "towards the end of 1909," [4] the story was printed in May. From this date on the group of stories now gathered under the title *The Wild Body* began to appear in *The English Review,* Goldring's *The Tramp, The Little Review,* and *Art and Letters.* They comprise Lewis' earliest work. Pound, in fact, introducing "Inferior Religions" in *The Little Review* for September 1917, says that the entire collection was "in process of publication" when war broke out. They were not published in book form until December 1927 by Chatto and Windus, but two letters from Lewis to Martin Secker in my possession, dated March 3 and 4, 1925, show him trying to make arrangements for publication of the volume under the general title of *The Soldier of Humour*.

It is interesting to establish the fairly early origin of *The Wild Body* stories for in them we already find a theory and practice of satire from which Lewis never swerved. The later satires enlarge his

3. David Garnett, *The Golden Echo* (London, Chatto and Windus, 1954), pp. 37–8; Richard Aldington, *Portrait of a Genius, But . . .* (London, Heinemann, 1950), p. 71.

4. Douglas Goldring, *Reputations* (New York, Seltzer, 1920), p. 135; and cf. Douglas Goldring, *Odd Man Out* (London, Chapman and Hall, 1935), p. 100.

scope, but there is nothing in *The Wild Body* which his subsequent practice contradicts. The ideal structure of satire is here from the first.

First, it must be remembered that in these early stories "humour" is usually satire. Lewis detests humor, of the cosy or *Punch* variety. In *Blasting and Bombardiering* he tells us that *Blast* allotted the first "blast" to humor. He is wrong; humor is given the fifth "blast" as "Quack ENGLISH drug for stupidity and sleepiness." Coffman rather carelessly observes that *Blast* blessed humor. Humor is given the third "bless" in *Blast No. 1* but only when *in the hands of* Shakespeare and Swift, i.e. as satire. *Blast No. 1* calls humor "Arch enemy of REAL" and "a phenomenon caused by sudden pouring of culture into Barbary." *Blast No. 2* reaffirms this emphasis: "The English 'Sense of Humour' is the greatest enemy of England." This second issue of *Blast* attacked *Punch* under this head (a charge repeated by Eliot in *The Sacred Wood*). And Lewis has kept up this dislike of the English "grin" until the present day.[5]

Book IV of *The Mysterious Mr. Bull*, devoted to "The Sense of Humour," further clarifies this dislike. Humor, we learn here, is something you do to yourself; it is a delightful dope, based on evasion of reality, which can be used as a political weapon to keep the masses quiet. It is, in brief, a subjective, romantic tool. So Tarr tells Butcher that humor and pathos (Joël's Romance) are the same. Satire, on the other hand, presupposes change and reforms society. It does something to you. It is accordingly hated by the indolent Many.

Lewis finds Shaw the perfect example of this kind of English humor. The many attacks he makes on Shaw boil down to the charge that Shaw evades reality and creates "safe" lovable characters that take the mind off any real social change. *St. Joan* is "the swan-song of english liberalism staged for the post-war suburbs of London." [6]

5. *Left Wings*, pp. 296–7; *Blasting and Bombardiering*, p. 42; *Rude Assignment*, p. 104.

6. *Art of Being Ruled*, p. 56; and cf. *Blast No. 2*, p. 9; *One-Way Song*, p. 48; *The Enemy No. 3*, p. 91; *Rude Assignment*, p. 202.

A feature of the onslaught Lewis makes on humor is that it is an especially English failing (like "playing the game"). Tarr tells Butcher this. Calling humor the "inveterate enemy of anglo-saxon mankind," Tarr says: " 'The University of Humour—that is what it is—that prevails everywhere in England for the formation of youth, provides you with nothing but a first-rate means of evading reality.' " This section of *Tarr* is expanded in the second edition, where we find Tarr saying: " 'Humour . . . does paralyze the sense for Reality, people are rapt by their sense of humour in a phlegmatic and hysteric dream-world, full of the delicious swirls of the switch-back.' "

There are many, many other such references. From the start of his literary career Lewis approaches satire as the correction of vice, as well as of folly, and as dissatisfaction with the *Zeitgeist,* or social status quo, rather than acceptance of it. In short—*"wherever there is objective truth there is satire."* [7] So one can say that the function of satire, as of graphic art, for Lewis is to depict reality.

Yet there are various kinds of satire. Here he makes two principal definitions. In "classical" (presumably Hellenic and Roman here) satire the abstract, or quintessence, of a vice is pilloried, and it is on this level that the spectators are involved. Although admitting that Jonson of course created dramatic individuals, Lewis feels that the Jonsonian "humour" is the caricature of impersonal vice, of a human flaw common to all. It is the reverse of the caricature of a politician in a contemporary newspaper, which is attached to a definite leading individual. Lewis does not pass judgment on the "classical" form of satire, but in calling *The Apes* his only "pure" [8] satire I think he is suggesting that he regards this book as nearest to classical satire. It is so, in that "humours," endemic to the human animal, are ridiculed. Now it will at once be objected that *The Apes* certainly chose recognizable adversaries from our midst. This is true, but these are selected as representatives of "humours," and *The*

7. *Rude Assignment,* p. 48 (he says the same also on p. 46).
8. Ibid., pp. 52–3.

Apes is not *only* aimed at contemporary vice in the way that *The Childermass, The Revenge for Love,* and *Tarr* tend to be. If asked to pick out Lewis' most Jonsonian satire, I would without doubt select *The Apes.*

But the modern satirist, Lewis pleads, must engage with reality on both abstract and concrete levels. That is to say, since Fielding —with whom satire in creative fiction begins for Lewis—the satirist's function is not only to caricature a "humour," it is to expose recognizably contemporary vice. Like Flaubert, he says, the modern satirist must show up his age far more than his classical antecedent was required to. To this end contemporary satire must be disinterested and cruel. It must be violently destructive. In *Men without Art,* which reprints parts of the important pamphlet *Satire and Fiction,* Lewis tells us that satire is degraded if it becomes moral, (a) because moral judgments are constantly changing and in flux, and (b) because ethics, as today tied to theology, should be eschewed. This raises a point.

Throughout his later pronouncements on the theory of satire Lewis constantly asserts that it must be amoral. "I am a satirist . . . But I am not a moralist." And so on. Yet of course he is a moralist, in the sense that the urge to change the status quo, which avowedly prompts his satire, has a moral intention. One presumes that Lewis is exposing the evils in our society by means of satire in an effort to correct them. But what he clearly desires is that satire should not be "edifying." Any overt connection with a system of contemporary morality, especially one embedded in a religion, will vitiate the work of art for Lewis. It will soften it and make it ineffectual. *"Perfect laughter,* if there could be such a thing, would be inhuman," he writes. To succeed satire must have a painful effect and, in passing, I should warn the reader that Lewis generally (though not always) refers in "laughter" to satire. However, in the early stories, he uses all these terms loosely. Ker-Orr, the "soldier of humour," is really a soldier of satire.

This satire must magnify ("in an heroical manner") small areas of reality; its characterizations must be vast, to occupy space; as he put it in an article in *The London Mercury* for October 1934, "in Satire you reach the great classic lines of the skeleton of things." [9] Satire, he again reminds us here, gives objective truth, the truth of natural science—"satire is the 'truth' of the intellect." [10]

As regards the cruelty of this satire, Lewis from the first sees himself as "an artist in destruction." This conceit he described nicely in a newspaper article: "there was Pancho Villa, with his best friend always on his hip—his gun, that is. (When I read that I put my hand to my breast-pocket and stroked my stylo.)" [11] This is exemplified by Ker-Orr, the central figure of *The Wild Body*. Ker-Orr is, we notice, a *soldier* of humor; for laughter and the militant are always close in Lewis' satire. Ker-Orr likens himself to Don Quixote. He is to be found "manoeuvring in the heart of the reality," and when he finds life his inclination is "to make war on it and to cherish it like a lover, at once." "Everywhere where formerly I would fly at throats, I now howl with laughter." It might be said that Bestre, of this book, combines manslaughter and man's laughter in his formidable eye, a combination also found in Beresin, a character of another story, "The War Baby." Tarr talks about his eye as his shotgun. Ker-Orr says: "Violence is of the essence of *laughter* (as distinguished of course from smiling wit): it is merely the inversion or failure of *force*. To put it in another way, it is the *grin* upon the Deathshead." [12]

What transpires from Ker-Orr's complicated explanations is that "laughter," or satire, is an attack on life, or "reality," forcing the laugher to become detached, to become artistic ("Any master of humour is an essential artist").[13] In other words, laughter is a lib-

9. Wyndham Lewis, "Studies in the Art of Laughter," *The London Mercury, 30,* No. 180 (Oct., 1934), 511–12.

10. Ibid., p. 511.

11. "What It Feels Like to Be an Enemy," *Daily Herald,* No. 5082 (May 30, 1932), p. 8.

12. *Wild Body,* p. 158.

13. Ibid., p. 239. He uses "humour" here to connote satire, of course.

erating force, a revelation of reality cleansing the organism and keeping the "thing," or primitive, at bay. Naturally, the primitive will provide the pabulum of satire, for by contrast the intelligent laugher will have a heightened sense of separation. It is thus significant that Lewis chose for the setting of his first stories a primitive Breton community. *The Wild Body*, that is, is Lewis' only satire that gives us real primitives to laugh at. Subsequently we are to be asked to laugh at intellectual primitives, persons whom we must agree to see as "things" owing to their (idiotic) ideological convictions. But in these early stories Lewis was clearly fascinated by the primitive Breton peasants he had met (and some of this material appeared as factual articles in *The Tramp*), because they defined for him certain literary values. This is well borne out in the tragic story "The Cornac and His Wife."

Ker-Orr explains that the primitive Breton peasant usually designs his laughter to wound. That is, his comic sense does not rise above his circumstances or environment; it remains one with them, brutal as his everyday existence in the fields, brutal even in its necessity for revenge on this life. This is one form of laughter, cruel laughter torn out of a truly primitive state. But the educated man, Ker-Orr continues, uses this same comic sense to transcend his environment; he is conscious, in other words, of necessity. This is what Ker-Orr means when he calls the educated man a greater realist than the common peasant, for in him a philosophic understanding, or imaginative appreciation (as in the artist), of the external world enables him to get at the essence of reality. His laughter feeds on the primitive and, by revealing reality to him, removes him from the primitive condition. "It is a realistic firework, reminiscent of war," Ker-Orr says. Like a firework, it transcends the human condition and explodes, as it were, in derision at such primitivity.

This realization, the fruit of experience on his travels coming soon after having heard Bergson's lectures on laughter at the Collège, led Lewis to a fundamental dichotomy, basic to his entire theory of satire: "First, to assume the dichotomy of mind and body is necessary here, without arguing it; for it is upon that essential separation that the theory of laughter here proposed is based." [14]

This "separation," which we find in *Matière et mémoire,* is between "person" and "thing," Nature and puppet, between true man and machine, between Not-Self and Split-Man, between, finally, the intellect, or "laughing observer," and "Wild Body." In the section of the work entitled "The Meaning of the Wild Body" Lewis tells us it is impossible for us humans to leap this gap between being and "non-being." Indeed, such an effort of self-observation as this would entail might be disastrous: "We are not constructed to be *absolute observers.*" In 1950 he repeats this: "No person, of course, is capable of perfect detachment: the effort to attain it would damage the observation." But it is in this dichotomy that the comic is located: "The root of the Comic is to be sought in the sensations resulting from the observations of a *thing* behaving like a person." [15] If we reverse this statement, as Lewis does in the example he gives following this remark, we have Bergson's words in *Le Rire: "Nous rions toutes les fois qu'une personne nous donne l'impression d'une chose.*" [16] Because of this superficial reversal, McLuhan claims that "His theory of the comic as stated in *The Wild Body* is the exact reverse of the Bergsonian theory of laughter." I cannot agree with this. Lewis' theory of the comic, here, is distinctly Bergsonian, with surface variations, and vagaries.

As his chief example of the comic in this sense Lewis provides the picture of a man running for an underground railway train and just catching it in time, the comic effect being produced by the sight of his eye (intellect) in contrast to his body, which resembles a sack of potatoes. This sight, a Kantian incongruity, is as funny, Lewis says, as a cabbage reading Plutarch. "The deepest root of the Comic is to be sought in this anomaly." [17] It is the anomaly of the "thing"

14. Ibid., p. 243.
15. Ibid., p. 246.
16. Bergson, *Le Rire,* p. 59.
17. *Wild Body,* p. 247.

trying to behave like a "person," the fat man catching the train trying to be as deft and calculating as his eye, which is coolly spectator
of the operation. However, since we know that Lewis regards the
main mass of mankind as things, or "Appropriate dummies," [18] we
can also say that the comic comes equally from a "person" behaving
as a "thing" (though an element of tragedy is present here). Lewis
himself suggests this in *The Wild Body;* the comic result arising
"because the man's body was not him" is a reciprocal affair. After
all, the "person" finds himself provided with a body in this world.
He must at times watch this "sack of potatoes" acting in a "thing"-
like manner, as much as the "thing" making for the train feels his
eye watching his own manipulations. In *The Wild Body* stories,
however, the dichotomy is usually effected outside the character.
That is, none of the peasants presented (except possibly Bestre)
really act as "persons." It is their clash with the intellect in the
person of Ker-Orr that provides the satire. In later works the comic
dichotomy is presented within character. All the apes of God are
essentially "things" trying to be "persons," or artists. Yet, although
Ker-Orr has this special role in *The Wild Body* then, he also fulfills
another function which Lewis seems to consider a necessity in all
his satire, namely that of "showman." [19]

It was necessary, of course, if the "thing"-like peasants of these
stories were to be artistically compelling, for Lewis to have some
intermediary. This intermediary is the reasonably rational man
Ker-Orr, who lends an added dimension to the scene and by means
of whom we are enabled to communicate: "To introduce my puppets, and the Wild Body, the generic puppet of all, I must project a
fanciful wandering figure to be the showman to whom the antics
and solemn gambols of these wild children are to be a source of
strange delight."

In *Rude Assignment* Lewis calls Ker-Orr "ringmaster of this
circus" and, indeed, one of the principal stories in the book concerns a circus. We must not think that the "showman" is the Not-

18. *One-Way Song,* p. 94.
19. *Wild Body,* pp. 232–50.

Self. If he were, we the readers would be unable to communicate through him. He is, rather, a particularly intelligent human being, someone aware of the comic (or tragic) dichotomy. Ker-Orr tells us that his approach to life is a sort of detachment midway between his body, or "gut-bag," and intellect, or his eyes, his "two bright rolling marbles . . . bull's-eyes full of mockery and madness"—"I hang somewhere in its midst operating it with detachment." [20] So Ker-Orr is qualified to observe the clash between "person" and "thing" in his own nature, unlike the others. Unlike them, but like all the other showmen Lewis creates. Thus Ker-Orr talks about his two selves, his two *"me"*'s; Lewis has done the same. René of *Self Condemned* "lived in two compartments." Tarr also has this theory of the two selves in man (which we find, again, in Bergson's *Essai sur les données*), admitting " 'Half of myself I have to hide.' "

Ker-Orr is the first of Lewis' showmen. Lewis must early have found this intermediary indispensable to the kind of satire he wanted to write, for he has always retained him. So we are told of Tarr, in the subsequently excised Egoist Ltd. Prologue: "Tarr is the individual in the book, and is at the same time one of the showmen of the author." [21] Arghol is the showman in *The Enemy of the Stars,* Zagreus in *The Apes.* Pierpoint, the master mind behind the scene in this latter satire, is more the Not-Self, or totally detached individual (so detached he never actually appears in the work). Zagreus is undoubtedly our means of communication; indeed, does he not act as showman, conjuror at Lord Osmund's, spiriting Dan away? In *The Revenge for Love* the Spanish gaoler Don Alvaro Morato enters the stage first and is a sort of showman, with his "clowns," the Communist prisoners. This "socratic turnkey," like most of Lewis' showmen, is gifted with strong eyes. Percy Hardcaster calls him " 'a lynx-eyed old devil,' " [22] and he sees through the first "false

20. Ibid., pp. 3–5.

21. *Tarr* (Egoist), p. x.

22. *Revenge for Love*, p. 19. Hardcaster threatens my theory by calling Alvaro false, in one place. But he may be lying here, as he later lies about Alvaro to Gillian. Eventually he says that Alvaro was " 'rather a fine man in his way.' " (*Revenge for Love*, p. 203).

bottom" in the book, the peasant girl's basket. Don Alvaro's eye, likened to a "bull's-eye" in one place, is reminiscent of Ker-Orr's "marbles." Snooty Baronet, yet another showman, also has eyes that shine like "marbles of freshly polished glass." Snooty frequently, perhaps too frequently, talks about himself as a showman, with the ridiculous characters Val and Humph as his "puppets." The narrator of *Rotting Hill* is another showman, as are, to some extent, Cantleman and the Enemy—while Shakespeare, Lewis alleges, was the supreme showman in this sense.[23] Here is Arghol playing this role in Lewis' play:

> *Arghol.* Existence. Loud feeble sunset—blaring like lumpish savage clown, alive with rigid tinsel, tricked out in louse-infested pantaloons, before a misty entrance, upon the trestled balcony of a marquee, announcing events in a stale programme of a thousand breakneck sports— . . . a showman who bellows down to penniless herds, their eyes red with stupidity, crowding beneath him clutching their sixpences.[24]

23. *Lion and the Fox,* p. 171.

24. *Enemy of the Stars,* pp. 18–19. The jacket of this publication claims that the first version of the play, which appeared in *Blast No. 1,* influenced Joyce in his Circe episode in *Ulysses.* Lewis suggests this himself in various places (e.g. *Time and Western Man,* p. 127), and Hugh Kenner supports the contention (Kenner, *Poetry of Pound,* p. 75). I have not personally been able to find any serious entertaining of this notion. There is no copy of *Blast No. 1* in Joyce's extant library as exhibited in Paris in 1949, though Joyce owned a copy of *The Caliph's Design.* Mr. Frank Budgen kindly tells me that Joyce lent him a copy of *Tarr* in Zürich, but that he never saw any copy of *Blast No. 1* in Joyce's possession.

In a letter to John Henry Quinn, dated January 7, 1921, Joyce says "Circe" is finished and being typed (there is a memoir in support of this from Mr. Sykes, Joyce's typist, in the Special Collections of the New York Public Library). The Slocum-Cahoon bibliography refers at p. 141 to the Circe MS as being in a notebook, and the Paris La Hune Catalogue confirms that this notebook was bought in Trieste (See No. 259 under "Les Oeuvres"). Yet, as Joyce tells Quinn that he wrote this episode nine times over, the notebook is likely to have been only one MS.

My own textual comparison, such as it is, reveals no real indebtedness on Joyce's part to *The Enemy of the Stars,* though both writers have in common verbal vitality and a certain distortion of presentation. Joyce could equally be

We do not, it is true, find a showman (unless it is Hyperides) in *The Childermass,* but this satire is exceptional. In *The Vulgar Streak* Vincent Penhale once more plays this role and ends, like so many of these characters, violently—Arghol is stabbed by Hanp, Hanp ending by drowning. The showman's function is the central one of observing and putting on the platform for us "things," puppets, or "wild bodies," creatures of such primitivity that they are no more than animal machines. The life of these creatures is so rigid, so circumscribed, that it takes on the character of religious ritual. It resembles the dance of an inferior religion. We recall Havelock Ellis claiming that Homer tried to convey the feeling of life at high tide as a dance.

The cryptic and arcane section of *The Wild Body,* called "Inferior Religions," where Eliot saw genius and Pound found "the most important single document that Lewis has written" in 1917, is to be interpreted this way. Lewis himself tells us it explains his title, thus answering the puzzled contemporary reviewer of *The Times Literary Supplement.* What it says is no more than that today the majority of mankind, unwilling and unable to act as "persons," is condemned to go through a routine of life which is like a caricature of religious ritual. In *Rude Assignment* Lewis tells us that he called his first writings "Inferior Religions," and writing to Lord Carlow with the Chatto and Windus edition of *The Wild Body* he explains this more clearly.

So in *The Mysterious Mr. Bull* we find Lewis calling humor "one of the Englishman's inferior religions." It is an obsession. And what

---

said to have been influenced in this last by Jarry's *Ubu Roi.* Who knows? What is interesting, however, is to find Joyce's answer to the charge of plagiarism in *Time and Western Man.* Professor Jones accuses Alderman Whitebeaver of plagiarizing his publications, of being "a barefooted rubber with my supersocks pulled over his face which I publicked in my bestback garden for the laetification of siderodromites and to the irony of the stars" (Joyce, *Finnegans Wake,* p. 160). William Frierson believes that "Lewis used many of Joyce's effects." William C. Frierson, *The English Novel in Transition* (Norman, Okla., University of Oklahoma Press, 1942), p. 269.

we find in these early stories is a number of fanatics possessed of obsessions, to which they are enslaved. This is the meaning of the "Wild Body." For these "creaking men machines . . . involved in a monotonous rhythm from morning till night" are possessed by some "set narrow intoxication" that deprives them of liberty. They are slaves ("abnormal") in the way he told us, in *Paleface,* the Roman *res* was a slave, or a lion, or a wild bee. All these are at the mercy of social or instinctual drives similar to a pseudoreligion: "I would present these puppets, then, as carefully selected specimens of religious fanaticism." [25] So the Frenchman, of "A Soldier of Humour," is intoxicated by, and enslaved to, his desire to be more American than Americans (a prescient critique, perhaps). The "Poles" are clearly at the mercy of their particular state of life, exile inducing a kind of poetic and parasitic indolence. Carl is enslaved to the "stupid madness, or commonplace wildness" of his crude appetites, Zoborov of the same story to his fight with Mademoiselle Péronette for the Beau Séjour pension. "The odious brown person of Bestre" is devoted to the absurd ritual of his ocular warfare with the painter Rivière, while the Cornac, with his wife and "haggard offspring," are slaves of their "implacable grudge" against their public, a "death struggle" with a brutally peasant audience which nightly longs for them to break their necks.

Although Lewis gives other interpretations in "Inferior Religions," the above are the chief sources of these characters. Helplessly impelled by some uncontrolled wish, they turn into mechanisms, "shadows of energy, not living beings." The stories at the end of the collection, and drawn from more educated levels of society, do not refute this analysis. In "You Broke My Dream" (a skit on J. W. Dunne, who is mentioned at the end of *Self Condemned*) a character called Will Blood, formerly Will Eccles in *The Tyro No. 1,* wakes up and—"The play begins." Life for these machines is stifled to a charade. They are not really living at all; they are novices, or Tyros—indeed, the religious pun is perhaps intended

25. *Wild Body,* p. 234.

here. Lewis defines a Tyro as "An elementary person: an elemental in short . . . a puppet worked with deft fingers with a screaming voice underneath." [26] And what else does Bergson require of a comic character in *Le Rire* than this?

In this work comic rigidity, produced in a character by "des mouvements de pantin," is what Bergson thinks funny. The laugher looks on at his comic character as at "une marionette dont il tient les ficelles." [27] There is no difference between Bergson and Lewis here. "Machines," "insects," "things," these are the satirist's material for Lewis and he has never had more of it on hand than today! Hazlitt, in *The English Comic Writers,* finds it a failing in Ben Jonson that his characters are so like "machines." Lewis finds this Jonson's strength. Only the detaching power of unholy laughter can free us from the spurious philosophies of our day, for Lewis; only such laughter can reveal to us man as he truly is: "Laughter is the brain-body's snort of exultation." [28] It is objective truth since it shows us, as can nothing else, man's egoisms and absurdities. It is not, apparently, concerned with revealing man's kinder qualities, though these (one might argue) form part of human reality.

This animality, the "thing"-like condition, which acts like a tonic on Lewis' satiric gift and which is seen at its most endearing in *The Wild Body,* is described by Bergson in *L'Évolution créatrice* as follows: "Ce qui constitue l'animalité, disons-nous, c'est la faculté d'utiliser un mécanisme à déclanchement pour convertir en actions 'explosives' une somme aussi grande que possible d'énergie potientielle accumulée." [29]

In *Le Rire* there are, of course, many ideas which any satirist might be expected to hold: the idea of the indifference ("insensibilité") of satiric laughter as opposed to the benevolence of humor,

26. *Tyro No. 1,* p. 2.
27. Bergson, *Le Rire,* pp. 143, 202.
28. *Wild Body,* p. 238.
29. Bergson, *L'Évolution créatrice,* p. 130.

the need for some human target for laughter to be truly affective, these are two. And there are distinctions to be made between Lewis and Bergson here; when Bergson writes of our laughter being the laughter of a group, Lewis would probably say this was humor rather than satire. But Bergson is speaking in a sociological, rather than literary, sense here; laughter, he suggests, is a social gesture which knits us together, usually against a character who is comic *by being antisocial.* And Lewis would not accept any more readily Bergson's conception of the comic in words and sentences. Beyond such minor reservations, Bergson's *Le Rire* is a primer of Lewisian satire.

For Bergson man becomes funny when the "élan vital" runs down in him, or when he deliberately arrests it. When this happens he atrophies to a machine and we laugh at *"un effet de raideur"* or *"raideur de mécanique . . .* ou l'on voudrait trouver la souplesse attentive et la vivante flexibilité d'une personne." [30] This rigidity—"Automatisme, raideur, pli contracté et gardé"—is the basic comic deformity for Bergson, as it is for Lewis. It is a lack of consciousness, of human awareness—"Le comique est *inconscient"*—which is actually corrected by laughter: "Cette raideur est le comique, et le rire en est le châtiment." [31]

This idea, of the retarding of the "élan vital" to the status of machine, is also given in *Matière et mémoire,* but Bergson develops it fully in *Le Rire.* One example he gives of such mechanical rigidity is an assassin getting out of a train and thereby infringing local company rules. It is interesting that Lewis also uses a train episode to illustrate his comic theory in *The Wild Body.* In *Le Rire* the formula for laughter is summarized as follows: *"Les attitudes, gestes et mouvements du corps humain sont risibles dans l'exacte mesure où ce corps nous fait penser à une simple mécanique."* [32] I have already

30. Bergson, *Le Rire,* pp. 4–10.
31. Ibid., pp. 17, 21.
32. Ibid., p. 30.

quoted Bergson's emphasis on the "pantin," a word that recurs throughout *Le Rire*. Here, in this character ("mécanique plaqué sur du vivant") we have the Wild Body; Bergson even suggests that the comic artist accomplishing this effect is classic! So Bergson lends Lewis his comic type, "la transformation d'une personne en chose." But he does more. For the rigid automatism and "distraction" of the comic type also furnish the comic situation or theme: "Le comique est un côté de la personne par lequel elle ressemble à une chose, cet aspect des événements humains qui imite, par sa raideur d'un genre tout particulier, le mécanisme pur et simple, l'automatisme, enfin le mouvement sans la vie." [33] A rigid mechanism in human affairs, Bergson says, also produces a comic effect similar to that produced by rigidity in the human personality. What he calls "distraction" (absent-mindedness, or lack of awareness) produces a logic of the absurd in events as in men. As well as informing us that they were based on paintings,[34] Lewis tells us that the characters in *The Wild Body* are "little monuments of logic." Bergson even mentions Don Quixote, with whom Ker-Orr feels affinity: "Toute distraction est comique . . . Une distraction systématique comme celle de Don Quichotte est ce qu'on peut imaginer au monde de plus comique." [35]

Thus, Bergson says, a function of comedy is to restore awareness to the human animal and to society. It must wake men up, stop them living in dreams. The only point on which Lewis could quarrel with *Le Rire* is the "insociabilité" of the comic, for what Lewis castigates is too much sociability. Bergson, however, sees the comic in a generous spirit, uniting mankind, whereas Lewis sincerely feels that today the satirist's function is to disrupt the group-rhythm and startle the individual out of it.

So I must conclude that nearly all Lewis' basic convictions about

33. Ibid., p. 88.
34. "Wyndham Lewis," *Beginnings* [by various hands], ed. L. A. G. Strong (London, Thomas Nelson, 1935), p. 98.
35. Bergson, *Le Rire,* p. 148.

satire are found in Bergson. If this shows anything, it surely shows once again what an inspiring teacher Bergson must have been, and how catholic a mind to have inspired artists as dissimilar as Lewis and Proust. It may be that Bergson owes this comic theory to Kant or Nicole, but he lent it directly to Lewis, with minor exceptions.

Chapter 15: A Failure of Energy

"A comic type is a failure of a considerable energy, an imitation and standardizing of self, suggesting the existence of a uniform humanity —creating, that is, a little host as like as ninepins." [*The Wild Body,* pp. 235–6.]

IN *Rude Assignment* Lewis admits that his later satire grew out of Bestre and Brotcotnaz of *The Wild Body,* and if so this must be in the development of the comic type, for there are few hints in these stories of the kind of theme he was to find comic. Naturally, however, the comic theme grows out of the comic type, as Bergson observed in *Le Rire.*

The satiric type for Lewis must excite disgust, as he feels Jonsonian characters do, rather than cosy laughter. The comic type is a "thing," machine, or puppet (Bergson's "pantin"), a failure in intellectual energy and thus a robot governed by routine—for "All difference is energy." Nearly all the characters of the early stories Lewis wrote act out a hollow charade, as their creator thinks most men do today. Roland, in the story "A Breton Innkeeper," "never departs from his *rôle* of buffoon," while Le Père François, in the story of this name used for the later "Franciscan Adventures," equally has his *"rôle"* to play, as again has Pringle in "Unlucky for Pringle." [1] To those of us engaged in this charade that is life, the picture presented of our activities will seem to be a deformation, and such deformation, giving true reality, is exactly what Benda

1. Wyndham Lewis, "A Breton Innkeeper," *The Tramp* (Aug. 1910), p. 411; Wyndham Lewis, "Le Père François (A Full-Length Portrait of a Tramp)," *The Tramp* (Sept. 1910), p. 518; Wyndham Lewis, "Unlucky for Pringle," *The Tramp* (Feb. 1911), p. 413.

asks of the inspired intelligence in *Belphégor*. In Lewis' case this deformation is founded both on the puppet-like rigidity required by *Le Rire* and on Cartesian animal automatism.

I have mentioned this above. Animal automatism is one aspect of the seventeenth-century war between the mechanists and vitalists and it is well covered by Leonora Rosenfield in her *From Beast-Machine to Man-Machine*. Descartes was not the first, as Miss Rosenfield shows us, to be fascinated by the regularity of animal behavior, but under the growing pressure of scientific discovery in his age, especially of physiological discovery, he took the idea ahead and drew reactions to it from other thinkers. Briefly, one may say that in the Cartesian metaphysic soul is identified with reason. The author of *cogito, ergo sum* meant that we exist inasmuch as we reason consciously. Descartes came to deny such conscious reasoning, and so free will, to animals: "Ex animalium quibusdam actionibus valde perfectis, suspicamur ea liberum arbitrium non habere." [2]

The perfectly mechanistic physiology Descartes observed in beasts made it seem unlikely to him that they were capable of thought; and although he did not apparently deny that beasts "existed," as might Lewis, they were for him (a practicing Catholic, after all) closer to plants, and matter, in the great chain of being, than to human beings, and spirit. There are hints in the *Discours de la méthode* that a machine in the shape of an animal was no different, in Descartes' eyes, from the animal itself, and he actually planned to construct such beast-machines. What worried him, and other mechanists engaged on this side of the controversy, like Fontenelle, Gassendi, and the early Henry More, was that beasts evidently felt pain. Father Nicolas Malebranche, a partisan of animal automatism, kicked a pregnant bitch, and it yelped. Descartes met this difficulty by proposing that dogs felt a pain that was different in *kind* from human pain, being merely corporeal and therefore

2. René Descartes, *Oeuvres de Descartes, publiés . . . sous les auspices du Ministère de l'Instruction Publique,* ed. Charles Adam and Paul Tannery (L. Cerf, 1897–1913), *10,* 219.

still mechanistic. In *Les Passions de l'âme* he further developed the idea that perceptions are of two sorts, from the soul and from the body. Animals did not have souls. Yet men certainly had bodies, and the "machine du corps," with its highly mechanical blood circulation shown by Harvey (to name only one such typical discovery), influenced Descartes profoundly. The Church, meanwhile, condemned him for the idea that he could construct beast-machines, for how might God-made and man-made creatures exist on the same level?

The whole of Lewis' approach to the comic type can be found in this controversy. And for her purposes Miss Rosenfield does not investigate Descartes' theories of the physiology of the eye, which are so interesting to a student of Lewis; in the so-called "pineal" gland, receiving immediate stimuli from the eyes, Descartes believed (as Norman Kemp Smith has demonstrated) that here resided "le principal siège de l'âme." Thus the less "mental," or in the Lewisian sense "visual," a man is, the more stupid he becomes. And the more stupid a man is, the more primitive he is; and the more primitive, and lower on the chain of being, the more mechanical. This is one reason accounting for Lewis' constant use of machine imagery, as we shall see below, but it is also the basis of his characterization. Of course, he takes Descartes to absurd extremes. In this he is probably closer to the eighteenth-century French materialist, and friend of Frederick II of Prussia, Julien Offray de La Mettrie, author of *L'Homme-Machine* (1748), which eliminated nearly all nonmechanical elements in the corporeal universe and accused man of being as much a machine as was the Cartesian animal. Evidently La Mettrie conceded a soul, but as this was one totally conditioned by the body it was scarcely a spiritual possibility. La Mettrie, in short, seems to have taken Descartes' idea of the beast-machine to the ridiculous (though still, apparently, debated) conclusion of manmachine, so that perhaps Lewis' lineal affinities in this respect lie with this philosopher, rather than with Descartes, for La Mettrie supposed just that sort of mechanical puppets who parade in clockwork packs through Lewis' fiction. In connection with the hero of *Self Condemned,* incidentally, Kenner notes that René means reborn; it is more to the point to observe that this is Descartes' name and that Lewis' René "was inclined to furrow up his forehead à la Descartes."

No reader can pick up any one of Lewis' satires without noticing the man-machine in them. "The froth-forms of these darkly-contrived machines twist and puff in the air, in our legitimate and liveried masquerade" in *The Wild Body.* Arghol yawns in "mechanical spasms." What does Ker-Orr learn about the would-be American Frenchman but "the important secret of this man's entire machine?" Kreisler is often referred to as a machine. Bertha is "machine-like"—the breath exudes from her nostrils like "the slight steam from a contented machine." Anastasya is an "even more substantial machine." In Lewis' "Tyronic Dialogues," a character called X. defines himself as an "animal," calls his friends, Q. and T., "automata," and has the following exchange with his interlocutor:

F. "I feel that my words, as I utter them, are issuing from a machine. I appear to myself a machine, whose destiny is to ask questions."

X. "The only difference is that I am a machine that is constructed to provide you with answers. I am alive, however. But I am beholden for life to machines that are asleep." [3]

Jack Cruze, in *The Revenge for Love,* having a single obsession in life, is a "love-machine." Kemp exclaims, *"We must escape from the machine in ourselves!"* "Father" François (of *The Wild Body*), Humph (of *Snooty Baronet*), as well as many other characters, are described as "automata," while Mr. Patricks, the shopkeeper of *Rotting Hill* (who significantly resembles Jean-Paul Sartre in looks) "is himself like a wound-up toy." It would be possible to instance the man-machine in Lewis' satire almost indefinitely. No single

3. *Tyro No. 2,* pp. 48–9.

work deploys this characteristic as rewardingly, however, as *The Apes,* of which it might be said, in Lewis' own words in *The Caliph's Design,* "Every living form is a miraculous mechanism." [4]

Lord Osmund Willoughby Finnian Shaw, whose facsimile in real life has been remarked only too often, perfectly personifies La Mettrie, giving "the effect of the jouissant animal—the licking, eating, sniffing, fat-muzzled machine." Lady Fredigonde Follett, in the magnificent section at the beginning called "The Body Leaves the Chair," is a similar animal-machine. The whole of *The Apes* is conscious puppetry; "This was an all-puppet cast," we are told. Almost every character, except the Blackshirt, is described at some point as a "robot," "puppet," "machine," or "dummy"; this especially includes the Finnian Shaw family, Dan Boleyn, Betty Bligh, Ratner, Archie Margolin, and Mélanie Blackwell.[5] The fatuous play, enacted at Lord Osmund's, is thus a sort of charade of shams, a caricature of caricatures. The same idea of intellectual puppet, or "pantin," provides the theme for *The Revenge for Love,* while even Tarr is once described as such.[6]

Lewis' comic type is the human being lacking in awareness, guilty of Bergsonian "distraction," and approximating to the animal-machine. He is a romantic, of course, in his lack of proportion, his servitude to idiosyncracy. Roy Campbell claims that Lewis "accentuates mercilessly the ruling 'humour' of each of his characters." [7] The ape fulfills this role admirably. First, there is the Teutonic idea of the devil as the ape of God, the Simon Magus legend, what Luther called "Affenspiel." Then, the ape is the animal-machine most nearly related to man—and, as Lewis wrote in an entertaining essay on the London Zoo, "The animal world, of course, does not begin at the turnstiles of the Zoo. It begins right here, wherever this book is held in an ape-like and prehensile

4. *Caliph's Design,* p. 40.

5. *Apes,* pp. 65, 87, 108, 146, 349, 603, 625, gives some examples.

6. *Tarr* (Chatto), p. 62 (it is as Tarr rises from being close to Bertha that he experiences this otherwise unusual sensation).

7. *Satire and Fiction,* p. 15.

hand." [8] Further, he is a ghost of animality haunting man's efforts:
"Whenever we get a good thing, its shadow comes with it, its *ape*
and familiar." [9] Again, the ape is an imitator and of course all the
characters in *The Apes* are impersonators of the Godlike artists. In
this sense it is interesting to observe François Mauriac using a similar indictment in his *Le Romancier et ses personnages* of 1933:
"L'humilité n'est pas la vertu dominante des romanciers. Ils ne
craignent pas de prétendre au titre de créateurs. Des créateurs! les
émules de Dieu! A la vérité ils en sont les singes." Martin Jarrett-
Kerr, in his brief study of Mauriac, translates the last part of this as
"emulators of God—they are apes of God." And finally, Lewis uses
the word "ape" in the sense in which we find it in Hazlitt's essay,
"On Shakespeare and Ben Jonson." Hazlitt (who, as a clue, is mentioned at Lord Osmund's) writes as follows: "Man can hardly be
said to be a truly contemptible animal, till, from the facilities of
general intercourse, and the progress of example and opinion, he
becomes the ape of the extravagances of other men. The keenest
edge of satire is required to distinguish between the true and false
pretensions to taste and elegance; its lash is laid on with the utmost
severity." [10]

This is the key to the comic types in *The Apes*. Each has some
idiotic pretension, or "humour," as often as not sexual as well as
artistic, and these "humours" are symptoms of a sick society—boils
that Lewis lances. Two characters, however, stand somewhat apart
in a certain passivity, Dan Boleyn and Horace Zagreus.

Lewis has called Dan "an authentic *naïf*," and in *The Caliph's
Design* he describes the naïf as "a doll-like dummy that the trader
on sentiment pushes in front of him in stalking the public." Here
he goes on to explain that there are two chief types of the naïf in

8. Wyndham Lewis, "The Zoo," *London Guyed*, ed. William Kimber (London,
Hutchinson, 1938), p. 168. Was it by typographical error, or Freudian lapse, that
Lewis called the famous "animal man" Mr. Cess Smith throughout this article?

9. *Art of Being Ruled*, p. 225.

10. William Hazlitt, *Lectures on the English Comic Writers* (London, John
Templeman, 1841), p. 67.

the contemporary artistic world, the lover of the primitive and the lover of the child. In fact, much of the criticism of this pamphlet is behind the creation of Dan (whose original makes for some tempting guesswork); and there is behind him also Lewis' dislike of the swarming of young geniuses today, as expressed in *The Doom of Youth*. Zagreus is the showman. Some critics have seen him as a sympathetic autobiographical characterization, but I do not agree with this view. Zagreus is frequently ridiculed. In *The Criterion*, when he first appeared, Lewis called him "a central myth." [11] He is the emissary of Pierpoint who, if anyone is, may be the "Vorticist King"; and he is also described as Pierpoint's Plato. Hugh Kenner points out that Pierpoint was the name of the public hangman in England at this time, so that Lewis presumably thought of him as the executioner (and a Fascist one) behind the moribund society of the work. However, the executioner who has recently received such publicity in England was Pierrepoint [*sic*]; Lewis spells his character either Pierpoint or Pierpont. [12]

One could easily continue to involve oneself in these amusing obscurities, but it is more to my purpose here to conclude with two examples of the Lewisian comic type in action, Percy Hardcaster and Otto Kreisler. I take these, not only because they are often considered two of Lewis' best characters, but also because they have certain traits which lead us into the comic theme. The pure puppet in Lewis' satire, that is, usually yields to one interpretation only. Compare, for instance, Hardcaster with Agnes Irons in *The Revenge for Love*. Agnes, golf champion of Malaya, is straight out of *The Apes* in type (she belongs there in Part VIII perhaps). In *The Apes* this kind of rigid caricature suits the theme but, put beside Hardcaster, Agnes is fairly uninteresting.

For Hardcaster grows. Indeed, he is one of the few characters in Lewis' satire to do so. At the beginning of *The Revenge for Love*

11. Wyndham Lewis, "Mr. Zagreus and the Split-Man," *The Criterion*, 2, No. 6 (Feb. 1924), 124.

12. See *Apes*, pp. 267–70, for variant spellings; Kenner, *Lewis*, p. 100.

it appears that he is not wholly convinced of communism. He disagrees with Don Alvaro's anti-Marxist sentiments, but he does so "against his better judgment." It is this better judgment (his intellect) that puts Percy on bad terms with himself, as we learn he is. At the start of the work Percy seems to me entirely unsympathetic, "a brasshat in the class-war" with a "mock-proletario vocabulary." But on returning to London he undergoes a purgatory in the sham of Chelsea communism. For a while he plays with these political buffoons, "to whom a communist *workman* was distinctly an alarming notion," but he reaches a turning point when he confronts the shallow, treacherous, vindicative, and entirely phony Communist, Gillian. Typically, a woman was chosen for this role.

Margot, Hardcaster's alter ego, says of these salon Communists, "Spring up and face them, and they would give way before you." Hardcaster does just this. He tells Gillian the truth, via Machiavelli, and upon this unspeakable breach of political etiquette Gillian turns and sets her "natural man," Jack Cruze, on him. Percy is kicked when down, in a caricature of the English sporting spirit. Now this kicking seems to me important, and I find Kenner's interpretation of it, as an action of "irrelevant neutrality" like the kicking of Arghol at the beginning of *The Enemy of the Stars,* a misreading. We are explicitly told that Percy emerges from the illness following the injuries of this kicking physically drawn, and also *changed inside.*[13] What has happened in Hardcaster's development is that his intellect has triumphed. We are told that he now possesses will, the one thing the others have not got,[14] and indeed his eye confronting that of Jack Cruze is clearly intellect facing senses. Forged in this flame, Hardcaster is now "the real Communist." [15] He is Hard Castle, *castillo duro,* as he himself had put it earlier. At the end he is twice called "incorruptible," and the tear that rolls down his cheek in the last lines of all may be a tear of self-pity, but

13. *Revenge for Love,* p. 271.
14. Ibid., p. 174.
15. Ibid., p. 210.

it is equally (and Marvin Mudrick would seem to agree here) [16]
one of compassion for Margot.

Otto Kreisler, Lewis' finest individual characterization, is far
more subtle and significant, however. Of *Tarr* Lewis has recently
written: "The book should have been called 'Otto Kreisler,' rather
than 'Tarr,' who is a secondary figure." [17] Equally for Pound
Kreisler is the most important creation in the book.[18] Most reviewers agree with this. Yet Tarr, we read in the Egoist Prologue, is the
"hero." In fact, we approach Kreisler through Tarr.

Tarr is an intelligent English artist in Bohemian Paris, a part of
Paris possessed by Germans. His name was that of a famous crick-
eter of the day, thus introducing the recurrent "play the game"
motif to which I will return below. He is autobiographical: "In the
physical description of the young Englishman, Tarr, may be seen
a caricatural self-portrait of sorts." [19] At the opening of the work
Tarr has just broken off his engagement with Bertha Lunken
(Lewis himself was engaged to a German girl in Paris before the
war). This is an effort on the part of the English and intellectual
to disengage itself from the German and sensual which characterizes the whole. We are explicitly told that Tarr's intellect resented
his attachment to Bertha's sensuality.[20] Tarr is continually associated with the intellect. This man, " 'strong i' the head: and uncom-
monly swarthy,' " and whose art is "ascetic rather than sensuous,"
is engaged in a "long drawn-out struggle" between intellect and
senses, between art and life. And surely we are permitted to associate Bertha with Big Bertha, the artillery piece, for the latter is
mentioned in *Snooty Baronet*,[21] while in *Wyndham Lewis the*

16. Marvin Mudrick, "The Double-Artist and the Injured Party," *Shenandoah*,
4, Nos. 2–3 (Summer/Autumn 1953), 63.

17. *Rude Assignment*, p. 151.

18. Ezra Pound, *Instigations of Ezra Pound* (New York, Boni and Liveright,
1920), p. 217.

19. *Rude Assignment*, p. 151.

20. *Tarr* (Chatto), p. 203.

21. *Snooty*, p. 167.

Artist Lewis has confessed to the visual stimulus the great German siege guns gave him at this time.[22] His war drawings evidence this further. In passing, Lewis is unlike Joyce as a rule in his choice of names. Few of these, I think, make complicated puns. This belief is surely backed by the numerous minor name changes Lewis made in the second edition of *Tarr*—Knackfus becoming Vitelotte, Pfeifer becoming Kreutzberg, and so on—for which I cannot account, though Lewis has told us that Knackfus stands for Montparnasse.[23]

Bertha, then, this " 'high-grade aryan bitch, in good condition, superbly made,' " stands for the senses. Like Kreisler, her character has a self-immolating side that makes her love a possessive and devouring quality. Although so physically yielding, Bertha is predatory; in her frightful flat, "An intense atmosphere of teutonic suicide permeated everything." And, like Kreisler, Tarr "found it difficult to think of her as fleeing, and not pursuing." At the start of the book this personification of Romance is dragging Tarr down. And in this sense the story is one of the resurrection of Frederick Tarr himself. For at the end, "committed to the rôle marked out by reason," Tarr recovers balance. He meets Anastasya, even more physically opulent than Bertha ("a sort of super-Bertha," as Pound says), but remains uncommitted, though tempted. After he has kissed her, Tarr adjusts his glasses (intellect) and leaves her. Before doing so, he puts her in her proper, female place by treating her as a prostitute. He goes on to marry Bertha from duty (after all, we are told that her child resembles him), and she hopes that he is at last "denying reality" by doing so. His subsequent marriage to another girl shows that he is not. Mrs. Bertha Tarr, meanwhile, marries an eye-doctor, the one person, I would say, she ought to have seen in the first place! Thus Tarr gives us "the message of a figure of health"; he, the artist, has succeeded in conquering life, as the Egoist Prologue suggests.

22. *Wyndham Lewis the Artist,* p. 69.
23. *Beginnings,* p. 103.

Kreisler, however, with whom Tarr becomes involved over the duel, is rather more interesting because wider in implication. After all, not many of us are artists. But in Kreisler critics have seen a clever racial critique. Lewis frankly admits this. The Egoist Prologue says: "Kreisler in this book is a German and nothing else." In *Rude Assignment* Lewis re-emphasizes that *Tarr* is a novel about Germans and Germany, saying that "Otto Kreisler represents the melodramatic nihilism of the generations succeeding to the great era of philosophic pessimism." It is important to see *Tarr* as a criticism of this kind of Germany, and not a criticism thrown up by the first World War, as Pritchett mistakenly sees it. Kreisler's roots are in just that French antiromanticism examined in the first part of this study. Pound claims that *Tarr* was finished before the war, and Pound was responsible for having the work serialized in *The Egoist*. There is other evidence to support the idea that it was relatively uninfluenced by the war. According to the Egoist Prologue, which is dated 1915, the book was begun in 1910, and according to the Chatto and Windus Preface later, it was written during the first year of the war. This would all tie in with a letter to Sir William Rothenstein, alleging that it was completely written before Lewis enlisted, i.e. 1915.[24]

We first come across Kreisler, as we do another monumental philistine of modern fiction, Buck Mulligan, in the act of shaving. From this point on he is often to be found fatalistically sitting in cafés; as Lewis puts it in *Rude Assignment,* "he enjoys drifting with time, until they should reach the brink of the cataract." From the first, he is "Doomed Evidently."

This fatalistic nihilism in Kreisler's character is suggestively built up. From the start he is irrevocably committed to his *"Schicksal"* and his suicide at the end is both logical and compelling. It is, in fact, the subject of the book, an act of revenge upon society or a kind of "revenge for love." For the same fatality combined with erotic en-

24. Sir William Rothenstein, *Men and Memories, Recollections of William Rothenstein, 1900–1922* (London, Faber and Faber, 1932), pp. 378–9.

joyment that we meet in Kreisler is hinted at in a brief criticism of the German spirit in *Blast No. 2,* where Lewis writes of the "fantastic arrogance of a Prussian officer engaged in an amorous adventure. The Martinet and the Coquette are mingled. He is also a Samurai." Surely this is Kreisler. We read that he has a "prussian severity of countenance," a "martial tread," and the "frowning fixity of the Prussian warrior." So he advances on Bertha with a "fatal, martial monotony." As Lewis explains in *Rude Assignment,* "When the events of his life became too unwieldy 'he converted them into love.'" Bertha and Kreisler—"confederates beneath the same ban of the world's law"—personify together the German romantic nihilism that is the racial criticism of the work. Bertha, who has "'a nice healthy bent for self-immolation,'" according to Tarr, is often likened to Kreisler in her fatalism. And Kreisler, constantly referred to by the Liepmann ladies as a brute and a beast, is actually once called "Shicksal" [*sic*]: "Destiny had laid its trap in the unconscious Kreisler." Thus they are tellingly brought together in a brutal erotic clash, symbolic of the social rape Lewis thinks the Germans would like to effect in the society of nations. Indeed, Kreisler, who is called a pure German, is fascinated by suffering, we read, and demands to make society suffer also. This is admirably symbolized by the duel.

But Kreisler's "plan of outrage" is first shown in action at the Liepmann party. We notice that both Kreisler, at this party, and Zagreus, "Chez Lionel Kein," act abominably on purpose (like Knut Hamsun's Glahn), in an attempt to break up and disintegrate reality, though it is true that they do this from different starting points. Kreisler is, of course, the man of "action," in the Lewisian sense. He boasts of having violently beaten up a dun in Italy. He has already had a student duel and we are told that he either seeks out women to humiliate them, or to suffer by them. He keeps a dog whip in his apartment and has "the romantic stiff ideals of the german student of his generation." Lewis' period in Munich was most valuable to him here.

In Kreisler (Conrad's Schomberg, with his "grotesque psy-chology") we have the best example of "pantin" in Lewis' satire. For in this character he found a rigidity of ideology to raise Kreisler above the stereotypes of *The Apes*. Lewis' comic type here engages with a wide reality. In Forster's terminology Kreisler is "round," whereas the apes are "flat," or types (*the* lesbian, *the* millionaire-bohemian, *the* young genius, and so on); the apes are from Theo-phrastus. Hardcaster is also "round." He develops and shows some, if only minor, flexibility. And, like Kreisler, he is close to the tragic. But Kreisler perfectly personifies the social automatism of which Bergson wrote in *Le Rire:* "L'esprit qui s'obstine finira par plier les choses à son idée, au lieu de régler sa pensée sur les choses." [25] Kreisler does just this in his absurd duel, in which he injects reality with a nightmare of "action" and tries to make the world conform to his personality; not only is this duel, in its futility and needlessness, highly reminiscent of the duel in *Fathers and Sons* between Pavel Kirsanov and Bazarov, but it makes us think of other nihilistic duels, both before and after *Tarr,* involving Naph-tha, Stavrogin, Leverkühn. Blind commitment to Schicksal leads Kreisler to this useless duel, which no one really wants to fight, except perhaps Kreisler's second, the bogus-revolutionary Bitzenko. But Kreisler's rigidity is such that he is unable to swerve from his logical destiny (we are told that he really ought to have killed him-self at the beginning of the book), and he sees the duel as a fight for *Lebensraum:* "He, Kreisler, is insulted: he is denied equality of existence." What a compelling parallel this character makes with Hitler in so many ways! Kreisler, who craves discipline, wishes he could use swords, rather than pistols, in his duel. Blood is what he would like to see shed. He kills Soltyk "in a silly accident," bolts like a criminal knowing (we read) that he was beaten. His final suicide is reminiscent of Hardcaster's end in *The Revenge for Love* (and slightly duplicated by Penhale's suicide at the end of *The Vulgar Streak*). Both Hardcaster and Kreisler, in their respective prison cells, experience similar twinges of self-pity, both realize

25. Bergson, *Le Rire,* p. 189.

that they have been living a dream. Kreisler, however, unlike Hardcaster, kills himself and dies without dignity, "the last thing he was
conscious of his tongue," organ of the senses, while the last organ
of Percy's that is mentioned is the eye.

Kreisler is guilty of the romantic heresy, of injecting reality with
dream, and of mixing art and life. Tarr actually describes him as
a dithyrambic spectator at the end, when he says, " 'I believe that
all the fuss he made was an attempt to get out of Art back into
Life again.' " [26]

It was on the basis of the character of Kreisler that so many English reviewers likened *Tarr* to Dostoevsky that, writing in *The Egoist* for September 1918, T. S. Eliot could claim that it was "already
a commonplace to compare Lewis to Dostoevski." Calling Lewis,
as I have observed above, "the most fascinating personality of our
time," Eliot went on to praise the book highly,[27] if not quite so
highly as Pound who called it "the most vigorous and volcanic
English novel of our time." [28] Actually the contemporary reviews
of the book were by no means entirely eulogistic. Nearly every reviewer had some reservations, generally over the long talk between
Anastasya and Tarr at the end. On the whole the good reviews did
come from the more intelligent papers (*Morning Post, The Man-
chester Guardian, The Scotsman*), the poor reviews from the popular press (*Daily News, Observer, Aberdeen Journal*), and, as was
to become customary for a work signed by Wyndham Lewis, from
America. *The New Republic* for July 13, 1918, for instance, found
the work guilty of "inhumanity," and "an example of exasperated
self-consciousness, of town-mad art." (Hugh Gordon Porteus later
called it a "too-smart-to-last novel." [29]) *The Nation* thought it a

26. *Tarr* (Chatto), p. 305; on p. 113 of this edition Kreisler is further described
as a German "of the true antiquated grain." In the Carlow Collection there is
Lewis' card dated 1905, when he was staying at the Pension Bellevue, Theresien-
strasse No. 30, I and II Str., Munich.

27. T. S. Eliot, " 'Tarr,' " *The Egoist, 5,* No. 8 (Sept., 1918), 105–6.

28. Pound, *Instigations*, p. 215.

29. Hugh Gordon Porteus, "Wyndham Lewis," *The Twentieth Century, 2,* No. 7
(Sept., 1931), 5.

"dull rigmarole," while Henry B. Fuller, in *The Dial,* actually suggested that Lewis was sympathetic to the German element in the book! [30]

Eliot was referring to a number of references to Dostoevsky in the English reviews of *Tarr.* He endeavored to correct *The Times Literary Supplement*'s view of the lack of balanced method in the book by means of the ingenious suggestion that Kreisler and Tarr alternately imposed their own method on the narrative. (What happens, one wonders, when a stupid and insensitive character imposes a method on a work of art? Can it still remain a work of art?) *The Times,* for July 11, 1918, had indeed been critical, though by no means hostile. But *Tarr* was for *The Times* a document, rather than a work of spontaneous art, and a document that in its utter nihilism out-Dostoevskyed Dostoevsky. Two other reviewers, however, prior to Eliot's notice, had praised Lewis for his affiliations with Dostoevsky in the creation of Kreisler. Robert Nichols, in *The New Witness,* found the three masters of the author of *Tarr* to be Dostoevsky, Balzac, and Flaubert. He went on: "it will become a date in literature, not on account so much of the book's intrinsic value (though that is considerable) as because here we have the forerunner of the prose and probably of the manner that is to come, a prose that is bare and precise . . . Here the new writer takes definite and lasting leave of the romantic movement, not as in Mr. Joyce's '*Portrait of the Artist as a Young Man*' (also published by the Egoist Press) with a regretful wave of the hand, but with a most decided shake of the fist." [31] Nor has Nichols been alone in this large claim for *Tarr,* A. J. A. Symons writing in 1937 that the work was "the first signpost to the novel of the future." [32] One supposes that the critics who saw *Tarr* as a break from the traditional English novel

30. Henry B. Fuller, "A Literary Swashbuckler," *The Dial, 45,* No. 774 (Oct. 5, 1918), 261–2.

31. Robert Nichols, "An Exposé of the Hun," *The New Witness, 12,* No. 305. (Sept. 6, 1918), 371.

32. A. J. A. Symons, "The Novelist," *Twentieth Century Verse, 6/7* (Nov./Dec. 1937), unpaged.

were thinking of the author's scant respect for the usual narrative sequences and the deposing of the "hero" from a central position. Certainly the text is stripped of the normal aspects of narrative, in a way that reminds one slightly of *Howard's End* of 1910. The author, that is, will dismiss the narrative element of *Tarr* as an annoying necessity ancillary to the more pressing psychological interests of the novel; thus, of Tarr and Anastasya: "At that moment the drums began beating to warn everybody of the closing of the gates. They had dinner in a Bouillon near the Seine. They parted about ten o'clock." In a similar way there is more narrative in the last page of the book than in the whole novel put together. As Lewis has well observed, *Tarr* was composed at the height of his abstract sympathies.

One other reviewer besides Nichols seized on the Dostoevskyan depiction of Kreisler as German, and one should perhaps remember that Constance Garnett's translation of *The Brothers Karamazov* appeared in 1912. The anonymous reviewer in *The Nation* (London), who Lewis tells us was none other than Rebecca West, and whom he thus not for nothing calls "by far the best book-critic at that time," [33] was equally impressed by the psychological perspicuity shown in the handling of Kreisler. *Tarr* was here "a beautiful and serious work of art that reminds us of Dostoevsky only because it too is inquisitive about the soul, and because it contains one figure of vast moral significance which is worthy to stand by Stavrogin." [34]

The comparison with Nikolai Stavrogin of *The Possessed* is not one that should be pressed, however. Stavrogin is an aristocrat, and his nihilism has other implications. He has a wealthy mother, Varvara Petrovna, while Kreisler is kept continually short of funds by his father, and to some extent his actions are impelled by lack of cash. There is the same duel business and boorishness in respectable society. But Stavrogin is married when the story opens,

33. *Rude Assignment*, p. 148; *Blasting and Bombardiering*, pp. 92–3.
34. "Tarr," *The Nation* (London), 23, No. 19 (Aug. 10, 1918), 506–8.

and although presumably Verkhovensky, who organizes the Nihilists in Dostoevsky's work, is Lewis' Bitzenko, and the arson accomplished with Stavrogin's seemingly tacit consent is a Kreisler-like action, there are many aspects of *The Possessed,* such as the critique of godlessness, which have nothing to do with Lewis' satire.

Even so, it is odd that critics have not pursued this comparison, made by Pound and Eliot as well as by Rebecca West; but Kenner, Tomlin, Grigson, and Porteus all (perhaps wisely) avoid mentioning Lewis' indebtedness to Dostoevsky. It remained for Lienhard Bergel to deliver a most interesting paper at the annual meeting of the Modern Language Association of America in 1955 entitled "Wyndham Lewis, Dostoevsky, and Gide: The Demon of Progress in the Arts" (unpublished as this goes to press).

Professor Bergel does not find any real ideological similarity between Kreisler and Stavrogin. On the other hand, he sees *Tarr* in the perspective of the German artist-novel, and observes the borrowing of Kreisler's name from E. T. A. Hoffmann. *"Tarr* reads almost like a parody on German romantic artist novels, a parody that is executed in the style of Dostoevsky," writes Bergel, adding: "But it is the manner of *The Notes from the Underground,* rather than that of *The Possessed,* which is continued in Lewis's novel." It is *The Revenge for Love,* Bergel feels, that is really Lewis' *The Possessed.* Dostoevsky's criticism of Western "progressivism" (in Verkhovensky) is transposed by Lewis to his Chelsea dilettantes, and there are in this connection some very close similarities between the two books, as there are also between *The Revenge for Love* and Gide's *Les Faux-Monnayeurs.* "Gide's novel," Bergel suggests, "may well have served as an inspiration to Wyndham Lewis." The possession by Hardcaster of a genuine Juan Gris is made in the same context, Bergel shows, by Werfel, Gide, and Mann (Leverkühn): "The sections in Werfel's novel *Barbara* that deal with the Viennese Bohème of 1918 read like a preview of *The Revenge for Love."* In sum, Bergel supposes that all these writers —being themselves of the avant-garde—particularly suspect "the irresponsible toying with 'advanced' ideas for the thrill they provide," and "the symbiosis of sham culture and nihilism."

Carlo Linati, who has a laudatory section on Lewis in his *Scrittori anglo americani d'oggi*, and is rewarded by being called "Linati, that fine critic of Milan" in *One-Way Song*, has also some suggestive things to say about *Tarr*. For he has read Lewis with care and understands that Kreisler's tragi-comic flaw is his inability to come to terms with reality. Kreisler is incapable of realism (of "the realistic intelligence"); and we are also told that reality brings him up short, and that he hears laughter like a blow.[35] So Linati writes: "La figura di Kreisler, nella sua stortura, è magnifica. Questo satanico impotente par riassumere in sè tutte le disfatte degli artisti falliti, il febbrile disgusto dell'ideale non raggiunto, le vendette dell'uomo contro l'insufficienza della realtà e la mediocrità della creazione. Kreisler ha l'energia devastatrice di un Jago . . ."[36]

Personally, I cannot see *Tarr* as a signpost to the novel of the future. Lewis' work has not proved seminal in the way Joyce's has. But in this martial nihilist, who "hated powerfully," the comic type as envisaged by Lewis achieves real stature. No character he has created since matches Kreisler in importance, or suggests that need for social reform which the best satire presupposes. *The Apes*, though a larger and perhaps better written work, has a smaller subject. And in any case, like all great characters in fiction, Kreisler is wider in significance than the racial critique I have been suggesting here allows. There is something of Kreisler in every adolescent. But it is as a nationalist symptom that he makes an especially disturbing character to read today. With his hatred, bellicosity, paranoia, romanticism, and love of the *alt'deutsch*, Kreisler *is* Goebbels or Hitler. And the sexual side of the Nazi myth is in him also. So Lewis writes prophetically in this work: "Instead of rearing pyramids against Death, if you can imagine some more uncom-

35. *Tarr* (Chatto), pp. 87, 117.
36. Carlo Linati, *Scrittori anglo americani d'oggi* (Milano, Corticelli, 1932), p. 31.

promising race meeting its obsession by means of an unparalleled immobility in life, a race of statues, in short, throwing flesh in Death's path instead of basalt, there you would have a people among whom Kreisler would have been much at home." [37]

37. *Tarr* (Chatto), p. 157, a passage unaltered from the first edition.

Chapter 16: The Tragic Impulse

"Tarr's message, as a character in a book, is this. Under the camouflage of a monotonous intrigue he points a permanent opposition, of life outstripped, and art become lonely . . . He exalts Life into a Comedy, when otherwise it is, to his mind, a tawdry zone of half-art, or a silly Tragedy. Art is the only thing worth the tragic impulse, for him." [Prologue, *Tarr*, Egoist Ltd. edition, p. xi.]

"TRAGIC HUMOUR," Lewis wrote in *Blast No. 1*, "is the birthright of the North." As he put it in *The Enemy of the Stars*, there is a "unique point of common emotion from which these two activities arise." So Socrates, at the end of the *Symposium*, compels Agathon and Aristophanes, tragic and comic poets, to acknowledge that the true artist in tragedy is also a comic artist. For Lewis, Shakespeare combines the two ideally.[1] And he is defining his own satire, I feel sure, when he writes: "Satire, some satire, does undoubtedly stand half-way between Tragedy and Comedy. It may be a hybrid of these two, or it may be a *grinning* tragedy, as it were." [2]

Lewis seems to have felt this from the outset of his career. In *The Wild Body* we read, "Laughter is the representative of tragedy, when tragedy is away . . . Laughter is the emotion of tragic delight . . . Laughter is the female of tragedy." "There is laughter and laughter," he wrote later in *Satire and Fiction*, "and that of true satire is as it were a *tragic* laughter." Points 9 and 10 of the *Blast* manifestoes confirm this.

The satires themselves are full of such references. We are told

1. *Lion and the Fox*, p. 21.
2. "Studies in the Art of Laughter," p. 515.

that Bestre and Brotcotnaz are tragic organisms, that the Cornac and his wife tread a hairline of laughter and terror, and that the Frenchman of the first story "was convinced the greater part of the time that he was taking part in a tragedy." [3] In *Tarr* Bertha's face lights with a "happy tragic resolve," the farcical duel takes on a "tragic trend," while Tarr actually calls comedy the "embryo" of tragedy on one occasion. It is in the other satires, too. "We are tragic beings," Lewis writes in *Rude Assignment,* and he surely means by this that the spectacle of man acting as a machine or "pantin" is a sad affair.

On this relationship to the tragic his comic theme is based. In his book on Shakespeare Lewis accepted the definition of tragedy as a fall from high estate (only one of various forms, of course, yet apparently the most important to his purposes). Tragedy is directed against the fortunate, he claims, and after *The Wild Body* very little of his satire is directed against low life. The majority of his butts have a lot to lose; they are usually characters puffed up, by wealth or pretensions to talent, to a condition of spuriously high estate, from which they are then knocked down like ninepins by his pen. In the Shakespeare book, it is interesting to find him objecting that what usually deprives tragedy of the status of "the purest art" is its destruction of the colossus by means of the little man (the Jack the Giant-Killer theme). Certainly this is not a feature of Lewis' satiric approach.

But I do not mean that Lewis wants us to read the satires as tragedies. Far from it. *The Apes* is not tragic in the sense that a Shakespearian tragedy is. If Lewis had wished to achieve this effect, he would naturally have written tragedies of the dramatic sort. The fall from high estate of Dick Whittingdon, for example, a sort of burst bubble of inflated reputation, does not move us to tears, nor is it intended to; it is meant to arouse a savage dislike in us and move us to a pitiless correction of the society responsible for this automaton, who actually believes he can paint. (Richard Wyndham

3. *Wild Body,* pp. 8, 137, 239.

was, of course, a worthless society dilettante.) As we read in *The Ideal Giant,* "The terrible processions beneath are not of our making, and are without our pity." The tragedy lies behind the satiric presentation, in social implications. This is what Lewis meant when he wrote, "art cannot be 'tragic' in the intense fashion of life, without ceasing to be art." He would argue that Shakespeare could not write an *Othello* or *Lear* today. The heroic individual, the "person," who made the Shakespearian tragedy possible, has all but vanished. Consequently our tragedy, tragedy for us "things," can never achieve the stature of art, with the result that satire becomes the truest tragedy of our times. *The Apes* illustrates this.

The Apes is a merciless exposure of men and women as social symptoms. Lewis himself sees it from this point of view; it was about "the social decay of the insanitary trough between the two great wars," [4] and most of Lewis' criticism is to be found in it. He calls the book an inferno of social decadence, adding: "A society has premonitions of its end . . . Mortification already set in at the edges. They began to stink. I have recorded that stink." [5] Homosexuality, the youth cult (Dan has the "prestige of the 'under-twenties' "), the revolutionary orthodoxy, all are flayed in this unforgettable picture of a moribund society. But the balance is arranged against artistic (literary and graphic) amateurism. Although *The Apes* is a fictional digest of the critical works, it is, unlike them, *primarily* leveled against the class in which Lewis lived and by which he was most hurt, namely the literati—the "lettered herd." Then, it could be argued that artistic amateurism is for Lewis only one more example of the collapse of the authoritarian tradition which is the principal weakness of our societies today. The longing for irresponsibility in the child, artist, and imbecile (all three conveniently coalescing for Lewis in a figure like Gertrude Stein) is itself a social phenomenon against which Lewis inveighed in *The Art of Being Ruled.* All the same, *The Apes* is

4. *Rude Assignment,* p. 199.
5. Ibid., p. 171.

aligned against artists; it is as such that it is remembered. This, as I shall show, robs it of real importance for some critics, and I think one can safely say that it is in this way more satiric than tragic, whereas *Tarr,* which has wide social implications, fulfills far better Lewis' expressed desire that satire should act as a tragic cathartic. *The Apes* is aimed, in short, at a far more special target than Swift condescended to address. Lewis himself may be hinting at this weakness when he calls the book his only "pure" satire, but the work does show us the tragic fall from high estate. To cling to my original example, Dick Whittingdon is brought on to the stage as an admired, successful, wealthy amateur artist, and with his servants, motor cars, and leisure we might excusably envy him; but by the time we have finished reading about him we are—or should be—united in despising him as an empty, vain, and stupid painter, and a sexual pervert to boot. So Dick falls from grace and Lewis achieves a genuine satiric effect. He is a "sham-man."

The Apes is a satire of millionaire Bohemia, of what Horace Zagreus calls " 'the High Bohemia of the Ritzes and Rivieras.' " We are prepared for the attack by the previous criticism, in *The Art of Being Ruled* and *The Diabolical Principle,* of artistic amateurism today, rife now since monied men deprived of public life by the democratic conceit turn to art.[6] Yet he also told us, in *The Enemy No. 2,* that "The millionaire revolutionary proletarian of 1927 is, in short, disguised as a 'bohemian.' " *Time and Western Man* attacked "the moneyed throng of the 'revolutionary' High-Bohemia." Also, the same criticism is hinted at in *Tarr* and confined, with its "Noblesse of Gomorrah," to a gloomy purgatory in *The Childermass.* For instance, Tarr's friend Lowndes has "just enough money to be a cubist, that was to say quite a lot." (And Lowndes once looks at his watch with "apelike impulsiveness.") Tarr's dislike of Hobson equally prepares us for *The Apes.* Hobson, rotted with liberalism and Bohemianism, is told that he lacks all individuality and that any normal State would sterilize him. The easiest

6. *Art of Being Ruled,* pp. 151–9, 177; *Diabolical Principle,* p. 132.

breakthrough into *The Apes* itself, and a condensation of all this criticism, can be found in the encyclical delivered to Zagreus from Pierpoint.[7]

The satire of this moribund society—now dead?—begins appropriately with the prelude of Lady Fredigonde preening herself, getting ready, in fact, to die. "The especial effluvium of *death,* like a stale peach crept in her nostrils." [8] Then the society is exposed, man by man, or man-woman by woman-man. Obviously the work is a *roman à clef* with real life originals, the existence of many of whom today naturally prohibits overt speculation. But some of the subjects have acknowledged the gratuitous portraiture; thus Campbell says he sat for "Zulu" Blades, though "Zulu" is described as a "disgusting beast." It is this fatuous society, with its *Salonfähigkeit* (Lord Phoebus with his tower to show he was a poet, Lady Harriet "living period-piece in crazy motion" and author of *Sobs in Quad*), that the Blackshirt, Bertram Starr-Smith, symbolically kicks on the behind in the person of Colonel Ponto. He later kicks Dan himself, and "The Vanish," or conjuring trick by which Zagreus makes Dan disappear, is another symbol of what should happen to this society. We recall, too, that *starr* is the leitmotiv of Worringer's desiderata for art.

The destructive side of the book presents no difficulty and may give more or less satisfaction. It is on the work's constructive side that I find divergence among critics. Who, for instance, is Starr-Smith? Who is Pierpoint? How much may we take it that Lewis sympathizes with these two? Pierpoint, the man behind the scenes organizing the disintegration of this society, must remain obscure, though a confessed Fascist. But there are points of likeness between Lewis and Pierpoint, who is a " 'painter turned philosopher,' " we are told, his name but a pseudonym. His political secretary, or business manager, Starr-Smith, knows the dying society well; at Lord Osmund's he tells Dan he has a " 'map of the house.' " From

7. *Apes,* pp. 118–25.
8. Ibid., p. 16; cf. "this culture was dead as mutton" (p. 43).

his lips we hear many of Lewis' own criticisms; Old England is dead, the Ritz-Riviera culture of the Finnian-Shaws is stifling true art, Osmund and Harriet are perpetuating the child cult, and so forth. As opposed to the invert Osmund, Blackshirt is " 'masculine to a fault!' " However, Blackshirt is mildly satirized himself, as I have pointed out. He denounces Zagreus who, however, proves an obedient party disciple in the letter he hands to Dan; this is filled with lies and accuses Dan of the democratic conceit, of wanting to be *"no-bigger-than-anybody-else."* Finally, the society dies in the figure of Fredigonde, collapsing as Zagreus kisses her.

The Apes has been the most spectacular of all Lewis' productions. It is probably his greatest book. From its original appearance in the vast, beautifully produced Arthur Press edition, an edition that splendidly matches the character of the work, to the commercial publications in England and America, of 1931 and 1932 respectively, it drew with it a wake of lengthy reviews, libel writs, anonymous letters, and even a threat on the author's life by an airman! In *Satire and Fiction* Lewis has reprinted some of these reviews, such as those from Naomi Mitchison, L. P. Hartley, Montagu Slater, Cecil Roberts, and others, as well as a number of congratulatory letters from Augustus John, H. G. Wells, Montgomery Belgion, Richard Aldington, and so on. In *The Referee* Aldington called the book "one of the most tremendous farces ever conceived in the mind of man," adding that "The novel contains some of the most brilliant satirical writing ever committed to paper." J. D. Beresford and Augustus John saw genius in the book, while Yeats wrote that it brought back "something absent from all literature for a generation . . . passion ennobled by intensity, by endurance, by wisdom. We had it in one man once. He lies in St. Patrick's now under the greatest epitaph in history." [9] More recently, Pound has described the work as "a smashing big canvas of the boil on ole

9. Yeats, *Letters*, p. 776. This praise, often quoted, occurred, however, in the context of a reproof; in the letter from which it is drawn Yeats is first and foremost defending Edith Sitwell.

England's neck," claiming for it a place beside Smollett or Fielding but owning that "the peeve" limits it.[10] Elsewhere, Pound has been but one of many to compare Lewis with Swift.[11]

The Apes, of course, did not enjoy unanimous approval in England. Raymond Mortimer and Frank Swinnerton were two dissentient voices, while the contemporary review in *The Times Literary Supplement* has become a minor classic of misunderstanding, and was recently reprinted. This time, however, Lewis got far more praise from across the Atlantic than usual. *The New York Times* for April 17, 1932, was on the whole in favor, while *The New Republic* reviewer wrote on June 8: "*The Apes of God* is the most ambitious, and probably the greatest, piece of fiction published in English since *Ulysses.*" Geoffrey Stone, in *The Bookman* for March, went even further: "The greatest novels the twentieth century has so far produced, it is generally agreed, are James Joyce's *Ulysses* and Marcel Proust's *Remembrance of Things Past.* With the publication of Wyndham Lewis's *The Apes of God,* a third takes its place among them, and can claim superiority so far as intellectual content is concerned."

If evaluations of this sort must remain opinionative, we can surely be grateful to Yeats for pointing out that satire in the grand manner has certainly been missing from English literature. In this way *The Apes* is an authentic expression of the English genius, dormant for some time. Of all Lewis' works *The Apes* has for me the greatest artistic integrity. Hugh Kenner calls it Lewis' "worst-written" book. It is, of course, his best. Every page has been composed with honesty. Every page, despite one's immediate feeling to the contrary, is functional. Beside this work *Snooty Baronet* or *The Vulgar Streak* seems slipshod. Lewis' verbal vitality is here at its peak. In this respect (though perhaps in this respect only) it seems to me an improvement on *Tarr,* and certainly nothing he has written since approaches it.

10. Pound, *If This Be Treason,* pp. 5–7.
11. Pound, *Polite Essays,* p. 154.

Indeed, it is interesting to see how weak "The Roaring Queen" of a few years later, which reads like a bad chapter from *The Apes,* seems beside the bigger book. Some reference has been made to this unpublished satire. E. W. F. Tomlin, in his British Council pamphlet on Lewis, discusses the work authoritatively, as though he has read it, but one is understandably suspicious when he mis-spells the title.[12] Actually the characterizations, especially that of the principal figure, a literary dictator called Samuel Shodbutt, which Kenner probably rightly takes to be a skit on Arnold Bennett, are similar to those of *The Apes,* and the farce is equally ludicrous. (According to a letter to Hugh Walpole Lewis was still dining with Bennett in 1920.) But the later work is marred by silly puns and impossible exaggerations, the personages are moved clumsily and, at least in the proof copy I read, there is still a confusion of names. At its best "The Roaring Queen" reminds one of the early Waugh, which Lewis would call damning praise.

In theme the novel lampoons the London literary coterie, with its social tie ups and nepotisms: reviewers "puff" works from pub-lishers for whom they read, others "plant" anonymous reviews of their own books in London periodicals, and so forth. There is little in this side of the book that was not better said by Q. D. Leavis in her *Fiction and the Reading Public.*

The action takes place at an absurd literary house party given in an imitation Strawberry Hill in Oxfordshire by a Mrs. Wellesley-Crook (who, we learn, is one of the Crooks of Chicago). Samuel Shodbutt is to confer the much coveted Book-of-the-Week Prize that he controls on a homosexual youth, a shrinking hulking speci-men highly reminiscent of Dan Boleyn of *The Apes.* This young man, Daniel Butterboy (actually Butterby), is reluctantly engaged to the Hon. Baby Bucktrout, daughter of Lord and Lady Saltpeter, a sexually precocious miss who dislikes the idea of the false union and makes constant, but unsuccessful, assaults on the virtue of a local yokel on the estate, a lout-like gardener called Tom who is

12. The title is explained at pp. 73–4 of the Harvard proof copy.

frequently to be found in the tool shed. This is palpably a parody of *Lady Chatterley's Lover,* a book which, in fact, Baby carries with her like a Bible.

The fantastic house party also includes a Scottish Proustian, a painter called Dritter who reminds one of Augustus John, a Black Mammie, an Austro-Czech lady novelist (also log-rolling champion of Central Europe, in both senses of the word, it seems) whose name is—undisguisedly—Lilli O'Stein, a Mrs. Rhoda Hyman who has just won a prize for plagiarism, several girl and boy prodigies of the literary world, and sundry hangers-on. The plot is complex and artificial. The emphasis on plagiarism—Mrs. Hyman is awarded a prize for the Year's Cleverest Literary Larceny for thieving from Sonclair [*sic*] Lewis—and on the successful young gives evidence of how strongly Lewis, Wyndham, felt on these points. Eventually, after much jockeying for position and what the eighteenth century called "place" among the literary aspirants, the young hopeful Butterboy is shot in bed. I differ mildly with Kenner here in his thinking this death "as meaningless as a cinder in the eye," for there is a definite point to this murder, it is not an *acte gratuit* as at the end of *Snooty Baronet.*

The most damaging criticism of *The Apes,* and of Lewis' satire in general, is directed against his comic theme, rather than against his comic type, however. The theme of *The Apes* is too small for such gigantic literary effort; the targets for Lewis' satire are unworthy, Frank Swinnerton suggests.[13] T. S. Eliot has said the same: "Mr. Wyndham Lewis, the most brilliant journalist of my generation (in addition to his other gifts), often squanders his genius for invective upon objects which to everyone but himself seem unworthy of his artillery, and arrays howitzers against card houses."[14] V. S. Pritchett uses this criticism and the metaphor in which it is couched, when he recently calls Lewis' satires "old block-busting

13. Frank Arthur Swinnerton, *The Georgian Literary Scene* (London, Heinemann, 1935), p. 477.
14. Eliot, *Selected Essays,* p. 445.

guns and tanks skewed on the abandoned field, they stand still, fantastic without their thunder." Of *The Apes* Pritchett adds, "Its fatal limitation is triviality of subject." [15]

This is a serious charge, of course, and Lewis himself was aware of it. It is not merely a matter of overtopical references, such as that in the first *Tarr* to the Flatbush Vitagraph lot ("Vitagraph camp" is changed in the later edition to "Hollywood camp"). In *Satire and Fiction* he tries to answer it on the grounds that Dryden also chose insignificant targets to satirize. But there lurks in one's mind that there is more in the criticism than this. Will *The Apes* be deprived of the highest rank as a satire because of its lack of universality? For such universality is not only a question of subject matter; it is a matter of the creator's state of mind. *The Tale of a Tub,* even the *Drapier's Letters,* are satires in which we can share, despite their local references, because of the width of Swift's mind. Does *The Apes* already seem dated, as Pritchett suggests? Incidentally, its date, the period it condemns, is not the late twenties or even (as I have heard some say) the early thirties. The first drafts of the book appeared in *The Criterion* at the beginning of 1924. The "Bloomsburies" Lewis ridicules are far more of the vintage Roger Fry, Lytton Strachey, Virginia Woolf, Vanessa Bell, as well, of course, as the family against whom the satire is more obviously aimed, than the subsequent generation. Perhaps "the peeve" does limit *The Apes,* though both I. A. Richards and Geoffrey Stone defend Lewis' small targets. Is not ours a "mean" or "little" age, as Lewis describes it? Where are the big targets today, he would ask? Or, in his own words: "Art will die, perhaps. It can, however, before doing so, paint us a picture of what life looks like without art. That will be, of course, a *satiric* picture. Indeed it is one." [16]

It is when we turn to two minor satires, *Snooty Baronet* and *The Vulgar Streak,* that we at once realize we have been judging *The*

15. V. S. Pritchett, *Books in General* (London, Chatto and Windus, 1953), pp. 248, 252.

16. *Men without Art,* p. 225.

Apes by the very highest standards. These two works are far less consequential, though both illustrate the Lewisian comic theme in action. The first owes considerably to *The Apes;* it is, as it were, a skittish and erratic progeny of the larger satire. Literary London is again the target, but there are somber notes which announce *The Revenge for Love.* The book is told in the first person by "Snooty" himself, Sir Michael Kell-Imrie Bt., an author attached to an aging society Bohemian called Val (Mrs. Valerie Ritter), and in the clutches—so far as his writing is concerned—of his literary agent Humph (Captain Humphrey Cooper Carter). Both these last two characters are riddled with humbug.

Val is really younger sister of Fredigonde. Fredigonde, we recall, was "A Veteran Gossip-Star." Val is an "old imitation-society-'piece' " living in Chelsea and flattering herself she can write; she is "Chelsea Enchantress, *model* 1930." She has perhaps already been mentioned in *The Childermass* as "an ageing gossip-column Lido-tart with lifted face and gorgon-eye." Val is a total amateur, or ape of God ("It is seriously to be doubted . . . if any longer she realized what she was *saying,* so accustomed had she become to *write* it").

Apart from being a dithyrambic spectator, Val represents the emotion against the intellect, approving a Persian book Snooty picks up which condemns the mind and lauds the flesh. (Snooty, however, is by no means the pure intellectual of the Tarr type; his sexual appetite must be accounted for, disastrous as it is, and Rousseau's *Émile* is his *livre de chevet.*) Sexual intercourse makes Snooty sick, owing to his head wound received in the war. At the end of the book he takes revenge on Val, treating her with utter callousness, leaving her lying ill of smallpox, possibly dying, her looks to be marred forever.

Humph, equally called an "animal," "automaton," "puppet," "moron," and "doll," [17] lives in a continual dime-fiction atmosphere of his own invention; this man, "insufferably up-to-snuff," is the

17. *Snooty,* pp. 58, 59, 141, 287.

best character in the book and may not be met in the other satires. Riddled with sham, constantly acting in a play of his own devising, he becomes intolerable when the three go to Persia in search of an adventure that will provide the basis for a book. Eventually Snooty shoots him in the back, in an *acte gratuit*, when Humph isn't looking (and indeed when he is just about to leave Snooty). Like many of Lewis' characters, Humph has a physical counterpart to match his overblown "humor," in his case a huge chin.

The semi-autobiographical Snooty is an admitted misanthropist, by no means free of puppetry himself. With his mechanical leg, and plate in his skull, he is nearly a machine himself, as he often points out. So, watching a mechanical dummy in a shopwindow advertising men's hats by raising and replacing a hat on its head, Snooty wonders which is the more real, this puppet or the people round him in the Strand. This moment, incidentally, closely recalls Carlyle's famous "Hatter in the Strand" (*Past and Present,* Book III, chapter 1), an advertising device extremely similar to the one Lewis uses here, and equally ridiculous and detestable to Carlyle for the same reasons. Snooty sees mankind as "puppets," "machines," "insects," "moving morons," and dummies.[18] He is explicitly anti-Man, longing for the bull to gore the *torero* and for the whale to win in *Moby Dick*— Ahab represents the herd. Thus his actions at the end are consistent. He shoots the man who has befriended him and leaves his woman, suffering from smallpox, in the hands of a Persian bandit. These brief comments do not at all convey the disturbing note of the book's final scenes, nor the shocking brutality of the shooting of Humph.

But the tragic element concerns the fate of Rob McPhail, perhaps the first thoroughly sympathetic character Lewis had created in his satire (in *Broken Record* Roy Campbell accepts the attribution of McPhail). McPhail is a poet from the Veldt ("one of the few authentic poets now writing in English"), an expert bullfighter and fisherman, living in the south of France. Snooty meets him on

18. Ibid., pp. 64, 152, 186, 272.

his way to Persia. Both Snooty and McPhail are "in pursuit of the solid sensations," and both spit at the mention of Bloomsbury. McPhail, rather than Snooty, is the man of honor in the book, and his death is symbolical. For he dies in a bullfight into which he need not have entered, a fight itself a sort of sham, thus personifying death at the hands of the society Snooty sees as so sick. McPhail is "struck down in a fifth-rate bull-fight, defending the sportive honour of the Faujassers to whom he did not belong." It is a heroic, useless gesture, tragically betrayed by those he is trying to help. The bullfight scenes are powerful, even at their most ridiculous (as when the toreros fight each other, the bull looking on), and the symbolic manner in which the absurd catches McPhail in its grip is excellently achieved.

The same exasperation with sham, accompanied by a similar note of the macabre at the end, pervades *The Vulgar Streak*. Indeed, there are similarities between Martin Penny-Smythe of this work and Humph. And Vincent Penhale here has a Clark Gable smile, like Victor of *The Revenge for Love*. The narrative concerns itself with a type of sham, a Gidean counterfeiting of bank notes. The work is overtly a protest against class snobbery in England, against "the relentless pressure of the English class incubus."

Vincent is a class traitor, a treachery which society revenges at the end. He is a working-class man who steps into the upper classes and marries an upper-class girl. The moral of the story is the regenerating power of love, but as in *The Revenge for Love* the central character learns this too late. And, in fact, a tear slides down Vincent's cheek at the end, rather as it does down Hardcaster's. Vincent finds out that his wife is really in love with him, or that love is stronger than class, and there is no other end for him but the most tragic of all in this context, suicide. Vincent is a fairly sympathetic character. Although he has deserted his class, he has by no means left his family in want. He takes his beautiful sister Maddie with him into the new class and supports the rest of his family, sending back money, most of which is spent by his mother on drink. All around him Vincent discovers a sham or "pseudo" society; ten years after this book was published Lewis was to utilize, in *Rotting Hill,* this veritably obsessive theme to satirize Attlee socialism (I counted the word "pseudo," "sham," or "ersatz" five times in four pages of *Rotting Hill*).[19]

Further, *The Vulgar Streak* is a critique of "action." The cult of action, which Lewis associates with sensation or Romance, is to be thought of in different terms from energy. For instance, Lewis believes that disinterested intelligence should be filled with energy, but it should not be mixed in action. In 1927 he criticized the Futurists for their "evangile of *action,*" and a quarter of a century later, in *The Writer and the Absolute,* he laid the same charge at the door of Malraux, Sartre, and Camus—in varying degrees of severity. In passing, one must once again admit that Lewis takes this point up rather as it suits his immediate purpose. Thus, in *Hitler,* the Führer is praised as a man of "action," of precisely the kind one would expect Lewis to dislike. Lewis here actually champions Hitler's *Erfühlungspolitik,* as he calls it (actually the word used by the Nazis was *Erfüllungspolitik*), a view he directly contradicts in *The Hitler Cult.* The dislike of action of this type comes through in *The Vulgar Streak* when Vincent is sent by his mother-in-law to consult a psychiatrist (decidedly reminiscent of the delightful Dr. Frumpfsusan of *The Apes*), and by a play on words we are told that the more "action" takes over the personality—and it can do this by a man's being a sham, or "actor," of life—the less the individual lives. The theme is driven home by an easel, a "great futile easel, like the skeleton of a prehistoric bird," representing art, and the intellect, which haunts Vincent's room overlooking the Thames. Unused, its shadow mounts guard over his eventual suicide.

It is *Snooty Baronet,* rather than *The Vulgar Streak,* however, which leads us thematically to *The Revenge for Love,* the most tragic of all Lewis' satires. The book was originally entitled *False Bottoms* and changed, so he writes to Lord Carlow, for fear of offending

19. *Rotting Hill,* pp. 145–8.

"Mrs. J. Bull, the Boots Library Subscriber." We are prepared for this in *Snooty Baronet* when Snooty first sees Humph and is reminded of a box with a false bottom. And the "capture" planned for Snooty at the end is a sham capture, very similar to the sham delivery of arms at the end of *The Revenge for Love*.

This work, in which we have Lewis' nearest approach to direct tragedy in the form of satire to date, appeared in May 1937. Earlier the same year, in his article addressed to the British Fascist party, Lewis had called Marxism "an enormous sham." [20] And he was soon, in *Left Wings*, to indict the "sham-bulldog" of Great Britain. The theme of false bottom is continually mentioned throughout *The Revenge for Love*.[21] First, however, it provides the frame. The book opens with the warder's discovery of the false bottom in the peasant girl's basket (food covering seditious material), and it ends with Victor Stamp's discovery of bricks, instead of guns, in the false bottom of his car. Indeed, the image might be prolonged to cover Victor's and Margot's death by falling over a precipice, a natural false bottom in the treacherous mountains. In this connection, it is significant that the "slowly-ploughing traditional vessel of Old Spain," the peasant girl Josefa de la Asunción, should be the carrier of the first false bottom, for the civil war is seen in this work as Old Spain sabotaging herself. It is everywhere a "foreign freedom" that is being ushered into the West in the name of Marx, and into Spain too, in *Count Your Dead* as in *The Revenge for Love,* and this is what Stamp introduces into Old Spain at the end in the form of his "typewriters." Josefa herself, it might be added, has anything but a false bottom.

Equally, however, the title as we now have it describes the theme, one stated by the showman, Don Alvaro, on the first page: " 'we are only free once in our lives . . . That is when at last we gaze into the bottom of the heart of our beloved and find that it is false.' " Sham is here the human norm, and love therefore an

---

20. " 'Left Wings' and the C 3 Mind," p. 30.
21. *Revenge for Love*, pp. 49, 162, 177, 180, 253, 266, 272, 313, 368–71.

act of complicity with falsification. Hence, the warder is saying, we are only truly free when detached from such love by the very act of betrayal. For love implies attachment, and for Lewis detachment is all. The thesis of the book is that love attracts disaster in a world of sham, or that love will take revenge on false bottoms, and it is primarily enacted by Hardcaster and Margot. The rest of the characters, with the odd exception like Tristram Phipps, are socialist puppets or political marionettes, and we are forcibly reminded that T. E. Hulme wrote of socialism: "it has all the pathos of marionettes in a play, dead things gesticulating as though they were alive." [22] The Communists of *The Revenge for Love* are "wax-dolls," "ghost-persons," "sham-politicos," living "the machine-life of an hysterical, half-conscious, underworld," in brief, "sham-underdogs athirst for power: whose doctrine was a Sicilian Vespers, and which yet treated the real poor, when they were encountered, with such overweening contempt, and even derision." [23]

It is the false bottom of this unreality that underlies everything solid and sensible. Nor can it fairly be objected that this criticism is wildly exaggerated. Indeed, the very kind of sham socialism Lewis criticized in these parlor pinks is virtually admitted in Isherwood's *Prater Violet* where the hero, called Isherwood, thinks back on his generation at this time as "parlor socialists": "I cared . . . But did I care as much as I said I did?" [24] In his recent autobiographical *The Invisible Writing* Arthur Koestler refers to "the lotus-eaters of the British C.P." at this time.[25]

In Lewis' novel everyone, excluding the principals, is fake. Even Victor is a sham, a "deluded" man who does not give a jot for the people and whose painting is described as "vomit." It is no surprise when he joins the workshop producing faked modern masters. At

22. Hulme, *Speculations,* p. 255.

23. *Revenge for Love,* p. 160.

24. Christopher Isherwood, *Prater Violet* (New York, Random House, 1945), p. 104.

25. Arthur Koestler, *The Invisible Writing* (New York, Macmillan, 1954), p. 384.

the end, in the company of Margot with whom he has been living, he improves. Every other minor character is bogus (not Tristy). Sean O'Hara, who betrays his friend, has earlier absconded from Dublin with the Communist party funds. Abershaw, the signature forger, is a "highly bogus personage," and so on. Every minor character, every incident, follows this rule. Serafín, who helps Hardcaster escape, is paid by *both* sides. When Percy watches the funeral of an anarchist, we learn that the man has not died gallantly, in action, but from overeating caviar. At the end a beggar woman spits on Hardcaster when he gives her chocolate.

In such a world authenticity of any kind must pay a heavy penalty. There are two types of love in the book, intellectual (that of Hardcaster for a creed) and emotional (that of Margot, Gwendolen Margaret Savage, for Victor, her lover). In Margot's case, however, it must be admitted that there is an element of make-believe in her love for Victor. She wears a Kate Greenaway hat and reads Virginia Woolf avidly, and we are told that "she belonged to a 'period'—of her own manufacture." At the end the authenticity of this love is debated between Hardcaster and a Communist called Mateu. Hardcaster denies that Margot's love is genuine, but then he is not the man to approve of any emotional exhibition. Mateu, however, disagrees, and maintains that Margot's is a true passionate love.

Hardcaster's intellectual love brings equal disaster. Hardcaster introduces one motif dear to Lewis, namely that of playing the game. We explicitly read that Percy "played the game," and it is for this that he must pay. For to Lewis (whose name is also Percy) "playing the game" is a sort of English sham, like the sense of humor. He has actually called the English sense of humor "that maudlin twin-brother of the Sporting Spirit," [26] and at about the same time as he was writing *The Revenge for Love* he also wrote, " 'playing the game,' as too hypnotic a slogan, has perhaps rotted the sense of

26. Wyndham Lewis, "First Aid for the Unorthodox," *The London Mercury, 32,* No. 187 (May 1935), 31.

reality of the average Briton." [27] In *One-Way Song* he boasted: "The man I am who does *not* play the game!" This emerges in Major Corcoran of *America, I Presume* also; so when Corkers learns that his guide around a Canadian youth club is a rugger Blue he exclaims " 'You unspeakable cad!' " Lewis himself was educated—briefly—at Rugby, home of rugby football and thus of "playing the game," but as he put it in *Rude Assignment,* "I rapidly came to see that there was, in fact, no game there at all." The satire on "playing the game" occurs also in *The Childermass* where the fatuous Satters appears dressed for football, though in this case the cherished Rugby cap (like the Mons Star he wears) is really an emblem of what Satters would like to have been in life. Father Card of *The Red Priest* was a boxing Blue. Hardcaster's fatal mistake is to "play the game" in two senses: (a) he is honest, like McPhail, in a world of sham, and (b) he "plays the game" of salon communism with the Chelsea socialists without realizing that for them it is only a game. For this he must suffer. For a lack of recognition of reality, for failing to realize that Gillian and the others are unreal, he suffers the atrocious penalty of being kicked when down, itself the negation of the Sporting Spirit and of "playing the game." (Card, later, kicks a man when down.) Finally, we have a feeling of impending disaster as Hardcaster is approached by the sinister Abershaw and the corrupt O'Hara and asked to mix himself once more in the game. As Percy agrees and holds out his hand, it grows dark in the room, a moment of ominous threat paralleled for Margot as she bends over the brook and feels nature as hostile and unsympathetic.[28]

Victor and Margot are killed. Percy is put back in prison. All these, at the end, are people of honor in the work. At the conclusion Victor improves; he comes out to Spain "to give a hand," and must accordingly suffer. Margot calls Percy "a sincere man" at the finish, and for this he too must pay. When Percy, for instance,

27. *Left Wings,* p. 44.
28. *Revenge for Love,* pp. 284, 305.

hears of the chance of Victor being double-crossed he says, " 'I'm not so hard-boiled as to stand by and allow that.' " And he is taken prisoner in an act of unselfishness designed to protect Stamp—which it does, if only temporarily.

Margot is revenged for the truth of her love, takes Victor with her. But the most tragic revenge for love is upon the intellectual, Hardcaster. At the end he lies in prison, where we had first found him, "His integrity stiffened after each fresh buffet of fate." In the case of this character the "pantin" steps over into tragedy, and Lewis cannot ask us to remain unmoved by the end of the book. He himself has placed *The Revenge for Love* higher than *Tarr* and it is certainly a development from *Tarr* rather than from *The Apes*. (*The Times Literary Supplement* has seen *The Revenge for Love* as Lewis' finest work.) The inflexibility, the rigidity that the Marxist logic imparts—like the logic of Kreisler's nihilism—is seized upon and mercilessly satirized in the person of Percy. But it gives him a "hard cast" only (I allow myself this interpretation, as there is constant play on Percy's surname throughout). The act of belief has been pitifully human. Spurned by the other prisoners, spat on by a beggar crone, "this man of truth" with his "incorruptible intellect" at last lets a tear fall down his poker face. No physical suffering has brought this reaction from him, though he has experienced plenty of that—only the thought of Margot to whose kind, the weak and the tender, his politics has played Judas: this is the context of the last, brilliant passage of the book.[29]

In conclusion, there are two other satires by Lewis that should be briefly mentioned here. That they will only be briefly mentioned, however, is due to two convictions: first, in these works the critic has least need to act as interlocutor; and second, for one has to take one's stand somewhere, they do not constitute his important con-

29. Ibid., p. 377. I am aware that Hardcaster feels "self-pity" at this point, but do not feel that this qualifies my analysis here. It is, however, a complete misreading to claim, with Marvin Mudrick, that Hardcaster "cleverly betrayed" Victor and Margot at the end; he did the reverse.

tributions to literature. In asserting this, I am well aware that *Self Condemned* is considered very highly by some. For L. P. Hartley it has "the strongest fictional and human interest" of all Lewis' novels. T. S. Eliot has found it "a book of almost unbearable spiritual agony." E. W. F. Tomlin has called it Lewis' "most impressive performance in straight novel-writing." At the same time, in concession to my own estimate, which is not high, I would add that other critics equally sympathetic to Lewis are much more cautious: Walter Allen calls it "a novel of great intellectual distinction," but little more, while Hugh Kenner, who verges on the uncritical in some of his opinions on Lewis, writes that *"Self Condemned* is not a well-made novel but a slow and terrible wind, gathering force for 400 pages, dying to occasional doldrums in whose hush the novelist carries on out of habit."

For me the real disappointment of Lewis' first novel for thirteen years, between 1941 and 1954 that is, is its total lack of creative surprise and inventive vigor. After having read everything else by the same author to date, I could in all honesty find little of interest in *Self Condemned* (and even less in *The Red Priest* which followed). Why must we, for example, plough through a long interpolation on Arnold of Rugby in this novel when we can read Lewis' views on this figure, more coherently expressed, in *The Times Literary Supplement* a few months later? Too heavy a judicum should not be imposed on a work merely because it is predictable, however, and there are passages of great power in this novel of an intellectual engaged in an agonized struggle of disengagement and eventually "condemned" for refusing to preach contemporary ideology. For at the start of the book René Harding, a half-French history don, throws up his academic position in England and exiles himself to Canada for the duration of the second World War; both he and his wife Hesther know that this ultimate, indeed sepulchral, unorthodoxy is a symbolic gesture, a last *vale:* "Both of them knew that this was the last year of an epoch, and . . . that as far as that quiet, intelligent, unmolested elect life was concerned, they were both condemned to death." For there is a pun in the title. The two leave Europe only to find an inferno of fire and ice in the new world.

René is an "implacable perfectionist" (though "gaily capable of unregenerate behavior"), who winks at a bust of Bolingbroke, is falsely accused of being a Fascist by *The Times,* and on the way over to Canada tosses overboard a copy of *Middlemarch.* But this characteristically sharp-eyed persona cannot rid himself of Romance so easily as that, for Hesther is our old friend, the neoclassical conception of woman and a mild comeback of Bertha in *Tarr.* Hesther is, for instance, "classified under the head 'Erotics,' " René later calls her Hesteria, and it is with "what almost amounted to a shudder" that René is sexually attracted by her. "He always forgot that Hesther was a human being, because she was so terribly much the Woman." René, as usual, one might say by now, hates being "compromised with the silliness involved in the reproduction of the species," and the two get off the bed where they have been making love "like two flies dragging themselves out of a treacly plate." One level of the intellectual's degradation in philistine Canada, then, is to lose something of his necessary differentiation from this wife who shows "the remains of the child-mind" in her eyes, eyes which indeed "hung open like a gaping mouth." In this manner the hotel room in which most of *Self Condemned* takes place replies to the room of Barbusse's *L'Enfer.*

For three years and three months René and his Hesther live in the Hotel Blundell in the Canadian city of Momaco, "the never-never land . . . the living-death, the genuine blank-of-blanks out of which no speck of pleasantness or civilized life could come." It took the Canadian critic H. M. McLuhan to observe that Lewis probably intended by this name Mom & Co. Here, in Room 27A ("twenty-five feet by twelve"), a "lethal chamber" as they find it in every sense, the action of the novel hideously freezes. The two are "room-ridden" with a vengeance, "frozen in their tracks, as it were, by the magic of total war," as Lewis allows the tragic inertia of his crippled intellectual to atrophy symbolically.

For a retrospective, half-elegiac interval, the figures of Old

England cast their shadows across the arid landscape of Momaco. We meet characters of the other continent, of the earlier Lewis, such as Mr. Herbert Starr, the Momaco fairy, a throwback to *The Apes* (even in name, also), and Cedric Furber, who sits for Lytton Strachey and introduces Bloomsbury once again. Around this time, too, Lewis had had Strachey visited by "a certain novelist of my acquaintance" in a story in *Encounter* and described as a "perverse amorist." There is also Mrs. Plant, "the dazed and crippled mistress of all this," who possibly recalls Evelyn Waugh's own persona, John Plant, for there are references elsewhere to Waugh in *Self Condemned* and I have instanced Waugh's dig at Vorticism in *Vile Bodies.*

Furber hires René to help him with his library until an infatuation with a youth deprives René of this employment and drives him to write for the *Momaco Gazette-Herald* (Lewis himself had contributed to the Toronto *Saturday Night* at about this time). Like Hardcaster, René is kicked, and kicked when down, and this climacteric seems to set off his whole tragic annihilation until, as Hugh Kenner aptly observes, "he becomes the thing he rejected." He begins selling his books, he "modifies" his earlier "perfectionist" theories (expressed to a character called Rotter and paraphrasing *The Art of Being Ruled*), until we read: "Even, he had developed an appetite for this negation of life, and a sort of love for this frightful Room." Eventually the hotel (a "brisk little microcosm") goes up, like Europe, in flames; as the edifice is razed to the ground, René and Hesther "both stood dreamily at the window: their eyes seemed to be saying to the flames, 'Yes, all right. Leave nothing.'" Nothing is left. René collaborates with his anti-self, Momaco, accepting the Chair of History at the local university and Hesther, either in despair or with mind deranged, kills herself. At the very end René reaches rock bottom; he accepts a teaching position in America.

To resume *Self Condemned* in this summary fashion does scant justice to some really memorable minor characterizations, especially

René's superb London charlady, her face "eerily jeering," or his London plumber, Mr. Shotstone, "a prostatic elder" straight from *Rotting Hill*. There is also René's brother-in-law Percy Lamport, a sham liberal, a subscriber to *The New Statesman,* "an emissary of Nonsense in person." For David Paul, who reviewed *Self Condemned* in *The Observer* alongside Daphne du Maurier's *Mary Anne,* the book recalled "some of the novels of twenty-odd years ago." Is there, indeed, "twentyish" dialogue in *Self Condemned?* If so, the answer is: And so there should be! For here in Momaco, "the barren spot where you ceased to think," is a characterization of cultural lag; the Canadian general outlook is depicted as vulgar and sterile, with its smug philistinism, its inbreeding, its "anti-British bias," its detestation of "Pea-soups" ("No Nazi," René once remarks, "could feel more racial superiority than the English Canucks of Upper Canada").

It is the catty cleric of *Self Condemned,* if not of *Rotting Hill,* who announces Lewis' recent *The Red Priest.* The Reverend Robert Kerridge, engaged in the "god-business" in *Self Condemned,* prepares us for Father Augustine ("Teeny") Card, a skit on the side perhaps of both Donald Soper and Norman Vincent Peale.

The satire begins briskly enough. Poor Mary Chillingham is breaking with her suitor Arthur Wootton, "a child-like Grenadier, as dumb as his busbies," while Father Card is seen chucking dissenters out of his church. There is the old bravura in the vocabulary, too, as Lewis depicts the Knights of the Dustbin Lids, exaggerated juvenile delinquents, "elderly infants," or "mildewed midgets," waging constant warfare on rival gangs in the mews of London. Card and Mary marry and the story gradually bogs as it progresses—all too obviously—toward Card's hollow assumption of power and final death in the Arctic regions. The work contains a covey of nonfunctional and uninteresting characters, and Card himself is unconvincing; though educated at Eton, he uses Americanisms like "guy" and "dough." The prose itself slowly becomes more and more banal.

This may be intentional, of course; and it is possible that there is self-parody in *The Red Priest*. Certainly Mary Chillingham, whom *The Times Literary Supplement* found a "magnificent characterization . . . a finely conceived figure, drawn with an extraordinary certainty of touch," is a parody—probably of Woolf—"a heroine of romance," as she is called, who goes through a series of reactions as stock and as conventional as Card's are the reverse. "In each other's arms as never before," we read of Mary and Augustine, and surely such clichés are intended to convey the measure of Card's degradation. Card, we remember, is another *contra mundum* "enemy," a "stone-age man" who has committed one grave blunder in his life—the murder of Makepeace. And this haunts him, until he himself is killed by the Eskimos. *Blast No. 1* had called England "The Siberia of the Mind."

Chapter 17: The External Approach

"The *external* approach to things belongs to the 'classical' manner of apprehending . . . as for pure satire—there the eye is supreme."
[*Satire and Fiction*, p. 52.]

THE TECHNIQUE by which Lewis presents his satire is what he calls "the philosophy of the eye." Like Joyce's Shaun, he is an eye-man. How many times has he told us this? "I am an artist, and, through my eye, must confess to a tremendous bias. In my purely literary voyages my eye is always my compass," we read in *The Art of Being Ruled;* "I go about and use my eyes," in *One-Way Song;* "The ossature is my favourite part of a living animal organism," in *Satire and Fiction;* and so on. It has become a commonplace by now to remark Lewis' external approach, both in his graphic and literary work. He is a *"visuel,"* Montgomery Belgion claims. Pound has compared him with E. E. Cummings, presumably the Cummings of *The Enormous Room,* in this respect. W. G. Constable, in a not altogether friendly review, likened Lewis' drawing to his "hard, mechanical, jerky," and external literary style, attributing both to an obsessive anxiety to make his personality felt.[1] Of *The Apes* Lewis has claimed, "no book has ever been written that has paid more attention to *the outside* of people." [2] L. P. Hartley likened the prose of the book to sculpture in its effects. "The cortex, massive and sharply outlined, not the liquefaction within, I have always regarded as the proper province of the artist," Lewis wrote in his 1939 autobiography.

1. W. G. Constable, "Wyndham Lewis," *The New Statesman, 15,* No. 367 (April 24, 1920), 74.
2. *Satire and Fiction,* p. 46.

For this "specialist in *seeing*," [3] this "fanatic for the externality of things," [4] as he likes to style himself, has proposed in contemporary literature an altogether different technique to the "auriferous mud," as he puts it, of writers like Joyce, Henry James, and D. H. Lawrence, the writers of the "inside." The expressive form of satire, in other words, should match its metaphysical kernel: "Dogmatically, then, I am for the *Great Without,* for the method of *external* approach, for the wisdom of the eye, rather than that of the ear." This approach, Lewis claims (and claims with Benda's support), is closer to the classical than to the romantic.

It was in *Time and Western Man* that Lewis first adumbrated at length his "philosophy of the eye." The eye was "the crowning human sense." It alone gave reality, unaffected by the "darkness" of the aural and tactile world. Untroubled by the lower senses, the optic sense placed the world of common-sense reality as directly as possible before the intellect. In fact, the eye *is* the intellect, *"private* organ" of the senses, the "person" in the human organism.

This idea may be found also in *Belphégor*. Benda equates distinction with the eye, confusion with hearing.[5] The "philosophy of the eye" is deliberately anti-Bergsonian. For Bergson, true perception travels from the periphery to the center (the real self); the constantly changing external world only exists as the inner personality accords it existence.[6] Needless to say, Lewis opposes this view. Fernandez also opposes it in practice in Proust; though by no means an artistic failure for Fernandez, Proust's method suggests too much a constant collapse into sensation, it is "une manière de défaite spirituelle." Attacking introspection, Fernandez considers that the formation of personality may be accomplished outside the fictional character.[7] Lewis goes much further than these critics, of course. He summarized his dislike of the ear in *Time and Western*

3. *Jews,* p. 41.
4. *Blasting and Bombardiering,* p. 9.
5. Benda, *Belphégor,* pp. 189–95.
6. Bergson, *Matière et mémoire,* pp. 36 ff.
7. Fernandez, *Messages,* pp. 52–7.

Man as follows: "A world of motion is a world of music, if anything. No visual artist would ever have imagined (or had he imagined, he would have turned in horror from) such a world as the bergsonian, relativist world. The fact that Einstein comes from the country of music may not be without significance." [8]

All this is interesting enough, but to be of constructive value, and not to be written off as mere dislike for the interior monologue which was proving so fertile in the hands of Joyce, Larbaud, Döblin, and Woolf at this time, the "philosophy of the eye" must give us some positive suggestions concerning literary technique. Lewis pretends to give these in *Satire and Fiction*. Before approaching them, however, I would suggest that the vital distinction between Lewis' "philosophy of the eye" and the interior monologue, or *Strom des Bewusstseins*, is a metaphysical difference. Lewis' work is a retraction from, rather than mingling in, experience. Bergson stands for the opposite approach, that of Proust, when he says, in *Matière et mémoire*, that perception must be mixed with affection. Satire, Lewis replies, aims to give truth before pleasure: "If you want to be 'happy' you must not be a man, but a pig." [9] The more agreeable the art-form, he actually suggests in *Satire and Fiction*, the more false it is likely to be.

Rejecting what he calls "fiction from the inside," especially as exemplified by Lawrence, James, and Joyce, Lewis pleads that an injection of the satiric gift has stiffened all good art, since the grotesque will tend to correct the soft romantic imagining, and he goes on to ask for more "fiction from the outside." As for satire itself, there is no other way—"it must deal with the outside." A number of characters reiterate this opinion. To Ratner (James Joyce, after all) Zagreus says, " 'To be a true satirist Ratner you must remain upon the surface of existence.' " The Bailiff says, " 'The more highly developed the individual . . . the more the

8. *Time and Western Man*, p. 410.

9. *Art of Being Ruled*, p. 443; *Satire and Fiction*, p. 49. Lewis adds the caveat that all disagreeable art is not therefore satire.

exterior world is a part of him.' " Joyce comes in for his ration of scorn here. In 1929 Lewis lets himself go. The "unpunctuated" portions of *Ulysses,* he writes, ignoring his own large debt to Joyce on this score, are "merely a device . . . for presenting the disordered spurting of the imbecile low-average mind." In both *Satire and Fiction* and *Men without Art* Henry James is equally derided. James stands for "the art of the 'soul' " instead of "the art of the body." Though in one place a "New England old maid," James also is "a believer in mob-values." Once again, this attack is all the more eccentric if we turn to its victim. For James's severe review of Harriet Elizabeth Prescott's *Azarian: An Episode,* originally published in *The North American Review* for January 1865, actually hints at the "inside" and "outside" methods to come in modern fiction, in a heartfelt appeal for true observation in the novel. In fact, James here stresses action and narrative, rather than tedious description.

The "philosophy of the eye" belongs properly to satire, Lewis says, however, since its aim is to cure man of vices and that can best be effected by showing what he really looks like. (It is, of course, sarcastically that Mrs. Mallow advises Vincent Penhale to go to a psychiatrist who will tell him what he looks like from the outside.) Yet Lewis will, he says, allow the interior monologue to be employed in fiction for depicting (1) the very aged, (2) the very young, (3) half-wits, and (4) animals. "In my opinion it should be entirely confined to those classes of characters." [10] Class 1 would include a character like Fredigonde, whose thought-stream is certainly given us; Class 2 would include someone like the mentally young Dan; Class 3 would include the majority of Lewis' characters, and Class 4 remains unfilled in his satire, so far as I know. It has been left to Jules Romains to provide for us the interior monologue of a dog—if we except the special case of the interior monologue of a dog presented by a half-wit, in the case of Kipling.

10. *Men without Art,* p. 120. Lewis again confines the technique of the interior monologue to these four categories in his interview with Louise Morgan. Louise Morgan, *Writers at Work* (London, Chatto and Windus, 1931), pp. 43–52.

Yet there is a further category that permits the stream-of-consciousness style, though Lewis does not mention it, for obvious reasons. The interior monologue may be used, it is apparent, as a parody of the interior monologue. The "Stein-stutter" is the chief of these. But there are other parodies, too. There is a deliberate skit on Virginia Woolf's style at the beginning of Part VI of *The Revenge for Love,* when the highly feminine Margot is being characterized. In *Snooty Baronet* there is an obvious skit on the style of the maid's novelette. This occurs in the first chapter dealing with the London Lily (not to be confused with Shushani, the second Lily Snooty meets in Persia, a prostitute). The first Lily is a London shopgirl, salesgirl at a tobacconist's kiosk, a "mechanical dollie" whom Snooty uses when he pleases: "whenever I see her she was the dream-come-true that tumbled my heart about and shook my pulses in an idiot's tattoo." This pleasant take-off of a writer of the type of Ethel M. Dell is apparently taken seriously by Roy Campbell, who calls this section of the book fine lyrical prose in *Light on a Dark Horse*! *Snooty Baronet* also contains a less lighthearted parody of D. H. Lawrence, when Snooty picks up a book called *Sol Invictus,* purporting to be by Lawrence, and quotes from it; it is, of course, a mishmash of bulls and the Mithras cult. In *The Vulgar Streak* April Mallow's first kiss is described in cliché-ridden English, parodying fiction of the best-seller variety. But by far the most serious parodies Lewis presents are directed against Stein and Joyce, the monstrous offspring, so far as he came to be concerned, of the unspeakable *transition.* Interestingly, we find Babbitt criticizing *transition* as a semi-official organ of the stream-of-consciousness school in *On Being Creative.* This style, Babbitt writes, can never give us reality, being "below the human and rational level." [11]

Several characters "stein," to coin Lewis' verb. Dan is guilty of constant Stein-like repetitions. [12] The chief offenders, however, are

11. Irving Babbitt, *On Being Creative* (Boston, Houghton Mifflin, 1932), p. 125.
12. *Apes,* p. 114. Zagreus is reported as saying that Dan thinks the way Stein writes, " 'like a soft stammering ninny spelling out its alphabet' " (*Apes,* p. 420).

the inane Fredigonde, who "Steins away" like mad, and the appalling Satters of *The Childermass*. The Stein-stutter is not merely a matter of Lady Fredigonde's thought-stream in *The Apes*, however. As a type of idiotic repetition (precisely of the kind Bergson proposed as the comic) it crops up in dialogue; here is the Finnian-Shaw family talking to each other at Lord Osmund's:

> "I do believe I've pulled Lady Truncheon's train right off!"
> "I think you have!" Lord Phoebus cried.
> "How terribly careless of me—I do hope Lady Truncheon will excuse me, it was particularly clumsy of me."
> "*I* shouldn't if *I* were Lady Truncheon!"
> "I could hit myself!" the offender bayed at herself.
> "I'm sure she could!" crashed back Lord Phoebus.
> "If I had only known you were there Lady Truncheon!"
> "Couldn't you see that Lady Truncheon was there Harriet!"
> "I know!"
> "You must I think have been *blind* not to see that Lady Truncheon was there!"
> "I believe I must Phoebus!"
> "I'm quite positive you must Harriet!"
> "I know, mustn't I?" [13]

The effect is to freeze the action into a sort of unholy stasis. After all, Lady Truncheon is standing there in her underclothes. The same effect is achieved when Ponto is booted in the behind by Blackshirt. He flies through the air and—a long description follows. Ponto is left hurtling through the air, hand clasping the offended area. The point is that the Stein-stutter is not merely a critique of verbal anarchy and purposelessness, it is also a mental yawn, a rictus arresting sociological progress, symbolic of a suicidal vacuity embodied, in one instance, in the inane Finnian-Shaw family; nor is this purpose forgotten by Lewis in his recent *Self Condemned*, where an exchange like the following can desolatingly take place:

13. *Apes*, p. 488. (Possibly there is a mild skit on Henry James at p. 462.)

"I went to the window."

"Why do you go the window?"

"Why do *you* go to the window?" René retorted, in what seemed a silly *tu quoque*.

"I do not go to the window," Mr. Furber answered.

"Well, I *do*. I always go to the window if perplexed," René remarked.

"You went to the window? Why did you go to the window, Professor?"

It need only be added that René Harding is here talking to a character who is really a leftover from *The Apes*. And there is a similarly idiotic repetition in the ringing of a telephone in a Norwich flat in *The Red Priest*. So page after page of this repetitive dialogue, of the type instanced above, is perfectly functional. Nothing could be effectively subtracted. And in passing I would point out the way (in *The Apes*) nearly every one of the above speeches terminates in an exclamation mark. The drama is heightened. A rhetorical vigor is sculpted onto the page, and makes the hollowness of the characters talking all the more absurd. But the most obvious satire of Stein is to be found in *The Childermass* in the person of Satters. Satters continually "steins . . . for all he's worth," either by a direct stammer (" 'Y-y-y-y-y-you howwid blag-blag-blag-blag-blag-blag-blag-blag-' ") or by infantile repetition of sentences such as this: "Pulley has been most terribly helpful and kind there's no use excusing himself Pulley has been most terribly helpful and kind —most terribly helpful and he's been kind. He's been most terribly kind and helpful, there are two things, he's been most kind and he's been terribly helpful, he's kind he can't help being—he's terribly." [14]

It is interesting to compare this passage, which is a parody of Stein, with an extremely similar passage written in 1954 in which the technique can be seen in decay. It is a serious moment in Faulk-

14. *Childermass*, p. 37.

ner's *A Fable:* "because people are really kind, they really are capable of pity and compassion for the weak and orphaned and helpless because it is pity and compassion and they are weak and helpless and orphaned and people though of course you cannot, dare not believe that."

In *The Childermass,* too, the most extensive parodies of Joyce appear, though in *The Apes* Ratner's thoughts are often presented also in a Joycean stream of consciousness. But Joyce is so chameleon-like in *Ulysses* that these parodies are far less telling. When the Bailiff shouts out to his men, " 'Net Fret Tet! Tick tear, ant Mick! Howillowee Willee and Fretty Frocklip *ant* Oliv Erminster *ant* Chrisst Waltshut! lisserndt termee!' " Lewis is commenting on the names he had been reading in "Work in Progress." More explicitly, however, we find the Bailiff "Dickensjingling." Here we must keep in mind that Lewis likened Joyce's method in presenting Bloom's thoughts to Mr. Jingle's thoughts in *Pickwick Papers.* In the same way the Bailiff says: " 'Hipe!—this once!—having putter hand turrer plar—take no denial—Ime rights rain—one chance more— lovely ladies—beautiful bilgewater—bloomingasblooming—one of the best—never say die—top o' the morning—Kilkenny cats— very!' " [15]

In *Finnegans Wake* Joyce replied to this in the study period when Dolph (Shem) and Kev (Shaun) are interrupted by Professor Jones over their thorny problem of their mother's anatomy. Lewis is here "the beast of boredom" arresting literary progress, lurking in an "Eating S.S. collar." [16]

There are many other parodies in Lewis' work. There is a brief skit on Hemingway when René is kicked in *Self Condemned,* and

15. Ibid., p. 272.

16. Joyce, *Finnegans Wake,* p. 292. Sylvia Silence, the "girl detective," may be S.S.; Joyce's reference is surely too early for this to have been the Nazi political department. The Eton collar would be symbolical of a repressive Englishman of Lewis' class. In *The Apes* (p. 139) Willie Service has an aunt called Susan Service, reminiscent of Sylvia Silence, while S.S. is the nickname for Samuel Shodbutt, the principal character in "The Roaring Queen" of 1936.

there is a brilliant lampoon of murder mystery fiction at the end of "The Roaring Queen." Some reviewers saw a parody of Spender in *One-Way Song*. If so, it must be in something like the line "Ah ah! Ah ah! The Business of the Sun!" but Lewis himself denied that he had parodied Spender in a letter to *New Britain*,[17] and it is certainly not an extended one.

From the start of his work Lewis exemplified the external approach in depicting his characters. It is by now a platitude to point out the visual method of these descriptions. Yet it is interesting to compare his fictional descriptions of some characters in the early stories with their originals in the factual travel articles for *The Tramp*. The reworking shows a tremendous exaggeration of idiosyncrasies, reminiscent of the German Expressionist school in painting. But unlike a painting, a verbal picture must unfold before us on the printed page, bit by bit, feature by feature. This slows up the effect and deprives it at least of that dash to be found in Lewis' drawings, though it may have the compensating factor of achieving that necessary stasis I have mentioned. In the case of the peasant woman at the start of *The Revenge for Love* the slowly unfolding manner of her presentation harmonizes perfectly with her character and lends considerable suspense to the scene, too. But in principle Lewis' visual descriptions insist on the exact word, on the hard rather than the blurred image, and this we find a feature of Imagism (particularly in one of the later manifestoes, that prefacing *Some Imagist Poets* of 1915). One might call this Lewis' Vorticist description, for Hobson at the beginning of *Tarr* and the Frenchman of "A Soldier of Humour" seen from the hotel window in his desperately American suit are both fashioned for us in black and white outlines. Carl, of *The Wild Body*, also, is seen "black and white, dazzling skin and black patches of hair alternating." We notice the same clear lines with which Tarr is built up (white collar, black hat), and we find the same when Potter enters the Bailiff's Court in

17. Wyndham Lewis, "Shropshire Lads or Robots?" *New Britain*, 2, No. 33 (Jan. 3, 1934), 194.

The Childermass, or again at the funeral in *The Vulgar Streak,* to name only a few examples. What is not always noticed, however, is the way in which Lewis' ideological convictions color his descriptions of human physiology.

For to Lewis the mouth is the representative of one of the lower senses. So it is nearly always described as soft, wet, mushy, pulpy, never as clean or hard. A plethora of instances of this comes to hand. The bogus Franciscan Father's mouth is "like a burst plum in a nest of green bristle and mildewed down," and he puts a cigarette Ker-Orr gives him "into the split plum, which came out in the midst of his beard." A prostitute in *Snooty Baronet* has a mouth like a "plum," again, while Matthew Plunkett in *The Apes* has "plum-lips." Satters has a "wet cherry-mouth," and lips like "a ripe fruit" or "pregnant plum." Dr. Frumpfsusan, proud of his "inferiority complex" of being a Jew, allows his mouth "to flower contemptuously," reminding us of Zoborov whose mouth is seen "to flower rather dirtily," while Stella, Cantleman's "Spring-Mate," has lips like "a bull-like flower." Val's mouth in *Snooty Baronet* is "like an escaped plush lining of rich pink," [18] Gillian's in *The Revenge for Love* is like "the inside of something slit open with a scalpel." That this imagery is not accidental is surely testified by the roll call of unpleasant, emotional characters I have just enumerated. Indeed, of a hateful homosexual in *The Childermass* we expressly read, "The mouth, which is a coarse hole, promises complete absence of mind." Hanp, in Lewis' play, has a "hair-edged hole" for a mouth. But usually it is the female characters who have these squashy mouths. Lutitia, of "The War Baby," has a mouth like "some strenuous amoeba," [19] while of Anastasya we read: "Her lips were long hard bubbles risen in the blond heavy pool of her face: grown forward with ape-like intensity, they refused no emotion noisy egress if it got so far." [20]

18. *Snooty,* p. 1; she has, also, a mouth like a "muzzle" (p. 225).

19. Wyndham Lewis, "The War Baby," *Art and Letters,* n.s., 2, No. 1 (Winter 1918/19), 29, 31.

20. *Tarr* (Chatto), pp. 91–2.

Further, we have already seen how essential to Lewis' satire it was that the comic type be a puppet, dummy, or clown; consequently nearly all his characters, even the sympathetic showmen, are called one of such categories at some time. Nearly all of them are clowns, from the "Old Colonels" at the end of *The Apes* to Ker-Orr ("a large blond clown") or Rymer, the socialist parson of *Rotting Hill,* or Father Card of *The Red Priest.* Rymer is seen in one place as an "infuriated animal," in another as a "cabotin," while both Eldred, the eminent though ham historian of this volume, and Gartsides, art teacher né army sergeant, are described as clowns. (See, too, the "Kermesse" design for *Blast No. 2.*) And these clowns, condemned to act a show rather than real life, wear masks, like players. Of course, as suggested in my introduction, the mask may act as "anti-self" for some sympathetic character like Tarr, Penhale, or Penhale's sister Madeline.[21] But it is also used to indicate the condition of human dummy, or fathead. Anastasya is thus "a mask come to life." Harriet has a "waspish witch-mask" (can we doubt her original after this?). The mask is used in the imagery of *The Apes* throughout,[22] while the masked party at the end is itself a symbol of Lewis' purpose here. The word occurs continually in *Self Condemned.*[23]

But in contrast to the soft and squashy mouth of this mask the eye is generally clear and hard. Nearly all sympathetic characters have powerful eyes, including Tarr, Blackshirt, Snooty, and Corcoran. Even in the unsympathetic characters the eye is likened to something hard and metallic; often they are like discs, an object that has meant a lot to Lewis in his graphic work. Handley-Read sees the eyes of the figures in Lewis' painting "The Mud Clinic" as "discs," [24] and elaborates on Lewis' graphic style from this point of view. The Frenchman fixes Ker-Orr with his eyes—"with the blankness of two metal discs." Zagreus' eyes are like discs. Kemp stares at people

21. *Vulgar Streak,* pp. 106, 160, 166, 208, 224, 235.
22. *Apes,* pp. 195, 246, 250, 252.
23. *Self Condemned,* pp. 19, 25, 27, 321, 360, 400.
24. Handley-Read, *Art of Wyndham Lewis,* p. 57.

"with his blank red-rimmed disk of an eye." [25] In the recent *Self Condemned* we notice the "blank discs" of Mr. Furber's eyes.[26] But the disc, a mechanical object, began to be used by Lewis for other physical description. Bestre's hand is a "pudgy hieratic disc," while Deborah (in "Sigismund") reclines in bed, "a flat disc of face . . . sideways on the pillow." Gladys, "the dreary waitress, in her bored jazz" of "You Broke My Dream," is seen with a virtually Vorticist eye by Will Blood: "He models her with his blue eye into a bomb-like shape at once, associating with this a disk—a marble table—and a few other objects in the neighbourhood." [27] Interestingly enough, Val once sits down at "the metal disk of the table" in *Snooty Baronet*. One could give many more instances of this, but in passing it is only necessary to observe how thoroughly, once again, Joyce understood Lewis; Ratner's face is called a disc in *The Apes*. Joyce makes Shaun say, of his face, "I lift my disk to him." [28]

Perhaps, also, I should comment on a word that has occurred in this connection, namely "hieratic." It crops up frequently in Lewis' imagery. Matthew Plunkett has a "hieratic stiffness of limb," while the peasant girl in *The Revenge for Love* walks "with a hieratic hip-roll." Hieratic means consecrated to sacred uses—Lewis even describes himself with the word in *Blasting and Bombardiering*— and one presumes that it is linked with the idea of inferior religions. It is generally a word Lewis associates with rigidity, calling Dorothy Pound once "hieratically rigid." [29] This reminds us that Gaudier-Brzeska did a famous "Hieratic Head of Ezra Pound" that excited much comment. H. S. Ede's *Savage Messiah* shows a plate of Gaudier working on this bust which was originally to be a phallus, according to Horace Brodzky.[30] Epstein adds the information that

25. *Ideal Giant*, p. 11.
26. *Self Condemned*, p. 322.
27. *Wild Body*, p. 287.
28. Joyce, *Finnegans Wake*, p. 408.
29. Wyndham Lewis, "Early London Environment," *T. S. Eliot. A Symposium* (London, Editions Poetry London, 1948), p. 26.
30. Brodzky, *Gaudier-Brzeska*, pp. 58–62.

Ezra asked for it to be phallic and that Gaudier executed it in his famous workshop under the railway arch leading to Putney Bridge.[31] Aldington calls it also a "phallic statue." [32] This was the bust, still extant, which braved all weathers (and snails, according to Iris Barry [33]) in Violet Hunt's garden in London, until in the early thirties it was collected by some of Pound's admirers and erected at Rapallo. Possibly this controversial bust, to which Pound refers in his poem "Moeurs contemporains," [34] meant something to Lewis in his use of the word "hieratic."

In general, Lewis' satiric imagery fully exemplifies Bergson's idea of comic automatism. Nearly all his characters are called machines, at some stage or other, and the more often they are called mechanical, the less the reader may take it Lewis likes them. "Clockwork" is used constantly here. Kreisler has "clockwork-like actions," Fredigonde moves "the ruined clock-work of her trunk," Blackshirt calls Ponto " 'the stupidest clock-work.' " The peasant girl Josefa moves with "great clockwork hips" (like Doris, one of Jack Cruze's pretty secretaries, who walks in front of Tristy "in clockwork rhythm"). So the One-Ways, the idiotic progressives of Lewis' satiric poem, declaim:

Creatures of Fronts we are—designed to bustle
Down paths lit by our eyes, on stilts of clockwork muscle—

One can take this "clockwork" even further. Characters are often actually hinged like puppets; Dougal Tandish, of *The Vulgar Streak,* smokes his cigarette with "a hinged mechanical hand." The body of the Lewisian comic type is composed of latches, shutters, slides, blinkers (Lily's eyes are "poached blinkers"). To develop one example, here is Bestre closing his mouth: "With a flexible imbrication reminiscent of a shutter-lipped ape, a bud of tongue still showing, he shot the latch of his upper lip down in front of the nether

31. Epstein, *Let There Be Sculpture,* p. 37.
32. Aldington, *Life for Life's Sake,* p. 166.
33. Iris Barry, "The Ezra Pound Period," *The Bookman, 74,* No. 2 (Oct. 1931), 166.
34. Ezra Pound, *Quia Pauper Amavi* (London, The Egoist Ltd., 1919), p. 17.

one, and depressed the interior extremities of his eyebrows sharply
from their quizzing perch—only this monkey-on-a-stick mechanical
pull—down the face's centre." The same apparatus occurs again
and again. We find Arghol with his "upper lip shot down." Val
will "pull her upper lip down like a latch over the under one."
Humph's face is seen once as if shutters were working up and down
it. Blenner meets a sailor with eyes like "little billiard balls, lids
like metal slides." Kreisler's eyelids are caught "clapping to like
metal shutters." A mouth opens like a latch in "Cantleman's
Spring-Mate." La Mettrie would exult in this imagery.

It would be redundant to go on in this fashion. Only the "shell"
imagery should be further mentioned. For true satire, Lewis wrote
in his *London Mercury* article, should be "all constructed out of
the dry shells and pelts of things." Of the characters in *The Apes*
he wrote, "In it their shells or pelts . . . come first." He is quite
correct here. Dan's face is "a shell of mutton-fat." Ratner has a
"shell-face." A pun is made on this imagery when Matthew Plunkett,
who owns a collection of shells and sees people as shells, comes
across a poster advertising Shell petrol. Kreisler, Fingal (of *The
Ideal Giant*), the Franciscan "Father," Arghol, Hardcaster, Freddie
Salmon and Agnes (of *The Revenge for Love*), all are at some
time called shells. Uncle Thad, in the recent story "Doppelgänger,"
is left "only a shadow, a shell" on his Vermont mountain. René
Harding of *Self Condemned* ends as a "glacial shell" of a man.

How much has this "philosophy of the eye" been worth as a
literary method? This raises a problem at the heart of modern
literature. In answering it, I cannot be concerned here with Lewis'
minor syntactical effects. These are briefly studied by Bonamy
Dobrée in his *Modern Prose Style;* though finding in Lewis "an
almost panic-stricken avoidance of the cliché," [35] Dobrée admiringly
records Lewis' use of harsh, consonantal sounds (such as *t* and *ck*)
in the build-up of his sentences, in an effort, Dobrée feels, to goad
the reader almost physically.

35. Bonamy Dobrée, *Modern Prose Style* (Oxford, Clarendon Press, 1934),
p. 51; and see p. 103.

In his sympathetic little study of Wyndham Lewis called *A Master of Our Time,* Geoffrey Grigson takes his stand in the externalist camp, and pleads that Lewis' method in fiction has revitalized modern prose:

> *Tarr* outside, *Ulysses* inside. The divergence, the eccentricity of Lewis was not apparent. Compare once more a later pronouncement: "I have defined art as the science of the *outside* of things, and natural science as the science of the *inside* of things" (*The Art of Being Ruled,* 1926). In art the real life was, paradoxically, the deadness, the permanence, desiderated by Tarr: the warm moil and mess of the inside—in that there could be no proportion, no line, no simplicity of structural grandeur, no *art.* In the one camp Joyce, or Lawrence, or Virginia Woolf, flux which is captured; in the other Lewis and that which is made and made stiff. Obviously Lewis was going to be in isolation . . .[36]

And Grigson then goes on to accord the external approach in Lewis very high praise; *Time and Western Man,* first formulating this method for Grigson, is called "assured, deliberate, lucid criticism" —which is generosity itself. Finally we are told of Lewis' style: "Pick up a sentence, it does not bend or sag. But it *means,* this prose demands *reading:* it cannot be absorbed effortlessly like air."

In *The Destructive Element*—"Marxist-aesthetic criticism" according to Stanley Edgar Hyman— Stephen Spender puts the case for the prosecution. Spender is here as little in love with the interior monologue as Grigson. *Ulysses* provides only "monotony of style, thought, content, action, and characterization . . . Stephen is so disastrous a failure that he is only recognizable at all by being made inseparable from his ashplant." But in a chapter on "The Great Without" Spender takes up "fiction from the outside" and arrives at a rejection of everything Grigson appears to admire:

36. Geoffrey Grigson, *A Master of our Time* (London, Methuen, 1951), pp. 11–12.

The fact is that by imposing an external order on internal disorder, by ruggedly insisting on and accepting only the outsides of things, one does not improve matters. One merely shouts and grows angry with anyone who has a point of view different from one's own. For another point of view is sure to seem visceral, internal, decadent. One is, in a word, merely asserting that one is afraid of the symptoms which one dislikes in oneself, and more particularly in other people; not that one can cure them. Take this insistence on the external into the world of politics, and what is it but fascism? It is saying that we must suppress the effeminate, dark members of our society (the Jews), we must arrange our façade to look as well as possible, to appeal to the eye (the private armies), we must drive the symptoms of decadence underground.[37]

I am not prepared to argue out Spender's political parallel here, but it is not hard to support his contention concerning the intransigence of the neoclassical defense of external, or "hard," art. A fund of dogmatic statements is on hand. Hulme roundly states, "The sense of reality is inevitably connected with that of *space*." Yet Bergsonism, which Hulme championed, liberates for Lewis "a sightless, ganglionic mass." In Canto XLV (beginning "With *Usura*") of the *Cantos,* Pound goes so far as to suggest that the kind of hard-outline, external art he requires opposes usury. Lines 18 and 19 of the canto tell us this clearly:

> with usura the line grows thick
> with usura is no clear demarcation

Nor is this conceit uncommon to the neoclassicist, for it seems to have been independently in Lewis' mind in 1934 when he wrote, "the usurious banker-kings of the modern world . . . have extremely little to do with art of any sort, except perhaps music." [38]

37. Stephen Spender, *The Destructive Element* (London, Cape, 1935), p. 214.
38. Wyndham Lewis, "Tradesmen, Gentlemen and Artists," *The Listener, 12,* No. 298 (Sept. 26, 1934), 545. In *The Vulgar Streak* Penhale develops a money theory that seems to derive from Pound.

But the question is deeper than this. Of all literary forms in the comparatively modern world the early English novel, the picaresque novel of Fielding and Defoe, relied on time, owing to its strong narrative element. Lewis seems to be asking for a fiction that does not unfold in time, almost a contradiction in terms. Yet he is not unusual in so doing; in 1927 E. M. Forster's justly celebrated *Aspects of the Novel* takes up this matter and is obviously unhappy with aesthetic value being attached to time. Forster, however, concludes: "The time-sequence cannot be destroyed without carrying in its ruin all that should have taken its place; the novel that would express values only becomes unintelligible and therefore valueless." [39] Joseph Frank, writing in *The Sewanee Review* in 1945, grapples ably with this problem. Starting from Lessing's *Laokoön,* which saw form in the plastic arts as necessarily spatial, Frank argues that a number of outstanding contemporary writers like Eliot, Proust, Joyce, and Pound have actually refuted Lessing's definitions and produced a kind of "spatial form" in their work. As he puts it, "the reader is intended to apprehend their work spatially, in a moment of time, rather than as a sequence." [40] This is exemplified in the kind of concatenation (or vortex) of periods, cultures, and ideas latent in what Pound proposed as his "image." It is also to be found in Proust's highly charged "moment privilégié."

39. E. M. Forster, *Aspects of the Novel* (London, Edward Arnold, 1927), p. 42. This little classic was written shortly after, and possibly in response to, Percy Lubbock's equally brilliant *The Craft of Fiction* (1921). It was followed, in 1928, by Edwin Muir's *The Structure of the Novel* which takes pretentious issue with Forster (pp. 7–16, and Conclusion); Muir's third section deals with "Time and Space," and presents a thesis concerning the "spatial form" of literature which can hardly hold water after the experiments in this field of Joyce, Proust, Eliot, Pound, and others. Indeed, it is significant that Muir avoids reference to experimental writers in this section; his work concludes with a bitter fulmination against *Ulysses,* whose "design is arbitrary, its development feeble, its unity questionable." Joyce's symbolism for Muir is "hardly to be taken seriously." *Ulysses* is here "formless," "loose," "clumsy," "mediocre or meretricious," and has everywhere "an almost stagnant stillness."

40. Joseph Frank, "Spatial Form in Modern Literature; Part I," *The Sewanee Review, 53,* No. 2 (Spring 1945), 225.

A number of other examples of similar literary compression come to mind, particularly in poetry. Briefly, Frank feels that a spatialization of the contemporary novel has been achieved by writers like Joyce, Proust, and Djuna Barnes, by breaking up the ordinary chronological time-flow.

This may seem obvious enough to the reader, but Frank's article helped me to understand Lewis' real dilemma as a writer. As Lawrence Durrell has pointed out, in dealing with this problem in his *A Key to Modern British Poetry,* time has taken on a completely new significance in the novel of our age: "Time has become a thick opaque medium, welded to space—no longer the quickly flowing river of the Christian hymns, moving from here to there along a marked series of stages." [41]

It is easy to see that no author, writing after Einstein's theory of relativity, and wishing to be artistically honest, could ignore the implications of the space-time continuum. One could reject the idea, as Lewis did, in *Time and Western Man,* but one could not *as a writer* reject the innovations in language and the experiments in literary form dependent upon a whole new view of time for which Einstein (among others) is now considered largely responsible. The distortion of language to adapt itself to this new reality Durrell calls the "semantic disturbance." Eliot has made a famous comment on this. And it has been a real crisis for Lewis as a writer, one which in the final analysis he has failed to master.

Frank cites three works that have, as it were, overcome time by being ahistorical, by closely juxtaposing past and present, and by relying to a minimal extent on direct chronological narrative; these are the *Cantos, The Waste Land,* and *Ulysses.* One at once notices that two of these are poems and indeed Frank admits that the best contemporary novels are those moving toward poetry, for that total reorientation of language demanded by "spatial form" is most fruitfully achieved, he feels, in poetry. It is not hard to con-

41. Lawrence Durrell, *A Key to Modern British Poetry* (Norman, Okla., University of Oklahoma Press, 1952), 31.

cede this. Yet I cannot help feeling that Lewis would object to Frank's thesis that the chronology of the psyche (which need not at all be a forward narrative movement) introduces the old time-form under a new guise. Admittedly *Ulysses* takes place in one day, and there are epiphanic moments of "spatial form" with reflexive relationships for the reader in it, but the psyche of the characters still unfolds in time. Our eyes travel down the page. We read on, to learn what happens *next* in the thought-stream of this or that character. In other words, it seems to me that "spatial form," such as Frank suggests, would be intolerable if it obtained in the novel; in fact, the novel would cease to be a novel, and would become a poem. It is here, surely, that Frank's argument for the defeat of time, in the sense of chronological sequence, is most cogent. And indeed, in his brilliant article on Faulkner in *Situations I,* Jean-Paul Sartre seems to argue just this. In this essay, which among other things makes one feel that as a good English Parnassian Lewis should have been kinder to Faulkner than he was, Sartre suggests that Faulkner takes the infatuation with chronology to its logical conclusion in *The Sound and the Fury.* By a technique of *"enfoncement,"* by working backward (and around) in this novel, Faulkner has for Sartre pushed Proust's method to its ultimate conclusion and decapitated the future, the realm of free choice. In other words he has created the nearest thing to a static novel and—it is centered on a lunatic. Thus what Gide felt to be Faulkner's lack of soul is here seen by Sartre as a predominantly technical consideration. This goes on to raise a problem nuclear to modern literature, for it is by technics, by the *way* of saying something, that the great European writers of this century have felt impelled to project their vision —"technique as discovery" is the suggestive phrase Mark Schorer has used for this phenomenon.

Lewis was, then, in the quandary of disliking everything to do with a literary development like that of the interior monologue, but being unable, if he was to be a truly modern writer, to make himself independent of its dislocation of language. (The same might be argued of his attitude vis-à-vis Cubism.) *The Apes* is his attempt to create a new language, but even this work is highly dependent on innovations in language, and punctuation too, that were the result of the detested "time-philosophy." As Spender put it, not only did the classical Greeks have fine ears, but "the ossature is just as much inside an animal as the intestine; and the intestine of a human being is also just as much on the surface and affects the shell, as does the backbone." [42] As a consequence, there is a clash taking place in Lewis' imagery. In *The Wild Body,* and in parts of *Tarr,* he arrives in the literary arena beside the genius of the picaresque novel, like Fielding, exulting in human deformity and general extravagance. Like the early English novelist of this kind Lewis began by seeing life from below. Ker-Orr by no means looks down on the great "comic effigies" of these first stories; he himself is simply another type of alienated individual, equally antiromantic, though in his case an intellectual outlaw. This lends the eccentricity a note of affection, which we never find again in Lewis' satire. After about 1920 a lack of intellectual elasticity, even a doctrinaire bigotry, a necessity to play the part of "enemy," instead of feeling it instinctively, begin to weigh down on this potentially fertile ebullience. He sees life from above. For a moment, in *The Apes,* this actually helps, and we have the English comic masterpiece of the first half of this century. But we note that Lewis does not satirize himself in *The Apes,*[43] as Joyce was able to satirize himself in *Finnegans Wake.* The imagery atrophies. It becomes montonous, hectoring. The vocabulary shrivels. I took the liberty of documenting the use of favorite words in Lewis' imagery in *The Childermass,* for instance, and even a cursory inspection revealed the following:

Shell: pp. 3, 6, 14, 29, 41, 44, 231, 233, 262.
Disk: pp. 15, 26, 53, 58, 256.
Mask: pp. 3, 30, 41, 51, 57, 134, 148, 173, 232, 247, 258, 303.

42. Spender, *Destructive Element,* p. 209.
43. Some critics think he does, in Zagreus.

Doll: pp. 30, 36, 54, 302.
Clockwork: pp. 26, 34, 52.

The majority of these references, it will be seen, occur in the first part of the book, the descriptive part. In the ensuing dialogue characters are called puppets, automata, and machines about every third page. Indeed, *we heard you the first time!* is perhaps the most common criticism of Lewis' work I have come across.

Yet it would be churlish to end on an ungenerous note to this writer, at least two of whose productions are of the very highest rank. "Had we but world enough and time" we might know whether posterity will place these beside Swift or not. For Lewis, the eye is life, then. Ludo, the blind beggar of Rot—a word that combines the name for a Breton commune and a belch (in *One-Way Song* Lewis wrote, "I belch, I bawl, I drink")—represents death and is the only character in *The Wild Body* to die. The rest are vividly alive. In *Rotting Hill* we return to Rot, here a disease affecting Attlee's England, so that when Rymer arrives with a patch over one eye in this work and eructates, he is halfway to Ludo and an ironical comment on his creator who was rapidly going blind during the writing of these stories. For there is something savagely tragic about the fate that has now befallen the author, in *Blast No. 2,* of the comment, "My soul has gone to live in my eyes, and like a bold young lady it lolls in those sunny windows." Lewis has faced this fate with characteristic courage. "Pushed into an unlighted room, the door banged and locked forever," he writes, "I shall have to light a lamp of aggressive voltage in my mind to keep at bay the night." [44]

44. Wyndham Lewis, "The Sea-Mists of the Winter," *The Listener, 45,* No. 1158 (May 10, 1951), 765.

Chapter 18: Time Stands Still

" 'Time stands still in this land.'
'I said it was England' Satters answers." [*The Childermass*, p. 86.]

In 1928 Lewis published *The Childermass*, a fictional satire announced as the first section of a trilogy whose second and third parts were shortly to follow. It has been left to the conclusion of this study for two reasons. First, it contains so many of Lewis' critical opinions as to make it fall almost between his satires and his "pamphlets"; second, he himself has called it an exception in his canon in *Rude Assignment*. "It is about Heaven," he tells us there, "the politics of which, although bitter in the extreme, have no relation to those of the earth."

Meanwhile, the two subsequent sections did not appear, and only came out as recently as 1955 in a volume called *The Human Age*, a title intended to subsume what has now turned into four parts—*The Childermass, Monstre Gai, Malign Fiesta,* and *The Trial of Man*. (A revised version of the first section, *The Childermass*, appeared in 1956.) A writer in *The Times Literary Supplement*, praising the work in terms alluded to above, surmises that the earlier extensions of the 1928 book have "either been scrapped altogether or very radically revised." This may well be so. E. W. F. Tomlin, however, in his British Council pamphlet on Lewis, seems to hint at a tetralogical structure visible in the original volume:

> An important clue may be found in the elaborate description of the grotesque court in which the Bailiff conducts his business. The "Punch and Judy" structure in which he sits is

adorned with a variety of occult signs, chief among them being the symbol of the *Maha-Yuga*. Now the *Maha-Yuga* is the name in Vedanta doctrine for a complete cycle of history. Divided into four separate *Yugas,* it implies the successive decline in human righteousness, culmininating in the *Kali-Yuga* in which righteousness reaches its nadir. The representation of the "goat-hoof" underneath the sign in question, together with the recurrent imagery of the serpent's head (repeated on the Bailiff's banner in *Monstre Gai*) seems to imply that the world brought to judgement has reached its final phase.[1]

The whole work is difficult to the point of preciosity; Yeats, who called the first hundred pages of the first part "a masterpiece" in a letter to Olivia Shakespear, also said, "It is the most obscure piece of writing known to me." [2] Reviewing *The Human Age* (containing *Monstre Gai* and *Malign Fiesta*) for *The Sunday Times* for October 30, 1955, Cyril Connolly was appalled by "the immense tedium of the whole." Parts he found "disgusting and aesthetically wrong," and his conclusion was that "such a prosaic tapestry of banal dialogue, so much creative complacency, produces in the end only a bumbling in the ears." [3] Perhaps because it is such a cromlech of acrostics (not to say a dolmen of dullness) the work has repelled elucidators, by far the best exposition to date being that of Thomas Carter in *The Kenyon Review* for Spring 1956, in an extended notice of *The Human Age.*

Originally entitled "Hoadipip," and then "Joint," Lewis' most complex and single mystagogical satire opens on the fringes of

1. E. W. F. Tomlin, *Wyndham Lewis* (London, Longmans, Green, 1955), p. 30.

2. Yeats, *Letters,* p. 745.

3. At the start of this review Connolly writes: "Twenty-seven years ago Mr. Lewis produced 'The Childermass,' to which *The Human Age* is a sequel. I acknowledged it with pleasurable excitement in the 'New Statesman' and now find myself occupied with its successor." Mr. Connolly must surely imagine us unable to read, for his excitement in *The New Statesman* for July 7, 1928, may be turned up and found to be anything but "pleasurable."

"Heaven." This celestial city, lying to "the heavenly north" of the plain where we begin, and whose battlemented shadow haunts this twentieth-century slaughter of the "Holy Innocents," turns out to be anything but a Dantesque paradise; what one character calls the "human age" at the end of *Malign Fiesta* seems to be a ghastly compromise between angel and animal, and in the city that is only glimpsed in *The Childermass* Lewis later dramatizes a sort of immortal folly, an existence of contemporary Struldbrugs. Blood-red clouds emerge from the city in the first volume and, sure enough, we learn in the sequels that state socialism prevails there. And we also have a hint in the first section that Third City, as it is later called, is peopled by children, or childish adults.[4]

In *The Childermass* we are mainly concerned with the attempts of two characters, Satterthwaite and Pullman, to reach this city, and with a Punch-like Bailiff (the "monstre gai" of the second part), the slaughters at whose court parallel the massacre of the children by Herod (Matthew 2:16) from which the book takes its name. The second and third sections become increasingly Swiftian, Miltonic, and Dantesque: there are references to Gulliver and the absurd names are reminiscent of Swift; in *Monstre Gai* there is an exchange of epic insults between Pullman and Sentoryen which is only one of many such scenes reminding one of Satan and Gabriel squaring up to each other (or Satan and Death) in *Paradise Lost*, whereas in one such passage the very syntax becomes Miltonic— "He from Hell affected dignity"; finally, a set of torture cells in *Malign Fiesta* is "a kind of caricature of Dante's Inferno." In this last connection we have what Carter calls an "utterly debased version of Paola and Francesca." Yet this couple Pullman sees shows how little Lewis has visualized his final scenes: at p. 404 we read that his Paolo and Francesca are naked, "glued" together, and "the man exactly placed to facilitate *sinful* love" (my italics). Three pages later, we read that their posture is "lips to lips and sex to sex."

However this may be, the action of the whole opens, then, in

4. *Childermass,* p. 317.

"the suburbs of the wilderness, enclosed plots of desert, over each of which a peculiar solitary sun stands all day, glittering madly upon its apologetic fragments of vegetation." To the west of this "Plain of Death," as the Bailiff calls it, lies the "investing belt of Beelzebub," separated from the plain by a river, referred to once as the Styx. This is all the geography Lewis provides.

On this purgatorial plain two characters meet, Satterthwaite and Pullman, generally called Satters and Pulley. Both are appellants for Heaven, staying at the camp on the plain provided for such. But unlike Bouvard and Pécuchet, whom they somewhat resemble, these two have met before and we do not have the satirically ingenuous growth of acquaintance between the kindred souls which Flaubert provides. Their provincial reliance on each other also reminds one of Amédée and Blafaphas in *Les Caves du Vatican*.

The manner of meeting between Satters and Pulley recalls yet another work, Aristophanes' *The Birds*. Here we have two characters, Pithetaerus and Euelpides, entering an unknown and eccentrically peopled landscape far from the usual world, with all its follies. In the same way, too, Aristophanes' characters come to consult an authority of the new world on which they stumble, Tereus the Hoopoe (Lewis' Bailiff), and like Satters and Pulley they are nearly torn apart by the hostile birds at the beginning (the river peons in *The Childermass*). The Nightingale's chorus in *The Birds* makes a criticism of men as half-alive shadows compared with the vital, immortal birds, which we can find in the lines given to Lewis' Hyperides, and there is a general atmosphere of farce in the City of the Skies which is to be found in the Bailiff's Court also. This is about as far as one should go in the comparison. There is also a hint of *The Frogs* in the ferryman business and in the absurd master-slave relationship between Pulley and Satters, reminiscent of that between Dionysus and Xanthias at the start of Aristophanes' drama, as also of that between Brush and Menaechmus I in Plautus' *The Twin Menaechmi*.

The likeness to Flaubert's posthumous satiric masterpiece is

equally suggestive, but equally superficial. I noticed that at one
point, in his materialist reading, Bouvard soaks himself in La
Mettrie, and in another place Pécuchet has a conversation with the
doctor, Vaucorbeil, as to the substantiality of matter which is
Childermassian. It is true that Flaubert called *Bouvard et Pécuchet*
"mon vomissement," and wrote of it, "j'espère cracher là dedans
le fiel qui m'étouffe," but his work is far more amenable; the two
protagonists, though gullible and philistine, are seen with sympathy, indeed so much so that D.-L. Demorest sees the two as
examples of intellectual and moral probity. Satters and Pulley we
detest, and should detest, from the start. Flaubert's work is far more
universal. It is the contemporary world that *The Childermass* deplores.

Satters and Pulley, like the characters around them, undergo
changes of identity in keeping with the flux of "space-time" that
persists on the plain. Generally, however, they are both male homo-
sexuals and generally Pulley is the leader, or Virgil. He is a "guide"
and "little master" for Satters. He is frequently referred to as Miss
Pullman or as a governess or "Nannie." In one place he wipes
Satters' face for him. He is "the sage Pulley," and says, " 'Suffer
me to lead Apes in Hell.' " [5]

Actually, we learn that James Pullman is aged about twenty-
eight, but he is dressed in a far more adult way than Satters, whom
we meet in football kit and wearing a medal to which he is not
entitled. Satters is, I think, meant to be the less likable of the
two, is constantly referred to as a baby, and becomes more and more
babyish as time passes; once, however, he changes sex, if becoming
a female homosexual from a male homosexual can be considered
such, and seems to age slightly in the process, for as a woman he
has a wig, a paunch, and "two prominent sagging paps." Satters,
who above all characters in the work makes us think longingly of
the title, continually "steins" and stutters, and is obviously meant

5. Ibid., pp. 11, 22, 42, 43, 82.

to represent Gertrude Stein just as, on one level, Pulley stands for James Joyce.

Thus Pulley, to identify only one Joycean association, tells Satters: " 'When war was declared I was in Trieste—in Spandau, I should say, at the Berlitz, teaching.' " A few lines further on, he adds, " 'Some one pushed me over, and my glasses broke.' " [6] The parallel between Stein and Satters, meanwhile, is present on almost every page. This homosexual Jew, as we learn Satters is, turns out to be unpleasant as could be. To take one episode, a criticism of communism (and probably of what Lewis saw as *transition* communism at this time), the two return in time to various ages and on one occasion stumble across a Lilliputian Tom Paine. Speaking in a broad American accent, Tom Paine calls Satters " 'a disgusting lout,' " and when Satters seizes him bites his hand. Satters replies by symbolically stamping the author of the *Rights of Man* to death "in an ecstasy of cruelty."

The two sequels have not kept the acrimony behind these characterizations. As *Monstre Gai* opens, Pulley is still referred to as the "guide," or Virgil, but he longs to throw Satters off. The latter still "steins"—"Pulley, wha . . . wha . . . wha . . . wha . . . what!" and so on—but not nearly so much; however, Satters appears with face "twisted into the mask of a baby afflicted with wind," and at the end of *Malign Fiesta* Pullman says of his friend, "All his values are schoolboy values." [7] Pullman is still likened to Joyce by Lewis but now treated with more respect; in Third City Pulley carries (like Stephen) a "deceptively elegant" stick, and we are told that, like Joyce, he had once grown a beard, had been educated by Jesuits, and "had not come out of a top-drawer." He once remarks, "I began life in Ireland. I am a Catholic." [8] There are suggestions that on earth Pullman wrote for profit, and he is re-

6. Ibid., p. 94.
7. *Human Age,* p. 455.
8. Ibid., p. 205.

ferred to as "yellow"—"Didn't he run away when Plowden denounced him!" He is called a "hero-rat" in one place and is violently
assaulted by a belligerent Irishman named O'Rourke (the Mino-
taur), a real "citizen" of Third City. In two places in the sequels
two of Pullman's books are seen, but on the whole this is no longer
the Lewis who called *Ulysses* "the disordered spurting of the imbecile low-average mind" writing. The attitude to Pullman in both
Monstre Gai and *Malign Fiesta* is far more pleasant; as regards
their names, it may not be going too far to suggest that the name
Pullman recalls a sleeper, and so Molly Bloom. A "pulley," meanwhile, is in opposition to immobility, while Satterthwaite may be
derived from Sat-her-weight. "The Roaring Queen" opens in a
Pullman corridor.

Whatever the value of such speculations may be, these two then,
Satters and Pulley, who themselves change identity, come across
menacing and mysterious beings on their way to the Bailiff's Court.
They have various mirages, mostly returning them in time; thus
Satters comes across a schoolboy called Marcus Morriss with whom
he had had homosexual relationship. They also meet literary characters, like Bill Sikes (murderer, and the Dickens connection for
Joyce). They have a hallucination of Old England, which is
identified by ladies' underclothes; following this skit both on the
oversentimental idea of rustic England (the work is extremely
Anglophobe), as well as on the politics of the English Puritan movement, they see a "righteous phalanx of incestuous masculine ma-
trons" with Eton crops and "revolutionary cockades." These are
the Mothers, the new woman of the twenties we have seen Lewis
deriding above. They turn out to be on the side of children, communism, and indiscipline in all its forms. Pulley leaps to serve them,
"he is the gelded herd-dog." This vision of the Mothers, satirizing
the development of the suffragette movement and of female emancipation in general, gives way to a vision of the Fathers, "matronly
papas" who are Big Business, and dispense, "meat-pale sunkist
fleshings of celanese silk stuffed with chocolates, crossword-puzzles,

tombola-tickets for crystal-sets, and free-passes for war films, to the million-headed herd of tiny tots of all ages but one size." [9]

The two then enter the deepest clouds of "space-time" in which everything shifts and changes in a Bergsonian hell. Here Lewis puts the idea of "durée" into crazy practice. "La vérité est qu'on change sans cesse," [10] might be the epigraph for this section from *L'Évolution créatrice*. The objective world is here turned into a farce of flux, and perhaps Lewis was merely exaggerating Bergson's comment in *Le Rire:* "nous ne voyons pas les choses mêmes; nous nous bornons, le plus souvent, à lire des étiquettes collées sur elles." [11] One can even trace verbal similarities. Macrob, a Scottish appellant at the Bailiff's Court, opposes the idea of becoming and change advocated by the Bailiff and is stamped on and cut to pieces for his pains. In one place he says, " 'This static degradation is the opposite, even, of the *becoming* to which you are so partial.' " [12] In *L'Évolution créatrice* Bergson develops his thesis of reality losing in time the more it extends in space, and in this context writes of the extra-spatial "se dégradant en spatialité." [13]

Eventually Satters and Pulley make their way to the Yang gate; we later learn that there is a Yin, or female, gate, but no woman puts in an appearance in this first work, though of course most of the appellants are half-women. It is also notable that they generally wander around in crowds ("herds"). Here the Bailiff arrives, heralded by trumpets, and proceeds to hold court. From here until the end of the work the action takes place mainly in this one spot, becoming at the end a series of dramatic speeches. As I. A. Richards puts it: "In deliberate and extreme contrast with these minute particulars of the sensory action, intellectual action is flung wide open. Platonic socratic care is taken not to pin anything down,

9. *Childermass*, p. 92 (note the topicality of this, though of course for crystal sets we might today substitute television sets without damaging the criticism).

10. Bergson, *L'Évolution créatrice*, p. 2.

11. Bergson, *Le Rire*, p. 155.

12. *Childermass*, p. 227.

13. Bergson, *L'Évolution créatrice*, p. 226.

not to let any speech sum up, answer any question or, merely, put it fairly." [14]

This Bailiff should not be confused with the somewhat autobiographical Bailiff "billed" in the first section of *One-Way Song,* despite the fact that we read that his is "a one-way world" in *Malign Fiesta.* This latter character, whose habits, we are told, are Swift's, holds a sort of school class and criticizes "Backness" (cult of primitivity in the arts). He tells us, for instance, that he long ago advised his class to " 'Say it with locomotives!' " (i.e. advocated the assimilation of the machine into art) but now feels that this has gone far enough: " 'You said it with locomotives honies! That will do I guess for to-night.' " [15] It should be remembered that *One-Way Song* was written at the time of the New Signatures group who were showing such an uncritical infatuation with the machine in poetry.

The Bailiff of *The Childermass* is everything Lewis dislikes. " *'Le mob c'est moi!' "* is his admitted motto and he boasts of his Bill of Wrongs: " *'Primitive and proud of it* that's my motto.' " He is, of course, idolized by Satters and Pulley, especially in his debate with the Greek Hyperides, with whom Lewis himself identifies. Yet the emblem of the Bailiff is an eye, and he himself has an extraordinary eye; furthermore, Pulley tells us that the Bailiff recommends the intellect and will. If this means anything, I think it means that the Bailiff sails under a false flag, that he is an intellectual traitor, wearing the colors of clerc but betraying his office. This is seen directly he starts to deal with the different appellants and reveals his cynical, pseudo-revolutionary "time-philosophy." We later learn that the Bergsonian Bailiff has a French-speaking mother, that he is nonhuman (*Monstre Gai*) and yet "Oriental" (*Malign Fiesta*).

A number of arguments take place and the Bailiff becomes characterized as repressive, arbitrary, and Bergsonian. Some of these speeches, however, are highly puzzling. I. A. Richards writes, "to

14. I. A. Richards, "Talk," *B.B.C. Third Programme,* transmission, March 10, 1952, originally recorded, New York, November 4, 1951. Typescript.

15. *One-Way Song,* pp. 11–12.

an agonising degree we're not allowed to know what it is all about. That very ignorance may be, of course, what it is all about." I cannot help feeling that Richards, either consciously or unconsciously, puts his finger on a point here, for the book *is* about "ignorance" (or Bergsonism, for Lewis). Does not Pulley counsel Satters to hold in mind the maxim, " *'Nothing is but thinking makes it so' "?*

At times the Bailiff does phrase some Lewisian sentiments, especially at the end, in his clash with Hyperides and Hyperides' men. But this is presumably explained by Hyperides when he catches the Bailiff out thieving ideas (the theme of plagiarism, which began to obsess Lewis about this time). So Richards writes: "By these means the book disowns a doctrine. Of course, plenty of Pulleys will become completely and perfectly positive what its doctrine is, and what they think about it. They will tell us it is an attack on Bergson, on Christianity, on the time cult, on the child cult or on homosexualisticism [*sic*], and so forth. Good. Let them. That again is what Pullman Pulleys are for. Fine little governess dons they be." [16]

This is disarming. But one should not let such strictures deter one from the effort of finding out what the work is about, and in fact Richards gives a useful working catalogue of what *The Childermass* is attacking. For if it is really about nothing—and not, rather, about philosophical ideas which Lewis thinks equal nothing—then it is not worth reading at all. A work about "ignorance" in the true sense, a book composed of the lowing of cattle, say, or (as are some comic books) of the noises of guns, would make unrewarding study.

The Childermass is about "ignorance" in the form of "time-philosophy." The Bailiff explains "space-time," the element in which the purgatorial plain is cast, as precisely everything Lewis attacked in *Time and Western Man.* One can refer constantly from the Bailiff's speeches to the critical works Lewis wrote in the twenties

16. Richards, *loc. cit.*

and thirties, and vice versa. To do so here would be repetitive. It is much more interesting to glance at the positive side of the work.

The Bailiff is just giving a prevaricating answer to an appellant, who has dared to ask whether there is anything in the challenge recently made against Time, when a champion of this point of view enters "from the contrary pole." This is the Greek Hyperides, the "legendary enemy" of the Bailiff. The two are "the oldest opposites in the universe," and later we are again reminded that they are the opposing principles, and principals. The first question put by the direct and forthright Hyperides goes home: "'Would it not be true, sir, to say that in your magical philosophy there is only Time, that it is essentially with *Time* that you operate?'"

They have an exchange and there follows a series of speeches by Hyperides in which he puts his position.[17] It is one directly opposed to "time-philosophy" and it is, of course, greeted with derision, and shouts of "Bloody Male!" from the Bailiff's admiring audience.

Hyperides, however, is not alone. "The last aryan hero," he has his faction. He himself is carried about in a litter in the pose of Michelangelo's most famous "Nude Youth," we read that he has a "smashed michelangelesque nose"—Michelangelo's nose was broken by a fellow student, according to one theory—and again we are told that he resembles a "florentine painter." His face is, like Lewis' own, dark—"a mask of force, a dark cameo, in the centre of the crowds of faces." If Lewis partially identifies with Zagreus, as some critics like to believe, then this is the second work in which he has put himself into the position of privilege, by means of a classical name. Zagreus was the son of Zeus and Persephone, torn to pieces by the Titans. Hyperides was the Attic orator, many of whose speeches were only found in the last century. Both characters are partly incarnations of their classical namesakes.

For it is really a funeral oration over a moribund culture that Hyperides pronounces in his long speeches in *The Childermass*. So at once he challenges the Bailiff:

17. *Childermass*, pp. 150–7.

"Is not your Space-Time for all practical purposes only the formula recently popularized to accommodate the empirical sensational chaos? Did not the human genius redeem us for a moment from that, building a world of human-divinity above that flux? Are not your kind betraying us again in the name of exact research to the savage and mechanical nature we had overcome . . . That Time-factor that our kinsman the Greek removed, and that you have put back to obsess, with its movement, everything—what is that accomplishing except the breaking-down of all our concrete world into a dynamical flux . . ." [18]

He goes on to accuse the Bailiff of the cult of action. Pulley feels uncomfortable here, for of Pulley-Joyce we read that "action is everything; to keep moving is the idea, this is the law of his existence." This criticism of Joyce as a "Fidgety Phil who couldn't keep still" is the same as Plato's of the ideal of busy-ness in the *Phaedo;* of Joyce, of course, it is a view neither probative nor cogent. The Bailiff's position is now what Lewis conceives as Bergsonian: " 'there is no *you* apart from what you perceive: your senses and you with them *are* all that you habitually see and touch: I am a part of you at this moment: those battlements are becoming you.' " Again, the Bailiff says, " 'Time is the mind of Space—Space is the mere body of Time. Time is life, Time is money, Time is all good things!—Time is God!' " [19] To this philosophy Hyperides and his men object. Hyperides designates as its outriders the youth cult, the revolutionary orthodoxy, and the sex war: " 'The male principle is scarcely your favourite principle where the human herd is concerned . . . you would drive back mankind into the protozoic slime for the purposes of your despotism where you can rule them like an undifferentiated marine underworld or like an

18. Ibid., pp. 152–3.
19. Ibid., pp. 222, 227. The latter passage is similar to, and may be a parody of, George Gissing's words in *The Private Papers of Henry Ryecroft* (London, 1914), p. 287.

insect-swarm . . . you are drilling an army of tremulous earth-worms to overthrow our human principle of life, not in open battle but by sentimental or cultural infection.' " Until the end of the first book, as we now have it, this division obtains. Against the classical Hyperides stands the romantic Bailiff. The last fifty pages, however, are confusing. Here the Bailiff makes a long attack on Hyperides, indicting the Greek for being a Fascist "Crowd-master." The Hyperideans he calls "class-conscious herd-midgets." It seems that the Bailiff, at a loss for argument, is merely borrowing the notions of Hyperides himself. Hyperides indeed replies, " 'You wish to turn the tables on me, puppet, by suggesting that I am no more a person than yourself I see.' " The Bailiff replies and there occur suggestions that he is appealing to Hyperides as might one cynical power-politician to another.

Hyperides remains unimpressed by this appeal. One of his *ligueurs,* the Action Française Alectryon, speaks for him and then Hyperides returns to the debate himself. The Bailiff then objects that Hyperides is overdogmatic: "It is only when we *close our eyes* —and open our ears for instance—that we realize how strangely unlike the purely visual world our datum can be. You are so overwhelmed with the concrete reality of everything—your intellect has it all its own way." To which Hyperides answers, " 'You of course are the *philosopher.*' " He goes on to rephrase the visual point of view, and the two continue their acrimonious exchanges, incidentally calling each other apes.

In the sequel, *Monstre Gai,* Pulley and Satters enter Third (or Magnetic) City by permission of the Bailiff—upon which Pullman experiences "a tremendously violent romantic disillusion." The place, indeed, far from being a prelude to Heaven, turns out to be closer to a Lewisian Hell. It is peopled by vacuous youth cultists: "Perhaps fifty per cent of the city is the desiccated remains of the youth-propaganda of forty years ago," remarks a character called Mannock—and there is no work, only "an ideal of averageness." Money is free; there is a spoof of social credit in this connection.

The city is, in fact, an amalgam of almost everything Lewis has criticized in contemporary Western society: State socialism, the left-wing orthodoxy (Pullman discovers "there there would be no wings in a Bailiff-world except left-wings"),[20] Negro-worship (some of the Bailiff's henchmen are colored), homosexuality, and now even the new teddy-boys. In *Malign Fiesta* a weird, tortured figure, a "World Bird," appears, his back tattoed with a map of the world in which we see statism rampant. In the course of the book a conflict develops in intellectual terms between the detestable Bailiff (representing Hell) and an heroic Padishah (representing Heaven). Of this latter character we read, "Clearly everything to do with Man filled him with an immense fatigue," and he consigns women to a compound in which they are periodically tortured and brutalized. In *Malign Fiesta* a Jewish guard is seen kicking a woman prisoner of the upper classes in a parodistic reversal of the concentration camp horrors of our century. This punishment center is looked after by Sammael, a totalitarian Puritan who executes his office with gruesome efficiency. These horror scenes have been highly praised for their graphic power, and Thomas Carter writes of them as follows: "Some of the harrowing *presence* of these scenes undoubtedly comes from Lewis' knowledge of London during the Blitz." [21] Unfortunately, Lewis was in Canada during the Blitz.

Even so, Carter writes suggestively of *Malign Fiesta*, which ends, as he puts it, in an "ironic apotheosis of the banal," [22] a proposed liquidation of this Hell itself by mating angels and sinners in a final holocaust, a "humanization of the divine." Praying, in terror, Pullman is at the end of this work "rescued" by two storm-trooper angels from his fate. A spoof of science-fiction brings to a close what Tomlin believes to be "one of the most prodigious imaginative creations of the present century, perhaps the only great work to come

20. *Human Age,* p. 148.
21. Thomas H. Carter, "Rationalist in Hell," *The Kenyon Review, 18,* No. 2 (Spring 1956), 332.
22. Ibid., p. 335.

out of the Cold War, and the climax of Lewis' literary career." [23]

Here one is finally forced back on opinion; is the "nightmarish existence, where the supernatural was real," of *Monstre Gai* and *Malign Fiesta* (with their bad French and worse German) really anything more than a sort of *grand guignol* museum piece? Does it not in its "horrible nullity" boast of the author's own savage hatred of humanity, as no other works of Lewis have before? When we read of the Padishah that "there was no one good enough, or supernatural enough, for him to communicate with," we realize with a jolt that Swift cared, and that Lewis no longer seems to do so. Indeed, Lewis tells us at the end of *The Demon of Progress in the Arts* that "talking about the alarming outlook for the fine arts appears so trivial a matter when one has finished writing about it. It is infected with the triviality of everything else." [24] If you are in that mood, as William Barrett suggested in his review of the book for *The New York Times Book Review* of October 30, 1955, you are unlikely to be in the best frame of mind for writing enduring literature. Compare the nihilism of *The Human Age* with that of *Waiting for Godot*.

The first part of *The Human Age* ends, then, on what Macrob had called the ultimate question—the reality of the Bailiff, and of his detestable philosophy. The Bailiff had himself earlier denied his own reality, but had suggested that he was real in that even the Hyperideans accepted him as real. But at the very end, in the last lines, the challenge is flung like a glove at the reader by Polemon, a leading Hyperidean who recurs in *Monstre Gai:* " 'Who is to be *real*—this hyperbolical puppet or we? Answer oh destiny!' "

It is, of course, a gage flung in front of the reader implicating the whole of Lewis' work, and only destiny will decide it. Yet already, because Lewis has deliberately associated his creative work so closely with his critical, he has seriously endangered the former. At the start of this study I mentioned Lewis' claim that his criticism

23. Tomlin, *Lewis*, p. 27.
24. *Demon of Progress*, p. 97.

was merely written in defense of his creative work. But the critical has now swamped the creative, and indeed vulgarized it with propaganda. Of course, there is divergence of opinion here. *Self Condemned* has been called a "masterpiece." The story "Time the Tiger" from *Rotting Hill* is considered by Hugh Kenner "a triumph of poise," [25] whereas William K. Rose, writing in *Furioso,* calls it "a feeble story." [26] There will always be debates of this sort in the *philosophe* press, no doubt, yet *Rotting Hill*—the pun on Notting Hill being suggested by Pound [27]—seems to me not only one of Lewis' weakest satires but one which shows signs of defending his criticism. This would prove a table-turning, indeed. And what creative work was *The Writer and the Absolute* aimed to protect?

The contemporary reviews of *The Childermass* presaged this crisis. Lewis claims, in *Rude Assignment,* that the book had a singularly quiet reception. In fact, it was widely and usually derogatorily reviewed. Of course, much of this was Blimpish disapproval of the difficulty of the prose. *The Times Literary Supplement* for July 19, 1928, called it "difficult and disjointed," and L. P. Hartley thought it "unintelligible" in the London *Saturday Review* for July 28. Raymond Mortimer, who has never been charitable to Lewis' work, was driven into what can only be called a venomous review in *The Nation and Athenaeum* for June 23. For Mortimer *The Childermass* was diseased; it contained "a positively pathological absence of all intellectual control. No doubt the book will have a great success among those whose admiration for a writer increases in proportion to their inability to understand what he is saying." Apart from this sort of review, however, the work was judged far more on its critical than on its creative content. Joseph Wood Krutch, for example, reviewing it in *The New York Herald Tribune* for September 2, 1928, found it a "new classifica-

25. Kenner, "The War with Time," p. 49.
26. William K. Rose, "Rotting Hill," *Furioso* (Fall 1952), p. 55.
27. Wyndham Lewis, "Ezra: The Portrait of a Personality," *Quarterly Review of Literature, 5,* No. 2 (Dec. 1949), 140.

tion of the forces at work in modern society." Two of the most interesting reviews of this sort, on either side of the Atlantic, came from Cyril Connolly and Lionel Trilling. Writing in *The New Statesman* for July 7, 1928, Connolly took occasion to consider, and consider brilliantly, the whole neoclassical attack. He found it invalid, and *The Childermass* Fascist. Above all, Connolly found the antiromantic approach sterile: "The Age of Reason is past, and neither the balance of Greece, nor the detachment of China, the Action Française, the neo-Thomists, nor even Mr. Lewis and his virile desperadoes will ever put Humpty-Dumpty together again." [28] Lionel Trilling, writing in the *New York Evening Post* for September 22, 1928, and writing with his customary perspicuity, was even more severe in his judgment. Lewis' prose was "arrogant," his ideas traditional. And Trilling concluded: "There remains to Mr. Lewis a quality that must prevent him from being the considerable corrective and pedagogic force that it is his potentiality to be. That quality is his anger. His anger will not keep him from being read. But it will prevent him from being granted the accord which he must be seeking from the best spirits. He had far better, for effectiveness and safety, have chosen the Olympian calm or the humor he has doctrinated in his own *The Wild Body*."

If Lewis would object to this that he is seeking neither "accord" nor "safety," yet it is true that of all his works *The Childermass* has the least "Olympian calm." Philip Henderson equally criticizes Lewis' satires, not for being too close to his criticism so much as for being invalidated by the nature of that criticism: "Nor is vital satire possible except in relation to a substantial body of belief, and apart from Communism, which Lewis rejects, our age offers no belief that a man can hold without insulting his intelligence." [29] Here Lewis would say that he was one of those who never saw communism as anything but an insult to the intelligence. Henderson,

28. Cyril Connolly, "Chang," *The New Statesman, 31,* No. 793 (July 7, 1928), 427.

29. Philip Henderson, *The Novel Today* (London, John Lane, 1936), p. 98.

however, feels that this lack of real ideological root in Lewis' work robs it of creative power: "The fact remains that Joyce's Leopold Bloom and Virginia Woolf's Mrs. Dalloway are far more convincingly human creations than any of Lewis's grotesques." [30]

But it must not be thought, from criticism such as this, that Lewis has not had his supporters. He has had many, if few of them scholarly. And if one is to pass judgment on his work with any balance, one cannot approach it in the spirit of Hugh Gordon Porteus' *Wyndham Lewis: A Discursive Exposition,* so partial it seems to place its subject above every satirist in literature. Not only is Lewis here "more serious and profound" than Joyce, he possesses the instruments of satire more perfectly than anyone "in the known history of literature." [31]

What Lewis' ultimate position will be it is hard to say. It is principally hard because he is such an erratic writer. There are so many levels of achievement in his work, from the inspired verbal vigor of the best of *The Apes* down to the weak urbanity of *Rotting Hill* and the longueurs of *The Red Priest.* There is an equal range in his criticism, too, from the challenging and succinct sallies of *The Doom of Youth* to the turgid, repetitive, and contradictory *America and Cosmic Man.* Nor does it really help matters to be told that Lewis is a writer of the future, for I find references alleging that his external approach is just about to be discovered in contemporary letters since about 1920.

Is Lewis a great satirist? Is only his hatred creative, as Ernest Sutherland Bates and G. W. Stonier both suggest? Is he fatally limited by what Pound calls "the peeve"? Pound, indeed, has called satire "surgery, insertions and amputations." [32] We may concede Lewis the first and last of these abilities, but his "insertions" seem to me limited because of what I can only call critical bigotry. This

---

30. Ibid., p. 102.

31. Hugh Gordon Porteus, *Wyndham Lewis: A Discursive Exposition* (London, Desmond Harmsworth, 1932), pp. 195, 204.

32. Pound, *Pavannes, and Divisions,* p. 225.

will be, nay should be, set down to some decided disagreement with the wilder of this criticism, yet a satirist like Flaubert, Swift, or Rabelais may surely contribute positively through his *saeva indignatio,* through showing us literary coin whose reverse face holds out hope.

In any final estimate of Lewis he cannot be called an affirmative writer, yet no fully committed satirist can really be such. George Aitken wrote of Swift that "the satirist must, in the end, take a lower place than the creative writer." On the other hand, in his *Essay on Satire,* Dryden seems to oppose this prejudice and approve Heinsius' belief that satire must inevitably be severely destructive (and one thinks, too, of Dryden's pseudonymous references to living originals). For Kenneth Burke, Lewis is merely, however, a writer of "burlesque," a man full of "mannerisms" rather than "manner," or style. Is Burke's charge admissible, that Lewis' "excoriations arise from a suppressed fear of death, or, in other words, from religiosity frustrated by disbelief"? [33] Certainly Lewis' constant, almost paranoid lust for destruction seems to be a sign of insecurity in the spirit, of uncertainty in the belief.

There is one feature immediately apparent in any assessment of Lewis' performance, and that is a high degree of divergence among the intelligentsia. In the case of Joyce there is no such problem really, because the intelligence is all on one side. Detraction does not mean too much when it comes from such pens as occasionally scribble against Joyce, usually from England (the whole question of Joyce-baiting by the British is well taken up via V. S. Pritchett's recent attack by W. Y. Tindall in *The New Republic* for June 25, 1956). But in the case of Lewis there is considerable division within the educated public itself.

First, it can be said that his stock has gone up immeasurably in recent years. Studies of contemporary literature by younger British critics, such as G. S. Fraser or Walter Allen, almost invariably

33. Kenneth Burke, *Attitudes toward History* (New York, The New Republic, 1937), *1,* 63.

accord Lewis a very high place in letters today. Walter Allen has, in fact, called Lewis "one of the few original minds of our time." Hugh Kenner agrees: "No other living novelist has such power at his command." George Woodcock, in *The New Yorker* for June 4, 1955, thinks Lewis "the most resolute intellectual of our age." For Cyril Connolly, Lewis' work now contains "some of the most vigorous satire, original description and profound criticism produced by the twentieth century." [34] "The man of genius who possessed no talents," is Horace Gregory's neat summary of Lewis in *The New York Times Book Review* for August 22, 1954, while Russell Kirk has recently compared him with Coleridge and named him "one of the few English men of letters in our time whose books probably will be remembered, if books are remembered, a century from now." [35] T. S. Eliot's praise, already frequently quoted, must be by now the best known of all these various tributes; "the greatest prose master of my generation," Eliot called Lewis in 1955, "perhaps the only one to have invented a new style." [36]

Yet one does not have to look far to find Lewis not so much being attacked as being dismissed with utter contempt. Steven Marcus refers to Lewis in *Commentary* as a "highbrow know-nothing." "Stop to examine the breezy flow of Lewis' prose on any point," advises William Barrett, an associate editor of *Partisan Review,* "and the vulgarity of the mind behind it is startling." Irving Howe, author of some brilliant criticism in the contemporary field, writes: "when a charlatan like Wyndham Lewis is revived and praised for his wisdom, it is done, predictably, by a Hugh Kenner in the *Hudson Review*." [37] For F. R. Leavis, Lewis is equally little worth bothering about. In *The Common Pursuit* Leavis treats Lewis

34. Connolly, *Enemies of Promise,* p. 60.

35. Russell Kirk, "Wyndham Lewis's First Principles," *The Yale Review, 44,* No. 4 (Summer 1955), 521.

36. T. S. Eliot, "A Note on *Monstre Gai,*" *The Hudson Review, 7,* No. 4 (Winter 1955), 526.

37. Irving Howe, "This Age of Conformity," *Partisan Review, 21,* No. 1 (Jan./Feb. 1954), 17.

with the greatest contempt, but it must be noticed that he is only dealing with Lewis here in the context of adulation for D. H. Lawrence. Lewis is thus "excited," incapable of proper thought, and "as unqualified to discriminate between the profound insight and the superficial romantic illusion, as anyone who could have been hit on." [38] This criticism is followed up in Leavis' more recent study of Lawrence, where any note of consideration for Lewis disappears: "It may perhaps be suggested that, if Mr. Wyndham Lewis's brilliance illustrates a capacity for 'what we ordinarily call thinking,' then Lawrence's strength is to lack that capacity." [39]

Wyndham Lewis has been seen in these pages as a contemporary neoclassicist, and it is seriously to be doubted that this neoclassical approach is positive, especially as we find it in Lewis. Unwittingly, perhaps, he puts the case against himself: "the romantic traditional outlook . . . results in most men living in an historic past." [40] We are too "historical," he argues; even when we satirize ourselves, we do not satirize what we are, only what we have been. We tend to laugh at the foibles of our past, and so fail to progress. Only the laugher, therefore, lives for only he, the true "person" of Lewis' political ideal, sees all satirically, externally, nonromantically, in a perpetual present. Only this man is fully conscious. [41]

This would be all very well, if the exigencies of the present time permitted it. But not only does Lewis' critical position bind itself too closely to tradition to allow for the present at all, it also insists on continually assailing the present in a *parti pris* fashion. This insistence on particularities, on assailing our time and not all time, robs his satire of universality. Much of his work is contemporary in allusion, and some of it only contemporary. Is it just possible that

38. F. R. Leavis, *The Common Pursuit*, New York, George W. Stewart, 1952, pp. 243–4.

39. F. R. Leavis, *D. H. Lawrence: Novelist* (New York, Alfred A. Knopf, 1956), p. 11.

40. *Diabolical Principle*, p. 144.

41. *Paleface*, p. 270.

Lewis' loss in powers of observation may be due to the "apriorist heresy," to his approaching reality subjectively (not to say, romantically), selecting from it data to confirm his theories? There are large areas of twentieth-century experience left untouched by Lewis' work, voluminous though it may be. One cannot say the same of Joyce. The recent satires show a serious loss of control of his material by Lewis, and if this decline continues, as one earnestly hopes it may not, we shall be faced with the spectacle of a potentially great satiric genius vitiated by prejudice.

At the same time, lest these words seem unduly harsh, it must be remembered that I am not taking into account Lewis' graphic work. Secondly, this failure, if failure it be, is one of our age. As the true artist grows less important in society, so the pressure falls on him more and more to try to influence society by his writings. Pound, Eliot, and Lewis have all spent a considerable part of their energies in such activity. Alone, of the "men of 1914," Joyce had the heroic ability to stand apart. Perhaps unconsciously again Lewis writes his own epitaph for his work when the Finnish poet cribs from Boileau at Lord Osmund's Lenten party:

> Muse, changeons de style, et quittons la satire!
> C'est un méchant métier que celui de médire!
> A l'auteur qui l'embrasse il est toujours fatal—
> Le mal qu'on dit d'autrui ne produit que du mal!

BIBLIOGRAPHY

Checklist of the Writings of Wyndham Lewis

The following is a chronological checklist of the writings of Percy Wyndham Lewis. No attempt is made to list Lewis' graphic publications, such as his *Fifteen Drawings* (Ovid Press, Jan. 1920), his *Timon of Athens,* his illustrations for such works by other authors as Naomi Mitchison's *Beyond This Limit,* Ford Madox Ford's *Antwerp,* or Sacheverell Sitwell's *Doctor Donne and Gargantua,* nor his many drawings contributed to periodicals and newspapers. It is an attempt to collect his written work only.

1909

"The Pole," *The English Review, 2* (May), 255–65.
"Some Innkeepers and Bestre," *The English Review, 2* (June), 471–84.
"Les Saltimbanques," *The English Review, 3* (Aug.), 76–87.

1910

"A Spanish Household," *The Tramp: an Open Air Magazine* (June/ July), pp. 356–60.
"A Breton Innkeeper," *The Tramp: an Open Air Magazine* (Aug.), pp. 411–14.
"Le Père François (A Full-Length Portrait of a Tramp)," *The Tramp: an Open Air Magazine* (Sept.), pp. 517–21.
"Grignolles (Brittany)," *The Tramp: an Open Air Magazine* (Dec.), p. 246. [Poem.]

1911

"Unlucky for Pringle," *The Tramp: an Open Air Magazine* (Feb.), pp. 404–14.

1914

"The Cubist Room," *The Egoist, 1,* No. 1 (Jan.), 8–9.
"Epstein and His Critics, or Nietzsche and His Friends," *The New Age,* N.S., *14,* No. 10 (Jan. 8), 319. [Letter.]

"Mr. Arthur Rose's Offer," *The New Age,* N.S., *14,* No. 15 (Feb. 12), 479. [Letter.]

"Modern Art," *The New Age,* N.S. *14,* No. 22 (April 2), 703. [Letter.]

"A Man of the Week: Marinetti," *The New Weekly, 1,* No. 11 (May 30), 328–9.

" 'Automobilism,' " *The New Weekly, 2,* No. 1 (June 20), 13.

"Long Live the Vortex!" [Editorial]		pp. 5–6.
Manifestoes . . .	*Blast No. 1* (June 20), London, John Lane, the Bodley Head,	pp. 11–43.
"The Enemy of the Stars" [1st Version]		pp. 51–85.
"Vortices and Notes"		pp. 127–49.
"Frederick Spencer Gore"		p. 150.

[Copies of *Blast* with deletions by the U. S. Censors made in some of Pound's poems can be seen in the Houghton Library at Harvard University.]

1915

Editorial		pp. 5–6.
Notice to Public		p. 7.
"War Notes"		pp. 8–16.
"Artists and the War"		pp. 23–4.
"The Exploitation of Blood"		p. 24.
"The Six Hundred, Verestchagin and Uccello"	*Blast No. 2,* War Number (July), London, John Lane, the Bodley Head,	pp. 25–6.
"Marinetti's Occupation"		p. 26.
"A Review of Contemporary Art"		p. 38.
"The Art of the Great Race"		pp. 70–2.
"Five Art Notes"		pp. 77–82.
"Vortex 'Be Thyself' "		pp. 91–3.
"The Crowd Master" [1st Version. Title hyphenated on Contents page]		pp. 94–102.

Preface, "Mayvale" by H. E. Clifton and James Wood, *The Cambridge Magazine, 5,* No. 8 (Dec. 4), 173.

1916

"The French Poodle," *The Egoist, 3* No. 3 (March 1), 39–41. [Includes a drawing of Lewis by Roald Kristian.]

"Serial Story.—Tarr," *The Egoist, 3,* No. 4 (April 1), 54–63; No. 5 (May 1), 72–9; No. 6 (June 1), 90–4; No. 7 (July 1), 107–10; No. 8 (Aug.), 122–5; No. 9 (Sept.), 139–43; No. 10 (Oct.), 155–8; No. 11 (Nov.), 170–3; No. 12 (Dec.), 184–6.

1917

"Serial Story.—Tarr," *The Egoist, 4,* No. 1 (Jan.), 10–15; No. 2 (Feb.), 29–30.

"Serial Story—Tarr," *The Egoist, 4,* No. 3 (April), 39–41; No. 4 (May), pp. 60–1.

"Imaginary Letters, I," *The Little Review, 4,* No. 1 (May), 19–23.

"Serial Story—Tarr," *The Egoist, 4,* No. 5 (June), 75–8.

"Imaginary Letters, II," *The Little Review, 4,* No. 2 (June), 22–6.

"Serial Story—Tarr," *The Egoist, 4,* No. 6 (July), 93–5.

"Imaginary Letters, III," *The Little Review, 4,* No. 3 (July), 3–7. ["The Code of a Herdsman."]

"Serial Story—Tarr," *The Egoist, 4,* No. 7 (Aug.), 106–9; No. 8 (Sept.), 123–7.

"Inferior Religions," *The Little Review, 4,* No. 5 (Sept.), 3–8.

"Serial Story—Tarr," *The Egoist, 4,* No. 9 (Oct.), 138–41.

"Cantleman's Spring-Mate," *The Little Review, 4,* No. 6 (Oct.), 8–14. [The name Cantleman is variously spelt in *The Little Review;* the spelling given here is that usually adopted by Wyndham Lewis, especially in the later *Blasting and Bombardiering.* This issue of *The Little Review* was incidentally disallowed by the United States postal authorities on the grounds of obscenity in the story by Lewis. They were taken to court by the Editress, Miss Anderson, but won their case.]

"Serial Story—Tarr: and Epilogue," *The Egoist, 4,* No. 10 (Nov.), 152–3.

"A Soldier of Humour, I," *The Little Review, 4,* No. 8 (Dec.), 32–46.

The Ideal Giant, The Code of a Herdsman, Cantelman's Spring-Mate, privately printed for the London Office of the *Little Review* by Shield and Spring. [Reprints "Cantleman's Spring-Mate." P. 37 drops the hyphen in this title.]

1918

"A Soldier of Humour, II," *The Little Review, 4,* No. 9 (Jan.), 35–51. [Vol. *5* appears, but this and subsequent errata are corrected by the Editress in the August issue.]
"Imaginary Letters, VIII," *The Little Review, 4,* No. 11 (March), 23–30.
"Imaginary Letters, IX," *The Little Review, 4,* No. 12 (April), 50–4.
"The Ideal Giant," *The Little Review, 5,* No. 1 (May), 1–18. [Reprints this play from the 1917 publication of this name.]
Tarr. London, The Egoist Ltd. ⎫
Tarr. New York, Alfred A. Knopf. ⎬ *July.*

[Reprints and expands "Serial Story—Tarr." Ruthven Todd (*q.v.*) maintains that the Knopf edition antedated the British edition by three weeks. *The English Catalogue of Books* gives July as month of publication. The *United States Catalogue* does not record the publication. June appears on the verso of the title page of the Knopf *Tarr.* However, *The Times Literary Supplement* acknowledges The Egoist Ltd. edition, on July 4, and reviews on July 11, while the American *Publisher's Weekly* only acknowledges the Knopf *Tarr* on July 20, as does *The Nation* (which reviews August 17); the *New York Times* acknowledges July 21.]
"The War Baby," *Art and Letters,* N.S., *2,* No. 1 (Winter), 14–41.

1919

Foreword, *Guns, Catalogue of an Exhibition by Wyndham Lewis,* London, Goupil Gallery, February, unpaged. [Foreword is dated January.]
"The Men Who Will Paint Hell. Modern War as a Theme for the Artist," *The Daily Express,* No. 5,877 (Feb. 10), p. 4.
"Mr. Wadsworth's Exhibition of Woodcuts," *Art and Letters, 2,* No. 2 (Spring), 85–9.
"What Art Now?" *The English Review, 28* (April), 334–8.
"I. Nature and the Monster of Design," *The Athenaeum,* No. 4673 (Nov. 21), pp. 1230–1.

"Prevalent Design. II. 'Painting of the Soul,' " *The Athenaeum,* No. 4676 (Dec. 12), p. 1343.

"Prevalent Design. III. The Man behind the Eyes," *The Athenaeum,* No. 4678 (Dec. 26), p. 1404.

"Harold Gilman," *Harold Gilman: An Appreciation* by Wyndham Lewis and Louis F. Fergusson, London, Chatto and Windus. Pp. 7–15. [No entry in *The English Catalogue of Books.* Reviewed mid-December in *The Times Literary Supplement.*]

The Caliph's Design. Architects! Where Is Your Vortex? London, The Egoist Ltd. [Again no entry in *The English Catalogue of Books. The Publisher's Circular* acknowledges on November 1, but *The Athenaeum* notices on October 31, *The Observer* on November 2, and *The Times Literary Supplement* on November 13.]

[The following lecture was given this year by Lewis: "Modern Tendencies in Art," Conference Hall, Central Buildings, Westminster, London. October 22.]

1920

"Prevalent Design. IV. The Bulldog Eye's Depredations," *The Athenaeum,* No. 4681 (Jan. 16), pp. 84–5.

"Mr. Clive Bell and 'Wilcoxism,' " *The Athenaeum,* No. 4689 (March 12), p. 349. [Letter.]

"Mr. Clive Bell and 'Wilcoxism,' " *The Athenaeum,* No. 4691 (March 26), p. 425. [Letter.]

Foreword, *"X" Group,* London, Maddox Galleries, April. [?]

"Sigismund," *Art and Letters, 3,* No. 1 (Winter), 14–31.

1921

"Note on Tyros" [Editorial]		p. 2.
"Notes on Current Painting, i: The Children of the New Epoch"	*The Tyro: A Review of the Arts of Painting, Sculpture,*	p. 3.
"Notes on Current Painting, ii: Roger Fry's Rôle of Continental Mediator"	*and Design, No. 1,* London, The Egoist Press, April,	p. 3.
"Will Eccles"		p. 6.

"Foreword: Tyros and Portraits," Catalogue, *Exhibition of Paintings and Drawings by Wyndham Lewis,* London, Leicester Galleries, April, pp. 5–8.

"The Coming Academy," *Sunday Express,* No. 121 (April 24), p. 3.

"Paris Versus the World," *The Dial, 71,* No. 1 (July), 22–7.

1922

"The Credentials of the Painter—1," *The English Review, 34* (Jan.) 33–8.

"The Credentials of the Painter—2," *The English Review, 34* (April), 391–6.

"The Long and the Short of It," *Evening Standard* (April 28), p. 3.

"The Worse-than-Ever Academy," *Sunday Express,* No. 174 (April 30), p. 5.

Editorial		p. 3.
"A Preamble for the Usual Public"		pp. 3–9.
"Recent Painting in London. The *Finance Expert*"		pp. 9–10.
"Essay on the Objective of Plastic Art in Our Time"	*The Tyro: A Review of the Arts of Painting, Sculpture, and Design, No. 2.* London, The Egoist Press,	pp. 21–37.
"Tyronic Dialogues.—X. and F."		pp. 46–9.
"Bestre" [revises "Some Innkeepers and Bestre"]		pp. 53–63.

1924

"Mr. Zagreus and the Split-Man," *The Criterion, 2,* No. 6 (Feb.), 124–42.

"The Strange Actor," *The New Statesman, 22,* No. 563 (Feb. 2), 474–6.

"The Young Methusaleh," *The New Statesman, 22,* No. 567 (March 1), 601–2.

"The Apes of God," *The Criterion, 2,* No. 7 (April), 300–10.

"The Dress-Body-Mind Aggregate," *The New Statesman, 23,* No. 579 (May 24), 191.

"Art-Chronicle," *The Criterion, 2,* No. 8 (July), 477–82; *3,* No. 9 (Oct.), 107–13.

1925

[Review of G. Elliot Smith, *Essays on the Evolution of Man;* G. Elliot Smith and Warren R. Dawson, *Egyptian Mummies;* W. H. R. Rivers, *Medicine, Magic and Religion*], *The Criterion, 3,* No. 10 (Jan.), 311–15.

"The Dithyrambic Spectator: An Essay on the Origins and Survivals of Art, Introduction," *The Calendar of Modern Letters, 1,* No. 2 (April), 2–107.

"The Dithyrambic Spectator: An Essay on the Origins and Survivals of Art, Part II," *The Calendar of Modern Letters, 1,* No. 3 (May), 194–213.

"The Foxes' Case," *The Calendar of Modern Letters, 2,* No. 8 (Oct.), 73–90.

"The Physics of the Not-Self," *The Chapbook* (*A Yearly Miscellany*), ed. Harold Monro. London, Jonathan Cape. No. 40, pp. 68–77.

1926

"Britons Never Shall Be Bees" [review of Beaverbrook, *Politicians and the Press*], *The Calendar of Modern Letters, 2,* No. 11 (Jan.), 360–2.

"The New Roman Empire," *The Calendar of Modern Letters, 2,* No. 12 (Feb.), 411–20.

The Art of Being Ruled. London, Chatto and Windus. March.

"Creatures of Habit and Creatures of Change," *The Calendar, 3,* No. 1 (April), 17–44.

Tarr. New York, Alfred A. Knopf. July.

The Art of Being Ruled. New York, Harper. September.

1927

"Preliminary Note to Public"   *The Enemy: A Review*   pp. vii–viii.
"Editorial"   *of Art and Literature,*
"What's in a Namesake?"   vol. *1,* London, The Ar-   pp. ix–xv.
"The Revolutionary Sim-   thur Press. January (i.e.   pp. 19–23.
pleton"   February),   pp. 25–192.

The Lion and the Fox. The Rôle of the Hero in the Plays of Shakespeare.
London, Grant Richards. January. [Reprints "The Foxes' Case."]
The Lion and the Fox. The Rôle of the Hero in the Plays of Shakespeare.
New York, Harper. March.
"The Values of the Doctrine behind 'Subjective' Art," *The Criterion, 6,*
No. 1 (July), 4–13.

"Notes Regarding Details of Publication and Distribu- tion"   pp. vii–x.
"Editorial Notes"   *The Enemy: A Re- view of Art and Literature,* No. 2.   pp. xi–xxxi.
"Editorial"   London, The Ar-   pp. xxxiii–xl.
"Paleface: or 'Love? What Ho! Smelling Strangeness' "   thur Press. Septem- ber,   pp. 3–110.
"The 'Blessings of the Sophisti- cated School of Literature' "   pp. 111–12.

Time and Western Man. London, Chatto and Windus. September. [Re-
prints "The Revolutionary Simpleton."]
The Wild Body: A Soldier of Humour and Other Stories. London, Chatto
and Windus. December. [Reprints "A Soldier of Humour, I," "A Soldier of Humour, II," "Inferior Religions," and "Sigismund." Reprints
and revises "The Pole," "Les Saltimbanques," "Le Père François,"
and "Will Eccles." Incorporates and expands material from "A Spanish Household," "A Breton Innkeeper."]

1928

The Wild Body. New York, Harcourt, Brace. March.
The Childermass: Section I. London, Chatto and Windus. June.

The Childermass: Part I. New York, Covici-Friede. September.

Tarr. London, Chatto and Windus, the Phoenix Library. [Revises 1st edition.]

Time and Western Man. New York, Harcourt, Brace. [Adds new Preface.]

1929

"Enemy Bulletin"	⎫	⎧ pp. vii–viii.
"The Diabolical Principle"	⎪ *The Enemy,* No. 3, Lon-	pp. 9–84.
"Details Regarding Publica-	⎬ don, The Arthur Press. ⎨ p. 90.
tion and Distribution"	⎪ January,	
"Editorial Notes"	⎭	⎩ pp. 91–100.

"A World Art and Tradition," *Drawing and Design, 5,* No. 32 (Feb.), 29–30, 56.

[Answer to questionnaire.] *The Little Review* (Spring Number, May), p. 49.

Paleface: The Philosophy of the "Melting Pot." London, Chatto and Windus. May. [Reprints "The Values of the Doctrine behind 'Subjective' Art." Reprints and expands "Paleface."]

Preface, H. Somerville, *Madness in Shakespearian Tragedy.* London, The Richards Press. Pp. 1–8. July.

"*** !! -- . . . ? *** !!!," *Daily Herald,* No. 9,200 (Oct. 25), p. 10.

1930

"Sex and the Child," *Daily Mail,* No. 10,625 (May 15), p. 10.

The Apes of God. London, The Arthur Press. June. Limited edition. [Reprints "Mr. Zagreus and the Split-Man" and "The Apes of God."]

Satire and Fiction, also "Have with You to Great Queen Street!" The History of a Rejected Review, by Roy Campbell. London, The Arthur Press, Enemy Pamphlets, No. 1. September.

1931

"Hitlerism—Man and Doctrine; the Weimar Republic and the Dritte Reich," *Time and Tide, 12,* No. 3 (Jan. 17), 59–60.

"Hitlerism—Man and Doctrine: Berlin im Licht!" *Time and Tide, 12,* No. 4 (Jan. 24), 87–8.

"Hitlerism—Man and Doctrine: The Oneness of 'Hitlerism' and of Hitler," *Time and Tide, 12,* No. 5 (Jan. 31), 119–20.

"Hitlerism—Man and Doctrine: The Doctrine of the Blutsgefühl," *Time and Tide, 12,* No. 6 (Feb. 7), 151–2.

"Hitlerism—Man and Doctrine: Creditcrankery Rampant," *Time and Tide, 12,* No. 7 (Feb. 14), 182–5.

"Nebulae in Brussels Sprouts" [review of Britton, *Hunger and Love*], *Time and Tide, 12,* No. 9 (Feb. 28), 255–6.

Hitler. London, Chatto and Windus. April. [Reprints the "Hitlerism" articles.]

"The Son of Woman" [review of Middleton Murry, *Son of Woman*], *Time and Tide, 12,* No. 16 (April 18), 470–2.

The Diabolical Principle and the Dithyrambic Spectator. London, Chatto and Windus. May. [Reprints "The Dithyrambic Spectator" and "The Diabolical Principle."]

"Youth-Politics. Foreword: The Everymans," *Time and Tide, 12,* No. 24 (June 13), 703–4.

"Youth-Politics. The Age-Complex," *Time and Tide, 12,* No. 25 (June 20), 738–40.

"Youth-Politics. Youth-Politics upon the Super-Tax Plane," *Time and Tide, 12,* No. 26 (June 27), 770–2.

"Youth-Politics. There Is *Nothing* Big Business Can't Ration," *Time and Tide, 12,* No. 27 (July 4), 798–800.

"Youth-Politics. The *Class-War* of Parents and Children," *Time and Tide, 12,* No. 28 (July 11), 826–8.

"Youth-Politics. Government by Inferiority-Complex," *Time and Tide, 12,* No. 29 (July 18), 854–5.

"Youth-Politics. How Youth-Politics Will Abolish Youth," *Time and Tide, 12,* No. 30 (July 25), 883–4.

"Filibusters in Barbary. High Table: the Packet to Africa," *Everyman, 6,* No. 144 (Oct. 29), 437–8.

"Filibusters in Barbary. Turning Darks into Whites," *Everyman, 6,* No. 146 (Nov. 12), 492.

"Filibusters in Barbary. Islamic Sensations," *Everyman, 6,* No. 148 (Nov. 26), 583.

The Apes of God. London, Nash and Grayson. November. [Cheap edition, reproduced photographically.]

"Filibusters in Barbary. A Deserted African Lido," *Everyman, 6,* No. 150 (Dec. 10), 660.

"Filibusters in Barbary. Petrol-Tin Town," *Everyman, 6,* No. 152 (Dec. 24), 724, 726.

1932

"Filibusters in Barbary. The Mouth of the Sahara," *Everyman, 6,* No. 154 (Jan. 7), 793–4.

The Apes of God. New York, Robert M. McBride. January.

"A Tip from the Augean Stable," *Time and Tide, 13,* No. 12 (March 19), 322–4; No. 13 (March 26), 348–9. [Announced as an Enemy Pamphlet to deal with "the decay of literary standards," this last title has found its way in book form into records of Lewis' work. In fact, although a book of this name is advertised as "Ready Shortly" on the jacket of *The Enemy of the Stars,* only the above articles appeared.]

The Doom of Youth. New York, Robert M. McBride. April. [March appears on verso of title page. Reprints the "Youth-Politics" articles.]

"The Artist as Crowd," *The Twentieth Century, 3,* No. 14 (April), 12–15.

The Wild Body. London, Chatto and Windus, the Centaur Library. May.

"What It Feels Like to Be an Enemy," *Daily Herald,* No. 5082 (May 30), p. 8.

Filibusters in Barbary (Record of a Visit to the Sous). London, Grayson and Grayson. June. [Reprints the "Filibusters in Barbary" articles. Withdrawn after publication.]

"Fénelon and His Valet," *Time and Tide, 13,* No. 25 (June 18), 673–4.

"The Artist and the New Gothic," *Time and Tide, 13,* No. 26 (June 25), 707–8.

"Flaubert as a Marxist," *Time and Tide, 13,* No. 27 (July 2), 737–8.

The Doom of Youth. London, Chatto and Windus. July. [Withdrawn after publication.]

The Enemy of the Stars. London, Desmond Harmsworth. July. [Revises and reprints "The Enemy of the Stars" and "The Physics of the Not-Self."]

Snooty Baronet. London, Cassell. September.

Filibusters in Barbary. New York, Robert M. McBride. September. [Also New York, National Travel Club edition.]

"Notes on the Way," *Time and Tide, 13,* No. 41 (Oct. 8), 1072–3; No. 42 (Oct. 15), 1098–1100.

"Notes on the Way," "A Historical Close-up" [review of Collier and Lang, *Just the Other Day*], *Time and Tide, 13,* No. 43 (Oct. 22), 1129–32. Autumn Book Supplement, p. 1154.

"Notes on the Way," *Time and Tide, 13,* No. 44 (Oct. 29), 1174–5.

Thirty Personalities and a Self-Portrait. London, Desmond Harmsworth. November. [Limited edition. Three pages of text.]

Hitler und sein Werk in englischer Beleuchtung, einzig berechtigte deutsche Ausgabe. Berlin, Verlag von Reimar Hobbing. [Translates *Hitler*. No translator acknowledged.]

1933

The Old Gang and the New Gang. London, Desmond Harmsworth. January.

"Poor Brave Little Barbary," *Daily Herald,* No. 5508 (Oct. 10), p. 10.

The Apes of God. London, Grayson and Grayson. November. [Cheap edition.]

One-Way Song. London, Faber and Faber. November. [Title page reads, *Engine Fight-Talk, The Song of the Militant Romance, If So the Man You Are, One-Way Song, Envoi*.]

" 'One Way Song,' " *New Britain, 2,* No. 30 (Dec. 13), 121. [Letter.]

"What Are the Berbers?" *The Bookman, 85,* No. 507 (December Christmas Number), 183–6.

1934

"Shropshire Lads or Robots?" *New Britain, 2,* No. 33 (Jan. 3), 194.

"Shropshire Lads or Robots Again," *New Britain, 2,* No. 34 (Jan. 10), 226–7.

"The Dumb Ox: A Study of Ernest Hemingway," *Life and Letters, 10,* No. 52 (April), 33–45.

"In Praise of Outsiders," *The New Statesman and Nation, 7,* No. 168, (May 12), 709–10.

"A Moralist with a Corn Cob: A Study of William Faulkner," *Life and Letters, 10,* No. 54 (June), 312–28.

"The Dumb Ox: A Study of Ernest Hemingway," *The American Review, 3,* No. 3 (June), 189–212. [Reprints from *Life and Letters.*]

"Art in a Machine Age," *The Bookman, 86,* No. 514 (July), 184–7. [Abstracts an address delivered at Oxford University.]

"Keyserling" [review of Keyserling, *Problems of Personal Life*], *Time and Tide, 15,* No. 31 (Aug. 4), 984–5.

"Rousseau" [review of Cobban, *Rousseau and the Modern State*], *Time and Tide, 15,* No. 33 (Aug. 18), 1034–5.

"Nationalism," *The Bookman, 86,* No. 516 (Sept.), 276–8.

"A Communist Abroad" [review of Dos Passos, *In All Countries*], *Time and Tide, 15,* No. 37 (Sept. 15), 1141–2.

"Tradesmen, Gentlemen and Artists" [review of Eric Gill, *Art*], *The Listener, 12,* No. 298 (Sept. 26), 545.

Men without Art. London, Cassell. October. [Reprints "Fénelon and His Valet," "Flaubert as Marxist," "The Dumb Ox," "A Moralist with a Corn Cob," "The Artist and the New Gothic," and portions of *Satire and Fiction.*]

" 'Classical Revival' in England," *The Bookman, 87,* No. 517 (Oct.), 8–10.

"Studies in the Art of Laughter," *The London Mercury, 30,* No. 180 (Oct.), 509–15.

[Answer to an inquiry.] *New Verse,* No. 11 (Oct.), pp. 7–8.

"One Picture Is More than Enough," *Time and Tide, 15,* No. 41 (Oct. 13), 1252–3.

"Power-Feeling and Machine-Age Art," *Time and Tide, 15,* No. 42 (Oct. 20), 1312–14.

"Plain Home-Builder: Where Is Your Vorticist?" *The Architectural Review: A Magazine of Architecture and Decoration, 76,* No. 456 (Nov.), 155–8.

"Art in Industry," *Time and Tide, 15,* No. 45 (Nov. 10), 1410–12.

"Sitwell Circus" [review of Edith Sitwell, *Aspects of Modern Poetry*], *Time and Tide, 15,* No. 46 (Nov. 17), 1480.

1935

"Wyndham Lewis," *Beginnings* [by various hands], ed. L. A. G. Strong. London, Thomas Nelson. Pp. 91–103. March.

"Notes on the Way," *Time and Tide,* No. 9 (March 2), 304–6 [unindexed]; No. 10 (March 9), 332–4; No. 11 (March 16), 390–2; No. 12 (March 23), 425–7; No. 13 (March 30), 456–8.

"Art and Patronage (I)," *The B.B.C. Annual.* London, British Broadcasting Corporation. Pp. 184–7. April.

"First Aid for the Unorthodox," *The London Mercury, 32,* No. 187 (May), 27–32.

"Freedom that Destroys Itself," *The Listener, 13,* No. 330 (May 8), 793–4. [Broadcast talk. *B.B.C. National Service,* transmission 10.00 P.M., April 30.]

"Among the British Islanders—Art and Literature," *The Listener, 13,* No. 337 (June 26), 1108–9.

"Martian Opinions," *The Listener, 14,* No. 340 (July 17), 125. [Letter.]

1936

"V," *Freedom* [by various hands]. London, George Allen and Unwin. January. [Reprints the broadcast talk, "Freedom That Destroys Itself."]

"Mr. Ervine and the Poets," *The Observer,* No. 7,549 (Feb. 2), p. 13. [Letter.]

Left Wings over Europe: or, How to Make a War about Nothing. London, Cape. June. [2d printing August.]

"The Roaring Queen." London, Jonathan Cape. [This novel was withdrawn before publication. The Houghton Library at Harvard University has a re-cased proof copy, Crown 8vo, 256 pp., printed by the Alden Press Ltd., Oxford. The front cover bears the printed legend: "Duplicate Proof for Retention / Does not contain Proof Reader's marks."]

1937

" 'Left Wings' and the C 3 Mind," *The British Union Quarterly, 1,* No. 1 (Jan./April), 22–34.

Count Your Dead: They Are Alive! or A New War in the Making. London, Lovat Dickson. April.

The Revenge for Love. London, Cassell. May.

"My Reply to Mr. Aldington. A Defence of Style: The Novel and the Newspaper," *John O'London's Weekly and the Outline, 37,* No. 952 (July 9), 555–6.

"Insel und Weltreich," *Europäische Revue,* XIII Jahrgang, Heft 9 (Sept.), 699–707.

Blasting and Bombardiering. London, Eyre and Spottiswoode. October. [Reprints parts of *Blast,* with minor revisions.]

"A Letter to the Editor," *Twentieth Century Verse,* 6/7 (Nov./Dec.), 2¼ pages unpaged. [Letter to the Wyndham Lewis Double Number. Unindexed.]

[Introduction], Catalogue, *Exhibition of Paintings by Wyndham Lewis,* London, Leicester Galleries, December, pp. 7–9.

1938

"Pictures as Investments: A Straight Talk. Some Possible Gold Mines of Tomorrow," *John O'London's Weekly, 38,* No. 985 (Feb. 25), 852, 858.

"Lawrence von Arabien," "Der Tod des Ankou," *Europäische Revue,* XIV Jahrgang, Heft 3 (März), 200–5, 215–24. [Translates "The Death of the Ankou" from *The Wild Body.* The article on T. E. Lawrence is translated by Hans Wilfert, the story by the Editor, Joachim Moras.]

"Art and Nature," *The Times,* No. 47, 983 (May 2), p. 17. [Letter.]

The Revenge for Love. London, Cassell. August. [Cheap edition.]

The Mysterious Mr. Bull. London, Robert Hale. November. [In this book *The Roaring Queen* is announced as previously published "By the Same Author." This work, which Charles Handley-Read has picked up, and mis-spelt, did not in fact appear.]

"The Zoo," *London Guyed,* ed. William Kimber. London, Hutchinson. Pp. 167–88.

Die Rache für Liebe, trans. Hans Rudolf Rieder. Essen, Essener Verlagsanstalt.

1939

The Jews, Are They Human? London, Allen and Unwin. March.
Count Your Dead. London, Davies. March. [Cheap edition.]
"John Bright und die englische Aussenpolitik," *Europäische Revue,* xv Jahrgang, Heft 4 (April), 358–64.
Wyndham Lewis the Artist, from "Blast" to Burlington House. London, Laidlaw and Laidlaw. May. [Reprints "Notes and Vortices," *The Caliph's Design,* "Essay on the Objective of Plastic Art in Our Time," and "Art and Nature."]
The Hitler Cult. London, Dent. December.
Der mysteriöse John Bull. Ein Tugendspiegel des Engländers, trans. Hans Rudolf Rieder. Essen, Essener Verlagsanstalt. [Reprints "John Bright und die englische Aussenpolitik."]

1940

"Picasso," *The Kenyon Review, 2,* No. 2 (Spring), 196–211.
"The End of Abstract Art," *The New Republic, 102,* No. 14 (April 1), 438–9.
[Letter], *The New Republic, 102,* No. 21 (May 20), 675.
America, I Presume. New York, Howell, Soskin. August.
[The following lecture was given this year by Lewis: "Should American Art Differ from European Art?" Columbia University in the City of New York, February 14.]

1941

"How Would You Expect the English to Behave?" *Saturday Night: The Canadian Weekly, 57,* No. 4 (Oct. 4), 18–19.
"Reasons Why an Englishman Is an Englishman," *Saturday Night: The Canadian Weekly, 57,* No. 10 (Nov. 15), 34b.
The Vulgar Streak. London, Robert Hale. December. [No entry in *The English Catalogue of Books.* My date is derived from *The Times Literary Supplement,* where it is "ready" December 8, as advertised on December 6, and reviewed December 27.]
Anglosaxony: A League That Works. Toronto, The Ryerson Press. [Distributed in the U.S.A. by Bruce Humphries Inc., Boston. Pp. 208–9 reprint p. 162 of *The Hitler Cult.*]

1942

"That 'Now-or-Never' Spirit," *Saturday Night: The Canadian Weekly,* *57,* No. 40 (June 13), 6.
"What Books for Total War," *Saturday Night: The Canadian Weekly,* *57,* No. 5 (Oct. 10), 16.

1944

[The following lecture was given this year by Lewis: "The Meaning of Ugliness, in Rouault, Picasso, and others," The Arts Club of Chicago, February 29.]

1945

"The Cosmic Uniform of Peace," *The Sewanee Review, 53,* No. 4 (Autumn), 507–31.

1946

"Canadian Nature and Its Painters," *The Listener, 36,* No. 920 (Aug. 29), 267–8.
"De Tocqueville and Democracy," *The Sewanee Review, 54,* No. 4 (Autumn), 555–75.
"American Melting Pot," *Contact Books,* Vol. 2 ("Britain between East and West"). London, Contact Books, George Weidenfeld and Nicolson Ltd. October. Pp. 56–9.
"The Art of Gwen John," *The Listener, 36,* No. 926 (Oct. 10), 484.
"Moore and Hepworth," *The Listener, 36,* No. 927, (Oct. 17), 505–6.

1947

"Round the Art Galleries," *The Listener, 37,* No. 944 (Feb. 13), 283.
"A Crisis of Thought" [broadcast talk]. London, *B.B.C. Third Programme,* transmission, 8.00–8.20 P.M., March 16.
" 'Puritans of the Steppes' " *The Listener, 37,* No. 949 (April 3), 508–9.
"Round the Art Exhibitions," *The Listener, 38,* No. 978 (Oct. 23), 736.

1948

"The Brotherhood," *The Listener, 39,* No. 1004 (April 22), 672.

"The Pre-Raphaelite Brotherhood," *The Listener, 39,* No. 1006 (May 6), 743. [Letter.]

"Augustus John and the Royal Academy," *The Listener, 39,* No. 1007 (May 13), 794.

"Round the London Art Galleries," *The Listener, 39,* No. 1011 (June 10), 944.

"Round the London Art Galleries," *The Listener, 39,* No. 1012 (June 17), 980.

"Standards in Art Criticism," *The Listener, 39,* No. 1013 (June 24), 1009. [Letter.]

America and Cosmic Man. London, Nicholson and Watson. July. [Falsely entered as by D. B. Wyndham Lewis in *Whitaker's Cumulative Book List,* Part xcviii, Jan. to Dec., 1948, p. 138.]

"Standards in Art Criticism," *The Listener, 40,* No. 1014 (July 1), 22. [Letter.] No. 1015 (July 8), 61–3. [Letter.] No. 1016 (July 15), 99–100. [Letter.] No. 1017 (July 22), 133. [Letter.]

"Early London Environment," *T. S. Eliot. A Symposium.* London, Editions Poetry London, 1948. September. Pp. 24–32.

"Round the London Art Exhibitions," *The Listener, 40,* No. 1029 (Oct. 14), 572.

"The Rot: A Narrative," *Wales, 8,* No. 30 (Nov.), 574–89.

1949

"The Chantrey Collection at the Academy," *The Listener, 41,* No. 1042 (Jan. 13), 65.

"Round the London Galleries," *The Listener, 41,* No. 1050 (March 10), 408.

"Painting in America," *The Listener, 41,* No. 1054 (April 7), 584.

Introduction, Catalogue, *Exhibition of Paintings, Drawings, and Watercolours by Wyndham Lewis.* London, Redfern Gallery, May 5, 2 pages unpaged.

"Round the London Art Galleries," *The Listener, 41,* No. 1059 (May 12), 811–12.

Note, Catalogue, *Exhibition of Paintings, Drawings, Book Illustrations, and Designs for the Theatre by Michael Ayrton,* arranged by the Wakefield City Art Gallery, May, 1 page unpaged.

America and Cosmic Man. New York, Doubleday. June.

"The London Art Galleries," *The Listener, 41,* No. 1063 (June 9), 988.

"Edward Wadsworth: 1889–1949," *The Listener, 41,* No. 1066 (June 30), 1107.

"The London Galleries," *The Listener, 42,* No. 1068 (July 14), 68.

"Bread and Ballyhoo," *The Listener, 42,* No. 1076 (Sept. 8), 407.

"Round the Art Galleries," *The Listener, 42,* No. 1082 (Oct. 20), 686.

"Round the London Art Galleries," *The Listener, 42,* No. 1086 (Nov. 17), 860.

"Ezra: The Portrait of a Personality," *Quarterly Review of Literature, 5,* No. 2 (Dec.), 136–44.

"Round the London Art Galleries," *The Listener, 42,* No. 1088 (Dec. 1), 959. [Letter.]

1950

"Round the London Galleries," *The Listener, 43,* No. 1095 (Jan. 19), 116.

"Round the London Art Galleries," *The Listener, 43,* No. 1099 (Feb. 16), 298.

"Fernand Léger at the Tate Gallery," *The Listener, 43,* No. 1101 (March 2), 396.

"Round the London Galleries," *The Listener, 43,* No. 1104 (March 23), 522.

"Contemporary Art at the Tate," *The Listener, 43,* No. 1106 (April 6), 610–11.

"Round the London Galleries," *The Listener, 43,* No. 1108 (April 20), 685.

"Round the London Art Galleries," *The Listener, 43,* No. 1112 (May 18), 878–9.

"Round the London Galleries," *The Listener, 44,* No. 1120 (July 13), 62.

"A Note on Michael Ayrton," *Nine, 2,* No. 3 (Aug.), 184–5.

"Round the London Art Galleries," *The Listener, 44,* No. 1129 (Sept. 21), 388.

"Ezra Pound," *Ezra Pound. A Collection of Essays edited by Peter Russell to Be Presented to Ezra Pound on His Sixty-fifth Birthday.* London, Peter Nevill. October. Pp. 257–66. [Carries the date "1948." This work was subsequently published as *An Examination of Ezra Pound,* Norfolk, Conn., New Directions, 1950. Reprints "Ezra: The Portrait of a Personality."]

Rude Assignment: A Narrative of My Career Up-to-date. London, Hutchinson. November. [Reprints "A Crisis of Thought."]

"Round the London Art Galleries," *The Listener, 44,* No. 1132 (Nov. 9), 508.

"Henry Moore's 'Head of a Child' " [letter], "Round the London Art Galleries," *The Listener,* No. 1135 (Nov. 30), 647, 650.

"A Negro Artist," *The Listener, 44,* No. 1136 (Dec. 7), 696; No. 1137 (Dec. 14), 745. [Letter.] No. 1139 (Dec. 28), 839. [Letter.]

1951

"Nature and Art," *The Listener, 45,* No. 1140 (Jan. 4), 22 [Letter.] No. 1141 (Jan. 11), 63. [Letter.]

"Nature and Art," [letter], "Round the London Galleries," *The Listener, 45,* No. 1142 (Jan. 18), 106, 110.

"Nature and Art," *The Listener, 45,* No. 1143 (Jan. 25), 145. [Letter.]

"The Rock Drill" [review of *The Letters of Ezra Pound*], *The New Statesman and Nation, 41,* No. 1048 (April 7), 398.

"The Sea-Mists of the Winter," *The Listener, 45,* No. 1158 (May 10), 765. [Announces total blindness.]

Tarr. London, Methuen. June. [Reprints revised edition.]

Rotting Hill. London, Methuen. December. [Reprints "The Rot."]

1952

"Augustus John Looks Back" [review of John, *Chiaroscuro*], *The Listener, 47,* No. 1203 (March 20), 476–9.

Rotting Hill. Chicago, Henry Regnery. April.

The Writer and the Absolute. London, Methuen. June.

The Revenge for Love. London, Methuen. June. [Reprints the 1937 edition.]

The Revenge for Love. Chicago, Henry Regnery. October. [Reprints the 1937 edition.]

1953

"Imaginary Letters," "Cantleman's Spring-Mate," Answer to a Questionnaire, *The Little Review Anthology,* ed. Margaret Anderson. New
York, Hermitage House, 1953. Pp. 110–28, 137–43, 370. [Reprints
from *The Little Review.*]

"The Rebellious Patient," *Shenandoah, 4,* Nos. 2–3 (Summer/Autumn),
3–16.

1954

"Doppelgänger: A Story," *Encounter, 2,* No. 1 (Jan.), 23–33.

Self Condemned. London, Methuen. April.

"Matthew Arnold," *The Times Literary Supplement,* Special Autumn
Number, No. 2,740 (Aug. 6), p. xxii. [Review of *Matthew Arnold:
Poetry and Prose,* ed. John Bryson.]

"Meredith As a Novelist," *Time and Tide, 35,* No. 39 (Sept. 25), 1269–
70. [Review of Stevenson, *The Ordeal of George Meredith.*]

The Demon of Progress in the Arts. London, Methuen. November.

1955

"Monstre Gai (i)," *The Hudson Review, 7,* No. 4 (Winter) [but appears
January], 502–21.

"Monstre Gai (ii)," *The Hudson Review, 8,* No. 1 (Spring), 28–56.

Self Condemned. Chicago, Henry Regnery. March.

The Lion and the Fox: the Rôle of the Hero in the Plays of Shakespeare.
London, Methuen. June. [Reprints the 1927 edition. BNB entry adds,
"This ed. first published 1951." Messrs. Methuen state that Grant
Richards' existing stock of this book was taken over in May 1951,
but that it was only reprinted by themselves in June 1955.]

"A Very Sinister Old Lady," *Shenandoah, 7,* No. 1 (Autumn), 3–14.

The Demon of Progress in the Arts. Chicago, Henry Regnery. October.

The Apes of God. London, Arco Pub. October. [Limited edition of one
thousand signed and numbered copies. Photographically reproduces
the 1930 edition. Adds an Introduction.]

The Human Age. Book 2: Monstre Gai. Book 3: Malign Fiesta. London,
Methuen. November. [Reprints "Monstre Gai," i and ii, and "A Very
Sinister Old Lady."]

1956

"Pish-Tush," *Encounter, 6,* No. 2 (Feb.), 40–50.

Introduction, Catalogue, *Wyndham Lewis and Vorticism,* London, Tate Gallery. July.

The Red Priest. London, Methuen. August.

The Human Age. Book I: Childermass. London, Methuen. November. [Revises the 1928 edition.]

SECONDARY SOURCES

The following secondary sources list direct references to Wyndham Lewis and/or his work of especial interest. Ephemeral reviews, the more important of which have been mentioned in the text, are not recorded here; the *Book Review Digest* and Manly and Rickert's "bio-bibliography" list many of these.

Aldington, Richard. "Blast," *The Egoist, 1,* No. 14 (July 15, 1914), 272–3.

———*Life for Life's Sake.* New York, Viking Press, 1941.

Allen, Walter. *The English Novel. A Short Critical History.* New York, E. P. Dutton. 1955.

——— "Talking of Books" [broadcast talk, Studio 3B], London, *B.B.C. Home Service,* transmission, July 13, 1952. Typescript.

Anderson, Margaret. *My Thirty Years' War.* London, Alfred A. Knopf, 1930.

Armitage, Gilbert. "A Note on 'The Wild Body,' " *Twentieth Century Verse, 6/7* (Nov./Dec. 1937), 2 pages unpaged.

Armstrong, Terence Ian Fytton. See under "Gawsworth, John."

"The Art League of Service Travelling Portfolios of Pictures," *Artwork, 1,* No. 2 (Oct. 1924), 70–5.

"Art Which Makes for Emotion," *The Literary Digest* (New York), *53,* No. 22 (Nov. 25, 1916), 1406.

Ayrton, Michael. Introduction, *The Unfortunate Traveller* by Thomas Nashe. London, John Lehmann, 1948.

——— "Tarr and Flying Feathers," *Shenandoah, 7,* No. 1 (Autumn 1955), 31–43.

Baker, Carlos. *Hemingway: The Writer as Artist.* Princeton University Press, 1952.

Barry, Iris. "The Ezra Pound Period," *The Bookman, 74,* No. 2 (Oct. 1931), 159–71.

Bates, Ernest Sutherland. "A Cathedral of Gargoyles," *The Saturday Review of Literature, 5,* No. 11 (Oct. 6, 1928), 181–2.

Beevers, John. "I Read Lewis," *Twentieth Century Verse, 6/7* (Nov./ Dec. 1937), 1 page unpaged.

Bell, Clive. "The English Group," Catalogue, *Second Post-Impressionist Exhibition,* London, Grafton Galleries, October 5—December 31, 1912.

——— "Wilcoxism," *The Athenaeum,* No. 4688, March 5, 1920, pp. 311–12.

Bénézit, E. *Dictionnaire critique et documentaire des peintres, sculpteurs, dessinateurs, et graveurs.* France, Librairie Gründ, 1952. P. 559.

Bergel, Lienhard. "L'estetica di Cesare Pavese," *Lo spettatore italiano,* anno VIII, n. 10 (Ottobre 1955), 407–21.

Booth, Meyrick. *Youth and Sex. A Psychological Study.* London, Allen and Unwin, 1932.

Bowen, Stella. *Drawn from Life.* London, Collins, 1941.

Brinton, Christian. Introduction, *War Paintings and Drawings by British Artists,* exhibited under the auspices of the Ministry of Information, London, published New York, Redfield-Kendrick-Odell, 1919.

Brodzky, Horace. *Henri Gaudier-Brzeska, 1891–1915.* London, Faber and Faber, 1933. P. 166.

Brunius, Av Teddy. *Pionjärer och Fullföljare i Modern Engelsk Lyrik och Kritik.* Stockholm, Natur och Kultur, 1952.

Burke, Kenneth. *Attitudes toward History,* Vol. *1.* New York, The New Republic, 1937.

Campbell, Roy. *Broken Record. Reminiscences.* London, Boriswood, 1934.

——— "Contemporary Poetry," *Scrutinies by Various Writers,* Vol. *1.* London, Wishart, 1928.

——— *The Georgiad. A Satirical Fantasy in Verse.* London, Boriswood, 1931.

——— *Light on a Dark Horse.* Chicago, Henry Regnery, 1952.

——— "A Note on W. L.," *Shenandoah, 4,* Nos. 2–3 (Summer/Autumn 1953), 74–6.

[A printed book on Lewis by Roy Campbell was announced from Desmond Harmsworth some years ago, and has crept into checklists since, but in fact such did not appear.]

Coburn, Alvin Langdon. *More Men of Mark*. London, Duckworth, 1932. [A little known photograph of Lewis is included as Plate xxii.]

Coffman, Stanley K., Jr. *Imagism. A Chapter for the History of Modern Poetry*. Norman, Oklahoma, University of Oklahoma Press, 1951.

Connolly, Cyril. *Enemies of Promise*. Revised ed. New York, Macmillan, 1948.

Constable, W. G. "Wyndham Lewis," *The New Statesman, 15,* No. 367 (April 24), 1920, 73–4.

Cournos, John. *Autobiography*. New York, Putnam's, 1935.

Craig, Hardin. *A History of English Literature*. New York, Oxford, 1950.

The Criterion: A Quarterly Review, Vols. *1–18,* London, R. Cobden-Sanderson, 1922–39.

Cubism and Abstract Art. New York, Museum of Modern Art, 1936.

"O.R.D.," *The Nation and Athenaeum, 29,* No. 3 (April 16, 1921), 106–8.

Dekobra, Maurice. "The Art of Making Enemies," *Daily Herald,* No. 5075 (May 21, 1932), p. 8.

Dobrée, Bonamy. *Modern Prose Style*. Oxford, At the Clarendon Press, 1934.

Duncan, Ronald. "BLAST and About and About," *The Townsman, 1,* No. 1 (Jan. 1938), 26–7.

Earp, T. W. "The Leicester Galleries Exhibition," *Twentieth Century Verse, 6/7* (Nov./Dec. 1937), 3 pages unpaged.

Ede, H. S. *Savage Messiah. Gaudier-Brzeska*. New York, The Literary Guild, 1931.

The Egoist; an Individualist Review, Vols. *1–6,* London, The Egoist Ltd., 1914–19.

Eliot, T. S. *After Strange Gods*. New York, Harcourt, Brace, 1934.

——— [Review of James Joyce, *Ulysses*], *The Dial, 65,* No. 5 (Nov. 1923), 482.

——— "The Lion and the Fox," *Twentieth Century Verse, 6/7* Nov./ Dec., 1937), 3½ pages unpaged.

——— "A Note on *Monstre Gai,*" *The Hudson Review, 7,* No. 4 (Winter 1955), 522–6.

——— *Selected Essays*. New York, Harcourt, Brace. 1950.

——— " 'Tarr,' " *The Egoist, 5,* No. 8 (Sept. 1918), 105–6.

T. S. Eliot. A Symposium, by various hands. London, Editions Poetry London, 1948.

Epstein, Jacob. *Let There Be Sculpure.* New York, Putnam's, 1940.

———— to Arnold L. Haskell. *The Sculptor Speaks. A Series of Conversations on Art.* New York, Doubleday, 1932.

Ewart, Gavin. "Note," *Twentieth Century Verse, 6/7* (Nov./Dec., 1937), ½ page unpaged.

Fehr, Bernhard. *Das England von heute: Kulturprobleme, Denkformen, Schrifttum.* Leipzig, Verlag von Bernhard Tauchnitz, 1932.

Fiedler, Leslie. *An End to Innocence.* Boston, Beacon Press, 1955.

"Five." "Wyndham Lewis's 'Enemy,' " *Experiment* (Cambridge, England), No. 3 (May, 1929), pp. 2–5.

Fjelde, Rolf. "Time, Space, and Wyndham Lewis," *Western Review, 15,* No. 3 (Spring, 1951), 201–12.

Flint, F. S. "The History of Imagism," *The Egoist, 2,* No. 5 (May 1, 1915), 70–1.

Ford, Ford Madox. (Hueffer) "A Haughty and Proud Generation," *The Yale Review, N.S., 11,* No. 4 (July 1922), 703–17.

———— *It Was the Nightingale.* Philadelphia, Lippincott, 1933.

———— *The March of Literature: from Confucius to Modern Times.* London, Allen and Unwin, 1939.

———— *Mightier than the Sword. Memories and Criticisms.* London, Allen and Unwin, 1938.

———— *Return to Yesterday.* New York, Horace Liveright, 1932.

———— *Thus to Revisit. Some Reminiscences.* London, Chapman and Hall, 1921. [Published under "Hueffer."]

Fraser, G. S. *The Modern Writer and His World.* London, Derek Verschoyle, 1953.

Friedman, Melvin. *Stream of Consciousness: A Study in Literary Method.* New Haven, Yale University Press, 1955.

Frierson, William C. *The English Novel in Transition.* Norman, Okla., University of Oklahoma Press, 1942.

Frye, H. N. "Wyndham Lewis: Anti-Spenglerian," *The Canadian Forum, 16,* No. 185 (June 1936), 21–2.

Gallup, Donald. *T. S. Eliot. A Bibliography.* London, Faber and Faber, 1952.

Garnett, David. *The Flowers of the Forest.* London, Chatto and Windus, 1955.

Gaudier-Brzeska. A Memoir, by Ezra Pound, Including the Published Writings of the Sculptor, and a Selection from His Letters. London, John Lane, the Bodley Head, 1916.

Gaunt, W. "Contemporary Personalities by Wyndham Lewis," *The London Studio* (Nov. 1932), pp. 262–8.

"Gawsworth, John." *Apes, Japes, and Hitlerism*. London, Unicorn Press, 1932.

Gilbert, Stuart. *James Joyce's "Ulysses." A Study*. London, Faber and Faber, 1930.

Goldring, Douglas. *The Last Pre-Raphaelite. A Record of the Life and Writings of Ford Madox Ford*. London, Macdonald, 1948. (Published in 1949 as *Trained for Genius,* New York, E. P. Dutton.)

———— *Life Interests,* with a Preface by Alec Waugh. London, Macdonald, 1948.

———— *The Nineteen Twenties. A General Survey and Some Personal Memories*. London, Nicholson and Watson, 1945.

———— *Odd Man Out. The Autobiography of a "Propaganda" Novelist*. London, Chapman and Hall, 1935.

———— *People and Places*. Boston, Houghton Mifflin, 1929.

———— *Reputations. Essays in Criticism*. New York, Thomas Seltzer, 1920.

———— *South Lodge. Reminiscences of Violet Hunt, Ford Madox Ford and the English Review Circle*. London, Constable, 1943.

Gorman, Herbert. *James Joyce*. New York, Rinehart, 1948. [Unindexed references.]

Grigson, Geoffrey, ed. *The Arts Today*. London, John Lane, the Bodley Head, 1935. [Includes praise for Lewis from Louis MacNeice and Arthur Calder-Marshall, as well as Grigson.]

———— "Living Writers. 5: Wyndham Lewis" [broadcast talk, Studio 2B]. London, *B.B.C. Third Programme,* transmission, November 2, 1946. Typescript.

———— *A Master of Our Time*. London, Methuen, 1951.

Handley-Read, Charles, ed. *The Art of Wyndham Lewis,* with an essay on detail in the artist's style, a chronological outline and notes on the plates. With a critical evaluation by Eric Newton. London, Faber and Faber, 1951.

Hannay, Howard. "Photography and Art," *The London Mercury, 1,* No. 5 (Jan. 1920), 301–11.

———— "Tyros and Portraits by Wyndham Lewis," *The London Mercury,* *4,* No. 20 (June 1921), 204–5.

Häusermann, H. W. "Left-Wing Poetry," *English Studies: A Journal of English Letters and Philology, 21,* No. 5 (Oct. 1939), 211–12.

———— *Studien zur englischen Literarkritik, 1910–1930,* Kölner Anglistische Arbeiten, 34 Band, Bochum-Langendreer, Verlag Heinrich Pöppinghaus, O.H.-G., 1938.

Henderson, Philip. *The Novel Today: Studies in Contemporary Attitudes.* London, John Lane, the Bodley Head, 1936.

Hennecke, Hans. "Wyndham Lewis: Vision und Satire," *Europäische Revue,* xiv Jahrgang, Heft 3 (März, 1938), 205–14.

Herbert-Dell, Mollie. "An Introduction to the Work of P. Wyndham Lewis." Thesis in partial fulfillment for the requirements of Master of Arts, Leeds University, 1950. Typescript.

Highet, Gilbert. *A Clerk of Oxenford.* New York, Oxford University Press, 1954.

Hueffer, Ford Madox. See under Ford, Ford Madox.

Hughes, Glenn. *Imagism and the Imagists. A Study in Modern Poetry.* Stanford, Calif., Stanford University Press, 1931.

Hulme, T. E. "The Articles Contributed by T. E. Hulme to 'The New Age.'" Submitted in partial fulfillment of the requirements for the degree of Master of Arts, Faculty of Philosophy, Columbia University, by Philip J. Leddy Jnr., 1947. [Collects Hulme's prose outside *Speculations.*]

———— *Speculations. Essays on Humanism and the Philosophy of Art,* ed. Herbert Read, with a frontispiece and foreword by Jacob Epstein. London, Kegan Paul, Trench, Trubner, 1936.

———— *Further Speculations by T. E. Hulme,* ed. Sam Hynes. Minneapolis, University of Minnesota Press, 1955. [Virtually the same compilation as that made by Leddy above.]

Hunt, Violet. *I Have This to Say. The Story of My Flurried Years.* New York, Boni and Liveright, 1926.

Hyman, Stanley Edgar. *The Armed Vision.* New York, Alfred A. Knopf, 1948.

Innis, Harold A. *The Bias of Communication.* Toronto, University of Toronto Press, 1951.

———— *Changing Concepts of Time.* Toronto, University of Toronto Press, 1952.

Isaacs, Jakob. *An Assessment of Twentieth Century Literature*. London, Secker and Warburg, 1951.

───── "England," *Contemporary Movements in European Literature,* ed. J. Isaacs and William Rose. London, George Routledge, 1928. Pp. 6, 10, 15.

Jepson, Edgar. *Memories of an Edwardian and Neo-Georgian*. London, Richards, 1937.

John, Augustus. *Chiaroscuro. Fragments of an Autobiography*. First series. London, Jonathan Cape, 1952.

Jones, Glyn. "Satiric Eye," *Twentieth Century Verse, 6/7* (Nov./Dec. 1937), 1 page unpaged.

Keenan, Peter. "Memories of Vorticism," *The New Hope, 2,* No. 6 (Oct. 1934), 5–6, 18–19.

Kenner, Hugh. *Dublin's Joyce*. Bloomington, Indiana University Press, 1956.

───── *The Poetry of Ezra Pound*. Norfolk, Conn., New Directions, 1951.

───── *Wyndham Lewis*. Norfolk, Conn., New Directions, 1954.

Kirk, Russell. "Wyndham Lewis's First Principles," *The Yale Review, 44,* No. 4 (Summer 1955), 520–34. [Reprinted in *Beyond the Dreams of Avarice,* Chicago, Henry Regnery, 1956.]

Krutch, Joseph Wood. "Plastic and Temporal in Art," *The Nation, 105,* No. 3257 (Dec. 7, 1927), Holiday Book Section, 643–4.

Kunitz, Stanley J. ("Dilly Tante") and Haycraft, Howard, eds. *Twentieth Century Authors*. New York, H. W. Wilson, 1942.

Lambert, Constant. "An Objective Self Portrait," *Twentieth Century Verse, 6/7* (Nov./Dec. 1937), 2½ pages unpaged.

Laver, James. *Portraits in Oil and Vinegar*. London, John Castle, 1925.

Lawrence, D. H. *Phoenix*. New York, Viking Press, 1936.

Leavis, F. R. *The Common Pursuit*. New York, George W. Stewart, 1952.

───── *D. H. Lawrence: Novelist*. New York, Alfred A. Knopf, 1956.

Lee, Alwyn. "Henry Miller—The Pathology of Isolation," *New World Writing, Second Mentor Selection,* New York, New American Library, Signet Books Inc., 1952.

Levin, Harry. *James Joyce*. Norfolk, Conn., New Directions, 1941.

Linati, Carlo. *Scrittori anglo americani d'oggi*. Milano, Corticelli, 1932.

The Little Magazine: A History and a Bibliography, by Frederick J. Hoffman, Charles Allen, and Carolyn F. Ulrich. Princeton University Press, 1946.

The Little Review; . . . Journal of Art and Letters. Vols. 1–12. Chicago, M. C. Anderson (*q.v.*), 1914–29.

The Little Review Anthology, ed. Margaret Anderson. New York, Hermitage House, 1953.

Living Art. New York, The Dial Publishing Company, 1953. [Discussed by Lewis in *The Criterion* for October 1924.]

McLuhan, Herbert Marshall. *Counterblast.* Toronto, Canada, privately printed, 1954.

—————— *The Mechanical Bride: Folklore of Industrial Man.* New York, Vanguard Press, 1951.

—————— "Wyndham Lewis: His Theory of Art and Communication," *Shenandoah, 4,* Nos. 2–3 (Summer/Autumn 1953), 77–88.

Mallalieu, H. B. "Social Force," *Twentieth Century Verse, 6/7* (Nov./Dec. 1937), ½ page unpaged.

Manly, John M., and Rickert, Edith, revised by Millett, Fred B. *Contemporary British Literature.* New York, Harcourt, Brace, 1935.

Marcus, Steven. "The Highbrow Know-Nothings," *Commentary, 15,* No. 2 (Feb. 1953), 189–91.

Marriott, Charles. *Modern Movements in Painting.* New York, Scribner's, 1921.

Melville, Cecil F. *The Truth about the New Party.* London, Wishart, 1931.

Melville, Robert. "Portrait of the Artist, No. 7: Wyndham Lewis," *Art News and Review, 1,* No. 7 (May 7, 1949), 1, 3.

Miskin, Leonard. "Aspects of Modern British Painting," *Envoy, 4,* No. 16 (March 1951), 33–43.

Monroe, Harriet. *A Poet's Life.* New York, Macmillan, 1938.

Moore, Harry T. *The Life and Works of D. H. Lawrence.* New York, Twayne Publishers, 1951.

Morgan, Louise. *Writers at Work.* London, Chatto and Windus, 1931.

Mudrick, Marvin. "The Double-Artist and the Injured Party," *Shenandoah, 4,* Nos. 2–3 (Summer/Autumn 1953), 54–64.

Nash, Paul. "Modern English Textiles," *Artwork, 2,* No. 6 (Jan./March 1926), 83.

—————— *Outline. An Autobiography and Other Writings,* with a Preface by Herbert Read. London, Faber and Faber, 1949.

Nevinson, C. R. W. *Paint and Prejudice.* London, Methuen, 1937.

Newton, Eric. "Emergence of Mr. Wyndham Lewis," *The Listener, 41,* No. 1060 (May 19, 1949), 852. [See also under Handley-Read, Charles.]

O'Casey, Sean. *Sunset and Evening Star.* New York, Macmillan, 1954.

Orage, A. R. *Readers and Writers (1917–1921).* New York, Alfred A. Knopf, 1922.

———— *Selected Essays and Critical Writings,* eds. Herbert Read and Denis Saurat. London, Stanley Nott, 1935.

Palmer, Herbert. "The Chaste Wand," *New Britain, 2,* No. 34 (Jan. 10, 1934), 227.

Pelham, Edgar. *The Art of the Novel.* New York, Macmillan, 1933.

"Personality of the Week. Britain's Most Advanced Painter Leads a Return to Naturalism, But It Is a NEW Naturalism," *The World of Art Illustrated, 1,* No. 8 (June 7, 1939), 6–7. [Interview, with direct quotations.]

Porteus, Hugh Gordon. "Eyes Front (Ideogram)," *Twentieth Century Verse, 6/7* (Nov./Dec. 1937), 5¼ pages unpaged.

———— "Resurrection in the Crypt," *T. S. Eliot. A Symposium.* London, Editions Poetry London, 1948, pp. 218–24.

———— "Wyndham Lewis," *The Twentieth Century, 2,* No. 7 (Sept. 1931), 4–6.

———— *Wyndham Lewis: A Discursive Exposition.* London, Desmond Harmsworth, 1932.

"Portrait of the Artist. No. 7," *Art News and Review, 1,* No. 7 (May 7, 1949), 1.

Pound, Ezra. "Edward Wadsworth. Vorticist," *The Egoist, 1,* No. 16 (Aug. 15, 1914), 306–7.

———— *Guide to Kulchur.* Norfolk, Conn., New Directions, n.d.

———— *If This Be Treason.* Siena, privately printed for Olga Rudge, 1948.

———— *Imaginary Letters.* Paris, Black Sun Press, 1930.

———— *Instigations of Ezra Pound.* New York, Boni and Liveright, 1920.

———— *The Letters of Ezra Pound, 1907–1941,* ed. D. D. Paige. New York, Harcourt, Brace, 1950.

———— *Literary Essays of Ezra Pound,* edited with an Introduction (*q.v.*) by T. S. Eliot. London, Faber and Faber, 1954.

———— *Make It New.* London, Faber and Faber, 1934.

———— *Money Pamphlets.* London, Peter Russell. These consist of No. 1, *An Introduction to the Economic Nature of the United States,* 1950; No. 2, *Gold and Work,* 1951; No. 3, *What Is Money For?* 1951; No. 4, *A Visiting Card,* 1952; No. 5, *Social Credit: An Impact,* 1951; No. 6, *America, Roosevelt and the Causes of the Present War,* 1951.

―――― *Pavannes and Divisions.* New York, Alfred A. Knopf, 1918.

―――― *The Pisan Cantos.* Norfolk, Conn., New Directions, 1948–.

―――― "Vorticism," *The Fortnightly Review,* N.S., *573* (Sept. 1, 1914), 461–71.

―――― "Wyndham Lewis," *The Egoist, 1,* No. 12 (June 15, 1914), 233–4.

Pound, Reginald. *Arnold Bennett.* New York, Harcourt, Brace, 1953.

Pritchett, V. S. *Books in General.* London, Chatto and Windus, 1953.

―――― "Literary Letter from London," *The New York Times Book Review* (Sept. 28, 1952), p. 43.

Pryce-Jones, Alan. "Little Reviews and Big Ideas," *The Listener, 43,* No. 1099 (Feb. 16, 1950), 285–6.

Read, Sir Herbert. *The Philosophy of Modern Art.* London, Faber and Faber, 1952.

Rhys, Keidrych. "Celtic View," *Twentieth Century Verse, 6/7* (Nov./ Dec. 1937), 2 pages unpaged.

Richards, I. A. "Talk," *B.B.C. Third Programme,* transmission, March 10, 1952; originally recorded New York, Nov. 4, 1951. Typescript.

Rickword, Edgell. "Wyndham Lewis," *Scrutinies.* Vol. *2,* by various writers, collected by Edgell Rickword. London, Wishart, 1931. Pp. 139–61.

Roberts, Michael. *T. E. Hulme.* London, Faber and Faber, 1938.

Roberts, William. *The Resurrection of Vorticism and the Apotheosis of Wyndham Lewis at the Tate.* London, Favil Press, 1956.

Rodker, John. *The Future of Futurism.* London, Kegan Paul, Trench, Trubner, 1926.

Rodman, Selden. *The Eye of Man.* New York, Devin-Adair, 1955.

Rothenstein, John. *British Artists and the War.* London, Peter Davies, 1931.

―――― "Great British Masters—26. Wyndham Lewis," *Picture Post, 2,* No. 12 (March 25, 1939), 47–50.

―――― *Modern English Painters. Lewis to Moore.* New York, Macmillan, 1956.

Rothenstein, Sir William. *Men and Memories, Recollections of William Rothenstein, 1900–1922.* London, Faber and Faber, 1932.

―――― *Since Fifty. Men and Memories, 1922–1938. Recollections of William Rothenstein.* London, Faber and Faber, 1939.

Routh, H. V. *English Literature and Ideas in the Twentieth Century.* London, Methuen, 1946.

Russell, Peter. "Wyndham Lewis Today," *Shenandoah, 4,* Nos. 2–3 (Summer/Autumn 1953), 72–3.

Rutter, Frank. *Art in My Time.* London, Rich and Cowan, 1933.

———— *Evolution in Modern Art. A Study in Modern Painting.* London, George S. Harrap, 1932.

———— *Modern Masterpieces. An Outline of Modern Art.* London, George Newnes, 1940.

———— *Some Contemporary Artists.* London, Leonard Parsons, 1922.

Savage, D. S. "Lewis and Lawrence," *Twentieth Century Verse, 6/7* (Nov./Dec. 1937), 1 page unpaged.

Scott, J. D. "On Re-Reading Wyndham Lewis" [broadcast talk, disc No. SLO 92562], London, B.B.C. Third Programme, transmission, July 25, 1951.

Scott-James, R. A. *Fifty Years of English Literature, 1900–1950.* London, Longmans Green, 1951.

Shenandoah, Vol. *4,* Nos. 2–3 (Summer/Autumn 1953). Wyndham Lewis Number.

Sickert, Walter Richard. *A Free House, or the Artist as Craftsman, Being the Writings of Walter Richard Sickert,* ed. Osbert Sitwell (*q.v.*). London, Macmillan, 1947.

Sitwell, Edith. *Aspects of Modern Poetry.* London, Duckworth, 1934. [Reviewed by Wyndham Lewis above.]

Sitwell, Sir Osbert, Bt. *Great Morning.* London, Macmillan, 1948.

———— *Laughter in the Next Room.* London, Macmillan, 1949.

———— "A Short Character of Walter Richard Sickert," *A Free House.* . . . London, Macmillan, 1947. Pp. xlv–xlvi.

The Sketch. "Look Here," *The Sketch, 109,* No. 1405 (Dec. 31, 1919), 5.

———— "Wyndham Lewis as a Tyro," *The Sketch, 114,* No. 1473 (April 20, 1921), 89.

Soby, James Thrall. *Contemporary Painters.* New York, Museum of Modern Art, 1948.

Spender, Stephen. *The Destructive Element.* London, Cape, 1935.

———— *The Creative Element.* London, Hamish Hamilton, 1953.

"Spurious Art," by the Editor, *The Connoisseur, 56,* No. 223 (March 1920), 138.

Stone, Geoffrey. "The Ideas of Wyndham Lewis," *The American Review, 1,* No. 5 (Oct. 1933), 578–99; "Part II," *The American Review, 2,* No. 1 (Nov. 1933), 82–96.

Stonier, George Walter. *Gog Magog and Other Critical Essays*. London, Dent, 1933.

———— "That Taxi-Driver," *Twentieth Century Verse, 6/7* (Nov./Dec. 1937), 2½ pages unpaged.

Summers, Montague. *The Gothic Quest. A History of the Gothic Novel*. London, Fortune Press, 1938.

Swinnerton, Frank Arthur. *The Georgian Literary Scene*. London, William Heinemann, 1935.

———— *Background with Chorus*. New York, Farrar, Straus and Cudahy, 1957.

Symons, Julian. "Notes on One-Way Song," *Twentieth Century Verse, 6/7* (Nov./Dec. 1937), 2½ pages unpaged. [It is more than likely that the one-page editorial to this issue was also written by this author.]

Thieme-Becker. Thieme, Ulrich, and Becker, Felix, begründet von, *Allgemeines Lexikon der bildenden Künstler, 23* (Leipzig, Verlag von E. A. Seeman, 1929), 164. [Contains a useful list of reproductions.]

Time Magazine, 53, No. 22 (May 30, 1949), 60. [Contains an extended quotation from Lewis on his portraits of Eliot. Probably written originally by Marvin Barrett.]

Tindall, William York. *D. H. Lawrence and Susan His Cow*. New York, Columbia University Press, 1939.

———— *Forces in Modern British Literature, 1885–1946*. New York, Alfred A. Knopf, 1947.

———— *James Joyce. His Way of Interpreting the Modern World*. New York, Scribner's, 1950.

"Tis." "About Wyndham Lewis," *Colour, 10* (March 1919), 24–7.

Todd, Ruthven. "Check List of Books and Articles by Wyndham Lewis," *Twentieth Century Verse, 9* (March 1938), 21–7. [A supplement of articles, announced as forthcoming in the note prefaced to this list, did not appear.]

———— "Comments on a Critic," *Twentieth Century Verse, 6/7* (Nov./ Dec. 1937), 2½ pages unpaged.

Tomlin, E. W. F. "The Philosopher-Politician," *Twentieth Century Verse, 6/7* (Nov./Dec. 1937), 3 pages unpaged.

———— *Wyndham Lewis*. London, Longmans, Green, 1955.

transition. Eugene Jolas, Elliot Paul, Robert Sage, "First Aid to the Enemy," *transition 9* (Dec. 1927), 160–76.

Twentieth Century Verse, 6/7 (Nov./Dec. 1937). Wyndham Lewis Double Number.

Tschumi, Raymond. *Thought in Twentieth-Century English Poetry.* London, Routledge and Kegan Paul, 1951.

Vines, Sherard. Foreword, *Whips and Scorpions, Specimens of Modern Satiric Verse, 1914–1918,* collected by Sherard Vines. London, Wishart, 1932. P. vii.

——— *Movements in Modern English Poetry and Prose.* Oxford University Press, 1927.

——— *100 Years of English Literature.* London, Duckworth, 1950.

Ward, A. C. *The Nineteen-Twenties. Literature and Ideas in the Post-War Decade.* London, Methuen, 1930.

Warner, Rex. "Extract from a Letter," *Twentieth Century Verse, 6/7* (Nov./Dec. 1937), ½ page unpaged.

Waugh, Alec. See under Goldring, Douglas, *Life Interests.*

Wellington, Hubert. (Deutsch von Margarete Mauthner.) "Die neueste Malerei in England, II," *Kunst und Künstler,* Jahrgang 23, Heft 12 (Sept. 1925), 464–6.

Wickham, Harvey. *The Impuritans.* New York, Lincoln MacVeagh, The Dial Press, 1929.

Wilenski, Reginald Howard. "Lettre de Londres," *L'Amour de l'art.* 1re année (mai–décembre 1920), 223.

——— *Masters of English Painting.* Boston and New York, Hall, Cushman, and Flint, 1934.

Woolf, Leonard. "The World of Books," *The Nation and Athenaeum, 40,* No. 14 (Jan. 8, 1927), 539.

Woolf, Virginia. *Roger Fry, an Autobiography.* London, Hogarth Press, 1940.

——— *A Writer's Diary.* New York, Harcourt, Brace, 1953.

Yeats, W. B. *A Vision.* New York, Macmillan, 1938.

——— *The Letters of W. B. Yeats,* ed. Allan Wade. New York, Macmillan, 1955.

Index